ISRAEL'S
National
Identity

ISRAEL'S National Identity

The Changing Ethos of Conflict

Neta Oren

LYNNE
RIENNER
PUBLISHERS

BOULDER
LONDON

Published in the United States of America in 2019 by
Lynne Rienner Publishers, Inc.
1800 30th Street, Boulder, Colorado 80301
www.rienner.com

and in the United Kingdom by
Lynne Rienner Publishers, Inc.
Gray's Inn House, 127 Clerkenwell Road, London EC1 5DB

Library of Congress Cataloging-in-Publication Data
Names: Oren, Neta, author.
Title: Israel's national identity : the changing ethos of conflict / Neta
  Oren.
Description: Boulder, Colorado : Lynne Rienner Publishers, Inc., 2019. |
  Includes bibliographical references and index.
Identifiers: LCCN 2018046213 | ISBN 9781626377844 (hardcover)
Subjects: LCSH: Political culture—Israel. | National characteristics,
  Israeli. | Jews—Israel—Identity. | Arab-Israeli conflict.
Classification: LCC DS113.3 .O74 2019 | DDC 956.9405—dc23
LC record available at https://lccn.loc.gov/2018046213

British Cataloguing in Publication Data
A Cataloguing in Publication record for this book
is available from the British Library.

Printed and bound in the United States of America

 The paper used in this publication meets the requirements
of the American National Standard for Permanence of
Paper for Printed Library Materials Z39.48-1992.

5 4 3 2 1

To the memory of my parents,
Arie Barnea and Ruth Barnea

Contents

Tables and Figures

Tables

Figures

Acknowledgments

I have worked on this book, on and off, for several years. I am thankful for all the people who helped me on this long journey. I am grateful to Russell Stone, who shared data from the Guttman surveys that he had collected for his book *Social Change in Israel: Attitudes and Events, 1967–1979*. Thanks to Rafi Ventura, Mirit Cohen, and Erez Eden of the Israel Democracy Institute for their assistance in obtaining additional Guttman Institute data. A special thanks to Michal Shamir and Jacob Shamir who shared with me their database of surveys about peace and territories conducted during the years 1967–1991. Michal Shamir also provided access to National Security and Public Opinion Project survey data from 1986 to 2000 (with the permission of the late Asher Arian); she shared with me her extensive knowledge about public opinion in general and in the Israeli context. I am particularly grateful to Daniel Bar-Tal for advice, inspiration, and encouragement. My book is based on his conception of the ethos of conflict and the psychological repertoire of a society during an intractable conflict. I am also grateful to Oded Leshem, Dean Pruitt, Sara Cobb, Daniel Rothbart, and Karina Korostelina, all from the School for Conflict Analysis and Resolution at George Mason University, who provided me with valuable ideas throughout the various stages of the project. Thanks also to three anonymous reviewers who offered useful suggestions regarding an earlier draft.

Thanks are due to Lynne Rienner for her confidence and support and to the team at Lynne Rienner Publishers: Nicole Moore, Shena Redmond, and Sally Glover.

Finally, this project has depended on the support of my family. Thanks to my husband, Yair, for his superb editing and his smart remarks that often exposed me to a different perspective on Israeli society than my own. Further thanks to my sons: Ido, who always inspires me in his own way, and Nadav, the best research assistant I ever had.

I dedicate the book to the memory of my parents, Arie Barnea and Ruth Barnea, who were there for me with their unconditional love at the beginning of this project, but sadly did not get to see its completion.

1

The Israeli Ethos as an Ethos of Conflict

I was working on this book when I traveled from my home in Washington to Israel in 2015, during another tense period in the Israeli-Palestinian relationship. Every Israeli I met during my visit, including peace activists, was pessimistic about the chances of resolving this conflict. They all seemed to agree with Benjamin Netanyahu when he said, during his October 2015 appearance at the Israeli parliament (the Knesset), that Israel will "forever live by the sword"(Ravid 2015a).

This despair is not limited to Israeli and Palestinian societies and to the Israeli-Arab conflict.[1] Bitter and prolonged conflicts have dominated the life of many nations. In this phase of their history, these nations are comprised of generations upon generations who have only known the experience of conflicting with another society and being exposed constantly to violent acts that threaten their lives and the lives of their loved ones. In these nations, the conflict also dominates the discussion in the media and in politics, appears in school textbooks, and leaves its mark on popular cultural products such as literature and cinema. It shapes the way the past and present are presented, as well as affecting aspirations for the future. In other words, the conflict shapes the *ethos* of the society. What are the unique features of the ethos in a society with prolonged exposure to intractable conflict? To what extent do people in such a society embrace the content of the ethos that is transmitted to them from a young age? What are the types of changes typically observed in an ethos during a conflict? To what degree do attempts to resolve the conflict influence this process of change or are influenced by it? My aim in this book is to provide some answers to these questions based on a detailed analysis of the Jewish Israeli ethos.

1

Previous studies have noted the link between Israeli collective identity and the Israeli-Arab conflict. For example, Sucharov (2005) describes Israel's role identity as "defensive warrior"—a state with an ethical army involved only in self-defense wars. She argues that some major events in the 1980s (e.g., the 1982 Lebanon War and the first intifada—the 1987–1993 Palestinian uprising in the territories captured by Israel in the 1967 War) created a cognitive dissonance between Israel's identity as a defensive warrior and its actions; these events further dredged up "unconscious counternarratives" depicting Israel as an aggressive actor. The fear among Israelis from what they had become in turn pushed Israel to pursue the Oslo Accords. Sucharov uncovers important shared beliefs in Israeli society—regarding security and the image of Israel as a villa in the jungle—which I explore further in Chapter 3 and Chapter 4. Sucharov discusses some aspects of Israeli collective memory and the Jewish roots of Israeli identity, but only those aspects that are linked to Israel's role as a defensive warrior, and thus does not cover the full breadth of these components of Israeli identity. My analysis of Israeli identity covers a longer period than Sucharov's analysis; it shows that, for most of the period, Israeli society, by resorting to a variety of mechanisms, was actually more successful than Sucharov argues in coping with the potential dissonance between Israel Defense Forces (IDF) actions during wars and Israel's identity as a moral society. I further show that it was the need to confront the inherent dissonance *within* Israeli identity (e.g., the dissonance between the belief in Israel as a Jewish state and the values of democracy) that played the most significant role in shaping Israel's policy toward the conflict with the Palestinians.

Waxman (2006a) focuses on the way that the debate surrounding Israel's identity shaped Israeli foreign policy. He refers especially to the Jewish component of Israeli identity and to the debate between the "civic" definition of Israeli national identity (*Israeliness*) and "ethnoreligion" definition (*Jewishness*). He is by no means the only scholar to have looked at the diversity of groups that compose the Israeli polity—these issues are the focus of several other important works such as those of Kimmerling (2001).[2] Waxman's accounts that the Israeli-Arab conflict both shaped Israel's national identity and helped to sustain it (2006a, 6) and that identity can complicate peacemaking efforts, not just trigger such attempts (Waxman 2014), most closely resemble some of the arguments I advance in this book. However, the importance he assigns to controversies regarding Israeli identity and the divisions within Israeli society as animating factors underestimates the counterbalancing power of the ethos that these groups share. This ethos has helped Israel survive and prosper against what appeared at times to be great odds. It allows Israeli society to cope effectively with the stressful conditions produced by conflict, and for many years motivated Israelis to sacrifice on behalf of the state, including risking their lives.

Other studies have examined subsets of the components of the Israeli identity such as siege beliefs and the effect of the Holocaust on Israel's national identity (Zertal 2005; Amir 2011), or the belief in the existential threats faced by Israel and security beliefs more broadly (Abulof 2015; Ben-Eliezer and Al Haj 2003; Bar-Tal, Jacobson, and Klieman 1998). None of these studies, however, provides a broad depiction of Israeli identity, with its multitude of (potentially contradictory) shared beliefs. Using the framework of ethos of conflict, in this book I provide that much-needed comprehensive and updated account of the shared beliefs comprising the Israeli collective self, the complex relationship between those beliefs, and their effect on Israel's policies. As an Israeli-born woman, who has lived most of her life in Israel, I have a deep familiarity with Israeli society and its ethos. But most of all, this analysis is based on what I believe to be one of the most comprehensive studies ever undertaken of the Israeli ethos and its evolution since 1967.

The Concept of Ethos

This book relies on a definition of *ethos* developed by Bar-Tal (2013, 174): "a particular configuration of central societal beliefs that are enduring and shared by most members of society." Societal beliefs, then, are the building blocks of an ethos, defined as cognitions shared by and of interest to members of a society and contributing to their sense of uniqueness. While not every member of a society will agree with these beliefs, they do have to recognize their importance and role as a characteristic of their society. Not every societal belief is included in a society's ethos. The three main criteria for evaluating whether a societal belief is part of a particular societal ethos are (1) a majority of society members share the belief for long periods; (2) the belief is often invoked as part of justifications, explanations, and arguments in political debate, and it influences decisions made by leaders of the society;[3] and (3) it is imparted to the younger generation and to new members of the society (Bar-Tal 2013, 175). In the methodological section of this chapter I further elaborate on ways to measure and determine when an expression of societal belief in political rhetoric and public polls indicates that it is part of an ethos.

The definition of *societal beliefs* that are part of the ethos is broad and includes attitudes (positive or negative feelings about some object) and values (a perception of how things should be), as well as what people consciously understand about an object or action (Eagly and Chaiken 1993). Societal beliefs also include narratives—plots with a clear beginning and end that provide the sequence and cause of an event or a set of events (Bruner 1991). As I emphasize again and again throughout the book, narratives are usually grounded in reality but present one interpretation of that reality. Narratives about a collective shared past, for example, may present the collective as continuous through time, marginalizing any changes to its membership or rules (Hamilton, Levine, and Thurston 2014). The strategies of narrative construction, such as structures of time sequence (e.g., linear, circular, zigzag), separation of periods from one another, and selection of the historical starting point of the narrative, legitimize claims and acts in the past and in the present (E. Zerubavel 2003). For example, narratives about the beginning of a confrontation between the rivals ("who fired the first shot") might support beliefs about the rival side as the aggressor and one's own side as a victim. Setting a historical starting point for the narrative might play a vital role in establishing territorial rights ("We are the original inhabitants of this land"). From here on, unless otherwise specified, the term *societal beliefs* refers to all elements of an ethos: beliefs, attitudes, values, and narratives.

Another special case of societal beliefs is collective memory, which relates to the history of the society (Paez and Liu 2011; Wertsch 2002; Y. Zerubavel 1995). Often it conforms to a generic story about a golden age, a fall and decline, and then a process of rebirth and redemption. Such a narrative constitutes the Israeli collective memory—as I show in the next chapter. In addition, collective memory focuses on specific major events that become symbolic, commemorated events for the group. They often include "chosen traumas" and "chosen glories" (Volkan 1997, 48). In the following chapter I discuss in more detail the notion of the Holocaust as a chosen trauma in Israeli collective memory and its manifestation in how Israelis perceive the Israeli-Arab conflict—even though the Holocaust took place in Europe with no direct Arab involvement.

In his later work, Bar-Tal distinguished between ethos and collective memory, explaining that *collective memory* includes societal beliefs about the past while *ethos* refers to societal beliefs about the present and future. Regardless of this distinction, he notes that the main themes of collective memory and ethos are similar. In conflict, for example, both ethos and collective memory include themes regarding goals in the conflict, delegitimization of rivals, glorifying one's own society, and self-victimization (Bar-Tal 2013, 148–149). Likewise, ethos and collective memory of conflict have similar roles: providing an ideology through which to interpret the reality, encouraging sacrifices on behalf of the society, and allowing people to maintain a positive self-image. Finally, collective memory and ethos are highly connected and inseparable. Collective memory often justifies society's claims and actions in the present and provides guidance for the future. It follows, then, that a comprehensive understanding of a society must include a study of its collective memory as well as common beliefs about its present and future. Thus, in this book I analyze both the Israeli ethos and relevant narratives of its collective memory.

According to Bar-Tal (2013), a society that engages in a long intractable conflict with another society develops an ethos that is affected by the conflict. This ethos of conflict may include eight themes: beliefs about the goals in the conflict, security, one's own victimization, a negative image of the opponent, positive self-images, national unity, patriotism, and peace. Bar-Tal provides examples for these themes of ethos of conflict from societies as varied as the Catholic and Protestant societies in Northern Ireland, the Tutsi and Hutus in Rwanda, and the Greek and Turkish societies in Cyprus. The first goal of this book is to reveal the extent to which the themes of ethos of conflict identified by Bar-Tal serve as the pillars of the Israeli ethos. I refer to the following themes: the goal of establishing a Jewish state (which corresponds to beliefs about goals in the conflict in Bar-Tal's framework), security beliefs, Israeli victimization and siege beliefs, the perception of Israel as a villa in the jungle (which corresponds to a negative image of the opponent and positive self-image beliefs), Israeli patriotism and the belief in the need to maintain national unity, and beliefs about the value of peace.

My analysis of the Israeli ethos in this book, however, goes beyond a mere description of Bar-Tal's (2013) eight themes of ethos of conflict as they manifest in Israeli society. It adds ideas about the structure of an ethos (e.g., how these themes interact with each other), and about types of ethos changes that enrich the theoretical discussion about the concept of ethos and allow us to systematically compare the Israeli ethos *as a whole* across time. First, my analysis explores the hierarchy of the societal beliefs within the Israeli ethos—which themes are more and less central. Indeed, some themes may be more prominent in the ethos of a society, such that they are shared by more people than those who hold other themes of the ethos, they are subject to less public debate and challenges over the years, and they are mentioned in the nation's most cherished documents. Central beliefs in the ethos may also be perceived as *sacred goals or values*—a goal or value with "transcendental significance that precludes comparisons or trade-offs" (Tetlock 2003, 320). People ascribe to these goals and values importance above and beyond all others and, hence, refuse to compromise over them regardless of the costs or benefits (Sheikh, Ginges, and Atran 2013; Ginges et al. 2007). In the Israeli case, the theme about Israel as a Jewish state is a central theme of the ethos: the agreement with this theme in public polls was higher than for any other theme of the ethos over most of the study period, and few if any Jewish Israeli leaders ever opposed the goal of establishing a Jewish state and the collective memory that justified it. As I show in Chapter 2, this theme of the Israeli ethos is also the main idea in Israel's Declaration of Independence. Some aspects of this theme (e.g., the goal of maintaining a Jewish majority) were also portrayed in leaders' rhetoric and public polls as sacred values. Other themes in the Israeli ethos, such as siege beliefs, are not as central: their support in polls has been inconsistent, they did not figure prominently in the Declaration of Independence, and on occasion they were refuted by major political leaders.

Second, my analysis shows how the core themes of the Israeli ethos relate to each other and to other systems of beliefs and values in the society. Ethos themes may coexist in harmony, clash, or result in some combination thereof. Issues or events may reveal a conflict among the different themes of the ethos and other societal beliefs. In the Israeli case, the main tension exists between the societal belief in the value of democracy and the belief that it is necessary to ensure a Jewish nature for the state—a core theme of the ethos. This tension intensifies in the context of Israeli control of the territories captured by Israel in 1967, which are densely populated by Palestinians. Keeping masses of Palestinians under Israeli occupation may strain democratic practices. On the other hand, adding masses of Palestinians as new citizens to the Jewish state threatens the goal of having a Jewish majority and a Jewish state.

Third, my analysis identifies the strategies used to address perceived inconsistencies within ethos beliefs and between ethos and nonethos beliefs. Studies of cognitive imbalance or dissonance suggest that when people are aware of a contradiction between beliefs, the unpleasantness of the experience motivates them to eliminate or otherwise reduce the inconsistency (Festinger 1957). The psychological literature points to five main strategies for dealing with cognitive imbalance: denying the inconsistency, adding new cognitions to bolster one of the clashing beliefs, engaging in cognitive differentiation, changing one of the beliefs, or prioritizing one of the beliefs over the other(s) (Abelson 1968; Heider 1958). Several scholars have started to explore how states—and not just individuals—use strategies such as denial to deal with dissonance concerning their collective identity (Zarakol 2010; S. Cohen 2001). Lupovici (2012) suggests that states use another strategy commonly used by individuals to cope with dissonance—avoidance. Avoidance usually involves mechanisms of selective exposure to information that causes the dissonance. At the state level, this can be achieved by taking actions that self-restrict access to information, foster ambiguity, or create some distance from the source of identity threat. As such, avoidance usually does not eliminate the dissonance—it just makes it more tolerable.

My study continues this trend of exploring the strategies that are applied at the collective level to deal with dissonance between societal beliefs. I identified the use of such strategies in leaders' rhetoric and track the public's receptiveness as reflected in polls. For example, the Israeli public mostly has denied any potential contradiction between the value of Israel as a Jewish state and its ability to maintain a democratic nature. Israelis and their leaders also often have denied wrongdoing by the IDF that may contradict ethos themes presenting a moral self-image of Israel and the Israeli army (the villa in the jungle theme). I identified two additional strategies that were used by leaders and school textbooks in the latter context: *bolstering* (the claim that Israel is engaged in a type of war that makes some degree of civilian casualties unavoidable) and *cognitive differentiation* (the claim that only a few Israeli soldiers were involved in intentional attacks against Arab civilians and that they do not represent the spirit of the Israeli army). So, this source of potential dissonance was coped with rather successfully by Israeli society. In contrast, coping with the dissonance stemming from Israel's control of the territories proved far more complex, with the strategies significantly changing over time, as detailed later in this chapter.

In sum, in this book I provide a comprehensive framework for analyzing a society's ethos tracking its evolution over time, and comparing it to the ethos of other societies. In accordance with this framework, any study of an ethos must detail the central themes of the ethos, clarify the relationships between those themes and other societal beliefs, and describe strategies used by the society to resolve any inconsistencies. Societies may have similar themes in their ethos but may still differ in the specific content of these themes and their configuration. Societies may also diverge in the strategies they use at a given time to resolve inconsistencies among their central beliefs, ranging from total denial to changing their ethos. The framework of ethos that I present in this book also allows us to compare the ethos of the same society over time and to track the main changes in its identity. But before we can embark on this application of the framework, we need to discuss the issue of construction and transmission of an ethos.

The Transmission of Ethos and Collective Memory

As I emphasize throughout the book, the beliefs of the Israeli ethos are based on the reality of the conflict. In other words, by using the term *beliefs,* I do not mean to imply that their content is false or "invented" by the Israeli authorities. Neither am I suggesting that they represent an accurate and unbiased reflection of reality. Rather, like any other worldview, they present a prism through which to interpret that harsh and bloody reality. Any ethos or collective memory highlights some events, marginalizes others, and connects them in its own way. For example, societies tend to focus on their own suffering, brought about by acts of aggression by their opponents, and to marginalize or ignore the suffering of their rivals caused by their own actions. In this regard, H. Cohen (2015) shows that, while the killing of 133 Jews during the 1929 clashes between Palestinians and Jews is a central event in the Israeli collective memory of the Israeli-Arab conflict, it is mostly ignored in the Palestinian collective memory of the same conflict. Shapira (2000, 52) describes the way the Israeli society attempted to cope with the issue of expulsion of some of Palestine's Arabs by the

IDF in the 1948 War as "partial forgetting" or "memory dimming." Furthermore, even when focused on the same specific event, people can arrive at different conclusions, see numerous meanings, and interpret it in different ways. Consider, for example, the numerous meanings of the Holocaust and its potential learned lessons for the Jewish people. Some meanings and learned lessons were emphasized in different societies, and even by the same society at different times, while others were ignored or marginalized.[4] Therefore, my focus is on which main beliefs were adopted by the Israeli society and what purpose(s) they served, rather than the historical and factual accuracy of these beliefs.

Seen from this angle, the concept of ethos also helps us avoid a simplistic account of ethos construction—as content solely constructed by authorities for their own purposes. Indeed, societal beliefs are transmitted to the public by various channels such as leaders' speeches, school textbooks, and official symbols (e.g., the flag and anthem). An analysis of the production process of such official symbols and texts often reveals the intent of authorities in their effort to construct an ethos that would serve as a tool for the leadership to mobilize the masses (this by itself, however, does not necessarily imply that these beliefs are not valid). For example, Young (1990), who analyzed the debate among Israeli policymakers regarding the Israeli Holocaust Remembrance Day, which was first established in a 1951 parliamentary resolution and then in a 1959 law, shows how they intentionally tried to engender a particular meaning for this memorial day—Israel as the only safe place for the Jews—by choosing a specific date and a specific title for it. But leadership is not a monolith; there always may be voices in the periphery of the political elite who resist the ethos or try to present an alternative ethos. In addition, some of the channels that participate in the construction and transmission of ethos themes, such as media, art products, and academic publications, are not fully controlled or directed by the leadership of the state (especially in a democracy).

Regardless of the sources that define and transmit societal beliefs of ethos in a given society, it is important to note a fact that is often ignored in studies that analyze these products—that people are not necessarily passive "recipients" of such content. The public may accept some ethos content. They may internalize the ethos beliefs—that is, transform them into personal beliefs and personal narratives (Hammack 2009). But these are not the only options: people may doubt the ethos of their society, parody it,[5] or resist it altogether. In totalitarian societies, people resist the official ethos and collective memory in mostly latent ways.[6] In democratic societies, a resistance to the official ethos can take more visible or direct forms—people may avoid or ignore official events or memorial days, thereby refusing to adopt the beliefs and values that these events represent.[7] People may express disagreement with ethos beliefs or express their agreement with alternative beliefs in protests, demonstrations, and public polls. It must be noted, however, that the leadership (even in democratic societies) often makes efforts to maintain the dominance of the ethos and to prevent, or at least to minimize, dissemination of a competing ethos (see elaborate discussions about this trend in Bar-Tal, Oren, and Nets-Zehngut 2014; Oren, Nets-Zehngut, and Bar-Tal 2015).

The construction and transmission of an ethos, in other words, may be driven by top-down efforts by the leadership to transmit specific beliefs, but also may be shaped by bottom-up pressures—a change in public opinion that eventually forces the leadership to adjust its rhetoric and policy. A specific belief becomes part of the ethos only if these processes succeed— if beliefs that are transmitted by the authorities are embraced by the public, or if ideas shared by a majority of society members become part of leaders' rhetoric and influence their decisions.

It follows that analyzing only the content of official texts, such as speeches and school textbooks, is not sufficient for understanding the ethos of a society. It is essential to complement this analysis with a study of the level of agreement with it among the public. Unfortunately, most previous works focused on only one of the two aspects—usually the former[8]—and there are only a few comprehensive studies that compare the content of an ethos as it appears in formal texts with the way the public accepts it.[9] This study, then, is also unique in this regard: in each chapter, I compare the Israeli ethos as it appears in official products to data from public polls.

Change of Ethos

This book presents an original conception of changes in societal beliefs, including those that make up an ethos. According to this framework, these changes take one of two major forms. The first form involves changes in the *content* of beliefs over the years. For example, beliefs about Jewish rights to the land (which are part of the Jewish state theme discussed in the next chapter) changed during the 1980s and 1990s such that they no longer asserted *exclusive* rights for the Jews but recognized that Palestinians also had justified claims to the same land. Another example is the change in content of the belief about the nature of the threats to Israel (which is part of the security theme discussed in Chapter 3). The focus moved from the threat of conventional war and the danger posed by a Palestinian state to the threat of unconventional weapons in the hands of Muslim states and nontraditional security threats (the threat to the Jewish and democratic nature of the state).

The second form is a change in the extent of confidence in a societal belief. That is, people may lessen or increase their confidence in the belief—the belief may accordingly weaken or strengthen. When people increase or decrease their confidence in the bulk of the beliefs in the ethos, the ethos *as a whole* will strengthen or weaken (Oren 2004, 2005, 2016). In the case of the Israeli ethos of conflict, during the 1990s most of the component beliefs weakened, resulting in a weaker ethos. A weak ethos may be replaced by a new ethos. In the Israeli case, as I show in this book, an attempt was made during the 1990s to replace the ethos of conflict with a new ethos, but this attempt failed—its beliefs were not shared by more than 60 percent of the public and it was not imparted to the younger generation. Eventually, in the period after 2000 the Israeli ethos of conflict as a whole strengthened again, although it was not as strong as it was in the 1960s and 1970s.

The ethos as a whole can change in other ways over time: the hierarchy between the themes may change as a result of weakening of some themes along with strengthening of others, a change in content of specific beliefs in the ethos may create new contradictions with other beliefs, and a society may develop new strategies to deal with existing or new contradictions within the ethos beliefs or between the ethos and other societal beliefs. My study identifies changes over time in the strategies that were used to deal with the dissonance between core themes of the Israeli ethos and other societal beliefs, in the context of Israeli control of the territories. Initially, the main dovish party—Labor—denied any inconsistency between Israeli control of the territories and the value of democracy because, according to its 1969 platform, Israel's humane policy in the territories encourages the establishment of "democratic foundations" in the Palestinian society. The main hawkish party—Likud—used the bolstering strategy to cope with inconsistency between its belief in the need to maintain all territories under Israeli control (the value of Greater Israel) and the goal of Israel as a Jewish and democratic state. For example, its 1969 platform added the cognition that large Jewish immigration to Israel would enable Israel to preserve its Jewish majority while annexing the territories. But over time, both parties changed the way that they coped with the potential contradiction between core Israeli values in the context of Israeli control of the territories. Since the 1970s, Labor platforms have acknowledged a clash between Israeli control of the territories and main themes in the Israeli ethos such as the goal of security. They also have argued that in the context of permanent Israeli rule over the territories, or Israeli annexation, the values of a Jewish state and democracy could not coexist. As a result, a new strategy was advocated by the Labor party to cope with this inconsistency—changing the context within which the perceived inconsistency arises—for example, advocating giving up Israeli control of the territories that were captured in 1967 to resolve the clash that it creates between the values. As for the Likud party, in 1988 its platform stopped using any strategy to deal with the potential inconsistency between its goal of Greater Israel and the goal of a Jewish and democratic state and left the inconsistency unresolved. Since 1996, Likud platforms have not mentioned the goal of Israeli control of all the territories. That does not mean that the party no longer believes in Israel's right to the territories or that it completely abandoned its wish to keep it under Israeli control. But the failure to appeal to this goal in the platform does suggest that its salience had declined, and other goals had become more important at that time. Indeed, hawkish leaders like Ehud Olmert and Ariel Sharon applied a new strategy to cope with the inconsistency between the value of Greater Israel and the values of Israel as a Jewish and democratic state in their rhetoric and in the platform of their new party Kadima—they explicitly prioritized the value of a Jewish state over the value of Greater Israel.

Finally, in the period after 2000, following the collapse of the peace talks between Israel and the Palestinians and a failure to achieve agreement regarding the status of the territories, another strategy was used to cope with Israel's continuing control of the territories—avoidance. This was triggered by the building of a barrier that separates the territories from Israel while keeping Israeli settlements and IDF control of parts of the territories. The difference between avoidance and the previous strategy of changing the context within which the perceived inconsistency exists is that, in the latter, Israel's action aimed to solve the inconsistency while, in the former, the aim was only to make the inconsistency more tolerable.

As is typically the case in complex systems, multiple factors combined to bring about the above changes, and it is difficult to gauge the extent of the impact that each individual factor had on the ethos. My focus in this book is on changes in public opinion and the different factors that help explain how they came about. Changes in the society's configuration—for example, following mass waves of immigrations or intergenerational population replacement—may lead to changes of societal beliefs (Inglehart 1997). Specifically, the different experiences and socialization processes of new society members may lead them to embrace beliefs at odds with those of the older generation. In the Israeli case, I argue that the arrival of approximately 1 million Jewish immigrants from the former Soviet Union in the 1990s, as well as the increase in the number of ultra-Orthodox Jews as a proportion of the total population in Israel, explain some of the changes in the Israeli ethos.

But the reality may influence the ethos of the society even in the absence of major changes to the society's demography. New information (not necessarily directly related to the conflict) may cause people to reevaluate and adjust their current societal beliefs. In this vein, major wars and peace initiatives may play a vital role in changing societal beliefs (Deutsch and Merritt 1965; Sears 2002). The impact that an event may have has to do, in part, with the nature of the event itself—its duration, its threatening nature, whether it has a negative or positive meaning for the society, its ambiguity, and so forth (for an extended discussion about the characteristics of a major event that may enhance its potential for driving change in ethos of conflict, see Oren 2005). But the effect of major events is also determined by the way that the information regarding the events is presented by the media or by an *epistemic authority* (i.e., a source that exerts determinative influence on the formation of an individual's knowledge) (Kruglanski 1989). Throughout this book, I highlight the effect of major events in the Israeli-Arab conflict on the ethos. In the concluding chapter, I take a closer look at the factors that influenced changes in public opinion following the three most influential major events—the first intifada, the Oslo process, and the second intifada.

Ethos of Conflict and Conflict Resolution

My aim is not only to describe the changes in the Israeli ethos but also to explore the potential role they played in the efforts to resolve the Israeli-Arab conflict. In this analysis, I also rely on Zartman's (2000) ripeness theory and Rumelili's (2015) framework linking peace and ontological insecurity.

According to ripeness theory, resolution of a conflict usually follows a long process of searching for a formula that will satisfy both parties' aspirations (Pruitt and Kim 2004). The theory argues that "if the parties to a conflict (a) perceive themselves to be in a detrimental stalemate and (b) perceive the possibility of a negotiated solution (a way out), the conflict is ripe for resolution" (Zartman 2000, 228–229). Focusing only on material conditions that may bring the parties to perceive themselves to be in detrimental stalemate neglects to account for cases such as the Oslo Accords, when the stronger side in an asymmetrical conflict agreed to enter a peace process with its weaker adversary. This book elaborates on the sociopsychological price that brings a society to the perception of stalemate. I argue that one of the factors that made the Israeli-Palestinian conflict ripe for resolution in the early 1990s from the Israeli side was the perception of this conflict among some Israeli leaders and the public as being too costly in psychological terms; that is, because of the threat to the Israeli ethos that in turn threatened Israeli identity. In addition, changes to specific constituent beliefs of the ethos contributed to the perception that there was a formula to end the conflict. In particular, a decline in the belief denying Palestinian nationhood and in the belief that a Palestinian state would endanger Israel contributed to the shift of Israeli public opinion toward the option of a Palestinian state as a way out of the conflict. Thus, in this book I explore the potential impact of the ethos on motivation to solve a conflict (the first condition for ripeness) and optimism about the prospects of peace (the second condition); by doing so, I highlight some important and fundamental processes that set the stage for ripeness.

This book also joins a recent and ongoing scholarly effort to investigate the link between ontological security and peace. Studies in this scholarly field concern not just the conditions that encourage the parties to start negotiations but also those that move the parties from conflict resolution to peace and reconciliation. *Ontological security* refers to security of identity (of *being* rather than *surviving* or merely physical security) (Rumelili 2015; Mitzen 2006; Steele 2008). Rumelili (2015) argues that in societies that live under the conditions of intractable conflict, ontological security is achieved by establishing concrete objects of fear that help to cope with existential anxieties (unlike fear that is a response to a specific threat, one which can be faced and endured, the threats causing anxiety are unknown), and producing a system of meaning that provides a sense of self and differentiates friends from foes. As a result, "all conflicts, over time, become increasingly entrenched in narratives and conceptions of Self and the Other, and the maintenance of these narratives becomes critical for ontological security" (Rumelili and Çelik 2017, 2).

In recent years, the concept of ontological security has been applied to analyze specific cases of societies under conditions of intractable conflict such as Northern Ireland, Cyprus, and Israel (Lupovici 2015; Loizides 2015). Yet many of these scholars have used a vague definition of identity (if they used any definition at all) and there is a need to further theorize the link between identity construction and functions and ontological (in)security. Ethos of conflict, as I present in this book, can provide this needed link, in the sense that ethos is a major component of identity. More specifically, the security theme of the ethos may establish a definite object of fear and the means to cope with it. The creation of a clear differentiation between self and Others and between friend and foe is supported by themes such as beliefs about self, delegitimization of the enemy, siege, and society's goals. Furthermore, the ethos as a whole serves as a meaning system through which the conflict can be viewed and understood (Bar-Tal 2013, 211). Finally, the ethos of conflict, as I demonstrate in Chapter 2 and in sections that analyze school commemoration ceremonies on Memorial Days for fallen soldiers and the Holocaust Remembrance Day ceremonies, establishes routines that according to Mitzen (2006) are important in establishing ontological security. So, while the conflict may produce high levels of fear (in the personal and the national sense), the ethos of conflict as a whole can provide ontological security to the society. Rumelili (2015, 22–23) calls this situation a "stable conflict."

A threat to the ethos—a vital component of national identity—can produce ontological insecurity. Rumelili (2015, 23–24) defines a state of high levels of both fear and ontological insecurity as an "unstable conflict." She notes that ontological insecurity could have a positive potential for conflict resolution and that this anxiety may make a conflict ripe for resolution. This is because it may "pave the way for reconstruction of identity in a way that reverses the process that established the rival in the conflict as an object of fear" (Rumelili 2015, 24)—and this desecuritization of the rival transforms unstable conflicts into a "conflict in resolution" state that is characterized by high levels of ontological anxiety but low levels of fear. The high level of anxiety at this stage may be caused by the peace process itself since a peace process may "unleash high levels of ontological anxiety that were previously suppressed and generates ambiguities in the system of meanings" (Rumelili 2015, 24). Scholars have just started to study this aspect of a peace process and its implications for peace practice. Yet "further research is needed to trace precisely how ontological security needs hinder the advancement of the peace" (Lupovici 2015, 34). The study of ethos of conflict—in particular, the way that a peace process threatens the ethos—can contribute to this theoretical and empirical task by exposing the specific mechanisms that produce ontological insecurity during a peace process and the conditions under which peace can fail or succeed. I discuss these issues further in Chapters 7 and 9.

Ethos, Ideology, Culture, and National Identity

As noted above, ethos is a key component of national identity and, hence, the study of ethos of conflict contributes to our understanding of the link between identity and conflict resolution. Before proceeding, I want to clarify the relationships between ethos and national identity and other related concepts such as ideology and political culture. National identity is a popular concept that, like ethos, was for years vaguely defined. Brubaker and Cooper (2000) even went so far as to suggest that the concept of national identity is too ambiguous to serve the needs of social analysis and, thus, should be abandoned or restricted. More recently, David and Bar-Tal (2009) proposed a model for national identity that incorporates ethos as one of its components, along with other components such as language and customs. *National identity* can be seen, even under this more concrete definition to be too broad a concept for the purposes of conflict analysis and resolution. More so than other components of identity, much (although not all) of the ethos of conflict content is directly shaped by the conflict and, therefore, it provides a useful way to look at the link between identity and conflict. The ethos component of identity is also more dynamic than other components (e.g., language) and, thus, is especially important in explaining changes in the state's actions and policy regarding the conflict (Oren, Bar-Tal, and David 2004; Oren 2010; Oren and Bar-Tal 2006, 2014).

Another way to look at the societal beliefs of ethos is as "building blocks of the content that characterize culture" (Bar-Tal 2013, 175). Inglehart (1997, 52) defines *culture* as a coherent system of beliefs, values, attitudes, norms, and skills that are widely shared and deeply held within a given society. Others argue that ethos is a part of cultural knowledge (Bar-Tal and Oren 2000, 7; McClosky and Zaller 1984, 16). However, the culture of a society may also include societal beliefs that are not central enough to be part of the ethos. These beliefs are not widely shared as the themes of ethos, and are not systematically imparted to the younger generation as the ethos beliefs. For example, according to a 2001 survey that employed questions from Inglehart's World Values Survey, Israel was found to have a moderately postmaterialist culture (Yuchtman-Ya'Ar 2002). Democracy, tolerance, and multiculturalism are core postmaterial values and are associated with sensitivity to minority and women's rights and to the environment. Most of these cultural values are not part of the Israeli ethos. Indeed, postmaterialism in Israel is embraced mainly by younger, more secular, higher-income individuals who identify with the political left (Yuchtman-Ya'Ar 2002). It is also widely assumed that culture either experiences no change over time or changes slowly in response to long-term trends. This means that, in contrast to ethos, the concept of culture is not dynamic enough to explain changes in policy preferences.

A common definition of *ideology* as a highly consistent set of ideas (in the form of attitudes, values, and even ideological narratives) that provides an interpretation and a prescription as to how the order of society should be structured (Maynard and Mildenberger 2018; Jost, Federico, and Napier 2009; Haidt, Graham, and Joseph 2009) is close to Bar-Tal's definition of ethos. And indeed, according to Bar-Tal et al. (2009), ethos is a variant of ideology that influences perceptions and interpretations of social reality. Maynard and Mildenberger (2018, 567) point to a lacunae in current writing about ideology regarding the question of ideology's *scale*—the relationship between ideology and subideology phenomena and superideology phenomena. In this regard, ethos of a society is a superideology in the sense that it functions as a framework that overrides the various separate subideologies in the society. As I show in the following chapters, for most of the period that is covered in this book, the core themes of the ethos of conflict were shared by the main ideological subgroups in Israel (e.g., the political right and political left).[10] My analysis of the way that each group dealt with the contradiction between its ideology and the national ethos contributes empirically and theoretically to our understanding of the relationship between superideologies and subideologies in a society. It follows that changes in a society's ethos are more fundamental than are changes in any of its subideologies and, hence, may have a larger impact on that society's policies (e.g., toward conflict resolution).

In sum, rather than replacing the use of concepts such as national culture, ideology, and national identity, my goal is to contribute to the study of these concepts in the sense that ethos is an important component, albeit not the only one, of these constructs. Ethos can explain policy choices of a society, including those related to conflict resolution. However, I do not claim that ethos is the only factor shaping policy choices. It obviously is only one piece of the grand puzzle of politics.

Methodology

At this point, it would be useful to further elaborate on the methodology behind this study. As noted, my goal was to uncover the extent to which themes of ethos of conflict identified by Bar-Tal (2013) serve as the pillars of the Israeli ethos, the relationship between these themes, and the change in the ethos over time. Among the many types of sources that contribute to the construction of the content of the Israeli ethos or serve as reliable barometers, I decided to focus on the following:

1. Political leaders' speeches, interviews with the press, and writing;
2. School curricula;
3. Election platforms; and
4. Public polls.

In addition, anecdotal examples from Israeli popular songs and published opinion writing are used as illustrations to the themes of the ethos and as complements to the systematic analysis of the principal sources listed above. Since the transmission and change of the beliefs that construct the ethos could be top down or come from below, official sources such as leaders' rhetoric may shape and give expression to the ethos. Leaders can influence people's beliefs and groups' identity with their rhetoric, but leadership is also influenced and constrained by collective identity (Hogg, Knippenberg, and Rast 2012; S. A. Haslam, Reicher, and Platow 2010; Rhodes and Hart 2016). Changes in positions of specific leaders and political parties within the society can be explained by leaders' personality traits, personal beliefs systems, and the "evolutionary-dynamic" explanation for changes in core beliefs of nationalist movements (see a more extensive discussion in Chapter 8) (Aronoff 2014; Shelef 2010). One should keep in mind, however, that leaders and parties have to gain public approval and, therefore, need to be responsive to shifts in public opinion. Leaders often monitor public polls and adapt their rhetoric and policy to surveys' data (Auerbach and Greenbaum 2000). Furthermore, leaders can influence the society's identity, but only up to some point. They "can be ahead of the group, but never so far ahead that they are out there on their own" (S. A. Haslam, Reicher, and Platow 2010, 106). Thus, a change in rhetoric of the leaders, especially when analyzed within a broader context of changes in public polls, could be an indication of a decline or strengthening in the idea's hegemonic status in the society. That is also why I am less concerned with the authenticity of political rhetoric. True, politicians are not always honest but, even in this context, appeals to themes of the ethos matter since they convey the relevance of these themes to political discourse and, at the same time, can influence the public's preferences. Politicians from peripheral and tiny parties are less constrained by hegemonic ideas and often target only specific sectors within the society. Thus, my analysis focuses only on mainstream politicians and excludes leaders of groups on the periphery of the Israeli political system. Due to space limitations, I included the rhetoric only of leaders that served as prime ministers (with one exception—Yair Lapid, Netanyahu's current main political competitor, is included to get some insight into future trends).[11] These individuals obviously do not exhaust the variety of mainstream Israeli politicians, but we can assume that they played the most significant role in expressing and shaping the beliefs of the public.[12]

The curricula taught in schools can be seen as an institutionalization of the ethos—as attempts by the leadership to construct an ethos and transmit it to the students, especially in Israel where the state is highly involved in determining the curricula and in monitoring the content of school textbooks (Podeh 2002, 8). Indeed, changes in school curricula are often associated with a change in the identity (and political affiliation) of the minister of education, when the new ministers attempt to promote different ideological goals than their predecessors. Given that the person appointed to this position is usually a leading member of one of the parties that comprise the ruling coalition, the new priorities can be seen as a reflection of the leadership priorities and not just the minister's beliefs.

Since I focus on the hegemonic discourse, I excluded from my analysis the curricula of independent ultra-Orthodox schools and of the schools in the Arab sector because they are on the periphery of the Israeli education system and have their own ethos.[13] Note also that under the term *curriculum* I include both the "intended" curriculum, also known as the "official," "formal," or "explicit" curriculum (Cuban 1992) as well as the actual content of textbooks and extracurricular activities at school. The intended curriculum is expressed in official documents published by the Ministry of Education that conceptualize goals for teaching a given subject matter in schools. In Israel, one can find about three to four generations of curriculum documents for most school subjects, beginning with the foundation of the state in 1948 up to contemporary times (Hofman, Alpert, and Schnell 2007). As I show throughout the chapters in this book, the actual content of textbooks may or may not match the declared goals of the intended curriculum. The occasional discrepancies can provide some insight into which themes are central to the ethos—and, hence, are declared as explicit goals for education—and themes that are less central but still may be common in textbooks, even if implicitly.[14]

As noted, a theme is part of the Israeli ethos of conflict if it appeared in leaders' rhetoric, if it was transmitted to students in school curricula, and if most people in public polls agreed with it. I utilized an extensive database of Israeli public polls to determine the extent to which the Israeli Jewish public has embraced the ethos beliefs and to evaluate how those beliefs have changed over time (see the Appendix for more information about the main surveys used in this study, institutions that conducted these polls, polling frequency, and type and size of samples).[15] In keeping with the spirit of Bar-Tal's (2013) criteria of a belief deserving to be considered part of an ethos if shared by a majority of society members for "long periods," I set a benchmark in my analysis of at least 60 percent support for at least a decade. It must be noted that fluctuations in public opinion are common; hence, a one-time decline below the 60 percent threshold did not disqualify a belief from being part of the ethos since it could indicate a measurement error or an immediate reaction to an extreme event that occurred shortly before the survey was conducted.

Relying on public polls that were conducted in the past has some limitations. First, there is little polling data for the period before 1967, so my analysis of Israeli public opinion is limited to the period after 1967. Second, there is a lack of polling data regarding some of the beliefs of the ethos; for example, there are few time series questions that refer to victimization beliefs in Israeli society even though these are central beliefs in school curricula.[16] In addition, some questions were worded in such a way that it may have influenced their results. Yet if repeatedly asked over time, even questions with problematic wording can provide some indication regarding ethos changes. Despite the above limitations, then, the database of public polls provided valuable insight into the general agreement with the ethos beliefs within the Israeli Jewish public. Unless otherwise indicated, all public polling data presented in this book pertains to only the Israeli Jewish population. I chose to focus on the Israeli Jewish public and exclude the attitudes among the Israeli Palestinians for several reasons. The main reason is technical; another limitation of public polls prior to the late 1990s is that questions relevant to ethos beliefs were asked in surveys that were conducted among only the Israeli Jewish population. Comparing results from later surveys that included Israeli Palestinian respondents to earlier survey results that did not include them would give a misleading picture of changes over time. In addition, the core of the Israeli ethos (Israel as a Jewish state) addresses the Jewish population of the country and, for obvious reasons, is not shared by the majority of Arab citizens of Israel. The way that Israeli Palestinians deal with this ethos and their attempt to change the main ethos of the Israeli society is an important issue that should be studied; it is, however, beyond the scope of this book.

Structure of the Book

The first part of the book provides detailed analysis of specific themes of the ethos of conflict in Israeli Jewish society. It is important to note here that, while each chapter in this part focuses on an individual theme, the themes remain inseparable parts of a complex whole, and I refer to the ways they relate to each other throughout the book and especially in the last two chapters. In Chapter 2, I explore the theme of establishing a Jewish state in the historical land of Israel as well as the collective memory relating to the roots of the Israeli-Arab conflict and the justness of each party's goals in the conflict. In Chapter 3, I look at security beliefs—the perception of Israel as a small country that is under existential threat, the centrality of national security, and the public trust in the Israeli army. In Chapter 4, I present the dichotomy in the Israeli ethos between the positive self-image of Israel as an advanced, moral, and peace-loving country and the negative image of Arabs as backward, untruthful, and seeking Israel's destruction. The focus of Chapter 5 is siege and victimhood beliefs: Israel's self-image as a society that stands alone against a hostile world and how this theme relates to the Holocaust. In Chapter 6 I turn to the theme of Israeli patriotism, examining the extent of pride that Israelis feel for their country and their willingness to make the ultimate sacrifice on its behalf. I also discuss beliefs about the need for and extent of national unity. Then, in Chapter 7 I investigate the centrality of the value of peace in Israeli society, how achievable it was considered to be in different eras, and the nature of the perceived peace.

The second part of the book goes beyond study of each theme separately to elaborate on the relationship among these themes and the implications of changes in the ethos as a whole for policy preferences. In Chapter 8, I present the ethos of conflict as it was reflected in the election platforms of the two main Israeli parties (Labor and Likud) during the years 1969–2009, analyzing the relationship between the themes in the ethos and how those themes feed and sustain each other. I also discuss the extent to which there was acknowledgment of contradictions among the ethos themes and other core beliefs in society, and how the political parties dealt with such contradictions. Finally, I explore the connection between the ethos beliefs and policy preferences of the parties regarding the conflict with the Arabs. I offer specific conclusions in Chapter 9 regarding the Israeli ethos and its effect on future trends in the Israeli-Arab conflict. I also underscore the theoretical merit of this study and its potential contribution to other topics such as conflict resolution and leadership and social change in intractable conflicts.

Notes

1. I chose to use the term *Israeli-Arab conflict* rather than *Israeli-Palestinian conflict* since it more accurately reflects the wider historical context (in its earlier phases, including the early part of the period covered in this book, there were other Arab parties—Egypt, Syria, Jordan, etc.—actively involved in the conflict. To a lesser degree this is still true today). This term also reflects the way the conflict is framed within the Israeli ethos: viewing the entire Arab world as implacably hostile to Israel has been a relatively stable tenet of the Israeli ethos as I discuss further in this book.

2. Kimmerling (2001) wrote about the civil versus the primordial identity of Israel, and he also identified several subdivisions of the Israeli polity (traditionalists, Arab citizens of Israel, Russian-speaking immigrants, Ethiopians, noncitizen workers).

3. These two categories are used by McClosky and Zaller (1984, 4) to explain why capitalism and democracy are the two values that define the American ethos.

4. For the meanings of the Holocaust in Israel and the United States, see Novick (2000); Gorny (2003); Navon (2015); Klar, Schori-Eyal, and Klar (2013); and Lustick (2017).

5. Y. Zerubavel (1995), for example, shows how jokes that became popular among Israeli Jews during the 1970s and 1980s about the historic Tel Hai battle defied the myth about this battle in Israeli collective memory.

6. For example, Wertsch (2002, 117–128) shows how in the Soviet Union people applied what he calls "internal emigration" as a mechanism to resist the official collective memory. This internal emigration involved questioning official stories in a narrow circle of friends, and consuming underground literature that refuted these narratives.

7. An example for a state-directed ritual that was not adopted by the Israeli public is the Independence Day Haggadah that was circulated by the state to the Israeli public in 1952 to use in their homes during Independence Day. This text substituted God with Israel Defense Forces (IDF) while citing phrases from the traditional Passover Haggadah. In addition, the minister of education at that time offered a detailed proposal for the celebration of Independence Day in Israeli homes (reading of the Declaration of Independence at a family meal, decorating homes with olive branches), but none of these official proposals and texts were adopted by the Israeli public in its Independence Day celebration practices (Liebman and Don-Yihya 1983, 116).

8. For example, Ben-Shaul (1997), Shohat (1989), and Gertz (2000) analyzed Israeli films; Firer (1985) and Podeh (2002) analyzed school textbooks; and Urian (2013) analyzed Israeli theater. Sucharov's (2005) account of Israeli identity is based on examination of cultural symbols such as folk songs, plays, films, and school curricula. Arian (1995) and J. Shamir and Shamir (2000) analyzed Israeli public opinion.

9. Waxman (2006a) and Abulof (2015) use a variety of official and cultural sources such as political rhetoric and op-ed writing in Israeli newspapers, and occasionally cite anecdotal poll data. However, public polls are not their main focus and their analysis of public opinion is less comprehensive and systematic than the one that I present in this book.

10. McClosky and Zaller (1984) make a similar claim about the American ethos of democracy and capitalism that American conservatism and liberalism share.

11. Twelve people served as prime ministers of Israel: David Ben Gurion, Moshe Sharet, Levi Eshkol, Golda Meir, Menachem Begin, Yitzhak Shamir, Yitzhak Rabin, Shimon Peres, Ehud Barak, Ariel Sharon, Ehud Olmert, and Benjamin Netanyahu.

12. The analysis of leaders' rhetoric is based on published academic studies about these leaders, a search within the Prime Minister's Office archive of speeches on the internet (http://www.pmo.gov.il/MediaCenter/Speeches/Pages/default.aspx),

the archive of Rabin's speeches at the Rabin Center for Peace (http://www.rabincenter .org.il/Web/He/Archives/Subjects/Default.aspx), the Israeli parliament archive on the internet (http://main.knesset.gov.il/About/Occasion/Pages/BeginSpeeches.aspx), and Israel's Foreign Policy–Historical Documents (http://mfa.gov.il/MFA/Foreign Policy/MFADocuments/Pages/Documents_Foreign_Policy_Israel.aspx). For the purposes of this book, a theme is considered to be part of the Israeli ethos of conflict if it was mentioned by at least three leaders who served as prime ministers. Beyond this criterion, the strength of a theme within the ethos may vary on a spectrum ranging from a theme that was infrequently mentioned by only three leaders to a theme that was frequently mentioned by every one of these leaders over the years.

13. The Israeli school system is divided into Jewish and Arab sectors. The Jewish sector is divided into three tracks: state-secular, state-religious, and the independent ultra-Orthodox. The ultra-Orthodox system (with about 24 percent of Jewish pupils) is separate and autonomous and focuses almost exclusively on religious studies (Hofman, Alpert, and Schnell 2007). For many years the curriculum for the Arab sector was supposed to be identical to that of the Jewish sector, but since the 1980s large parts of the curriculum for Arab schools have been adapted to Arab cultural heritage.

14. The sections in this book that describe the content of the ethos themes in the Israeli school curriculum are based mostly on a review of the vast and rich literature devoted to the way that Zionism and the Israeli-Arab conflict have been depicted in the curriculum, much of it written in Hebrew and hence not accessible to non-Hebrew readers. In addition, I have provided my own analysis of the current school curriculum that to my knowledge has not yet been covered by other scholars.

15. This database was originally created by Jacob and Michal Shamir and included surveys on the issues of peace and territories conducted during the years 1967–1991. The database was a product of a systematic process: first, J. Shamir and Shamir conducted an extensive search of the archives of the two major newspapers in Israel at that time for references to public polls; then, they searched all published academic studies for polling data; and, finally, they directly obtained the survey data from major opinion research institutions that were operating during those years (J. Shamir, Ziskind, and Blum-Kulka 1999). I followed this procedure and updated the database with polls that were conducted during the years 1991–2017 as well as earlier polls that referred to issues in the ethos other than territories and peace.

16. There may be several reasons why public polls do not refer to specific beliefs. In some cases, it may indicate that a belief achieved a status of hegemonic belief in the sense that it is considered to be common sense, natural, and obvious (Lustick 1993). But this is not always the case. It also may happen because the topic is politically sensitive and, therefore, difficult to ask in many contexts. Or the reason may be technical; as Stone (1982, 7–8) explains, the questions in the survey reflected shifting interests of survey clients and sponsors as well as considerations regarding space limitations and the cost of interviewers and data processing. The meaning of the absence of a topic from public polls, then, should be determined in the context of other available information on this issue—for example, the way leaders referred to it.

PART 1

Themes of the Israeli Ethos

2

A Jewish State
in Eretz Israel

An ethos of conflict often includes a theme about the goals of the society and the legitimation of these goals (Bar-Tal 2013). Of course, this theme is a core element in an ethos of any society, including those that are not living under conditions of conflict. In fact, this is the focus of nationalist movements that are often consumed with beliefs about the territorial boundaries of the homeland as well as about the national "mission" (Shelef 2010). However, the theme in the ethos that defines society's main goals and justifies them is especially important in the context of intractable conflict since many conflicts revolve around competing goals. The conflicts between Israelis and Palestinians, Turkish Cypriots and Greek Cypriots, and Serbs and Albanians in Kosovo, to name just a few, all revolve at least in part around conflicting national goals and territorial rights to the same land. Each side highlights the justness of its goals over the opponent's goals. Indeed, a set of beliefs that justify these goals is part of the content of this theme of the ethos of conflict. Common justifications for territorial rights include arguments based on divine "promises" articulated in holy texts such as the Bible or the Quran, liberal arguments related to the principle of self-determination, arguments about rights derived from prior habitation, and assertions that their side makes the "most efficient use" of the land (Lustick 1996b). Furthermore, conflicts that involve goals that are perceived by one or more of the rivals as sacred, or revolve around sacred places, are difficult to resolve. People will kill and risk their lives and the lives of their loved ones in the name of sacred values. They tend to resist the rational give-and-take of negotiation and, therefore, such conflicts are rarely amenable to resolutions that call for dividing or sharing the disputed land (Hassner 2013; Sheikh, Ginges, and Atran 2013; Ginges et al. 2007).

This chapter, then, focuses on the main goal of the Israeli society—the goal of establishing a Jewish state in the ancient homeland of the Jews, as a main theme of the Israeli ethos and its specific justifications. I present the debate about the meaning of this goal and its status as a sacred goal, explore changes over time, and analyze references to tensions between the goal of establishing a Jewish state and other Israeli societal goals and values such as democracy.

As I noted in the previous chapter, this theme dominates the 1948 Israeli Declaration of Independence. Hence, before proceeding with analysis of leaders' rhetoric, school curricula, and public polls, I begin with an outline of the way this theme is presented in the 1948 declaration. As is the case in many other countries, the Israeli declaration was influenced by the American Declaration of Independence (Armitage 2007; Shachar 2009). First and foremost, the Israeli declaration borrowed its format from the American declaration, including both a narrative of past events leading to the creation of a new state and justifying its creation as well as a declaration of rights that defines the future form of the new state. Beyond the format, the last paragraph of the Israeli declaration resembles the last paragraph of the American declaration. More important, however, is how the end of both nations' declarations differ. The first difference concerns the entity that declares independence. In the American text, it is "the Representatives of the United States" while the Israeli version notes two groups: the representatives of the Hebrew community in Israel and the Zionist movement that represents Zionist Jews everywhere. In this sense, the State of Israel is not just a Jewish state, but a state of the Jews.

In both declarations, the state is man-made while "God was asked to keep an eye" (Shachar 2009, 591); however, the Israeli declaration does not use the term *divine Providence* that appears in the American text, even though it is a common term in Jewish texts. Neither does it use any other universal term for God such as *the Lord*. Instead, it uses the less common term *Rock of Israel*. This term appears in the Bible and in the Ashkenazi Jewish morning prayers in which God is the protector of the Jewish people on their return to their ancient homeland. In other words, God in the Israeli declaration is "strictly ethnic and territorial" (p. 591). This idea, then, leads us to another critical difference between the American and Israeli ethos. Unlike the United States' creation of a new nation, Israel's claim of independence is an act of restoring an ancient and lost Jewish sovereignty.

The Israeli Declaration of Independence declares the establishment of "a Jewish state," a striking edit to earlier drafts that described a "Jewish free independent and *democratic* state" (Shachar 2002, 563, emphasis added). While the declaration does not specifically declare Israel as a democratic state, it does include a paragraph that describes the nature of the future Jewish state as a liberal democracy:

The state of Israel will be open for Jewish immigration and for the Ingathering of the Exiles; it will foster the development of the country for the benefit of all its inhabitants; it will be based on freedom, justice and peace as envisaged by the prophets of Israel; it will ensure complete equality of social and political rights to all its inhabitants irrespective of religion, race or sex; it will guarantee freedom of religion, conscience, language, education and culture. (Israel Ministry of Foreign Affairs n.d.)

But even this paragraph, which defines Israel's commitment to democratic principles, starts with the definition of Israel as a Jewish state—it will be open "for Jewish immigration and for the Ingathering of the [Jewish] Exiles." So, even here, the Jewish character holds precedence over the democratic one as it is the first mentioned feature of the state, presumably the most important one. Note also that the term *Jewish state* may have other meanings than a state that is open to Jewish immigration. Another meaning is that the public life in Israel will conform to the Jewish tradition. A third meaning is a Jewish majority in Israel. The last meaning is especially important given the democratic character of the Jewish state. In this regard, despite the paragraph in the Israeli Declaration of Independence mentioned above, Israel is a *majority-hegemonic state*—a state that promotes the interests of the majority ethnopolitical group in a multinational setting, which does not meet the definition of a liberal democracy (I. Peleg 2007). More specifically, while Israel employs many formal aspects of democracy (e.g., free elections and limitations on executive authority) and it grants all citizens, including non-Jewish citizens, a substantial package of liberties and freedom, it limits group rights of non-Jewish groups (mostly Arabs), such as in the right of land control, and it acts to promote the collective agenda of mainly the Jewish population rather than treating all social groups in Israel equally or neutrally (I. Peleg 2007; I. Peleg and Waxman 2011).

Another omission in the Israeli Declaration of Independence is the absence of any references to the borders of the future Jewish state. At first sight, this does not seem odd. The Israeli declaration was written before the end of the 1948 War and, hence, before the 1949 borders of the new State of Israel were established (what is now known as the "Green Line"). But the writers of the declaration could have envisioned the borders of the future Jewish state, as they envisioned its future character. For example, they could have declared that the borders of this state would match the United Nations (UN) partition plan. Indeed, one of the earlier drafts of the declaration did exactly that (Shachar 2002). Or they could have stated that the aim is to establish a Jewish state in the whole land of the ancient homeland of the Jews. They chose to do neither. In other words, the declaration addressed only the *sovereign goal* (the establishment of a Jewish state) while leaving the *territorial goal* (what part of Eretz Israel will be included in the Jewish state) open.

Most of the Declaration of Independence is devoted to the historical justifications for the goal of establishing a Jewish state in Israel. It begins with a reference to ancient times and stresses that "the land of Israel was the birthplace of the Jewish people" and that this is where they achieved independence. Then it notes that during their generations-long exile Jews maintained a strong spiritual and physical link to the land of Israel. After that, the declaration moves to modern times. It states that, in recent decades, the Jews "returned in masses. They reclaimed the wilderness, revived their language, built cities and villages and established a vigorous and ever-growing community." The declaration also mentions the Holocaust that "proved anew the urgency of the re-establishment of the Jewish state, which would solve the problem of Jewish homelessness by opening the gates to all Jews." It also notes the contribution of the Jewish people in Palestine to the struggle against Nazi Germany. It ends with the 1947 resolution adopted by the UN General Assembly for the establishment of an independent Jewish state in Palestine and concludes that "it is the self-evident right of the Jewish people to be a nation, as all other nations, in its own Sovereign State."

The declaration of independence, then, presents a chronological linear story—from ancient times to current times. In terms of progress, it is a zigzag (rise, fall, and rise) story (E. Zerubavel 2003). Thematically it is a narrative of redemption—a story of suffering and success, and of the emergence of power and strength out of weakness and persecution (McAdams 2006). Indeed, such narrative of birth or rebirth of a nation can be found in ethos of many other nations such as Greece and Northern Ireland (A. D. Smith 1999). Handelman (1990) notes that redemption is also a central element of traditional Judaism, and the movement from low to high also characterizes the rhythm of time in traditional Judaism.[1] Note, however, that while the declaration refers to a period of 3,000 years, its focus is modern times. This can be seen, for example, in the number of words in the declaration that are dedicated to the ancient biblical period (only 28) compared to the number of words that refer to the nineteenth and the twentieth centuries (249 words).[2] In other words, the Declaration of Independence focuses more on the redemption of the Jewish people than on its glorious past.

The goal to establish a Jewish state and the historical narrative that supports it are constructed also by routines such as the development of the Israeli national calendar. The State of Israel adopted much of the annual cycle of Jewish holidays. This is not a unique situation. Eviatar Zerubavel (2003), who studied national calendars around the world, found that the births of Christianity and Islam are officially commemorated as national holidays that signal the spiritual origin of the country in 195 states. He mentions the inclusion of Jewish traditional holidays, such as Sukkoth and Shavuot, in the Israeli national calendar as another example for national religious holidays that frame the origin of a state. In these holidays, Jews commemorate events that happened during the biblical era when Jews lived in this land. Thus, the inclusion of these Jewish holidays in the Israeli national calendar implies *antiquity* of the origin of the State of Israel and *priority* of the Jews to the land, especially vis-à-vis the Palestinians, by stating that there was a Jewish presence in this land long before its conquest by the Arabs in the seventh century; hence, the Jews are the original inhabitants of this territory.[3]

Following the establishment of the state in 1948, alongside the traditional Jewish holidays, new memorial days were added to the national holiday calendar such as Independence Day and Memorial Day for the fallen soldiers.[4] Thus, the Israeli national calendar combines traditional Jewish holidays with new holidays in a way that creates collective memory that further supports the historical rights of the Jews for the land and their national inspirations. A collective memory of redemption is contrasted through the *order* of holidays within the annual cycle that "symbolizes a vast movement from bondage (Passover) and victimization (the Holocaust Remembrance) through a national struggle (the Memorial Day for Israeli soldiers) to national independence (Israel's Independence Day)" (Y. Zerubavel 1995, 219).

Leaders' Rhetoric

The redemption narrative and the justifications for the establishment of a Jewish state in Israel presented above were common themes in the rhetoric of David Ben-Gurion, Israel's first prime minister. Ben-Gurion often cited the Bible to justify the Jews' claim to the land. However, he looked to the Bible as a source of historical justifications (e.g., the historic link of the Jews to the land) rather than religious ones (divine promise). In this vein, the biblical figures he regarded as heroes were those who had conquered the land (Joshua), expanded the kingdom (David, Solomon, Jeroboam II), and held a nationalist vision (Saul, Uzziah)—despite the Bible's notion that some of these heroes did evil in the eyes of the Lord (Tzahor 1995). He argued that the land of Israel was never completely abandoned by the Jews, and that Jews continued to inhabit the land through the ages. At the same time, he described the land prior to the Zionist arrival as "a razed land" and "barren wilderness"—hinting that non-Jewish residents neglected it (Tzahor 1995, 75). He presented Jewish life in the diaspora as unsustainable and emphasized that, to survive, the Jewish people needed a state. In this context, he referred to the Holocaust as a "Zionist proof-text"—that shows what happens to a people in diaspora when they have no country of their own (Lustick 2017, 130–140; see also Stauber 2007). For example, he stated in an interview in 1961 following Israel's trial of Adolf Eichmann that the Holocaust "revealed the whole tragic depth of a people in foreign country, at the mercy of strangers and abandoned to the arbitrariness of despots and Jew haters" (Weitz 2013, 247).

These narratives that justify the goal of establishing a Jewish state in Israel appeared in all of Ben-Gurion's successors' rhetoric. Here are some typical examples. Levi Eshkol said in 1964, "With our exodus from Egyptian bondage, we won our ancient freedom; now, with our ascent from the depths of the Holocaust, we live once again as an independent nation" (quoted in Handelman 1990, 199). Menachem Begin justified Israel's right for the land based on the history of the Jewish people in this land and the Holocaust (Naor 2003, 136; Peleg 1987, 64). For example, in a 1982 speech, he mentioned the West Bank—the land captured by Israel in 1967 and the core of conflict with the Palestinians—as "Judea and Samaria," and as a place "from whence we once came [and which] was the cradle of our faith, where our civilization was created and developed and which we took with us on our global wanderings, its greatness within us, and with which we turned home." He further declared that "this is the foundation—and there is no other—of our rights" (Begin 1982). In a speech given during the 1977 historical visit of Egyptian president Anwar Sadat to Jerusalem, Begin maintained that "anyone who has not seen the exhibits at Yad Vashem [Israel's World Holocaust Remembrance Center] cannot understand what happened to our people when we were deprived of our land. Nobody came to our rescue, neither from the East, nor from the West" (Begin 1977). Like Begin, Yitzhak Rabin evoked Israel's historic rights to the land when he said in a 1995 speech:

> Thousands of years of exile and the dream of generations have returned us to our historic home in the Land of Israel, the Land of the Prophets. Etched on every vineyard, every field, every olive tree, every flower is the deep imprint of Jewish history, of the Book of Books that we have bequeathed to the entire world, of the values of morality and justice. Every place in the Land of the Prophets, every name is an integral part of our heritage of thousands of years, of the Divine Promise to us and to our descendants. Here is where we were born. Here is where we created a nation. Here we forged a haven for the persecuted and built a model democratic state. (Rabin 1995e)

In a speech to the Knesset in March 2001, Ariel Sharon said that "after 2000 years of exile and persecution. This is the only place in the world where Jews can defend themselves, by themselves" (Ariel Sharon 2001). Ehud Olmert cited in a 2007 speech "the great miracle of the Jewish people, which clawed its way out of the abyss of the Holocaust to the height of national rebirth" (Olmert 2007b). A content analysis of all of Benjamin Netanyahu's speeches during 2013 revealed that historical narratives justifying the goal

Table 2.1   The Existence of Ethos Themes in Benjamin Netanyahu's Speeches in 2013 (percentage of speeches that refer to each theme)

	Audience		
Theme	Domestic ($n = 50$)	Foreign ($n = 8$)	Total ($N = 58$)
Jewish state	26	63	31
Historic rights to the land	20	63	26
Secure place for the Jews	8	38	12
Security	68	88	71
Existential threat	56	63	57
Security as a value	50	88	55
Siege	28	38	29
Villa in the jungle			
Negative perception of Arabs	46	88	52
Not moral/not democratic	14	50	19
Do not want peace	10	50	16
Want to destroy Israel	32	75	38
Backward	4	13	5
Nazis	6	38	10
Positive perception of Israel	62	100	67
Light into the nations	28	25	28
Moral, democratic	12	63	19
Modern, advanced	30	75	36
Peace-loving	38	88	45
Strong	34	25	33
Unity	22	25	22
Patriotism	6	13	7
Peace	2	50	9

of establishing a Jewish state in Israel appeared in 31 percent of his speeches (see Table 2.1).[5] In 12 percent of these speeches, he justified the establishment of the state by asserting the need for a secure place for the Jews. But he tended to focus more on the historical connection of the Jewish people to the land (26 percent of his 2013 speeches included this justification).

The elevation of the "Jews are the original inhabitants of the land" argument over other justifications is apparent in the well-known speech given by Netanyahu at Bar-Ilan University in 2009: the Bar-Ilan speech started with ancient times and claims that "the connection of the Jewish People to the Land has been in existence for more than 3,500 years." (Netanyahu 2009a). It specifically referenced the West Bank ("Judea and Samaria") as the homeland of the Jewish people. Netanyahu next described "the series of disasters that befell the Jewish People over 2,000 years" when the Jews were in exile that "reached its climax in the Holocaust." He then arrived at the conclusion that these tragedies demonstrate that "we need a protective state." He concluded by returning to biblical times and the birth of the Jewish nation. So, while it is still a redemption story, the historical narrative is in a sense also a circular story. I return to this point and its significance for historical progress or lack thereof in Chapter 5, focusing on the victimhood theme. For now, it is important to note that the early period—the glorious past—was more central in Netanyahu's Bar-Ilan speech than Jewish history in modern times. Netanyahu explicitly said the "right of the Jewish People to a state in the Land of Israel *does not* arise from the series of disasters that befell the Jewish People over 2,000 years" and that this right arises "*only* from one simple fact[:] Eretz Israel is the birthplace of the Jewish People" (emphasis added).

Public debate among mainstream leaders about the goal of establishing a Jewish state in the land of Israel focused mainly on the ways in which this goal is interpreted and applied by the state rather than its essence. Beliefs regarding the application of the goal to establish a Jewish state changed significantly, albeit most of these changes predated 1967; that is the starting point of the period covered by this book. First, regarding the meaning of "Jewish state" as a state that conforms to Jewish traditions, leaders from the two main Zionist movements—Labor and Revisionist—initially rejected the idea that religion should dominate the public realm of the Jewish state. But over time, they came to accept that it should govern significant aspects of public life[6] (Shelef 2010). A second area of change concerned the meaning of a Jewish state as the "state of the Jews" and the connection between Israel and diaspora Jews. Initially, Ben-Gurion and the Labor movement envisioned a goal of eradicating the Jewish diaspora—that is, having all Jews emigrate to Israel. But starting in the late 1930s, the goal slowly shifted to one that accepts the continued existence of these communities (Shelef 2010).

Third, the beliefs related to the territorial goal of the Jewish state also underwent major shifts in the period before 1967. The Labor Zionist movement's initial view of the desirable borders of the homeland were the Litani River (currently part of Lebanon) as the northern boundary, the East Bank of the Jordan River to the east (Transjordan), and the international border with Egypt in the south (the western boundary was the Mediterranean Sea). But in the late 1930s and early 1940s, a shift began to take place in Ben-Gurion's and the Labor movement's position regarding the borders: the East Bank of the Jordan River and southern Lebanon were no longer defined as parts of the land of Israel. So, the new map referenced the international borders with Lebanon and Egypt to the north and south and the Jordan River to the east. Similarly, the Revisionist movement's rhetoric about the borders shifted over time. Until the mid-1950s, it included both banks of the Jordan River, but gradually the references to the eastern bank disappeared, giving way to a perception of the "whole land of Israel" that is limited to the area west of the Jordan River (Shelef 2010, 5).

Currently, the territorial goal that is part of the Israeli ethos concerns the 1949 armistice lines: the Green Line mentioned above. Since 1949, this area has never been referred to by an Israeli prime minister as anything but an integral part of the state of Israel[7]—hence, it could be seen as hegemonic belief that is taken for granted in Israeli society (Lustick 1993). In the period after 1967, political debate about the territorial goal was between two groups in Israeli society, which Kimmerling (2008, 98–99, 1985) called the "state of Israel" and "Eretz Yisrael." According to the Eretz Yisrael group, the territorial goal of Israel is to establish Jewish political sovereignty over all of the land under Israeli control, including the territories captured in the 1967 War. This more hawkish perspective uses narratives rooted in biblical times to legitimize this goal and is especially prominent in the rhetoric of leaders such as Begin and Yitzhak Shamir. The "State of Israel" approach uses numerous justifications for Israel's existence, including the longing of the Jews for their ancestral homeland, the persecution of diaspora Jews as proof of the need for a state of their own where they can find safety, the existence of a Jewish Zionist community in the land, and the recognition by other states of the world. It is also more pragmatic regarding the territorial goal of Israel and supports territorial compromise with the Palestinians (see a detailed discussion in Magal et al. 2013).

Despite their differences, the two groups share the goal of establishing a Jewish state in Israel and the collective memory that supports this goal. Indeed, beliefs about the historical rights of the Jews to the land of Israel, including the territories, also appeared in rhetoric from less hawkish Israeli leaders. For example, Ehud Barak stated in 2000 that the territories are "parts of the homeland from which we had been separated by a hostile border and to which we returned. . . . A natural expression of our love for and historic bond with this land, which has been our patrimony and homeland since antiquity" (Barak 2000). Ehud Olmert said in 2006, "We insist on the historical right of the Jewish people over the whole of Eretz Israel. Every hill in Samaria, every valley in Judea, is a part of our historical homeland. We do not forget this fact, even for one moment" (Olmert 2006a).

Israeli leaders in the period after 1967, then, did not differ much on the question of whether the Jews had a right to the territories, but rather on whether controlling the territories represents a sacred goal on which any compromise is unacceptable. Hawkish leaders, such as Shamir and Begin, referred in the period after 1967 to territorial compromise of the land as a taboo (Landman 2010, 145). In a 1992 speech Shamir said, "*Eretz Israel* is not another piece of land; it is not just a place to live. Above all, *Eretz Israel* is a value; it is *holy*" (Waxman 2014, 143, emphasis added). For many other leaders, including hawkish leaders in the period after 2000, such as Netanyahu,[8] this was no longer a sacred goal—they expressed a willingness to negotiate Israel's control of the territories, and indicated the need for exchanging the territorial goal with other goals and societal beliefs such as the goal of Jewish majority, peace, and democracy. For example, Rabin said in 1995, "We had to choose between the Greater Land of Israel, which means a binational state and whose populations would comprise, as of today, 4.5 million Jews and more than 3 million Palestinians . . . and a state smaller in area, but which would be a Jewish state. We chose to be a Jewish state" (Waxman 2008, 78). In a 2005 speech, Sharon prioritized peace and the Jewish state goal over the territorial goal: "For peace we are willing to give up part of our right. When we had to choose between the completeness of the land without a Jewish state or a Jewish state without the completeness of the land, we chose a Jewish state" (Brom 2007, 10). Olmert said in 2006 that "the choice between the desire to allow every Jew to live anywhere in the land of Israel [and] the existence of the State of Israel as a Jewish country— obligates relinquishing parts of the land of Israel" (Olmert 2006a).

While not all Israeli prime ministers considered keeping the territories under Israeli control a sacred goal, there was virtual unanimity (dovish leaders included) in their rhetoric regarding the sanctity of the goal of maintaining a unified Jerusalem under Israeli control. Begin, for example, said, "United Jerusalem—the one—is Israel's eternal capital and will never again be redivided. It will remain one for generation unto generation" (Begin 1979a).

Some background is necessary before proceeding with analysis of this issue. After the 1967 War, without ever declaring a formal annexation, a complex series of laws was passed that extended the jurisdiction of Jerusalem's municipality to comprise a 70-square-kilometer portion of the West Bank that included the Jordanian municipality of East Jerusalem (where the Old City and holy sites such as the Western Wall are located) and lands from twenty-eight West Bank villages. Unlike other Palestinians in the West Bank, Palestinians living within the new municipal boundaries were granted permanent resident status and were permitted to apply for Israeli citizenship. In addition, after 1967 several Jewish neighborhoods were built on large tracts of land in the extended eastern sector of Jerusalem. In July 1980, parliament passed the Basic Law: Jerusalem, officially declaring that Jerusalem— "Whole and United"—was Israel's permanent capital and that Israel exercised exclusive sovereignty over it.

It is in this context that, for years, Israeli leaders have presented the current Jerusalem municipal borders—"united Jerusalem"—as a sacred goal. Rabin, for example, told the Knesset in 1993 that "united Jerusalem is not subject to bargaining, is and will forever be the capital of the Jewish people, under Israeli sovereignty" (Rabin 1993b). Looking closer at Rabin's rhetoric regarding Jerusalem, however, Lustick (1996a) concluded that "united Jerusalem" was not presented in Rabin's rhetoric as a natural and inevitable goal (while referring to united Jerusalem, Rabin also referred to Palestinians in East Jerusalem as "Palestinians from the territories").

Indeed, in later years, Israel negotiated the status of Jerusalem with the Palestinians. The 2000 negotiations between the Barak government and the Palestinians at Camp David and at Taba focused on changing the boundaries of Israeli Jerusalem. In 2008, Olmert offered the Palestinians sovereignty in East Jerusalem's Arab neighborhoods and proposed a multination nonsovereign trusteeship for the Old City. Netanyahu, however, still declared "united Jerusalem" as a non-negotiable goal. For example, speaking at an official Jerusalem Day ceremony in 2015, he vowed that "we will *forever* keep Jerusalem united under Israeli sovereignty. . . . The future belongs to the complete Jerusalem that shall *never* again be divided" (Miller 2015, emphasis added). Yair Lapid, Netanyahu's main political rival, also pledged in 2017 that Jerusalem will not be divided and that he would never discuss splitting the city: "If there's no peace because of that, then there won't be" (N. Landau 2017).

The sovereign goal of maintaining Israel as a Jewish state—especially when defining Jewish state as one that has a Jewish majority and that allows every Jew in the world to settle in it—is still considered a sacred goal by all Israeli leaders. Thus, they all have opposed negotiating the Palestinian demand that refugees from 1948 and their descendants be allowed to return to the area within Israel's 1949 borders (the so-called Right of Return), as that would endanger the Jewish majority in Israel (Landman 2010; Segal 2001).

When it comes to Israel's goals, the one aspect on which there have been noticeable changes over time in the rhetoric of Israeli leaders is the question of whether Israel has *exclusive* rights to the land; that is, negating the legitimacy of the Palestinian claim for the same land. During the 1960s and the 1970s, Israeli leaders held Palestinians to be part of the "Arab nation" and not a separate people; therefore, they were denied their right to the land. For example, in the Knesset in 1975, Begin said, "There is no entity, no identity, and no nation that is called Palestinian" (quoted in Auerbach and Ben-Yehuda 1987, 330). However, since the late 1970s, and more explicitly following the Oslo Accords, progressively more Israeli leaders have legitimized Palestinian self-determination, at least in principle. For example, in a 1995 speech Rabin said, "We are not alone here on this soil, in this land. And so we are sharing this good earth today with the Palestinian people" (Rabin 1995e). Similarly, Olmert said in December 2008, that "our Palestinian neighbors also have dreams, memories and a feeling of belonging to this piece of land" (Olmert 2008).[9] In his 2009 Bar-Ilan speech, Netanyahu accepted the Palestinian claim to their own state while still discussing the land as belonging mostly to Jews: "In the area of *our* homeland, in the heart of *our* Jewish Homeland, now lives a large population of Palestinians. . . . In my vision of peace, in this small land *of ours* two peoples will live freely, side-by-side, as good neighbors with mutual

respect. Each will have its own flag, its own anthem, and its own government" (Netanyahu 2009a, emphasis added).

School Curricula

The 1950s Through the Early 1990s

The State Education Act (1953) declared that Israeli schools should focus
on the commitment to uphold the Jewishness of the state and use education
to strengthen Jewish collective memory and myths, as well as values such
as freedom and equality (Naveh and Yogev 2002). Documents published by
the Ministry of Education regarding goals for the teaching of a given subject matter in schools (e.g., the intended curriculum) also emphasized
national goals, especially from the 1950s to the 1980s. For example, Podeh,
who analyzed the declared goals of history curricula from 1954 through the
late 1990s, shows that the declared intention was primarily to instill respect
for Zionism and the belief in the justness of Israel's claims for the land
(Podeh 2002, 42).

This trend was not unique to history curricula. Hofman, Alpert, and
Schnell (2007) analyzed the curriculum documents of the Ministry of Education in ten disciplines from the 1950s to 2000. They found that during the
1950s and 1960s curricula tended to promote "unified, hegemonic national
goals" and, although curricula in the 1970s and 1980s increased the emphasis on academic and scientific values, national values continued to be presented. Likewise, Resnik (2003), who studied the intended curricula in
Bible, history, literature, and civics from the 1950s to the early 2000s, found
that national goals were the main goals of the curricula.[10] Focusing on the
teaching of specific justifications for the establishment of a Jewish state in
Israel, she found that the main goal during the 1950s was to impart the belief
that Jews are a national entity with the right to a state and to emphasize the
attachment of the Jews to the land of Israel. During the 1960s, another goal
appeared—to deepen Jewish consciousness among Israeli students—thus
supporting the definition of the term *Jewish state* as a state that conforms to
the Jewish tradition. However, the teaching of this goal found expression in
mainly nonformal activities at school.[11] During the 1970s, the curriculum
linked the Holocaust to the establishment of the State of Israel and it has
been the dominant intended justification since the 1980s.

Historical justifications for the right of the Jews to the land also found
expression in the actual content of textbooks, written following official
instructions from the Ministry of Education. Firer (1985) found that history
textbooks from 1930 to 1984 emphasized the collective memory and the
justifications for the Jewish claims to the land as they appear in the Decla-

ration of Independence: that the Jews have a right to the land based on their historical origin, having lived there until they were exiled,[12] having maintained close spiritual and physical ties with the land during exile, and having maintained a constant Jewish presence in the land throughout the exile. Also important is the threat to Jews during the diaspora, indicating their need for the establishment of a state.[13] In this vein, history textbooks often rejected Jewish life in the diaspora as unsustainable. This idea was promoted by Ben-Zion Dinur who served as minister of education during the years 1951–1955. In a 1955 speech, he said that exile is "a sin" and that "exile always includes destruction" (Lustick 2017, 133).

Firer (1985) found that in general, history textbooks from 1930 until 1984 presented Jewish history as a deterministic—the Law of Redemption. According to this law, Zionism and the establishment of the State of Israel is more than a "solution" to anti-Semitism in the diaspora; it is an expression of an eternal historical force that has directed Jewish history since the expulsion of Jews from the land. Until the end of the 1960s, history textbooks focused on anti-Semitism as the main catalyst for the Zionist movement and the awakening of the Law of Redemption. However, history textbooks published during the 1970s and early 1980s, while still referring to anti-Semitism as a factor in Zionist awareness, now emphasized the connection between the Jewish people and the land as the central justification. Firer also found that history textbooks commonly presented the land as a divine promise to the Jews until 1948, but less so thereafter.

Podeh (2002) provides supplementary evidence to Firer's (1985) findings. Focusing treatment of Palestinian claims to the land by history textbooks, he found that Israeli textbooks from the 1950s until the mid-1980s refuted all Palestinian claims to the land. For example, these textbooks described "a country without people for a people without a country," and presented the land as deserted prior to the arrival of the Zionist pioneers.[14] In addition, history textbooks tended to minimize the importance of Arab nationalism, describing it as a monolithic movement without distinctions between Egyptians, Syrians, Palestinians, and other Arab groups, and as a mere reaction to Zionism rather than a development within the Arab society.

While Firer (1985) and Podeh (2002) analyzed only history textbooks, arguments legitimizing the Jewish right to the land and refuting Palestinian claims appeared in other subjects' textbooks as well. Textbooks written following the 1976 introduction of civics as a separate compulsory curriculum "put the Jewish-Zionist ethos at the center of civic education" (Pinson 2007, 359).[15] David (2012) analyzed readers used to teach Hebrew literature and found that justifications for the establishment of a Jewish state were aligned with those in history textbooks. Both readers and history textbooks presented Israel as the Jews' fatherland ("Eretz Avot") and included many texts linking the State of Israel to the ancient biblical land.

The readers also addressed historical rights of the Jews to territories in the West Bank. Readers for secular schools from the 1970s stressed mostly the Jewish connection to Jerusalem. Readers for state religious schools after the 1967 War also emphasized the Jewish link to other places in the territories such as Hebron and Bethlehem.

Readers from the 1950s and 1960s emphasized the national political significance of Jewish holidays over their traditional religious meanings. For example, text about Hanukah emphasized the Maccabees' success in liberating the Jews over the divine miracle of the flask of oil and the renewal of services at the Temple. Texts about Passover likewise emphasized the national liberation of the Jews. They also highlighted links between the Jews and the land through emphasis on natural and agricultural aspects of the holidays over religious ones. Passover was celebrated as the spring holiday, and Sukkoth as the harvest holiday. Otherwise minor holidays with connections to the land like Tu-Bi-Shvat (the Holiday of the Trees) became central holidays in the readers while traditionally central holidays without such a connection—such as Yom Kippur and Tisha B'Av—were ignored for the most part. As David (2012, 268) notes regarding Tisha B'Av, this omission has an ideological symbolism: the renewed Jewish state eliminates the adversity of the destruction of the Temple and the exile (as commemorated by Tisha B'Av) and, thus, makes it unnecessary to focus each year on the ancient loss of Jewish independence.

The readers also included texts about a deserted land yearning for its original inhabitants to return. In describing the country during Jewish exile, a 1955 reader for third grade said: "The Land of Israel was crying: Who will plant a tree for me? Who will give me back my glorious days?" (David 2012, 116). Another common theme was the persistent experience of anti-Semitism in the diaspora, which demonstrates that a Jewish state is necessary for a secure existence. For example, a 1978 reader for seventh grade included the poem "About the Child Avaram" by Nathan Alterman. This poem describes the Jewish child Avaram sleeping on the stone steps of his house in a Polish city. He cannot sleep in his bed like other children, for he saw his mother "asleep with a slaughtering knife in her heart," his father "sleeping still with no head on his shoulders," and his sister "sleep with tears of the dead on her cheek." The poem then describes how "the seventy nations of the world" forced the child Avaram to return to the house where his family was murdered: "We will place you in your waiting bed / And there you shall sleep as still as your father." Invoking the biblical story of God commanding Avaram to go to the ancient land of Canaan, in the poem God approaches Avaram the Jewish Polish boy: "God spoke to Avaram, to Avaram / Who slept in the corridor of his home. / Saying: do not fear / Do not fear, Avaram, / For I will make your name great, / Go, through a night of butchery and blood, / To the land which I will show you / . . . And Avaram was afraid and fell on his face / And he left his home and gate / For the command that thundered over Avaram the father (man) / Thunders too over Avaram the boy."[16] The poem, then, references several justifications for establishing a Jewish state in Israel: the hostility of the world toward Jews, the biblical roots of the Jews in the land, and the divine promise.

Reliance on the Bible to legitimize Jewish claims to the land was not limited to readers. Even today, teaching the Bible remains mandatory in all Jewish schools in Israel. Hofman, Alpert, and Schnell (2007, 317) conclude that in the early decades of the state, the Bible was "considered, in a sense, as the historical document justifying Zionist settlement in the Land of Israel."[17] Schnell (2013) found that, like history textbooks, geography textbooks from the early years of the state emphasized the historical biblical right of the Jewish people to the land (see also Bar-Gal 1993). The study of geography textbooks is important because they addressed territorial goals (ideal borders of the state) as well as the sovereign goal (the establishment of a Jewish state). In this regard, Bar-Gal (1993) found that Israeli geography textbooks generally have presented an unclear map of the borders of Israel and avoided discussion of the precise borders. In other words, school textbooks have emphasized the sovereign goal of establishing a Jewish state in Israel and the historical narratives supporting this goal, but have kept an ambiguous position on borders and territorial questions.

The Late 1980s and the 1990s

Most of the studies mentioned above also documented significant changes during the late 1980s and the 1990s. Hofman, Alpert, and Schnell (2007) found that during the 1990s, the declared curricula in most subjects of learning promoted multiple, sometimes conflicting, goals rather than endorsing goals that were primarily national. For example, the new 1994 civics curriculum guidelines declared that one aim of civics studies was that students would "acknowledge the existence of the Israeli state as the state of the Jewish people and understand its commitment to the Jewish people in the Diasporas." Yet it also presented a common definition of citizenship based on the exploration of "Israeli society's diverse political and social perspectives" (quoted in Pinson 2007, 364), not just the Jewish perspective.

In some disciplines' textbooks, the content changes were noteworthy and mostly in line with the new declared goals, but in others only minor changes were made despite those official goals. Hoffman, Alpert, and Schnell (2007, 319) note that the literature curriculum went through dramatic changes in the 1990s as textbooks began selecting literary works according to students' interests and psychological needs rather than national aims. David's (2012) analysis of 1990s Hebrew literature readers came to similar conclusions, including a notable decrease in references to the goal of establishing a Jewish state and its justifications.

Pinson (2007) identifies some major changes in 1990s textbooks, this time for civics. A book entitled *To Be a Citizen in Israel: A Jewish and Democratic State,* written and approved following the new 1994 civics curriculum guidelines, became the most widely used civics textbook in high schools. Unlike earlier civics textbooks, this book recognized competing definitions of the State of Israel (from a state that fully adopts the Jewish religious laws to a secular democratic state that does not identify with the Jewish religion). It also acknowledged the tension between Israel as a Jewish state and Israel as a democratic state, in contrast to prior versions. However, while the body of the textbook engaged the students in discussions about the problems inherent in the dual definition of Israel as a Jewish and a democratic state, it ended with a chapter that aimed to "assist" the students in concluding that this definition was still the most desirable one. Likewise, the book justified the establishment of the State of Israel with more liberal democratic language—that it was an expression of the "natural right" of each Jew—rather than the biblical or historical justifications employed in earlier versions. Changes to the civics textbook, then, represented the multiple conflicting goals of the intended curriculum while still emphasizing and justifying the goal of establishing a Jewish state in Israel (Ichilov 2004).

Some studies found a notable change in history textbooks from the late 1990s, especially regarding the exclusivity of Israel's claim for the land and their presentation of the Palestinian claim for it. A new generation of history textbooks was published during the late 1990s (the Oslo Accords years—when Yosi Sarid, a politician from the dovish party Meretz, became the minister of education), including books such as *The 20th Century: A History of the People of Israel in the Last Generations, for Grades 10–12* (Bar-Navi 1998); *Modern Times, Part II: The History of the People of Israel, for Grades 10–12* (Bar-Navi and Naveh 1999); *Journey into the Past: Chapters in History for Grades 8–10* (Tabibyan 1999); and *A World of Changes: A History Book for 9th Grade* (Ya'akobi 1999). These books presented a revised history of the conflict and recognized the existence of a Palestinian national group (Podeh 2002). Bar-Navi's (1998) history textbook taught the evolution of Palestinian nationalism from the disintegration of the Ottoman Empire to the first intifada and the Oslo process. It acknowledged that Zionism shaped a Palestinian nationalism but noted a similar process during consolidation of the Spanish and German nations (see a review of this book in Podeh 2002, 94).

Peled-Elhanan (2009, 2012) analyzed the same history books but arrived at a different conclusion, due possibly to a different methodology. Inspired by Van Leeuwen (2005) and Kress and Christie (1989), Peled-

Elhanan (2009, 2012) employs a critical discourse analysis that goes beyond the books' explicit content and into latent meaning. Examining semiotic and visual cues, such as the layout or arrangement of elements (e.g., pictures and text on a page, chapters in a book), the use of specific words and verbs to describe events and groups, and the questions that the students are asked about the text, she drew conclusions about messages that were implied but not overtly articulated. For example, a two-page spread in Bar-Navi's (1998, 78–79) textbook included two pictures from 1905 of Jewish pioneers who were "sun-tanned, healthy and well-built, wearing Arab *kafiehs,* mastering Arab horses and familiar with the art of cultivating the Land" with the caption "Land of Israel types." In other words, the Jewish immigrants were presented as "indigenous natives and not as the newcomers from Eastern Europe that they were at that time," which supports arguments that the Jews were the original inhabitants of the land (Peled-Elhanan 2009, 97). Likewise, the verb that was most frequently attributed to the Palestinians in the new textbooks was "abandon"—that they "abandoned" the land. So, even though the content had been broadened to include multiple perspectives, the implied message was consistent with earlier textbooks.

Firer, 'Adwān, and Pingel (2004) provide a critical analysis of the history textbooks written by Bar-Navi (1998) and Bar-Navi and Naveh (1999) similar to Peled-Elhanan's (2009, 2012). Firer, 'Adwān, and Pingel note that the Palestinians who lost their homes in the 1948 War were referred to as "Arabs," a "phenomenon," and, most frequently, as "Eretz-Israel Arabs." Analyzing the maps in these textbooks, Firer, 'Adwān, and Pingel also note that a map in Bar-Navi's textbook of the first Zionist immigration presented the thirty-two established Jewish settlements and some mixed Jewish Arab towns (e.g., Jaffa and Jerusalem), but did not show the hundreds of Arab villages already in existence. Thus, the land was presented as less populated, and claims of settling deserted lands were reinforced. Firer, 'Adwān, and Pingel also identified this narrative about deserted land with regard to the 1967 War; the description of this war ignored the Palestinian inhabitants of the territories, "as if the conflict between Israel and the Arab states was unfolding on empty land" (2004, 63).

Examining geography textbooks, Hofman, Alpert, and Schnell found a discrepancy between the declared goals of the formal curriculum, published in the late 1990s, and the actual contents of the textbooks used during that period. While the intended curriculum called for teaching environmental aspects, social and economic inequalities, and respect for other cultures, the textbooks hardly covered these goals and instead were "saturated with a narrow nationalistic narrative and interpretation of culture that undermines other narratives" (Hofman, Alpert, and Schnell 2007, 316).

Finally, a 2000 study of 360 Israeli textbooks in Hebrew language, literature, history, geography, civics, Bible, and Judaic studies used in Grades

1–12 from 1999 to 2000 found that the texts recognized the national aspirations of the Palestinians and did not ignore the deep attachment of the Arabs to Jerusalem. However, they presented it as a religious issue and not a political one. Some books described the attachment of the Jews to Jerusalem as much deeper than that of the Muslims and Christians, therefore both acknowledging and undermining the Palestinians' claim to the land as less just. In addition, the textbooks maintained prior narratives in which the land was deserted prior to the arrival of the Zionist pioneers, "leaving the pupil with a distorted impression of the Jews having been the majority since the beginning of their settlement" (IMPACT-SE 2000, 7).

Thus, evidence shows that textbook content did change in the 1990s, especially about Palestinian rights to the land, but scholars differ about the intensity of this change, and it seems that old narratives did still exist, at least latently. It is also important to note that studies of early childhood education in Israel conducted since the 1980s found that strong nationalist messages were conveyed to young children earlier than first grade. Handelman (2004, 70–74) describes a celebration of Jerusalem Day in an Israeli kindergarten class of three-, four-, and five-year-olds. The celebration began with songs about King David making Jerusalem the capital of ancient Israel, describing rejoicing in Jerusalem, and calling for rebuilding of the Temple. The celebration concluded with the teacher telling the children that Jerusalem was and always would be the capital of Israel. The three-year-old children then built a wall of their own height (representing the Western Wall), formed a circle, and danced around it. Nasie, Diamond, and Bar-Tal (2016, 374) report observations from eight secular kindergarten classes that documented teachers telling the three- to six-year-old kindergarten children: "We [the Jews] have no other country to go to." Some referred to the 1947 UN resolution as justifying the Israeli claim to the land: "There was a UN decision, in which it was decided that Arabs and Jews will live together in Israel. The Arabs did not agree, and we had no choice but fight." Others refuted the justness in the Palestinian claim for statehood, telling the children that the Palestinians "have many countries and we have one, and they still want our country."

The Period After 2000

There are several indications of strengthening in the theme of Israel as a Jewish state in textbooks and nonformal activities in the period after 2000. Some of the books from the late 1990s were later banned or revised by the Ministry of Education. In 2000, the Ministry of Education recalled two previously approved books—*The 20th Century on Threshold of Tomorrow* by Eyal Naveh and *A World of Exchanges* by Danny Ya'akobi—due to their critical presentation of the Zionist narrative (Resnik 2003; Schnell

2013; Yogev 2010). The Education Ministry's pedagogical committee also decided to rewrite parts of *To Be a Citizen in Israel: A Jewish and Democratic State* (Kashti 2010). Analysis of those revisions found that "the definition of Israel as both Jewish and democratic is hardly mentioned in the revised chapters and, when it appears, "the way the material is framed and organized sends a clear message to the students that the Jewish element of Israel's definition takes precedence over the democratic one" (Pinson 2013, 1–2). Revised chapters also refuted Palestinian nationality, presenting Palestinian national identity as part of a pan-Arab entity and thus "giving students the impression that Palestinian self-determination can and has already been achieved in the context of Israel's 22 neighboring Arab nations"—a return to an argument that was common in leaders' speeches during the 1970s (Pinson 2013, 3).

Firer (2005) refers to 2000–2005 as the "retro period" and states that during this period new textbooks were written with content resembling that published before the Oslo Accords. In an analysis of second grade Bible studies textbooks published in 2000 about the book of Joshua, Zalmenson-Levy (2005) found that the textbooks blurred the difference between the country's biblical borders and its current borders by using the biblical expression "Promised Land" with photos of current cites in Israel, the territories, and Lebanon, without mentioning that the territories were currently occupied or that millions of Palestinians live there. The textbooks also build an analogy between Joshua's army and the IDF. In one exercise, which presented photos of both a soldier's backpack from the days of Joshua and an IDF soldier's backpack, students were asked to compare the two soldiers' equipment, thus linking current Israeli soldiers serving in the West Bank to Joshua conquering the land based on the divine promise. Overall, the textbooks promoted the justification of the Jewish rights to the land (including the territories) based on the ancient Jewish connection and on divine promise—a return to a claim common in earlier periods. This trend of emphasizing Jewish rights to the land and refuting the Palestinian historical narrative was also apparent in maps in other school textbooks from this period. A study of maps in all approved books for the year 2009 found that of those depicting the area between the Jordan River and the Mediterranean Sea, 76 percent did not distinguish between Israeli and Palestinian areas or mention the Palestinian Authority. As a result, these maps can be seen as implying that the Palestinian areas are part of the State of Israel (Adwan, Bar-Tal, and Wexler 2016).

This trend extends to extracurricular activities, as evidenced by a master plan program from the Ministry of Education regarding school field trips (Ministry of Education 2008). According to this program, students must visit Tel Aviv once and Jerusalem three times from kindergarten through twelfth grade. During those visits to Jerusalem, students must see the Western Wall, the Knesset, Month Herzl (Israel's national cemetery—a resting place of Israel's presidents, prime ministers, speakers of the Knesset, and other dignitaries—and national military cemetery), and the Holocaust memorial site Yad Vashem. Students should also travel to at least eight sites related to Jewish and Zionist history. Sites related to Jewish history must include at least one site related to the biblical area of the Israelites' conquest of the ancient Canaan, one site connected to the Destruction of the Temple, one site from the Tana'anic or Mishna period, and one site representing the old pre-Zionist Jewish community such as Tiberius or Tsfat. Related to Zionist history, students must visit at least one site that represents Zionist settlement of the land, one site that represents the Zionist Jewish immigration to Israel, one site that "illustrates the [Jewish] struggle for the country" (e.g., a battle site), and one site that represents the success of the Zionist development of the country (e.g., a power plant). Together, these eight field trips are expected to reinforce the collective memory and the justifications for Jewish rights to the land, especially that the Jewish nation was founded in the ancient land of Israel and that the Jews maintained close physical ties with the land of Israel even during their exile. Additionally, the teacher of the Bible classes must take part in the preparation for and instruction about the field trips to reinforce the "deep connection between the Jewish people and the land" (Ministry of Education 2008, 26). However, the master plan program does include two field trips to sites representing what are defined as "other cultures" in the history of the land (schools can choose Roman, Crusader, Muslim, or Ottoman sites), but the emphasis is that the land belongs first and foremost to the Jews. Visiting West Bank cities (the territories) is optional, but they are presented in the master plan program as integral areas of the State of Israel, with no mention of their special status as an occupied territory.[18]

In sum, the school curricula tended to promote belief in the goal of establishing a Jewish state in Israel and the justifications for that, and these were conveyed even to children in kindergarten. Over time, the centrality of each justification differed: the curricula since the 1980s emphasized the connection to the land in ancient times and the link between the Holocaust and the establishment of the State of Israel. The main change over time, however, was in the presentation of the Palestinian goal of establishing their own state in this land. Until the 1990s, school textbooks mostly refuted Palestinian rights to the land and maintained that Palestinians were not a national group. During the 1990s, new textbooks recognized the existence of a Palestinian nationality and presented the conflict as one between nations, although prior perceptions of the superior rights of the Jews continued to exist, latently at a minimum. Finally, textbooks and extracurricular activities from the period after 2000 indicate a return to earlier beliefs and messages that explicitly refute Palestinian claims and argue for an exclusive Jewish right to the land.

The Public

Agreement with Zionism
and the Goal of Israel as a Jewish State

Since Zionism defines the goal of establishing a Jewish state, analyzing questions regarding identification with Zionism can give us an indication about public agreement with this theme of the ethos. Such questions were asked annually in public surveys, and the results are presented in Figure 2.1. (See the Appendix for details about sample type and other relevant information about the surveys in Figure 2.1 and all of the other figures.) Figure 2.1 points out that, during 1970 to 2015 more than 70 percent of the respondents identified themselves as Zionist. Public polls conducted by the Dahaf Institute indicated that the percentage of respondents identifying themselves as Zionist dropped from 87 percent in June 1985 to 72 percent in 1997. Since there is no data about this question in the intervening years, we cannot determine when exactly this change took place or what might explain it.[19] One possible explanation is the arrival of new immigrants from the former Soviet Union in the beginning of the 1990s who had not gone through the same socialization process as those born and educated in Israel. Data showed that 48 percent of the new immigrants did not identify themselves as Zionist. Surveys from the the period after 2000, however, revealed

Figure 2.1   Identification with Zionism, 1970–2015

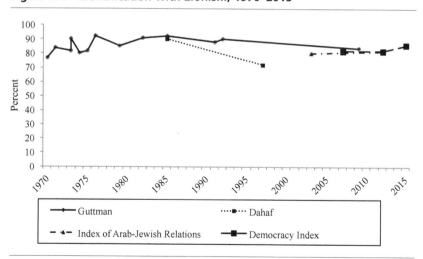

Sources: Guttman, Dahaf, Index of Arab-Jewish Relations, and Democracy Index; see Appendix for survey details.

that around 80 percent of the respondents identified themselves as Zionists (see Figure 2.1).

The common identification with Zionism in the Israeli Jewish society, as described above, does not distinguish between the specific goals that result from Zionism—the sovereign goal (the establishment of a Jewish state) and the territorial goal (the borders of the Jewish state). Questions regarding the sovereign goal indicated strong agreement with the general goal of Israel as a Jewish state. For example, according to a 1982 survey, 93 percent of the Jewish population affirmed that the State of Israel must be a Jewish state (Liebman and Don-Yihya 1983). Several questions addressed the three specific meanings of this goal (a state with a Jewish majority, a state with special ties to diaspora Jews, and a state with public life that conforms to Jewish tradition). In the same 1982 survey, 62 percent of respondents believed a Jewish state meant a state whose public image conforms with the Jewish tradition, 83 percent of the respondents thought that a Jewish state was one in which a majority of the population was Jewish, and 87 percent believed that a Jewish state is one that senses a special responsibility for diaspora Jews (Liebman and Don-Yihya 1983). Later surveys also addressed the specific meanings of a Jewish state (see Table 2.2). All surveys indicated that the principle of Israel as a Jewish state is a common belief in the Israeli society. The belief in a Jewish state as one with a public life that conforms to the Jewish tradition seems to have strengthened (from 44 percent who agreed with this principle in 1991 to 61 percent in 2009).

Another indication of belief in the three meanings of a Jewish state can be found in a 2011 Israeli Democracy Index survey that included the following open question: "Israel is defined as a Jewish state. Different people attach different meanings to the term 'Jewish state.' What do you think is the most important characteristic of a Jewish State?" I recoded the answers according to the three main meanings for "Jewish state," as discussed above, and the findings are presented in Table 2.3.[20] Note that most respondents (74 percent) chose one of those three meanings (a state with a Jewish majority, a state with special ties to diaspora Jews, and a state with a public life that conforms to Jewish tradition) as the most important characteristic of a Jewish state. Among the answers alluding to other meanings, the most common were a "Zionist state," "a state that is safe for Jews," or "the current situation in Israel." In addition, 9 percent of the respondents referred to democracy and universal values such as equality and tolerance as the main characteristics of a Jewish state. Only 1 percent of the respondents expressed negative attitudes toward "Jewish state" and associated it with words such as "religious coercion," or specifically commented that they preferred a state that is not exclusively Jewish.

Among the three main meanings of "Jewish state," the most common meaning in the 2011 survey was a state that conforms to the Jewish tradi-

Table 2.2 Agreement with Different Meanings of *Jewish State*, 1991–2014 (percentage who agree)

	1990	1991	1999	2002	2003	2004	2007	2009	2014
Jewish character									
Israel should keep its Jewish character[a]	95	93	–	–	–	–	–	–	–
Israel should have a Jewish character not necessarily religious[a]	–	–	78	79	–	–	–	–	–
Public life in Israel should conform with Jewish tradition[b]	–	44	52	50	–	–	61	61	–
Jewish majority									
Israel needs to maintain a Jewish majority[c]	–	–	–	–	95	97	–	–	–
State of the Jews									
Israel should maintain the Law of Return[c]	–	–	–	–	91	94	–	–	–
Support allowing Jewish immigrants to Israel immediate acquisition of Israeli citizenship[c]	–	–	–	–	–	–	–	87	–
Jews around the world should have the right to make aliyah[d]	–	–	–	–	–	–	–	–	87

Sources: a. Guttman; b. Guttman and Democracy Index; c. Index of Arab-Jewish Relations; d. Pew. See Appendix for survey details.

Note: The Israeli Law of Return grants the right to settle in Israel and automatic citizenship to every Jew who has expressed a desire to settle in Israel.

tion: 35 percent mentioned this characteristic as the main meaning of a Jewish state. Some of those who chose this option mentioned keeping the Sabbath as a rest day, having Jewish traditional holidays serve as national holidays, teaching a Jewish curriculum in Israeli schools, and so on. Eight percent of the respondents thought that "Jewish state" means full adoption of the Jewish religious laws (Halacha) as the law of the land. Twenty-eight percent of the respondents indicated that the demographic or sovereign meaning (Jewish majority or Jewish government) is the main characteristic of a Jewish state. In this regard, 4 percent of the respondents thought that the main meaning of a Jewish state is a state with Jewish residents *only* or without non-Jews.

In sum, the results of the 2011 survey are different from results of earlier surveys regarding this topic. This difference could be explained by dissimilarities in the format—the fact that the 2011 question was an open question and that the respondents had to choose the most important meaning of a "Jewish state" (as opposed to simply indicating their agreement

Table 2.3   The Most Important Meaning of the Term *Jewish State*, 2011

Most Important Meaning	Percentage Who Agree
Jewish majority	28
State according to Jewish religion	35
Relationship with diaspora Jews	11
Other	26

Source: Democracy Index.

with each given meaning of the term). While facing this format in 2011, the most common meaning of a "Jewish state" in respondents' answers was a state that conforms to the Jewish religion. Only a small percentage of the 2011 respondents (11 percent) chose the meaning of a state with special responsibility for diaspora Jews.

The territorial aspect of the Jewish state was often unclear in Israeli school textbooks, as noted in the prior section. Most Israeli surveys from 1967 to the 1990s focused on Israeli willingness to give up territories captured in 1967, especially the West Bank. Except for the first few years after the 1967 War, when nearly all Israelis wanted to keep these territories, the Israeli public has been divided on this issue, with gradually greater willingness to give up the territories (J. Shamir and Shamir 2000). We can conclude, then, that public polls, like school textbooks and leaders' rhetoric, showed that keeping the territories under Israeli control was *not* part of the Israeli ethos.

Sacred Values

We have seen the general agreement among Israeli Jews regarding Israel's goal of establishing a "Jewish state" in Israel. But does the public perceive any aspects of this goal as non-negotiable sacred values? Recall that, in my review of leaders' rhetoric, I identified two main aspects mentioned as sacred goals in the period after 1967: keeping "united Jerusalem" under Israeli control (this was a sacred goal in leaders' rhetoric mostly until 2000, although Netanyahu keeps presenting it as such), and opposition to the Palestinian Right of Return—a demand that is perceived as endangering the goal of preserving a Jewish majority in Israel.

Regarding Jerusalem, public polls indicated that an overwhelming majority during the years 1974–1990 thought that Israel should not give up its control of East Jerusalem under any conditions (see Figure 2.2). Figure 2.2 also shows that more than 70 percent of respondents in National Security and Public Opinion Project (NSPOP) surveys during the years 1975–1999 opposed negotiating the status of Jerusalem, albeit in declining percentages.

Figure 2.2   Israeli Control of Jerusalem as a Sacred Value, 1975–1999

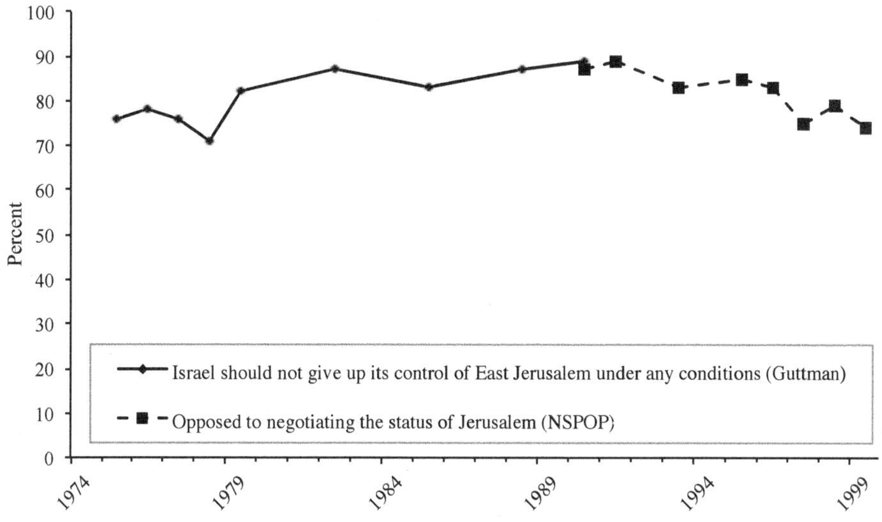

Sources: Guttman and NSPOP.

The data, then, indicate that keeping Jerusalem unified was considered by the public a sacred goal until the late 1990s. However, at that point things started to change. As early as 1996, a Guttman survey revealed mixed results: on the one hand, 78 percent of the respondents opposed any negotiation on the status of Jerusalem. On the other hand, 45 percent of the respondents were prepared to consider the idea of Palestinian control over Palestinian neighborhoods in East Jerusalem (Segal et al. 2000).[21] Indeed, in later years the question about willingness to negotiate the status of Jerusalem was dropped altogether, and instead the NSPOP included a new question about giving up Israeli control over specific parts of East Jerusalem. This change was a rather strong indication that "whole Jerusalem" or "united Jerusalem" was no longer a sacred goal for the Israeli public. The same can be said of the fact that more than 40 percent of respondents in NSPOP surveys during the years 2005–2017 were willing to compromise regarding the Arab neighborhoods of East Jerusalem (in 2017, 51 percent). However, only around 20 percent were ready to compromise regarding the Temple Mount (without the Wailing Wall) (Ben Meir and Bagno-Moldavsky 2013; Israeli and Dekel 2018).

In addition, polls indicated that objection to the Palestinian goal of the Right of Return retains its "sanctity." For example, NSPOP data indicate that during the years 1990–1999, around 90 percent opposed negotiating with the Palestinians about the Right of Return. Data from the 2000s indicated opposition to compromise on this matter even in the context of a peace agreement: in an August 2003 Peace Index poll, 66 percent of respondents were not prepared to recognize the Right of Return in principle, even if this recognition would not mean that refugees would be able to return to Israel and even if such recognition were the last obstacle to reaching an agreement with the Palestinians. This trend continued in later years and even strengthened. According to a September 2007 Peace Index poll, a considerable majority (87 percent) of the Jewish public opposed the return of a single refugee to Israel itself, even in exchange for a permanent peace agreement.[22]

Finally, Landman (2010) provides the most current and accurate account of sacred goals among the Israeli Jewish public. Her 2010 survey among 525 respondents that constituted a representative sample of the adult Jewish population in Israel was designed specifically to measure the existence of sacred goals among the Israeli Jewish population.[23] She found that within this sample, 47 percent considered opposing compromise on the holy sites in Jerusalem a sacred value, and 60 percent held a similar view regarding the return of any Palestinian refugees. In other words, according to Landman's survey, the only sacred value is the opposition to the Palestinian Right of Return, perceived as endangering the goal of keeping Israel a Jewish state.

Agreement with Historical Narratives That Justify Israel's Claim to the Land

A 1982 survey asked respondents to rate different justifications for the existence of Israel (Liebman and Don-Yihya 1983). I repeated this question in my 2016 survey and the results are presented in Table 2.4. The results indicate a change over time in the centrality of each justification: justifications chosen most frequently in the 1982 survey were "the suffering of the Jews in the diaspora as people without homeland" and "the yearning of Jews throughout the generations to return to the land." In 2016, fewer respondents chose these justifications, despite the increased emphasis in school curricula on the suffering of the Jews in the diaspora (and especially during the Holocaust) as the main reason for establishing Israel. The most common justification in 2016 was "recognition of the nations of the world of the idea of Jewish state"—a justification that was emphasized in the Declaration of Independence, but was less central in textbooks and leaders' rhetoric.

Only 9 percent of the respondents in 2016 (similar to levels in the 1982 survey) thought, like Netanyahu (2009a) in his Bar Ilan speech, that the settlement of the land by the Jews in ancient times was the main justification. Yet an increase appeared in the percentage of respondents who chose as the

Table 2.4   The Main Justification for Israel's Right to Exist, 1982 and 2016

Justification	1982	2016
Recognition by the nations of the world of the idea of a Jewish state	9	27
The suffering of the Jews in the diaspora as people without a homeland	30	14
The yearning of Jews throughout the generations to return to the land	24	11
The settlement of the land by the Jews in ancient times	8	9
The settlement of the land in modern times and the 1948 War	6	11
God's promise to the fathers of the nation that the land of Israel would be given to them people of Israel	16	24
Other response	5	3

Sources: Liebman and Don-Yihya (1983) and Oren's 2016 Survey.

main justification the divine promise that the land of Israel would be given to the people of Israel (from 16 percent in 1982 to 24 percent in 2016). These findings are in line with above documented trends of increasing centrality of the belief in a Jewish state as one that conforms to the Jewish religion.

When specifically discussing Jewish rights to territories captured in the 1967 War, some polls indicated that the public perceived that the land belongs to the Jews and, therefore, is not an occupied land. Others indicated the public regarded the territories as occupied. In an August 2004 Peace Index poll, 51 percent of the respondents regarded the West Bank and the Gaza Strip as occupied territories, while in a March 2008 Peace Index poll 55 percent of the respondents regarded the West Bank as "liberated territory," rather than "occupied territory." Finally, 72 percent of the respondents in April and May 2016 Peace Index polls stated that Israel's control of the West Bank is not an occupation.

Tension Between the Goal of a "Jewish State" and Other Societal Beliefs

Since the late 1980s, public polls have included questions about potential contradictions between the goal of a Jewish state and other goals. A NSPOP annual survey begun in 1988 was one of the first to address this issue. Respondents were asked, "In thinking about the various paths along which Israel can develop, there seem to be four important values *which clash to some extent,* and that are important to different degrees to various people: Israel with a Jewish majority, greater Israel, a democratic state (with equal political rights to all) and peace (that is, a low probability of war). Among these four values, which is the most important to you?" (emphasis added). During the years 1988–2013, keeping Israel as a Jewish state was almost always ranked higher than Greater Israel and democracy[24] (Ben Meir and Bagno-Moldavsky 2013; M. Shamir and Arian 1994). A similar trend appeared in December 2011 and December 2012 Peace Index polls, when 66 percent and 70 percent, respectively, preferred maintaining the Jewish majority of Israel over keeping the territories under Israeli control. A 2014 survey found that 88 percent of the respondents preferred a state with a clear Jewish majority while only 12 percent preferred to continue controlling the West Bank and Gaza and to become a half-Jewish and half-Arab state over time (Midgam Research and Consulting 2014).

A question that was asked in the Index of Arab-Jewish Relations in Israel during the years 2003–2012 revealed that around 70 percent of the respondents stated that "in case of contradiction between the democratic character and the Jewish character of the state, I would prefer the Jewish character." The Democracy Index also addressed this issue during the years 2010–2015; it offered three options: "Jewish," "democracy," and "both." It found that the proportion of those who favored the two components equally decreased from 48 percent in 2010 to only 27 percent in 2015. In 2015 the most frequent response (37 percent) was "Jewish state" and 35 percent said that the democratic component was more important. It seems, then, that "the Jewish public is shifting toward a specific preference at either end of the spectrum—'Jewish' or 'democratic,' rather than 'Jewish and democratic'" (T. S. Hermann et al. 2013, 62).

Several surveys asked respondents whether there is a contradiction between the idea of "Jewish state" and democracy. In a 2009 Guttman survey, 73 percent of respondents thought that Israel can be both Jewish and democratic. In a November 2014 Peace Index survey, 73 percent of Jewish respondents said that there is no contradiction between Israel being both a Jewish state and a democratic state. Finally, 76 percent of respondents in a 2015 Pew survey thought that Israel can be both a democracy and a Jewish state (Pew Research Center 2016).[25] So, Israeli Jews did not see a contradiction between the belief in Israel as a Jewish state and democracy but, when they were asked to choose between the two values, they preferred the goal of a Jewish state.

Do the Palestinians Also Have Rights to the Land?

As shown above, for a long time Israeli leaders and school curricula rejected the Palestinian claim to the land, maintaining that Israel has exclusive rights to it. Public polls about reasons to refute the Palestinian claims focused only on whether the Palestinians are a nation. Yet 2002 interviews with 100 fifty-five- to seventy-five-year-old Israeli Jews provided deeper elaboration of public beliefs regarding this issue (Bar-Tal, Raviv, and Abromovich forthcoming). Some participants in this study raised the idea that the land was deserted before the Zionists arrived—a claim popular mostly in the pre-1970s textbooks used when the participants in this study attended school. "This country was empty," declared Participant 504. Participant 604 in the study of Bar-Tal, Raviv, and Abromovich (forthcoming) asked "What was here in the land of Israel?" and answered "Just swamps and sand dunes and such. And they [the Palestinians] have the nerve to come and demand the land that we cultivated and the swamps that we drained." Others acknowledged that there were non-Jewish inhabitants in the land before the Zionists arrived but argued that most were new to the country, whereas the Jews were the original authentic inhabitants of the land. Participant 212 made these statements: "There are very few [Palestinians] who [their families] lived here for hundreds of years. Most [of the Palestinians] come with the [Zionist] Jews, because here they found livelihood. When the Jewish people started to come back to the land, Arabs from all over the Middle East followed. From Egypt, Saudi Arabia, from Iraq, from all the Middle East [Arabs] followed Jews, because [the Jews] provided livelihood [to the Arabs]." Indeed, many participants argued that the Palestinians were mainly nomads that did not settle in the land and that they lacked any national and political consciousness—again, a description that matches textbooks from earlier years. Participant 210 said, "They had no Palestinian or national consciousness, no, they were not like that." Participant 607 declared that "the Palestinians are not a people, there is no such people at all." Following arguments that the Palestinians are not a nation and that Jews can live safely only in their own country, many participants repeated statements from textbooks and speeches that the Jews have only one state while the Palestinians can choose any Arab country as their homeland. For example, Participant 108 complained that "they have so many countries, so many places, whole deserts. They could settle there as we settled here. Yes, they can go to other countries, they do not have to stick with us. They have so many places to live in other countries, and they specifically stuck with us in our place, specifically with us in our place."

Some participants dismissed all debate about the authenticity of the existence of Palestinians in the land prior to the Zionist immigration. According to this view, since the Palestinians rejected the 1947 UN resolution and the Israeli Jews won the 1948 War and conquered the land, according to the "law of history" it belongs to the Jews. This argument, although not common in textbooks and speeches, was quite popular among the participants. Participant 101 argued "that they lived here a thousand, three hundred or two hundred years and the Jews came and expelled them, so we expelled them. So Canada also expelled the Indians and Americans expelled Indians too and there are many [countries] like them. Then what? So what? It happens all the time." Participant 212 continued this line of argument: "From what I know in a war [countries] conquer, take land. That what it is. It's like that all over the world. That is what I know. So why should we be any different? It [the land] belongs to us. We took it and it is ours."

How common were these beliefs over the years? As noted, public polls referred only to the general idea that the Palestinians are not a nation. Recall that we saw a decline of this view in leaders' rhetoric and in textbooks from the 1990s, and a strengthening of this narrative since 2000. A review of public polls on this belief indicates some similar trends. More than 60 percent of the respondents from 1974 to 1977 thought that Palestinians did not constitute a separate people, but rather were a part of the Arab nation and that Jordan already served as a state for the Palestinians (see Figure 2.3). However, the data also show that fewer Israeli Jews held this view after 1979: the percentage of respondents agreeing that "the 'Palestinian Arab Nation' is an artificial concept that has only emerged in the last years due to developments in our area" dropped from 70 percent during the years 1973–1977 to around 50 percent during 1979–1983. Note that this trend *preceded* similar trends in school textbooks and leaders' rhetoric. This trend continued in later years. In a June 2009 Peace Index poll, 62 percent of respondents agreed with the statement "There is such an entity as a Palestinian people." In addition, most respondents in 2007 and 2008 Peace Index polls (62 percent in November 2007 and 61 percent in November 2008) thought that the Palestinians' demand for an independent state was just.

Yet there are indications that while willing to recognize the Palestinian claim to the land as just, many Israelis think that Israel's claim is stronger.

Figure 2.3   Beliefs Regarding Palestinian Nationhood, 1974–1983

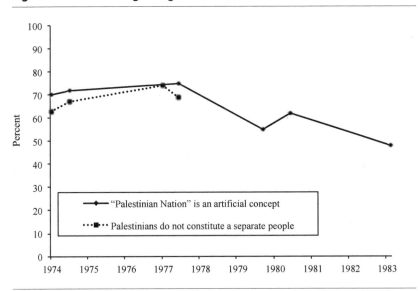

Source: Guttman.

In a survey conducted by the Dahaf Institute in 1986, 70 percent of the respondents thought that "Jews have the rights to the Land of Israel that are more just and compelling than those of the Arabs" (Zemach 1987, 30). Similarly, a large majority of Jewish respondents (72 percent) in a December 2015 Peace Index poll thought that the Jews' historical, religious, and cultural bond to the land is stronger than that of the Palestinians.

Finally, recent polls have indicated a strong agreement with old perceptions of exclusively Jewish rights for the land (a trend that also has appeared in some recent textbooks). For example, polls conducted as part of the Index of Arab-Jewish Relations in Israel in 2011 and 2012 found that most Israeli Jews agreed that "the Palestinians are Arabs that settled in the land of Israel that belongs to the Jewish people" (66 percent in 2011 and 64 percent in 2012). The percentage of those who thought that both Arabs and Jews have historical and national rights to the land dropped to 41 percent in 2013 (compared to 69 percent in 2006). A majority also thought that Palestinians have no national rights to the land because they are not its original inhabitants (62 percent in 2011 and 61 percent in 2012) (Smooha 2013).[26]

Conclusion

Ethos tends to outline the goals of the society, indicate their crucial importance, and provide their justifications. Since intractable conflicts often revolve around competing claims or around disputed land, societies in such conflicts develop special societal beliefs about the exclusivity of their claims that refute the legitimacy of their rival's goals. In this chapter, I focused on the goal of establishing a Jewish state in the ancient homeland of Eretz Israel. The term *Jewish state* has three main meanings: (1) having a Jewish majority in Israel; (2) having public life in Israel conform to Jewish tradition; and (3) having Israel serve as a state for world Jews. Israeli collective memory includes several justifications for this goal. First, Israeli collective memory references the Jewish nation founded in the ancient land of Israel. It also asserts that during their exile from Israel, Jews continuously aspired to return to it. In addition, it highlights the persistent experience of anti-Semitism in the diaspora as demonstrating the need for a secure existence in a Jewish state. A legal argument claims that international law, as expressed in the 1947 resolution adopted by the UN General Assembly for the establishment of an independent Jewish state, recognized Jewish legal rights to rule the country. A religious justification cites God's promise of the land to the Jews. Further arguments include the claim that the land was sparsely populated and neglected prior to the Jews' return, which calls into question the Arabs' attachment to the land. Other beliefs deny Palestinians' distinct nationhood, insisting instead that Palestinians are a part of an Arab nation that already has twenty-two states.

A review of leaders' rhetoric and school curricula indicated that the goal of Israel as a Jewish state and the collective memory justifying Israeli claims to the land mentioned above were dominant in these texts, but without agreement among the leaders on the territorial boundaries sought. Public polls also indicated that over the years more than 60 percent identified themselves as Zionist and agreed with the goal of Israel as a Jewish state. We can conclude, then, that these beliefs are societal beliefs in Israel that are part of the Israeli ethos. Furthermore, the theme that I discussed in this chapter is a *central* theme in the ethos, as agreement with this theme was high relatively compared to other themes (see Chapters 8 and 9 that analyze the whole ethos) and it also dominated the Israeli Declaration of Independence. Some beliefs that compose this theme—such as the opposition to Palestinian Right of Return that is perceived as endangering the goal of keeping a Jewish majority—were also considered sacred goals.

Finally, Israelis did not see potential contradictions between the goal of a Jewish state and democracy, and preferred a Jewish state over other goals, including democracy. This is important, given Israel's nature as a *hegemonic state*—a state that promotes the interests of the majority ethnopolitical group in a multinational setting—which makes it at best a "flawed" liberal democracy (I. Peleg 2007). During the 1990s, there has been a move toward strengthening the liberal democratic nature of the state including the passing of the 1992 Basic Law: Human Dignity and Liberty designed to protect individual rights such as "life body and dignity," property, privacy, and intimacy, and the 2000 Supreme Court ruling in the Kadaan affair that in principle no discrimination in land allocation to Jews and non-Jewish citizens of Israel is legal.[27] However, since 2000, an opposite tendency in legislation—of strengthening the Jewish character of the state—appeared. The latest example of this trend is the 2018 Basic Law: Nation-State Law. This law declares that Israel is the Jewish nation's historic homeland and that this nation has the singular right to national self-determination in it. The law anchors the flag, menorah, anthem, Hebrew calendar, Independence Day, and Jewish holidays as national symbols and states that the "whole and united" Jerusalem is the state's capital. It omits any mention of democracy or the principle of equality. It also includes several clauses that weaken group rights of non-Jewish groups in Israel and, hence, strengthen the hegemonic (nonliberal) nature of the state of Israel. It downgrades Arabic to a "special status" instead of an official language alongside Hebrew, and it declares the development of "*Jewish* settlement" as a "national value." The final law is a compromise between ethnonationalists and more liberal politicians within the political right. An early draft of the law included a clause that required the Supreme Court to set the state's Jewish character above its democratic character in rulings where the two clashed. Another controversial clause, which appeared to pave the way for the creation of communities segregated by nationality or religion, was stripped before final passage by a vote of 62–55. Indeed, the political right and the political left are divided over this law.[28] But these debates between the political right and political left within the Israeli-Jewish society are "more a matter of degree than of kind" (I. Peleg 2007, 178) since, as I showed in this chapter, that Zionist liberal leaders are committed to the Jewish state goal as well.

While all Israeli leaders were committed to the Jewish state goal, the relative strength and prominence of specific interpretations of the term *Jewish state* varied over time, as did the relative prevalence of specific justifications for Jewish rights to the land. The belief in a Jewish state as one that conforms to Jewish tradition increased. The justification that links the establishment of the state to the Holocaust has become dominant in school textbooks since the 1980s. Likewise, justifications emphasizing the glorious past of the Jews in the land was more prevalent in the period after 2000 in leaders' rhetoric and in school curricula. Polls from the period after 2000 also indicated an increase in the belief of a Jewish state as one that conforms to the Jewish tradition. These polls also indicated a strengthening of the belief about the divine promise as the main justification, and an increase in the belief about international recognition of the idea of a Jewish state as the main justification—two justifications that were less common in current textbooks and leaders' rhetoric.

Some of these changes in public opinion are probably best explained by demographic trends such as the increase in the proportion of more devout Jews.[29] Indeed, religious respondents tend more to believe in the meaning of "Jewish state" as a state that conforms to Jewish tradition and in the divine promise as the main justification for the Jewish right to the land. In my 2016 survey, 79 percent of ultra-Orthodox and 68 percent of religious respondents chose this justification as the main justification, compared to only 6 percent of nonreligious respondents. Still, this argument was not the most common argument because ultra-Orthodox Jews are a minority among Israeli Jews.

Among nonreligious respondents—the largest group of Israeli Jews— the most frequent justification in my 2016 survey for the Jewish right to the land was international recognition of the idea of a Jewish state (35 percent of nonreligious respondents chose this option compared to only 2 percent of ultra-Orthodox and 7 percent of religious respondents). Lustick (2015) suggests that this justification for Israel's right to the land became more dominant among Israelis because of scholarly works, including Israeli scholars, that refuted previous narratives about history of the land and the conflict over it. These studies described the development of Palestinian society and culture in the Ottoman and British periods. The argument about international recognition legitimizes Israel's right to the land regardless of Palestinians' existence in the land prior to the Zionist immigration.

Another change that began in the 1990s was the weakening of the goal of a united Jerusalem as a sacred goal, first seen in public polls and then acted on by some leaders (Barak, Olmert) who agreed to negotiate the status of Jerusalem with the Palestinians. While public polls in the mid-1990s showed that the status of Jerusalem was perceived as non-negotiable, they also showed a willingness to cede the Palestinian neighborhoods in East Jerusalem. This shift, then, demonstrates that sacred values are sometimes "merely pseudo-sacred" (Tetlock 2003, 322). Indeed, Tetlock (322) argues that often sacred values are essentially rhetorical devices and, therefore, they are easily compromised when having to cope with "the real world of scarce resources." In the case of Jerusalem, public opinion may have been influenced by "stubborn realities" that challenged the notion of a united Jerusalem (Lustick 1996a, 164). The overwhelming majority of Israeli Jews rarely visit Palestinian neighborhoods in East Jerusalem,[30] and the international community refuses to accept Israeli sovereignty over East Jerusalem. However, sacred goals are not always pseudosacred in the minds of people. In their studies, Ginges et al. (2007) showed that at least some groups among Israeli Jews, such as settlers, did hold the goal of keeping the territories under Israel control as sacred. Introducing material incentives to compromise actually intensified the opposition to compromise among this group. In addition, some sacred places in Jerusalem, such as the Western Wall, may be perceived as sacred goals among the general Israeli Jewish population.[31] Thus, more studies are needed to differentiate among sacred and pseudosacred goals within the general Israeli Jewish public.

The most notable change in the theme about Jews' right to the land, however, concerns attitudes toward the exclusivity of Israel's claims and the justness of the Palestinian ones. The 1980s and 1990s saw a significant erosion in the belief that Palestinians do not constitute a separate people and even a partial acceptance of the Palestinian demand for their own state. Public polls showed erosion in those beliefs during the 1980s and 1990s—*predating* similar trends in leaders' rhetoric and school textbooks. But since the 2000s, levels of resistance to this Palestinian narrative and the perception that Israel has exclusive rights to the land have grown again in leaders' rhetoric, school curricula, and public polls. These changes in public opinion were probably driven by major events in the conflict—for example, a major shift appeared following the 1979 Camp David Accords between Israel and Egypt that included Israel's recognition of the "legitimate rights of the Palestinian people" (although this was not acknowledged in the rhetoric of then prime minister Begin). Public opinion may also had been influenced by cultural products that refuted this belief. As noted above, academic studies since the late 1970s, as well as Israeli media, repeatedly have refuted historical narratives that deny Palestinian existence in and attachment to the land (Nets-Zehngut 2012). Israeli films and literature from the 1980s also questioned this belief (Shohat 1989).

What are the implications of these trends to the resolution of the Israeli-Arab conflict? On the one hand, any peace treaty should address the goal of establishing a Jewish state because this is a central theme in the Israeli ethos that defines its identity. This realization makes the task of peacemaking challenging given the competing goals of the rivals. On the other hand, the specific operationalization of the goal of a "Jewish state" did change over the years. With time, a willingness to compromise even on goals that were considered sacred (united Jerusalem) emerged. Thus, this central theme in the ethos is not set in stone. Of course, support among the Israeli public for any potential peace agreement with the Palestinians is also dependent on how that agreement deals with other themes of the ethos, as I discuss in the next chapters.

Notes

1. For example, this rhythm of time could be found in the way that traditional Jewish holidays are celebrated. Purim is preceded by a fast day commemorating the period when Jews in Persia were under threat. On the eve of the holiday, the story of their salvation is read and the following day is a day of celebration. The same pattern appears in Passover and Hanukah.

2. The number of words refers to the original Hebrew version of the declaration.

3. The Palestinians, from their part, go further back and claim to have even earlier roots—the indigenous Philistines and the ancient Canaanite peoples who had lived in this land, according to the Bible, prior to its conquest by Joshua. The Jews then claim a priority based on God's alleged promise of the land to Abraham. This situation of two sides in a conflict trying to outpass each other by invoking an earlier origin is a common phenomenon in protracted conflict and can also be found in other conflicts such as the conflict between Serbs and Albanians over Kosovo (E. Zerubavel 2003,107).

4. These new memorial days were established by laws and their content was mostly constructed by the state.

5. All speeches given by Netanyahu during 2013 that appeared in the Prime Minister's Office archive of speeches on the internet (http://www.pmo.gov.il/MediaCenter /Speeches/Pages/default.aspx) were analyzed. The coding was based on Bar-Tal's (1998) coding of ethos themes in school textbooks; the final coding book is available on request from the author. The analytical procedure was composed of several steps. First, the speeches were carefully reviewed, and all text that appeared to describe one or more of the coding categories was highlighted and labeled with the appropriate code(s). In many cases, each highlighted part of the text described more than one coding category. During coding of each highlighted part of the text, the entire speech was treated as a single segment to enable a holistic analysis of meaning according to context and circumstances (Krippendorff 2012). Next, all highlighted text in a speech was reviewed to identify themes. Software for qualitative data analysis, Atlas/TI, was used to efficiently facilitate the coding. I coded all of the speeches. An additional reader (an Israeli) analyzed about 20 percent of the speeches, where categorization was ambiguous. In most cases, there was agreement between us. In the few cases of disagreement, we discussed the matter until reaching an agreement.

6. For the Labor movement—Ben-Gurion's movement—this shift started in the 1930s. For the revisionist movement—Begin was the first prime minister who was associated with this movement—the shift started in the mid-1950s. Indeed, many aspects of public life in Israel are governed by the Jewish religion. For example, based on the 1953 Rabbinical Courts Jurisdiction (Marriage and Divorce) Law, all matters of marriage and divorce of Jews in Israel are under the exclusive jurisdiction of the rabbinical courts. Hence, there is no civil marriage in Israel and the only forum competent to decide the personal status of an Israeli Jew is the rabbinical court. Another example is the 1951 Hours of Work and Rest Law that declares Saturday as the day of rest in Israel. In coordination with Jewish laws and tradition, Jewish labor, without first obtaining a permit, is forbidden during this day and violations may constitute a criminal offense. There is also no public transportation in Israel on this day.

7. Lustick (1993) shows how some areas that are included in 1949 borders, such as Galilee and the Negev, were transformed from areas referred to in Israeli public debate as "occupied territories" in 1948 and 1949 into territories whose status as integral parts of the state of Israel is not a subject of dispute.

8. Netanyahu said that he would be willing to seriously consider an establishment of a Palestinian state within the framework of a permanent agreement (Blum 2006).

9. Ehud Barak said, "The whole world understands that 'the legitimate rights of the Palestinian people' includes the right for self-determination, the right for a state" (Shavit 2005). In a 2004 speech, Sharon said that he supports the establishment of a Palestinian state (Ariel Sharon 2004). He argued, in a 2005 speech, that the Palestinians "are also entitled to freedom and to a national sovereign existence in a state of their own" (Aronoff 2014, 80).

10. More specifically, her analysis is based on (1) booklets issued by the Ministry of Education and Culture; (2) the teacher's guide for high school final examinations; and (3) circulars issued by the director-general of the Education Ministry referring to the subjects mentioned above.

11. Teachers were asked to encourage pupils to attend synagogue on Yom Kippur, to build a sukkah at Sukkoth, and to accompany their pupils on a visit to Kfar Chabad (an ultra-Orthodox village) to view the matzah-making process for Passover (Resnik 2003, 306). Schools were also asked to send as many high school classes as possible to seminars on Jewish and Zionist history (Podeh 2002, 41).

12. In this regard, the textbooks emphasized the fact that the Jews were forced to leave the land and did not just desert it.

13. The textbooks referred not only to the physical threat but also to a spiritual threat of decline in the diaspora.

14. Kizel (2008) notes that when dealing with world history, Israeli textbooks from the early period of the state related American pioneers to the narrative about the Zionist pioneers.

15. These findings are in line with Resnik's (2003, 303) study that indicates that besides some basic universalist account of citizenship displayed in the first subsection, being a good citizen according to this 'quasi-Civics' course means accomplishing Jewish-Zionist goals in Israel."

16. The English translation was taken from Caspi (2001, 253) and Szobel (n.d.).

17. Likewise, Resnik (2003, 303) concluded that, in teaching the Bible at Israeli schools during the 1950s: "Biblical texts of a historical character were chosen, almost to the neglect of the far more numerous chapters containing religious injunctions. The Bible curriculum was formulated with a view to summarizing the history of the Jewish people in the Land of Israel. Beginning with Abraham leaving his ancestral land at God's beckoning and reaching Canaan (afterward the Land of Israel), the historical narrative relates the bondage of the people of Israel in Egypt,

followed by the Exodus and the conquest of the land and the settlement of the Israelite tribes and so forth."

18. Another relevant extracurricular activity that signals the strengthening of narratives that justify the establishment of the State of Israel as a Jewish state is the increase of popularity of school field trips to Holocaust sites in Poland with a message about the link between the Holocaust and the need for a strong Jewish state. An elaboration of this trend is provided in the next chapter.

19. Both surveys were conducted only among the Jewish population and used the same wording. The sample type, however, was somehow different: the 1985 survey was conducted among 1,200 respondents in 33 representative places in Israel. The 1997 survey was conducted among 802 respondents who were a representative sample of the adult Jewish population. In both surveys, the young respondents tended to be less Zionist.

20. The answers were coded by two Israelis with 95 percent intercoder agreement. The coding book is available on request from the author.

21. The national survey, conducted among a sample of 1,500 respondents, represents all Israeli Jewish adults aged twenty years and older in all types of communities except Kibbutzim.

22. In a 2014 Smith Survey among 500 people as a representative sample of the adult population of Israel, 33 percent of Jewish respondents agreed that Israel should accept on a humanitarian basis a limited number of Palestinian refugees into Israel, and 67 percent opposed (Smith and Paniel 2014).

23. In Landman's (2010, 154) survey, those who agreed with the statement that compromise on a given issue is "not permissible under any and all circumstances" were defined as those who held this issue as sacred. The other options were "compromise is permissible only in extreme cases where it would lead to sufficient gain or would prevent harm" and "I do not oppose compromise on this issue."

24. The exception is 2000 when democracy ranked higher than Jewish state (32 percent chose it as main value compared to 29 percent who chose Jewish state).

25. The survey includes a nationally representative sample of 3,789 Israeli Jews who were surveyed in six districts (Jerusalem, North, Haifa, Center, Tel Aviv, and South) and in the West Bank.

26. In 1994 poll, only 38 percent of respondents thought that the State of Israel belongs to the Jews exclusively (Yuchtman-Yaar and Peres 2000, 124).

27. The Supreme Court in the Kadaan affair has partially upheld an appeal of an Arab Palestinian family, which has asked to purchase a house in Katzir—a Jewish communal municipality.

28. A 2018 July Peace Index poll found that 52 percent of Jewish Israelis thought it was important to pass the Nation-State Bill "at this time"; 60 percent thought the law should have included equality. In addition, 51 percent of Israeli Jews supported changing Arabic's status from an official language of the state to a language with special status while 40 percent of Israeli Jews opposed this.

29. In 2017, 9 percent of Israeli Jews (twenty years old and older) identified as ultra-Orthodox and 11 percent as religious. The annual growth rate of the ultra-Orthodox population was 4 percent as opposed to 1 percent among other Jews.

30. Already in a 1996 survey about Jerusalem, 70 percent of the Israeli Jews said that they "never" visited Arab villages that are included within the borders of Jerusalem, 9 percent said that they visited there only "once," and 2 percent claimed that they never heard of these neighborhoods (Segal et al. 2000, 226).

31. Tetlock (2003, 223) notes that some sacred values, such as "the sacred soil of Jerusalem," are more entrenched and resistant to compromise.

3

A Small Country Surrounded by Enemies

Two of Israel's most popular political commentators—Ephraim
Kishon and Yair Lapid—devoted much of their work to describing the uniqueness of Israel. Kishon (1961, 2004) mentions the informality of daily life in Israel ("It's the only country where the man with the open, stained shirt is the honorable minister, and the one next to him with the suit and tie is his chauffeur"); the gap between Israel's advanced technology and often unproductive economic system ("it is the only country where you can easily get computer programs to build and send satellites, but you have to wait seven days for your washing machine to be repaired"); and the variety of the Israeli experience, from the country's cultural variety to the diverse nature of security threats facing Israel. In this regard, he points out that Israel is the only country threatened by "Scud [ballistic missiles] from Iraq, Katyusha rockets from Lebanon, explosives from Gaza and bombs from Syria." He also notes that "Israel is a country so tiny that there is no room to write its name on the world map." He feels these factors mean that Israel "is a country whose survival is permanently endangered" and "a country where every human being is a soldier, and every soldier is a human being." To Kishon, the security threat and the Israeli army, then, are central in the national identity of Israel.

This sense of national and personal danger is also pronounced in Lapid's (2001) essay that begins with a long description of what an Israeli feels after a terrorist attack: he watches TV news, he hopes that he does not know the victims, he checks on his sleeping kids, and he realizes that he just visited the site of the attack two weeks before. This feeling of severe threat pervades the essay. In some parts, concerns about security remain latent and perhaps hidden from the non-Israeli, but they stand out clearly to any Israeli reader. For example, Lapid writes, "To be an Israeli is to say 'more people are killed in traffic accidents' and not to be sure that this is still the case." Elsewhere in the essay, he explicitly states that Israelis live under constant security threats: "To be an Israeli is to go to the mall like you go to military reserve duty, and it is also to go to military reserve duty like you go to a war" (Lapid 2001). Lapid's essay, then, presents what some scholars describe as a condition of "dormant war" (Horowitz 1993).[1]

The security theme in ethos of conflict indicates the society is under severe threat. It describes not just the level of threat but also the kind of threat to the society, which might include military conventional threat, nuclear threat, threat to identity, and so forth. Because of the perception of high threat, security becomes one of the central values of the society, and the organizations that are responsible to ensure security are glorified and enjoy high prestige (Bar-Tal 2013). The analysis of this theme of the ethos overlaps with studies of *securitization;* that is, a process of framing an issue through a speech act (usually by a political leader) as an existential threat and the acceptance of this framing by a target audience, which leads to endorsement of employing extraordinary measures to address this issue (Buzan, Wæver, and Wilde 1998; Gad and Petersen 2011). Little has been written about Israel in the context of securitization studies (see a review and an explanation for this situation in Lupovici 2014a). In this chapter, then, I enrich our understanding of securitization in Israel. More specifically, I contribute toward an understanding of the attempts to securitize some issues in Israel through a speech act (of leaders) and analyze the acceptance of this securitization by the public. By the end of the chapter, I refer to some policy implications of this situation.

The Israeli belief regarding existential threat is, of course, grounded. The Israeli-Arab conflict included numerous full-scale wars, major military operations, and terrorist attacks. Israel's small size (20,770 square kilometers within the 1949 borders and 26,630 square kilometers with the West Bank) (CIA n.d.) could allow an invading army to overrun the country in hours or destroy it with just a few nuclear bombs. Almost all major Israeli cities are within the range of conventional missiles, thus increasing the probability of civilian casualties. Neighboring states and groups have repeatedly and openly called for the destruction of the State of Israel, as I discuss in the next chapter. Yet in most wars, Israel enjoyed aerial superiority and equipment advantages over its rival. Israel is likewise believed to be the only country in the Middle East with nuclear capabilities (A. Cohen 1998). As I show below, while beliefs about the kind of threat to Israel have changed over the years, the beliefs in severe threat, the centrality of security as a core value, and the prestige of the army have remained strong throughout the years.

Leaders' Rhetoric

David Ben-Gurion expressed the belief that Israel is under severe threat in his speeches and writing. For example, in 1959 he wrote that "the scope of our defense is wider than any other country" (Brecher 1972, 266). The main threat in his rhetoric was a permanent risk of war with Arab states. In a 1955 speech he said, "If tomorrow there will be war that we would win, we would risk a third, fourth and fifth round" (Saltzman 2016, 57). Furthermore, on some occasions, Ben-Gurion used the analogy between the existential threat to Israel and the Holocaust, an analogy that intensified the threat (Pedatzur 1998, 145; Zertal 2005).[2] It is not surprising, then, that on another occasion Ben-Gurion declared, "There is nothing more important, more precious and more sacred than the security of the state of Israel" (Liebman and Don-Yihya 1983, 86). Ben-Gurion was also known for his glorification of the Israeli army, by comparing Israel's achievements in battle to major Jewish victories from biblical times (Pedatzur 1998). In a 1956 speech, he went as far as declaring that Israel's victory in the 1956 War against Egypt was "the greatest and most glorious military campaign in the history of our people, and one of the greatest in history of the nations" (Bar-Zohar 1979, 451).[3]

Such beliefs appeared in the rhetoric of many other Israeli leaders. Levi Eshkol said, "Security is our first concern, and I may say that it has become, to a certain extent, a sacred value in its own right. . . . Behind the apparently tranquil borders . . . stand armed forces awaiting the hour of action. And it is not merely a question of potential danger, but of actual peril" (Brecher 1972, 297). Similarly, Menachem Begin emphasized the existential threat to Israel (Gertz 2000). Even in a speech that was given during the 1977 historical visit of Egyptian president Anwar Sadat to Jerusalem—a visit that started the Israeli-Egyptian peace process—Begin noted the existential threat to Israel when he said, "We defended our right, our existence, our honor, our women and our children against recurrent attempts to crush us by brute force, and not on one front alone" (Begin 1977). Like Ben-Gurion, Begin often invoked the analogy to the Holocaust to emphasize the threat and the need for Israeli self-defense (Naor 2003). For example, Begin justified the 1982 Lebanon War (a war in which Israel had a clear superiority over its rivals) as an attempt to prevent another Jewish Holocaust (Segev 2000, 399). A feeling of existential threat and the centrality of security also appeared in speeches of Yitzhak Rabin who often glorified the IDF. Indeed, Rosler (2012) found that 27 percent of Rabin's speeches during the years 1987–1991 referred to security beliefs. Ariel Sharon also emphasized the security challenge of Israel. For example, he wrote that "nowhere else do four million people carry on their lives in the midst of hundred million hostile people" (Aronoff 2014, 83).

The existential threat to Israel and the importance of Israeli military power are especially central themes in Benjamin Netanyahu's speeches. Seventy-one percent of Netanyahu's speeches in 2013 included reference to these issues. In fact, security beliefs were the most common theme in Netanyahu's speeches (see Table 2.1). Fifty-seven percent of his speeches pointed to severe threats to Israel in the past or in the present. Like previous leaders, Netanyahu also often stated that no other country faces as many security threats as Israel. For example, he said in a speech in the Knesset in 2013: "Why I say that we are the most threatened country in the world. Why? Because it is true" (Netanyahu 2013a).[4] Merom (1998) questions this statement and notes that other states and groups have been facing similar threats or even more severe threats to their existence than Israel—Taiwan, Lebanon, Poland, the Baltic states, to name just a few (and of course the Palestinians who have also suffered severe losses because of the conflict with Israel).

This review, then, reveals that the existential threat to Israel and the importance of security as a value were common among various Israeli leaders. There were, however, some changes over time in perception of the *nature* of threat to Israel, as well as disagreements regarding the means to achieve security among the different speakers. As can be seen from the quotes above, the main threat mentioned by Israeli leaders over the years was the danger of physical destruction of the state during a conventional war with Arab states. Since the 1980s, another existential threat appeared in reality and in leaders' rhetoric—the threat of the existence of unconventional weapons in the possession of Muslim states. Already in 1981, Begin described to the Knesset the demolition of Iraq's nuclear reactor by Israel in terms of an existential threat:

> They could have destroyed completely, utterly, the Dan district: the basis of our industrial, commercial, agricultural and cultural life . . . there was a direct danger that hundreds of thousands of our little children may be poisoned by that radioactivity as a result of using even three Hiroshima-type bombs which Saddam Hussein had an ambition to create in order to try to destroy our country and our people. . . . Then this country, and this people, would have been lost, after the Holocaust. Another Holocaust would have happened in the history of the Jewish people." (Begin 1981)

Since the 1990s, with the advancements in the Iranian nuclear program, leaders linked the threat of unconventional weapons mainly to Iran. The Iranian nuclear program was presented as existential threat by Rabin in 1995 (S. A. Cohen 2008, 40). Netanyahu especially emphasizes this threat since his second term in office (2009–) (Lupovici 2014b). For example, in a 2012 speech in a ceremony for Holocaust Remembrance Day, he argued that "a nuclear-armed Iran is an existential threat of the State of Israel" (Netanyahu 2012b).

The security threat of the Palestinians in the territories and of the establishment of a Palestinian state (or any compromise regarding the status of the territories) was another issue that appeared over the years, mostly in the rhetoric of hawkish leaders. Between the 1967 War and the 1973 War, they argued that holding all the territories occupied by Israel in 1967 would eliminate the danger of another war. For example, in a 1970 speech in the Knesset, Begin maintained that a territorial compromise with Jordan would bring Fatah rockets capable of striking almost every town in Israel. He said that Israel would then have to retaliate and that this would probably lead to "a war of destruction and bloodshed of a cruelty unprecedented in human history" (Naor 1999, 157). Naor, however, identifies this argument mainly as a rhetorical tool "aimed at effective persuasion toward a policy [the settlement policy] whose real basis is elsewhere" (p. 155). As I showed in the previous chapter, hawkish leaders based the legitimization of Israel's right to the territories on mainly historical and religious justifications, but they failed to establish the goal of Israeli control of the territories as part of the ethos. These leaders, then, tried to securitize the issue of the territories to legitimize Israel's control of the territories among the public.

When the claim that Israeli control of the territories would prevent war with the Arabs proved wrong with the eruption of the 1973 War, hawkish leaders focused on a different threat—terrorism—arguing that "if the territory were to be relinquished, there would be no personal security for anyone and, thus, holding the territories is necessary for personal security" (Naor 1999, 151). In a 1979 speech, Begin presented the threat from a Palestinian state as both a personal and a national threat to Israelis. He emphasized that a Palestinian state "will endanger our children in Tel Aviv" and "our women in Petah Tikva. . . . It is our very existence which is at stake" (Begin 1979a). After the Palestinian uprising in the territories during the years 1987–1991 (the first intifada) that involved mass demonstrations, strikes, and attacks on Israeli security forces and civilians,[5] some leaders again presented the Palestinians in the territories as a national (not just a personal) threat. Yitzhak Shamir, for instance, suggested that the first intifada was a "war against Israel's existence" (Aronoff 2014, 38). During the years 1987–1991, Rabin also presented the Palestinian uprising in the territories as an existential threat to Israel (Rosler 2012, 139). Yet in 1995, he said that "the Palestinians were not in the past, and are not today, a threat to the existence of the State of Israel" (Rabin 1995f).

Following the collapse of the Oslo process in 2000 and the second intifada (which included Palestinian suicide bombings in public places throughout Israel)[6] and the 2009 and 2014 Gaza Wars (which included rocket attacks from Gaza),[7] the threat of the Palestinians in the territories and of a Palestinian state have become common in leaders' rhetoric—especially Netanyahu's. For example, referring to the 2009 Gaza War in a 2009 speech, Netanyahu stated that "there is only one example in history of thousands of rockets being fired on a country's civilian population. It happened when the Nazis bombed British cities during World War II" (Netanyahu 2009b). By comparing Hamas rocket attacks—that caused the death of ten Israeli civilians between the years 2001 and 2007—to the London Blitz when more than 40,000 British civilians were killed (and ignoring the numerous Palestinian civilians who were killed in the 2009 Gaza War), Netanyahu blurred the fact that in the Gaza War Israel was the stronger side and, hence, intensified the threat the Palestinians posed to Israel. Netanyahu also often argued that a Palestinian state could become "an Iranian proxy" state (Netanyahu 2013n) and endanger life in Israel.[8]

The discussion about the nature of threat to Israel, however, goes beyond the "traditional" security threat to the existence of Israel and its residents to also include references to threats to national identity and themes of the ethos. Leaders often talked about the threat of an intra-Israeli-Jewish rift (threat to national unity) as a threat to the existence of Israel (Abulof 2015; Waxman 2006b). Speaking one month after the outbreak of the second intifada, Ehud Barak said: "We are splintering among ourselves into groups and communities that define themselves by their enmity to the other. That process is more dangerous to us than any enemy or external war" (Waxman 2006b, 212). Similarly, Sharon said in a 2002 speech: "We will stand together because we wish to survive" (Ariel Sharon 2002). I return to this issue in Chapter 6, where I discuss the theme of national unity.

The loss of a Jewish majority especially in case of annexation of the territories—what is called the *demographic threat*—was a major issue in political debates, especially after the first intifada when the argument about the status of the Palestinians in the territories intensified. For a long time, hawkish leaders discounted this threat. Begin asserted that annexation of the territories would change the demographic balance in Israel between Jews and non-Jews only by a few years and Jewish immigration to Israel would continue to ensure a Jewish majority (Shelef 2010, 175). Shamir maintained in 1987 that "people exaggerate what's called the demographic problem. . . . This problem has been with us for thousands of years, since the Israelites entered their land at the time of Joshua. Yet despite this problem we still exist" (Abulof 2014, 406; Aronoff 2014, 32). Netanyahu during the 1990s also marginalized this threat, arguing that Palestinian birthrate in the territories was declining and thousands of Palestinians would eventually emigrate from the territories so that in the long term there would be more Jews than Palestinians in the territories (Aronoff 2014, 46).[9] Dovish leaders, by contrast, argued that this was a major threat and that annexation of the territories without giving the Palestinians in the territories full rights of citizenship might turn Israel into Rhodesia or apartheid South Africa.[10] Rabin argued, in this context, that annexation of the territories will transform Israel to "a racial state with Apartheid" (Magal et al. 2013, 147). Some Hawkish leaders expressed similar concern in the period after 2000. Sharon stated in a 2005 speech that the demographic balance made it "impossible to maintain a democratic Jewish state while ruling over all parts of the Land of Israel" (Abulof 2015, 151). Ehud Olmert said that he wanted to avoid a situation in which Israel became either a binational state or an "apartheid" state (Rynhold and Waxman 2008, 24). Even Netanyahu in 2011 reacted to a report that argued that in a number of years there would be a Palestinian majority between the Jordan River and the Mediterranean Sea; he said that "I want to separate from them [the Palestinians in the territories] so that they will not be Israeli citizens. I am interested that there be a solid Jewish majority inside the State of Israel" (Ravid 2011).

Netanyahu has emphasized since the 2000s two additional demographic threats. The first focuses on Israel's Palestinian citizens within the 1949 borders as a demographic threat to the existence of the Jewish state, which peaked following the October 2000 Events, a wave of violent protests by Israeli Palestinians during which thirteen citizens were shot and killed by Israeli police officers. For example, Netanyahu said in 2003, "True, we have a demographic problem. But it's not about the Palestinian Arabs in the territories, but about Israeli Arabs . . . even if they integrate among us marvelously, and reach 35–40%, the Jewish State is gone, becoming instead a bi-national state" (Abulof 2014, 409). The second demographic threat that Netanyahu mentioned was the threat to the existence of Israel as a Jewish state because of non-Jewish illegal immigrants who were coming to Israel from Africa. A 2013 speech by Netanyahu is a typical example: "First 3,000 came, then 6,000 every month. Multiply that by 12 and you have 80,000 per year. You all know the meaning of this. It would pose a threat to the future of the State of Israel as a Jewish and democratic state" (Netanyahu 2013l).

Looking at this issue from a broader perspective, hawkish politicians (like Netanyahu) saw the existential threat to Israel as an eternal phenomenon that had started before the establishment of the state and was doomed to continue forever, given the extent of hatred from non-Jews in general and the Arabs in particular toward the Jewish people and Israel (e.g., the villa in the jungle theme discussed in Chapter 4 and siege beliefs discussed in Chapter 5). In contrast, dovish politicians saw the conflict situation as one that could be changed, even in the foreseeable future. For example, in a 1994 speech, Rabin noted that "promising signs appear on the horizon" and that "it may indicate the end of the Arab siege on Israel." But even he admitted that "it is still too early to return the sword to its sheath. Not just yet" (Rabin 1994c). Also, while the more hawkish politicians emphasized the Israeli necessity to live by the sword, dovish segments tended increasingly to express a desire to live a "normal life," to be "a nation like all the nations," and to stop the subordination of all goals to the security goal. However, this was seen more as a wish and even they admitted that it could not yet be achieved given the present situation of the Israeli-Arab conflict.

For both hawkish and dovish leaders in Israel, "making peace is a military matter" (Kimmerling 2001, 215). The main disagreement between doves and hawks, however, is about the relationship between security and peace and the main means to achieve security. In hawks' rhetoric, security is usually presented as the main condition to achieve peace and it is to be achieved through mostly military means. For example, Shamir suggested that security could be achieved through military means alone while peace based on territorial compromise would endanger Israel's security (Aronoff 2014, 28). Netanyahu argued that "a fundamental condition for our existence and for the existence of peace, to achieve peace and maintain it, is security" (Netanyahu 2013i). He repeatedly expressed the belief that Israeli concessions for peace would be perceived by the Palestinians as acts of weakness, encouraging more demands (Aronoff 2014, 52), and that "the IDF was and remains the thing that stands between us and annihilation. This is always true, even when we reach peace agreements" (Netanyahu 2013n). Rabin shared Netanyahu's view about the importance of military power in maintaining peace when he said: "Only a strong army can bring peace. Only a strong army can keep the peace"(Rabin 1994b). In contrast to Netanyahu, however, Rabin stressed that security could not be achieved through only military means. He even pointed out the limitations of military means in providing security to Israeli citizens: "Military cemeteries in every corner of the world are silent testimony to the failure of national leaders to sanctify human life. There is only one radical means of sanctifying human lives. Not armored plating, or tanks, or planes, or concrete fortifications. The one radical solution is peace" (Rabin 1994d).[11]

Accordingly, Rabin also discussed peace as a main means to achieve security. For example, he said that peace "is the solution for the long term, and for terrorism" (Rabin 1995b). Likewise, he repeatedly stated that the Oslo agreements with the Palestinians guaranteed Israel's security and that Israel could take calculated risks in a peace process with a weaker rival (Rosler 2012). In sum, Israeli leaders shared the core beliefs that the security of the state and of its Jewish citizens was under a serious threat (since the late 1980s, threats to Israel's identity were especially emphasized) and that security was and should be a central value. They also uniformly glorified the Israeli army. Their differences were over whether Israel's control of the territories threatened the Jewish and democratic identity of the state, how long Israel must live by the sword and how best to achieve security, especially whether a peace agreement could guarantee Israel's security.

School Curricula

The 1950s Through the Early 1980s

The perception of existential threat, the centrality of security as a value, and the glorification of the army dominated Israeli school curricula as well. David (2012) shows that Israeli readers from the 1950s until the 1970s included stories and poems that glorified the Israeli army. The readers contained real sto-

ries about battles—such as the 1948 War battles in Jerusalem—and fic-
tional stories about children who took part in the fighting. A 1962 reader for
fourth grade, for example, included a story about a child—David—who
fought alone against the Arabs and blew up an Arab tank. Readers used in
a religious school referred to the IDF as a holy entity. The poems in the
readers presented war and army service as a natural part of the Israeli life.
For example, Neomi Shemer's "We Are Both from the Same Village" tells
a story about two friends who grew up together: "We went to the same
places / We went to the same wars / We crawled over thorns and thistles /
But returned together to the village." The song continues and describes how
one of the young men was killed in the battle and his friend brought him
home to the village. The end of the song describes present life in the village
when "almost everything remains the same" and, as one of the friends
walks in the field, the other one glares at him behind the graveyard fence.
In this song, then, "war is treated as something so common that it becomes
routine" (Gadish 2009, 71); just as young Israelis attend high school and
hang out together ("going to the same places"), so do they fight in wars.
Gadish further notes that in this poem "the option of preventing war is
nowhere to be seen; war is implicitly unavoidable" (p. 72).

Podeh (2002, 145) points out that in history books, especially until
1967 but also in the period after 1967, "the fear of a second round of war
with the Arabs, and the threat of annihilation, was genuine and not theoretical." Major wars—such as the 1948 War—were described in history textbooks as wars of survival. This description was supported by the tendency
to present these wars as wars of a few (Jewish fighters) against many (Arab
armies). Accordingly, Israeli victories, such as in the 1948 War, were presented as "miraculous triumphs" (p. 103), even though studies have
revealed that in many battles of the 1948 War, the Jews attained superiority in manpower and in military equipment (Tal 2004). As Bar-Tal (2007)
notes, the perception of Israeli victory as a miracle may increase the feeling
of existential threat since it implies that such a victory is exceptional and,
hence, might not happen again.

This content was found in more than school textbooks. Furman (1999)
analyzed kindergarten rituals during the years 1982–1988 that revealed
messages about war as inevitable and glorification of military heroes that
were transmitted to young children who could not yet read (see Chapter 6
for further examples from her study). Likewise, Ben-Amos and Bet-El
(1999), who studied commemoration ceremonies on Memorial Days for
fallen soldiers in elementary, middle, and high schools, found that these
ceremonies often involved the children acting as soldiers on a military
parade ground. They had to snap to attention and then move to parade rest.
Ben-Amos and Bet-El also note that the Memorial Day for the fallen soldiers ceremony and the Holocaust Remembrance Day ceremony begin with

a siren that sounds like one during a war and, hence, remind children about the danger of a war. Texts read during these ceremonies encouraged the feeling of a dormant war. These texts did not refer to one specific war, and were read without noting even the date or author. Thus, war was presented to the children as an inevitable phenomenon.[12]

The Late 1980s and the 1990s

The emphasis on war as imminent and the notion of severe threat declined somewhat in the late 1980s and 1990s. Podeh (2002) and Firer, 'Adwān, and Pingel (2004, 44) found that several history textbooks from the 1990s included studies refuting the image of a few against many. Some books even asserted that the Jewish forces outnumbered Arab forces in the 1948 War, indicating that the perception of threat was less acute than presented in earlier textbooks. Yet Bar-Tal (1998), who analyzed the content of textbooks used in Grades 1 through 12 in history, geography, and civics studies as well as Hebrew readers that were approved by the Ministry of Education for use in 1994–1995, found that security beliefs were the most prominent theme, especially in readers and history textbooks, which focused on the need to defend the country and the glorification of the Israeli army.

Some changes appeared also in extracurricular activities at school. Ben-Amos and Bet-El (2003) note that while the army was still presented in school ceremonies during the 1990s, it was less notable than in earlier years. Lomsky-Feder (2004), who studied Memorial Day for the fallen soldiers ceremonies in fifty schools from 1994 to 2003, elaborates on changes during this time. Many ceremonies were held indoors, as opposed to on outdoor pseudomilitary parade grounds. Furthermore, some of the readings in these ceremonies challenged the inevitable nature of the state of war. A headmaster at one Jerusalem high school said, "We must ask ourselves, 'Have we done enough for peace, for life?'" Even when criticism of security beliefs was voiced, however, "the students always mentioned their duty to serve in the army and their belief that the State of Israel could not exist without the might of the Israeli Defense Forces" (Lomsky-Feder 2004, 301). It is also important to note that these trends are mostly from high school ceremonies while elementary schools tended to retain the existing format's military nature and security messages.

The Period After 2000

Two trends in current years may suggest a strengthening of the feeling of existential threat and glorification of the army. The first trend is the intensifying of premilitary preparation at high schools, which is discussed in Chapter 6. The second trend is the strengthening of Holocaust studies and the way that it is taught in Israeli schools. While this is discussed in depth in Chapter 5, it is worth noting here as it is especially well illustrated by high school trips to Holocaust sites in Poland. From 1988 to 2007, more than 370,000 students participated in these trips (Vergun 2008), and their message impacts have been debated by educators and scholars (see a review in Soen and Davidovich 2011). Especially relevant are messages about the need for a strong Israeli army, and that only such an army can prevent another Jewish Holocaust. Indeed, periodical memorandums by the Ministry of Education explicitly stated that one aim of the tours was for the students "to take away the lesson about the need of a *strong* sovereign Jewish state" (Glickman et al. 2011, emphasis added). J. Feldman (2002, 2008) found that this belief was transferred to the students during the visit explicitly and implicitly through sensory experiences. For example, she notes that the world of the voyage was sharply divided into two spaces: interior spaces (such as the bus and the hotel) and exterior spaces (Poland and its Holocaust visiting sites). The interior spaces were in many ways an extension of Israel since Israeli snack food was passed among participants, Israeli music played on the buses' audio systems, and so on. The Israeli guard accompanying each bus "always sits in the front seat by the door, scanning the road ahead." Any possibility for casual contact with the Poles was eliminated because of security concerns. These security measures suggested to the children that Poland is a dangerous place and that only representatives of the State of Israel could provide security to the Jews. In the words of the 2001 Holocaust Remembrance Day speech delivered by Israel's minister of education at that time, Limor Livnat: "We shouldn't suppose that we differ from our grandfathers and grandparents who went to the gas chambers. What separates us from them is not that we are some sort of new Jew. The main difference is external: we have a state, and a flag and an army: caught in their tragedy, they lacked all three" (J. Feldman 2002, 84).

Indeed, a nationwide study conducted among 2,506 students from 55 schools that participated in a Poland trip between 2007 and 2009 found that 83 percent of students returning from the journey reported that the trip contributed to their belief in the indispensability of the IDF (Glickman et al. 2011). These findings are in line with Ben-Amos and Bet-El's (2003, 382) interviews with high school students who participated in these trips in 1996, which revealed that one of the main lessons these students said they learned from the trip was that "we need a strong army." In sum, my review of leaders' rhetoric and school curricula revealed that the belief that Israel is under existential threat, the centrality of security as a main value, and the high prestige of the IDF dominated these texts. There was some decrease in the glorification of the army in school curricula, especially in the 1990s, but the general mood of high threat and the necessity of a strong army was rarely questioned even in those texts most critical of security beliefs.

The Public

The Nature and Magnitude of the Threat

Israeli public polls often included questions about security issues. Given the many wars in Israeli history and the centrality of the belief about dormant war in Israeli texts, it is not surprising that numerous questions referred to the possibility of another war between Israel and Arab states. Neither is the fact that during most of these years the majority of respondents thought another war with an Arab state was probable sometime in the distant future (ten years or more) or near term (within three years).

Polling data also revealed some changes. After Egyptian president Sadat's visit to Jerusalem in 1977, the percentage of respondents who thought that war was probable decreased dramatically. This percentage eventually rose again, but it took six years to return to pre-1977 levels. The percentage of respondents who thought war was probable in three years decreased during the early 1990s and from 2004 to 2005, when less than 40 percent expected a war. In 2007 and 2009, this rate sharply increased to 70 percent (see Figure 3.1).[13]

When surveyed about their main worries, Israeli Jews perceived a potential war as a threat on a national and a personal level. A 1962 international study about main hopes and fears in thirteen nations, including Israel, illustrated just how unique Israel is on this matter. In this study, only Israelis and Americans expressed concern about war as a personal worry. In Egypt, one of Israel's main adversaries at that time, none expressed such a fear on a personal level. Regarding national level fear, 49 percent of the Israeli Jews were worried about war with Arabs (again, none of the Egyptians expressed concern about war with Israel) (Antonovsky and Arian 1972). A follow-up study indicated that by 1975 (after the 1973 War), war was still Israelis' main fear on the national and personal levels (Katz 1980). Personal-level concerns about war also appeared in later surveys. In a 1990 survey, most respondents (58 percent) chose war as their main concern (over a car accident, family crisis, or unemployment) (*Hadashot* 1990). In 1997, they reported worries about (in declining order) terrorism, the security situation, and war (S. Landau 1998, 302). Importantly, comparisons with data from other countries revealed that Israelis worry more about war than citizens of other countries, even those with ongoing war or conflict. In the 2007 Pew Global Attitudes project[14] (shown in Table 3.1), Israel had the highest rate of respondents who reported "war/terrorism" as a main personal problem, with Lebanon in second place. This might be explained by the war between the two nations eight months before the survey. Yet in other countries involved in a war at the actual time of the survey, or countries that had recently suffered major terrorist attacks (e.g., the United

Figure 3.1   Perceived Likelihood of War, 1973–2009

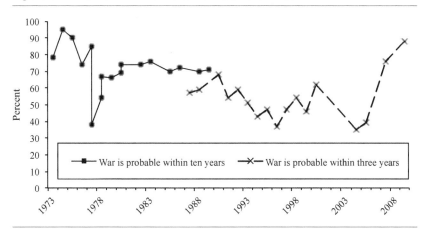

Sources: War is probable within ten years: Guttman. War is probable within three years: NSPOP.

States, Pakistan, Turkey, and Spain), the percentage of respondents reporting "terrorism/war" as a personal concern was notably lower.

Another indication of how much terrorism occupied Israelis' personal
worries is shown in Figure 3.2. From 1967 to 2015, usually more than 60
percent of the respondents expressed worry that they or their family members would be hurt during an act of terror. The National Resilience Survey
conducted by the National Security Studies Center in Haifa University from
2000 to 2011 also found that levels of fear of terror among Jews in Israel
were high and stable throughout this decade. On a scale of 1 (low fear) to
6 (high fear), levels of fear from terror never dropped below 4.43, even in
periods when the frequency of terrorist attacks dropped dramatically (Ben-
Dor, Canetti, and Lewin 2012; Ben-Dor and Canetti 2009).

Furthermore, terror was perceived as not only a personal threat, but also
as a national threat. For example, in 2000 85.5 percent of the respondents
thought that ongoing terror attacks might cause a strategic and even existential threat to the State of Israel, 86.6 percent thought so in 2002, and
83.0 percent in 2006 (Ben-Dor, Canetti, and Halperin 2007). A 2010 international survey—the International Social Survey Programme (ISSP)—
provides a comparative perspective and is presented in Table 3.2. The rate
of respondents in Israel who thought terrorism was the main national
problem was one of the highest rates of any country surveyed (only
Turkey had a higher rate). This rate is three times more than in Spain and
four times higher than in Russia, although those countries also coped with
terrorism at that time.

Table 3.1 Terrorism or War as the Most Important Problem Facing Self and Family, 2007

State	Percentage
Israel[a]	27
Lebanon	25
Morocco	13
Spain	11
Turkey	8
Côte d'Ivoire	7
Poland	4
Egypt	4
Jordan	4
Pakistan	4
India	4
Ethiopia	4
United States	3
Italy	3
Bangladesh	3
Uganda	3
Britain	2
Germany	2
Ukraine	2

Source: Pew Research Center (2007).
Notes: Combined responses are shown for the top three answers. a. Israel includes non-Jewish respondents.

Figure 3.2 Fears About Terror, 1967–2015

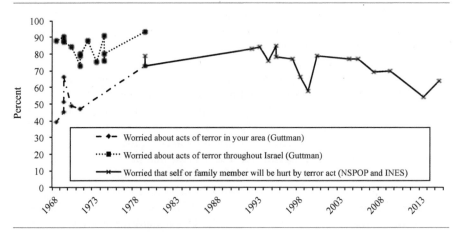

Sources: Guttman, NSPOP, and INES.

The Palestinian state is a unique issue for the Israeli-Arab conflict which, as we saw above, was mentioned by leaders as a severe threat over the years. This issue has also appeared frequently in Israeli public polls regarding potential threats to the State of Israel (see Figure 3.3), and the data showed that from the mid-1970s to the early 1990s the public expressed concerns similar to its leaders: during the years 1975–1981 the percent of respondents who perceived the Palestinian state as a threat to the State of Israel was about 90 percent, with a small variance. From 1985 to 1992 (the years of the Lebanon War and the first intifada), these percentages were steady around 80 percent. During Oslo process years, the data indicated a clear decrease in this belief (around 50 percent perceived the Palestinian state as a threat in 1997). Recall that a similar trend appeared in leaders' rhetoric during the 1990s—especially that of Rabin, who said that the agreements with the Palestinians did not endanger Israel's existence and may contribute to its security. Recall also that Netanyahu expressed much more concern over the threat from a Palestinian state, and the data revealed that in 2015 57 percent of the Jewish respondents shared his view.

At the same time, the public seemed to share Netanyahu's and other leaders' concern regarding the existence of unconventional weapons in Muslim states. The fact that questions on this issue appeared only after 1990 (shortly before the Gulf War) may indicate the growing awareness of this issue in Israeli society because of the war. In addition, from 1990 to 2012, between 70 and 80 percent of respondents perceived the existence of unconventional weapons in Arab states as a very threatening issue. In the 2012 survey 66 percent of the respondents "ranked the nuclear threat level as 7, that is, the highest level possible" (Ben Meir and Bagno-Moldavsky 2013, 64). Furthermore, this fear ranged higher in those years than any other threatening issues. It was perceived as more threatening than the establishment of a Palestinian state or a potential war with Arab states (Arian 1995; Ben Meir and Bagno-Moldavsky 2013).[15] Fear of these unconventional weapons was also mentioned in European surveys from that time (which did not include Israel), and the data showed a growing concern from this threat among European respondents as well.[16]

As for a less "traditional" security threat, leaders often mentioned the "demographic threat"—the loss of a Jewish majority—as an existential threat. Questions about this issue were less common in public polls than questions about military threat, but the data indicated that the public was concerned about this issue. For example, 83 percent of respondents in a 1991 NSPOP survey said that an equal number of Arabs and Jews in the country posed a threat to the country; similar results appeared in the 1992 NSPOP survey (86 percent). Unfortunately, the question was not asked again in NSPOP surveys. In a Peace Index survey from October 2003, 67 percent said that they strongly or moderately feared that without a solution based on the

Table 3.2   Terrorism as the Most Important Issue for One's Country Today, 2010

Country	Percentage
Turkey	39.0
Israel (Arabs)	13.0
Israel (Jews)	12.0
United States	7.9
Spain	3.5
Russia	2.7
Mexico	2.6
Germany	2.4
Czech Republic	2.1
Great Britain	2.0
France	1.6
Philippines	1.0
Slovak Republic	1.0
Average (in 32 countries)	3.0

Source: ISSP Research Group (2012).

principle of two states for two peoples, and with continued Israeli control of the territories, the Palestinians would turn from a minority to a majority and a de facto binational state would emerge west of the Jordan. In a December 2003 Peace Index survey, 71 percent agreed with Netanyahu's statement that the Israeli Arabs constituted a demographic danger. In a 2003 survey of the Index of Arab-Jewish Relations in Israel, 70 percent of Jewish respondents argued that "the Arab citizens endanger the state because of their high fertility." However, in 2012 only 52 percent thought so (Smooha 2013).[17]

Finally, a Peace Index time series survey addressed the general level of perceived threat to Israel. During the years 2001–2013, respondents were asked, "How would you characterize the level of security-military risk to Israel at present?" During most of this period, over 60 percent thought that the security-military risk to Israel was high.[18] Ben Meir and Bagno-Moldavsky (2013, 58) obtained similar findings while analyzing NSPOP data. Based on a question about the different potential threats to Israel, they created an index and concluded that "on the whole, the average Israeli feels more threatened than less threatened."[19]

War, terrorism, the Palestinian state, and unconventional weapons in the hands of Arab states were perceived as main threats to the State of Israel, and most respondents thought that Israel was under a high security threat. But what was the actual chance that they attributed to the possibility of the annihilation of their state? Questions regarding the possibility of the destruction of the state have been rare in public polls in most countries, but have appeared from time to time in Israeli polls. In a 1978 survey of Israeli students, 34.4 percent thought that there was no danger of dismemberment of Israel by the Arabs within the coming twenty years, 38.8 per-

Figure 3.3   Perception of Palestinian State as a Threat to Israel, 1974–2015 (percentage who think Palestinian state is a threat)

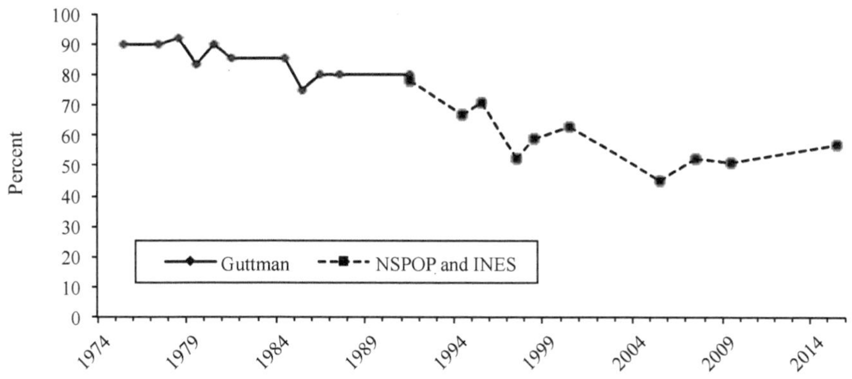

Sources: Guttman, NSPOP, and INES.

cent saw the probability as between 0.1 and 10.0 percent, 14.9 percent as an even chance, and 4.6 percent saw the chances as greater than even (Kimmerling 1984). On the one hand, 66 percent of the respondents thought that there was some chance that Israel would be destroyed in twenty years. On the other hand, most respondents thought the chance was low or not likely at all. Eight years later, in a 1986 survey, 18 percent of respondents agreed with the statement that "there's a reasonable possibility that the Arabs will destroy the State of Israel in the next 20 years," while 16 percent were not sure, and 66 percent disagreed (Zemach 1987). In an NSPOP survey from that period, most respondents (85 percent in 1986 and 74 percent in 1987) assessed the probability that the State of Israel would be destroyed as nonexistent or low (Arian 1995). Additionally, in a 1998 survey, 7 percent of the respondents thought that Israel would not exist in the coming fifty years and 11 percent were not sure (*Haaretz* 1998). Finally, a Democracy Index time series survey showed that during the years 2007–2010, most respondents had high trust in Israel's future existence, and the percentage of respondents with low trust in Israel's future existence never exceeded 22 percent.[20] Thus, Israeli Jews were worried about the security situation, but they did not think that Israel would cease to exist in the foreseeable future.

Security as a Core Value

Leaders' rhetoric and school textbooks attributed significant importance to security as an end in and of itself and not only as a means to achieve other aims. Numerous questions in Israeli polls referred to the importance of security as a main value and to its prioritization over other values. Respondents were asked to name their most important values, and always referred to security as one of the most important ones. This was clear even by April 1971 when, in a survey that was conducted by Bar-Ilan University, respondents were asked to rank their three most important values from a list. Seventy percent chose security, 33 percent chose freedom, 38 percent chose settlement of the land of Israel, and 8 percent chose equality (A. Peleg 1971). Later, in a 1993 survey by the Guttman Institute, respondents were asked to indicate the importance of five domains: security, health, employment, education, and peace. Most respondents (59 percent) chose security as the most important domain (Shor 1993).

Lastly, the Joint Israeli-Palestinian Poll (JIPP) included a question in 2000 (before the second intifada) and 2001 that I also included in my 2016 survey, which referred to ranking of the following goals: security, economic prosperity, democracy, peace, and a Jewish state (see Table 3.3). Again, security was chosen as the first choice more than any other goal.

The uniqueness of this situation was shown in the 2001 World Values Survey (WVS) that was conducted among forty-three nations (Israel participated in only the 2001 round). Israel was the only country that ranked strong defense forces as its first aim. In most countries, even those in a prolonged conflict, most respondents chose economic growth as the first choice (see Table 3.4). The only country close to Israel's prioritization of strong defense forces was China and, even there, economic growth was the more common first choice. These results were likely influenced by the survey's administration during the first year of the second intifada.[21] Yet the large gap between Israel and other countries, and the similarity of findings in surveys from other years, indicates that the centrality of security as most important goal for the state was stronger in Israeli society than in most other societies.

Table 3.3   The Most Important Goal for Israel, 2000–2016 (percentage who ranked this goal as highest)

	2000	2001	2016
Security	48	51	47
Economic prosperity	6	4	17
Democracy	6	6	10
Peace	12	14	12
Jewish state	26	23	14

Sources: JIPP (2000–2001) and Oren's 2016 Survey.

Table 3.4 The Objectives of the Country: First Choice in Different Countries, 2001 (percentage)

Country	Strong Defense Forces	Economic Growth
Israel[a]	43.0	41.0
China	39.4	40.0
Saudi Arabia	29.2	46.6
Egypt	24.6	54.8
Uganda	24.1	65.0
Jordan	21.7	65.8
India	17.5	54.3
Iran	16.8	55.6
Pakistan	16.4	76.3
Philippines	16.3	56.9
United States	16.0	48.6
Morocco	15.8	52.9
South Africa	12.7	60.5
Nigeria	11.7	70.7
Turkey	11.3	65.5
South Korea	9.4	50.5

Source: Inglehart et al. (2014).
Note: a. The number refers to Jewish and non-Jewish respondents. Among Israeli Jews, 47 percent chose strong defense forces and 39 percent economic growth.

Tension Between the Goal of Security and Other Societal Beliefs

Since the 1980s, several questions have addressed potential trade-offs between security and other values. In May 1986, 74 percent of the respondents preferred security over rule of law (*Yedioth Ahronoth* 1986). In a 1986 survey by the Guttman Institute, 95 percent of respondents preferred security over citizen's rights. In a September 1986 poll, 55 percent of respondents agreed with the statement that "in defending its security, it is sometimes necessary for Israel to violate liberties of innocent bystander[s]," and 21 percent were not sure whether they agreed (Zemach 1987).[22] Finally, NSPOP and Israel National Election Studies (INES) time series surveys that were conducted during the years 1987–2015 asked respondents to express their opinion regarding the dilemma between security considerations and observance of the principles of the rule of law. Almost all surveys pointed out a slight preference for security considerations. In the first year of the intifada, the percentage of respondents who preferred security over observance of the principles of the rule of law rose to 66 percent and then stabilized around 55 percent. Surprisingly, a slight decrease was observed during the Gulf War (1991).[23] Another increase appeared in 2009—probably because of the Gaza War that year. In 2015, 50 percent thought that a national security interest should always prevail, and 31 percent thought that it should prevail sometimes.

Means to Achieve Security

As I showed above, all Israeli leaders agreed about the importance of the army and a military means of ensuring security. However, they debated whether peace can serve as main means to achieve security or if security must rely on military means. A time series survey from 1986 to 2015 asked respondents what was the most effective policy to avoid further war with Arabs—peace talks or increased military strength (see Figure 3.4). From 1986 to 2000 (except for 1995), most respondents preferred peace talks over military capacity. Since then, however (in the 2001, 2002, 2007, 2009, and 2015 versions), more respondents thought that strengthening military capacity would be more effective in preventing war. Respondents at that time, then, tended to agree with Netanyahu regarding this issue.

Trust in the Israeli Army

As outlined earlier, another frequent trend in textbooks and leaders' speeches was high trust in the IDF and other security forces. In a 1990 poll, 94 percent of the respondents expressed trust in the IDF (Y. Peres and Yuchtman-Yaar 1992). Since 1994, two time series surveys (the Peace Index and Democracy Index) have addressed this issue annually (see Figure 3.5), and both showed a high and stable percentage of respondents expressing trust in the army. Additionally, in all public polls conducted in Israel, the army received more public trust than any other institution—higher than the parliament, or the Supreme Court. In 2015, for example, 93 percent of Jewish respondents said

Figure 3.4   Military Power or Peace Talks, 1986–2015

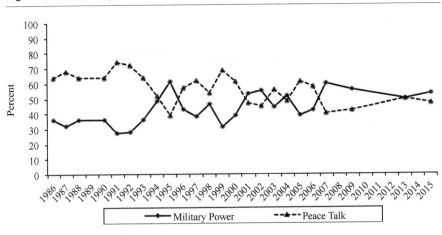

Sources: NSPOP and INES.

Figure 3.5   Trust in the Army, 1994–2016 (percentage who trust the army "to a large extent" or "to some extent")

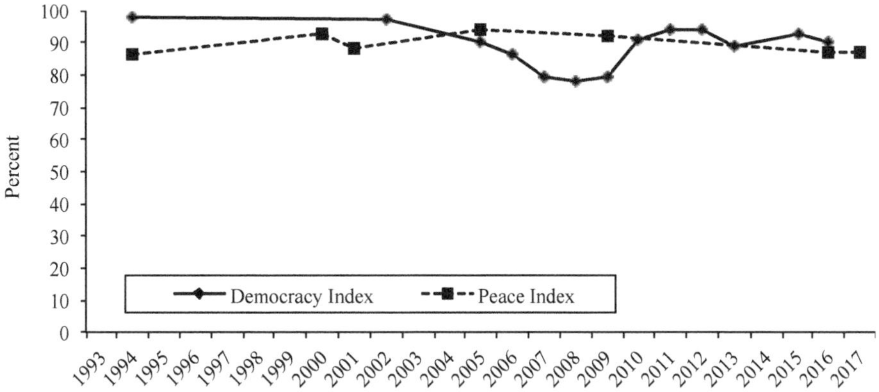

Sources: Democracy Index and Peace Index.

that they trusted the army "very much" or "quite a lot," compared to 62 percent who declared such trust in the Supreme Court and only 38 percent in the government (T. S. Hermann et al. 2015). This, however, is not a situation unique to Israel. Armies seem to inspire greater confidence than other national institutions in many states (Beetham 2006; Hattis Rolef 2006). Beetham (2006) found that trust in the military was the highest compared to other institutions in most countries in East Asia, Africa, and Eastern Europe. Yet the trust in the army is relatively high in Israel compared to other countries. Similar questions about trust in the army were included in the 2010–2014 WVS poll.[24] Comparing data from fifty-seven other nations, Israel was among those with the highest trust in its army, as 88 percent of Israeli Jews expressed trust in the army in 2014. Only Uzbekistan (96 percent), Qatar (95 percent), China (93 percent), and Jordan (91 percent) had higher levels of trust, and Armenia's and Australia's levels were comparable to Israel's. All other countries had lower levels of trust in the army (e.g., 83 percent in the United States, 76 percent in Turkey, and 56 percent in Taiwan).[25]

Additional questions studied the level of criticism toward the army. Shortly after the 1973 War, in June 1974, 91 percent of the respondents in a Guttman survey said that they trusted the IDF high command in its preparations for the next war, and 81 percent agreed with the statement that "the people in the IDF high command are the right people for this task." Since this was the first time that those questions were asked, we cannot know if these attitudes toward the IDF high command changed because of the war. Yet this high level of trust in the army came despite the release of a report (the Agranat Report) so critical of the army chief of staff that he immediately resigned. A series of questions from the 1980s, two years into the Lebanon War, still indicated high trust in the high command of the army. For example, in a 1984 survey by the Guttman Institute, 84 percent of the respondents said they trusted the judgment and decisionmaking of senior commanders in the army. In 1985, the percentage of respondents who trusted the judgment and decisionmaking of senior commanders dropped to 72 percent but then rose again to 80 percent in 1986.

However, another time-series of questions by the NSPOP and Peace Index indicated an increase in criticism toward the army in later years. The percentage of respondents in the NSPOP survey who thought the decisions of the high command of the army ignored relevant factors rose significantly from 53 percent in 1986 to 74 percent in 2009. In a 2010 survey, only 44 percent agreed with the statement that the IDF was an economically efficient organization (Eran Jona 2015). In a July 2015 Peace Index poll, respondents were asked to rate the IDF's combat operational and administrative organizational capabilities on a scale from 0 (poor) to 10 (excellent). While 72 percent chose the three highest scores (8, 9, or 10) regarding the IDF's combat operational capability, only 38 percent chose these scores about its administrative organizational capabilities. There is, then, an indication of increasing criticism toward the IDF's efficiency and decisionmaking in the period after 2000.

Conclusion

The security theme in the Israeli ethos reflects Israel's geopolitical situation as a small country surrounded by many enemies. Accordingly, the main security-related beliefs held that Israel is under existential threat and that it lives under conditions of latent (and periodically active) war. These beliefs also emphasized security as a value (not just a means to other goals) and glorified the IDF. While these beliefs were grounded in Israeli reality, they were also sustained by continual socialization emphasizing the threatening aspects of that reality and the potential consequences of these aspects for the state and the individual. Israeli Jews are socialized to believe not only that Israel is under existential threat and that security is the most important value but also that the essence of "being Israeli" is to always be preoccupied with security concerns, and that this is one of their main distinctions as a nation.

While the dominance of security beliefs within the ethos has not fluctuated much over time, there have been shifts with respect to the perceived nature of the threats. The focus (mostly in leaders' rhetoric and in public polls) moved from the threat of conventional war and the danger posed by a Palestinian state to the threat of unconventional weapons in the hands of Muslim states and nontraditional security threats (threats to identity). As I showed, these changes followed major events in the conflict such as the Gulf War and the second intifada. Since the 1980s, polls have shown a mild decline in the reverence toward the military and a growing willingness to criticize it. Yet the army's prestige remained high, as did the prevalence of beliefs holding that Israel is in a state of latent war and the centrality of security as a main value. These beliefs were rarely challenged in official discourse or in public polls.

In terms of securitization theory, Israel is an example of deep securitization whereby "widespread public discourses explicitly frame threats as probable, protracted, and endangering the very existence of the nation/state" (Abulof 2014, 412). Abulof argues that "if some securitizations are deeper than others, Israel's is one of the deepest" (p. 397). In most countries, when leaders discuss threats to the nation, they usually do not mean its literal disappearance or annihilation (Abulof 2014). Israeli leaders, as I have shown, often described the threat to Israel as existential—potentially leading to the country's destruction or disappearance. Abulof (2015) further argues that the Israeli public shared this anxiety. He based his conclusion on media discourse and a few anecdotal polls. My analysis of public polls, however, showed that the Israeli public agreed that the threat was severe, but not to the degree that it would lead to Israel's destruction in the foreseeable future. This is probably due to the positive image the public held of the Israeli military and its prowess (see Chapter 4, which analyzes Israel's self-image as a villa in the jungle). Note, however, that this confidence can be sustained only as long as the state continues to invest significant resources and attention in security.

A broader view of the dichotomy between the pervasive political discourse about the tangible existential threat to Israel on the one hand and the high confidence among the public in Israel's survival prospects on the other hand is provided by the theoretical framework of ontological security—security of identity—discussed in Chapter 1 (Rumelili 2015; Mitzen 2006; Steele 2008). Rumelili (2015) argues that ontological insecurity is caused by existential anxieties (unlike fear that is a response to a specific threat that can be faced and endured, the threats causing anxiety are unknown) and that, during a conflict, societies cope with ontological insecurity by establishing concrete objects of fear (through securitization) and producing a system of meaning that provides a sense of self and differentiates friends from foes. The security theme of the ethos of conflict establishes a definite object of fear and a means to cope with it. Whether it is conventional war or terrorism, leaders and army generals (who enjoy high prestige and trust) offer specific means to cope with these threats. The security theme with other themes in the ethos, like the villa in the jungle theme, also establish routines (that according to Mitzen 2006 are important in establishing ontological security) and legitimize employing extraordinary measures. In the Israeli case, those measures include, for example, a "state of emergency" that has been in place for seventy years and affords the government broad emergency powers to derogate from the rule of law, as well as a universal draft system that is perceived as a normal situation by the Israeli public and is even considered to be the essence of Israeliness. So, while the conflict may produce high levels of fear (in the personal and the national sense), the ethos of conflict provides ontological security to the society. On the other hand, a threat to the ethos (with or without securitization of traditional military threats)—a vital component of national identity—can produce ontological insecurity and provide powerful support in legitimizing collective actions.

A case in point is the 2005 disengagement from Gaza—a unilateral Israeli withdrawal from the Gaza Strip with evacuation of all Israeli settlements there and four settlements in the West Bank. Some of the justifications for this plan were based on securitization of traditional security threats such as the threat of terror. Sharon, for example, maintained that "disengagement can assist us in curbing terror, and will certainly allow us to fight terror in a better and more effective way" (Lupovici 2012, 828). He also has implied that the withdrawal would enhance Israel's deterrent posture by increasing the legitimacy of using extensive force if needed. But the main justification for this plan was based on securitization of the demographic trends regarding the proportion of Palestinians among the population west of the Jordan River that threatens the goal of a Jewish and democratic state and the ontological insecurity that is associated with such a threat (Abulof 2014). Sharon said in a speech immediately following his government's approval of the disengagement plan, "It is a resolution that is good for . . . the demography of the Jewish people in the Land of Israel" (Lupovici 2012, 823). Olmert—one of the architects of the disengagement plan—summarized it as "above all hovers the cloud of demographics" (Rynhold and Waxman 2008, 23). The public initially supported this plan.[26] As Ben Meir and Shaked (2007, 36–37) note regarding an increase in the percentage of respondents who chose the value of "a Jewish majority" as the most important value in 2006 and 2007: "This is probably due to the heightened salience of the demographic factor as a result of the Gaza disengagement." Ben Meir and Shaked further argue that the rationale behind this plan "was the vital need for Israel to preserve and maintain a strong and solid Jewish majority in order to guarantee its character as a Jewish and democratic state. The results confirm . . . that for more and more Israelis demography has become more important than geography" (pp. 36–37). It can be argued that the takeover of Gaza by Hamas and the persistent rocket fire from Gaza undercut the argument about the merit of this plan in providing physical security. Indeed, the support for the disengagement from Gaza after the fact decreased in later years.[27] Yet there is no public support for returning to the previous situation of full Israeli control of Gaza.[28] This is at least in part because of the concern about the demographic threat that is still dominant in the Israeli society.[29] As a well-known columnist wrote in 2006: "Even today, with the disengagement crumbling before our eyes, it should be justified. Even today, with the Israel Defense Forces returning to northern Gaza and Gush Katif, it should be argued that liberating 1.3 million Palestinians from the yoke of the Israeli occupation was fundamentally the right move" (Shavit 2006).

Notes

1. Abulof (2015, 137–138) provides numerous examples of the belief that Israel is under existential threat in the writing of prominent Israeli writers such as Ari Shavit and David Grosman.

2. For example, Ben-Gurion said in 1967, "None of us can forget the Holocaust. And if some Arab rulers declare day and night that Israel must be annihilated—this time referring not to the entire Jewish people in the world, but to the Jews living in their land—it is our duty not to take these severe statements lightly" (Zertal 2005, 119).

3. In fact, in this war Israeli forces were superior, and Egypt, that did not anticipate the attack, withdrew many forces from the Sinai Peninsula before the war (Morris 2001, 291).

4. In another speech, Netanyahu says, "Jewish state is a beleaguered democracy in a hostile region, threatened like no other country on earth" (Netanyahu 2013q).

5. Overall, between 1987 and 1993, more than 1,200 Palestinians in the territories were killed by Israeli troops and about 150 Israelis were killed by Palestinians (Arian 1995).

6. By April 14, 2004, the violence had claimed over 2,720 lives and 25,000 wounded on the Palestinian side, many of them civilians, and 943 lives (276 members of the security forces, 667 civilians) and 6,300 wounded on the Israeli side.

7. During the 2009 Gaza War, 3 Israeli civilians and between 300 (according to the IDF) and 900 (according to the Palestine Center for Human Rights) noncombatant Palestinians were killed (Anshel, March 26, 2009).

8. For example, "We must ensure that while we pursue our aspirations to achieve peace with our neighbors who are not partners to this goal, we do not, God forbid, allow that kind of enemy a foothold in those essential territories which are located very close to the heart of the State of Israel" (Netanyahu 2013m). Already in the 1990s, Netanyahu argued that a Palestinian state would work with Iran and Iraq to endanger Israel's existence (Aronoff 2014, 63).

9. During the early 1970s, even some dovish leaders did not see this issue as immediate threat. For example, Shimon Peres said in 1972 that "our path, and that of our forefathers, is that faith is always stronger than statistics" (Abulof 2014, 405).

10. Ehud Barak said, "Israel cannot afford and shouldn't try to govern over another people. . . . I think we should separate ourselves from the Palestinians. We do not need here either a kind of apartheid, or a Bosnia" (Magal et al. 2013, 159).

11. This idea was also expressed by Barak in 1999 (see Chapter 9) and Sharon in 2004, who said, "As one who fought in all of Israel's wars, and learned from personal experience that, without proper force, we do not have a chance of surviving in this region, which does not show mercy towards the weak, I have also learned from experience that the sword alone cannot decide this bitter dispute in this land" (Ariel Sharon 2004).

12. Lomsky-Feder (2004, 298) reported a similar observation.

13. There was also an indication for an increase in expectation for war in the less distant future at that time: 75 percent of the Jewish respondents in a March 2008 Peace Index survey thought that there were high chances that in five years Israel would find itself at war with one or more Arab states.

14. The question was asked only in the 2002 and 2007 rounds. The data from Israel includes also non-Jewish respondents.

15. Also, 79 percent of respondents in an August 2006 Peace Index survey thought that there was "a real threat to Israel's existence from Iran."

16. According to Eurobarometer, 62 percent of the respondents in 2000 and 79 percent in 2001 were afraid of spread of such weapons (European Commission 2002).

17. The public perceived Israeli Palestinian citizens as a current security threat—not just as a potential demographic threat. For example, 72 percent in 2003, 65 percent in 2012, and 60 percent in 2013 said that Arab citizens endanger Israel due to their struggle to change its Jewish character (Smooha 2013).

18. In November 2001, 62 percent of Jewish respondents thought that the security-military risk to Israel was high; in November 2003, 64 percent; May 2005, 51 percent; October 2013, 67 percent; May 2014, 68 percent; and July 2015, 81 percent.

19. In a January 2016 Peace Index poll, 61 percent of Jewish respondents opposed the view that "the Israeli-Palestinian conflict can continue for many more years without posing a threat to Israel's security and existence."

20. Abulof (2015, 140–141) presents data that indicated greater concern in these years, although the wording of the questions did not explicitly mention the annihilation of Israel. A Gallup poll in September 2001 showed that 70 percent of respondents said that they were anxious about the future of the country. Fifty-four percent in an October 2006 Ma'ariv poll and 57 percent in a November 2006 Yedioth Ahronoth poll said that they were anxious about the State of Israel. The data of these polls are taken from Abulof 2015, 140–141.

21. Fieldwork was conducted from September to October 2001.

22. In a 2016 Democracy Index poll, 62 percent agreed with the statement: "In the fight against terror, there is no room for ethical considerations, and it is permissible to use any means to prevent terrorist attacks."

23. Similar findings were documented in another survey that studied the dilemma between security considerations and democracy. In 1987, 61 percent of the respondents agreed with the statement: "A marginal threat to security does not justify curtailment of democracy." In 1988 (the first year of the intifada), the percentage of respondents who agreed with that statement decreased to 56 percent, and in the years 1989–1990 it decreased further to 43 percent (Y. Peres and Yuchtman-Yaar 1992). This survey also documented a decrease in the security preference over democracy during the Gulf War.

24. While Israel did not participate in this round, an identical question was asked in the 2014 Democracy Index.

25. In a 2014 Gallup World Survey Israel was ranked in twenty-ninth place among 127 states in the percentage of respondents who indicated confidence in the army. However, this survey was conducted among Jewish and non-Jewish Israelis.

26. According to NSPOP, in 2004 a clear majority supported the plan. In 2005 and 2006, six months after its implementation, Israeli public opinion was evenly split about the plan (Ben Meir and Shaked 2007). A May 2005 Peace Index survey indicated that 57 percent supported the plan.

27. In 2007 and 2009, less than one-third of Israeli Jews said that they supported the plan after the fact (Ben Meir and Bagno-Moldavsky 2010).

28. The public strongly objected to reoccupation of the entire Gaza Strip during the 2014 War. In an NSPOP survey conducted on July 27–28, 2014, only 28 percent preferred "Occupy the Gaza Strip and overthrow the Hamas regime." In a Rafi Smith survey, conducted on August 6, only 16 percent believed Israel should have "occupied the Gaza Strip and overthrown the Hamas regime" (Ben Meir 2014).

29. While a military reoccupation might improve somewhat the security of Israeli civilians, it is widely understood that a reoccupation would result in significant casualties among Israeli troops. As I discuss in Chapter 6, there is a high level of sensitivity among the Israeli public to military casualties, and it is therefore reasonable to assume that this is another reason for the public's reticence.

4

A Villa in the Jungle

In a 1996 speech, then foreign minister Ehud Barak described Israel as a "modern and prosperous villa in the middle of the jungle" (Barak 1996). Twenty years later, Benjamin Netanyahu elaborated on this idea: "At the end, in the State of Israel, as I see it, there will be a fence that spans it all. I'll be told, 'this is what you want, to protect the villa?' The answer is yes. Will we surround all of the State of Israel with fences and barriers? The answer is yes. In the area that we live in, we must defend ourselves against the wild beasts" (Ravid 2016).

This metaphor of a villa in the jungle of wild beasts exemplifies a negative definition of collective identity (Eriksen 1995). In this case, the focus is the *distinction* of one group from other collectives ("us-hood" vs. "them"), rather than the commonality within one group ("we-hood"). Both types of identity formation are usually in play with regard to national identity (David and Bar-Tal 2009), but the negative type dominates in societies that are involved in prolonged conflict and that tend to define their identities in opposition to their adversaries' identity. Bar-Tal (2013) argues that ethos of conflict includes two themes: a positive collective self-image, and societal beliefs delegitimizing the opponent that attribute to the opponent "extremely negative social categories that exclude it from the sphere of human groups" (Oren and Bar-Tal 2007, 112). Of course, the tendency to form a positive view of the in-group can be found in many societies and groups, not necessarily only in those involved in intractable conflicts (Roccas et al. 2008). The tendency to delegitimize out-group members has been studied in many different contexts such as nationalism, ethnicity, and related topics like immigration (N. Haslam 2006; Wimmer 2002). Nevertheless, in societies that are involved in intractable conflict, self-image and image of the opponent often appear as mirror images. Each side sees itself as peaceful, aiming only toward self-defense, while the enemy is seen as evil, aiming toward aggression. In this vein, the enemy's aggression is viewed as inherent in its nature while aggressiveness on one's own part is explained in situational terms (Huddy, Sears, and Levy 2013; White 1968). In this chapter, then, I explore the self/enemy images as a theme in the Israeli ethos. More specifically, I refer to beliefs that present Israel as an advanced, moral, and peace-loving society, as well as a regional military superpower, that is in sharp contrast to the backward and aggressive Arabs who are motivated only by their desire to destroy Israel.

As in the previous chapter, this perception is influenced by reality. I noted Israel's military superiority in the previous chapter. Israel is also a developed country in both a regional and global sense ("Human Development Index (HDI) Human Development Reports" n.d.). Israel likewise employs many formal aspects of democracy such as political participation and limitations on executive authority. As of 2014, Israel had the world's second-highest rate of political participation, and ranked relatively high in government functioning (alongside Spain, the United Kingdom, the Czech Republic, India, and France) (T. S. Hermann et al. 2015). On democratic principles, Israel ranked much higher than its neighboring states.

However, there are limitations to Israeli democracy, especially as a liberal democracy, that are often marginalized by the Israeli ethos. These limitations include relatively high military intervention in politics, discrimination against Arab citizens of Israel, and the presence of strong and influential antidemocratic groups (Neuberger 2000; Pedahzur 2004). As I showed in Chapter 2, rather than being a liberal democracy, Israel is a *hegemonic state*—a state that promotes the interests of a single ethnopolitical group in a multinational setting (I. Peleg 2007), which makes Israel at best a "flawed" democracy (I. Peleg and Waxman 2011; for more critical discussions about Israel's democracy, see Jamal 2007; Peled 2008; see also Smooha 1990). Indeed, in 2012 Israel ranked as only "partly free" in scales assessing perception of corruption, the electoral process and pluralism, gender inequality, economic freedom, and freedom of the press. Israel also had a low ranking for military intervention in politics (between China and Turkey) and civil liberties (Israel's scores were like those of Lebanon) (T. S. Hermann et al. 2013).[1]

The simple picture of Israel as a peace-loving society facing a united, homogeneous, and bloodthirsty rival is also far more complex in reality. Certainly, there is cause for belief in the negative intentions of the Arabs toward Israel in the past as well as the present. Major Arab and Muslim leaders and organizations have openly called for the destruction of the State of Israel.[2] Furthermore, the history of the Israeli-Arab conflict goes beyond rhetoric to actual joint coordinated hostile and aggressive actions against it—including full-scale wars, economic embargos, and terrorist acts against Israeli and Jewish targets in Israel and abroad. However, there have also been positive cooperative interactions between Israel and Arab nations. In the late 1940s and the 1950s, there were several bilateral secret peace negotiations between a single Arab state and Israel.[3] In most of these negotiations, the Arab nations called for major Israeli territorial concessions, so a consensus could not be reached. Secret negotiations between Israel and Arab leaders have continued in the 1960s and 1970s.[4]

Several major peace negotiations were held and some peace agreements even were reached between Israel and Arab countries and groups—the 1979 Israeli-Egyptian peace treaty, the 1993 Israeli-Palestinian Oslo Accords, and the 1994 Israeli-Jordanian peace treaty. Some Arab leaders made moderate public statements that were in sharp contrast to the declarations mentioned above from the 1960s. For example, Egyptian president Anwar Sadat told his parliament in November 1977 that "I am prepared to go to the ends of the earth for peace, even to the Knesset itself" (Shlaim 2000, 359). Similar changes appeared in Palestinian rhetoric. In November 1988 in Algiers, the PNC officially accepted the 1947 UN partition plan that called for a two-state solution to the conflict (Muslih 1997); and, a month later in Geneva, Palestine Liberation Organization (PLO) chairman Yasser Arafat denounced terror attacks against Israel. The PLO labeled these two actions its "peace initiative"—an idea that previously would have been unthinkable for Palestinian leaders (Stein 1991). These more moderate statements continued in the 1990s and into the 2000s and included a Saudi plan, adopted by the Arab League in March 2002, calling for peace with Israel in return for a full Israeli withdrawal from territories occupied in 1967 and the return of Palestinian refugees (Laqueur and Rubin 2008, 583–584). However, violence and hostile statements continued from other Arab leaders, groups, and media. The 1988 Hamas Charter, for example, aimed to "liberate" every bit of Palestine, condemned all compromise with Israel as a violation of divine law, and used anti-Semitic language to describe Jews (Laqueur and Rubin 2008, 341–48). Hezbollah and Iran's leaders (especially former Iranian president Mahmoud Ahmadinejad, who denied the Holocaust) also called for Israel's demise.

As for perceptions of Israel as a peace-loving country, while Israeli leaders repeatedly expressed a desire for peace, that was not always Israel's priority. During the 1950s and 1960s, attaining peace often meant inducing the Arabs to accept Israel's terms (see Chapter 7). In addition, several times Israel responded devastatingly and disproportionately to Arab violence, including with attacks on civilian targets. The Israeli society, as I show in this chapter, used several strategies to cope with potential contradictions between these and other actions and Israel's self-image as a peace-loving country.

Assessment of the "real" or actual Arab intentions toward Israel and Israel toward Arab nations (assuming that the "Arabs" are one group driven uniformly by one unchanging motivation) is in the eye of the beholder, and beyond the purposes of this book. My focus is on the content of beliefs in the Israeli ethos regarding Israel and the Arabs, and the way they had changed considering trends in the conflict mentioned above.

Leaders' Rhetoric

Leaders' rhetoric commonly contrasted negative images of the Arabs with positive images of the Israelis in terms of both aggression and morality. David Ben-Gurion, for example, maintained that geographically Israel is part of the Middle East, but it is quite different from its neighbors from a moral-cultural aspect (Podeh 2005). Ben-Gurion also often delegitimized the Arabs by identifying them as Nazis. In a 1961 nationwide Independence Day broadcast, he said that hate like that which led to the Holocaust "is still simmering among the rulers of our neighboring countries, plotting to eradicate us, and dozens of Nazi experts are their tutors and advisers in their hatred for Israel and the Jews of the world" (Zertal 2005, 114).

Ben-Gurion argued that Arab rulers aimed to "obliterate Israel for the map of Earth" (Pedatzur 1998, 144), most notably in a speech following the 1956 War. In the speech, he said that "it was our duty to take urgent and effective measures for self-defense" against "the noose" that had been prepared for Israel by the Arabs who "would neglect no means serving to destroy us" (Ben-Gurion 1956). Thus, he presented the 1956 War—when Israel invaded Egypt and took control of the Suez Canal, Gaza, and parts of Sinai—as a defense against Arab aggression. In the same speech, he cited a Czech arms deal that had supplied Egypt with "a tremendous flow of heavy armaments." He referenced Egypt's denial of Israel's right to navigate the Suez Canal, and mentioned the Fedayeen units, Egyptian-trained Palestinians who carried out a series of terrorist acts inside Israel. Finally, he referenced the "tripartite military alliance that was concluded among Egypt, Jordan, and Syria, which had one clear goal in view: War to the death against [Israel]."[5] Based on these hostile Arab actions, Ben-Gurion justified Israel's initiation of the war, arguing that "there are not a people in the world so deeply concerned for the principles of peace and justice contained in the United Nations Charter as is the Jewish people" (Ben-Gurion 1956).

This justification omits, however, that since 1955, several large arms deals with France (Shlaim 2000, 165; Morris 2001, 284) guaranteed Israeli military superiority over Egypt, regardless of the Czech deal, and there was no need to launch an urgent preemptive strike (Shlaim 2000, 165; Morris 2001, 288). Ben-Gurion also did not reveal that the 1956 War was an outcome of a secret agreement between Israel, France, and Britain. In fact, the war was initiated by France, following Egyptian president Gamal Abdel Nasser's nationalization of the Suez Canal Company. As the company's principal shareholders, the Egyptian takeover hurt France and Britain the most. In a secret meeting in France before the war, the three parties agreed to a plan in which Israel would attack Egypt and try to reach the canal zone. Britain and France would appeal to the parties to stay clear and, when Egypt presumably would not comply, Britain and France would have cause to attack Egyptian forces. In fact, Ben-Gurion presented a postconflict plan to reorganize the Middle East to serve the three nations' interests, dividing up territory in Jordan, Lebanon, and Egypt (Shlaim 2000, 172; Morris 2001, 290). This detailed plot to acquire territory was far removed from the defensive justification provided to the public. The full picture behind the 1956 War, then, reveals a more complex story than Ben-Gurion's simplistic narrative of Israel as merely a peace-seeking country. It is an example of the way that leaders in intractable conflict tend to emphasize only information supporting their side as defensive and peace-loving.

The distinction between Israel as an advanced, moral, and peace-loving country faced with Arabs intent on destroying it appeared in other speeches by Ben-Gurion (see a review in Brecher 1972) as well as many other Israeli leaders. For example, the narrative of Arabs aiming only to destroy a peaceful Israel was also used by Levi Eshkol, who was considered to be a relatively moderate leader. In a speech following the 1967 War, he said that while Israel perceived the 1949 armistice agreements as "a transitional stage on the road to peace," the Arabs saw them as "an expedient for gaining time in order to prepare for renewed aggression, with the aim of destroying Israel" (Eshkol 1967). Similarly, in 1970 Golda Meir stated that "we have not abandoned hopes of finding a way into the hearts of our neighbors, though they yet dismiss our appeals with open animosity" (Meir 1970).

This belief about hostile Arabs aiming to destroy Israel ignored the peace negotiations between Arab states and Israel discussed above, which were known to Israeli leaders (but unknown to the Israeli public). It also ignores the possibility that Arab hostile statements and actions were, among other things, a reaction to Israel's own aggressive actions and provocations in the conflict, including Israel's retaliation policy during the 1950s and the 1956 War. Nasser, the second president of Egypt, stated that Israel's aggressive actions during the 1950s had caused him to change his attitude toward Israel (Morris 2001, 283). Of course, this assertion might have been propaganda to justify Egypt's actions, but the fact is that a clear radicalization in the rhetoric and actions of Arab states appeared following the 1956 War (Morris 2001, 301). In Arab eyes, the collaboration between Israel and ex-imperialist states against Egypt in the 1956 War "validated" their own belief about Israel as imperialist agent aiming to take control of their land.

Arab declarations about destroying Israel, in return, "proved" to Israeli leaders that this was Arab intention all along, creating a cycle of reinforced negative perceptions.

This situation continued in later years. All Israeli-Arab wars following the 1967 War, even those initiated by Israel, were presented by Israeli leaders as defensive wars that were forced on Israel. A related belief presented Israel as a victim of its enemies, who was "forced" to kill them to defend itself. As a famous quote that is attributed to Meir said, "We can forgive you for killing our sons. But we will never forgive you for making us kill yours."[6] The perception of Arabs as a single homogeneous group united in their enmity for Israel also appeared in Israeli leaders' rhetoric in later years. Yitzhak Shamir is known for his observation in 1989 that "the Arabs are the same Arabs and the sea is the same sea. The goal [of the Arabs] is the same goal—liquidation of the state of Israel" (Man 2012). Shamir, then, dismissed both the positive change in Arab rhetoric at that time and the Israeli-Egyptian peace treaty. For him, the Arabs' aim to destroy Israel was an unchangeable fact—like the sea that the Arabs were said to want to throw the Jews into. However, Shamir's remark was outdated: since the mid-1970s Israeli leaders' rhetoric had shifted away from describing the "Arabs" as one united group, instead focusing specifically on the Palestinians.

Even with a narrowed focus on only the Palestinians, Israeli leaders' negative attitudes remained. Auerbach and Ben-Yehuda's analysis of four Israeli prime ministers' perceptions of the Palestinians from the mid-1970s to the mid-1980s—Menachem Begin, Shimon Peres, Yitzhak Rabin, and Ariel Sharon—indicated that these leaders believed the PLO's intention was to destroy Israel as a state and kill its Jewish population. These leaders delegitimized the PLO and its leaders, often by using symbolically evil labels like "Nazis." Begin stressed that the PLO was a "murderous Nazi organization" (Auerbach and Ben-Yehuda 1987, 336), and Peres said that "its Nazi characteristics are inherent to its nature, not only to its behavior" (Ben-Yehuda and Auerbach 1991, 527). However, most of these leaders distinguished between the PLO and the Palestinian population. Peres, Rabin, and Sharon thought that most Palestinians rejected the PLO's violence and wanted to live peacefully (under Israeli rule).[7] This view attributed less inherent destructive intent to the Palestinians as a group, somewhat moderating the image of violent Arabs, but it also marginalized any desire among them for self-identification or statehood.

During the Oslo Accords period (1993–2000), a significant erosion in the dichotomous view of the "good" Israelis against the "bad" Palestinians appeared in the rhetoric of Israeli dovish leaders such as Rabin and Peres. Negative stereotypes and delegitimization of the PLO and its leader Arafat almost disappeared from the rhetoric of these leaders. Rabin called Arafat and King Hussein of Jordan "ex-enemies" and insisted that they wanted peace like Israel did.[8] In contrast to previous leaders, Rabin argued that Palestinian actions were influenced by Israel's actions and the occupation situation:

> I want to tell the truth. For twenty-seven years, we have controlled another people that does not want our rule. For twenty-seven years, the Palestinians—who now number 1,800,000—have risen in the morning and cultivated a burning hatred for us as Israelis and as Jews. Every morning, they awake to a difficult life and it is partly our fault . . . but not completely. It cannot be denied: The continued rule of a foreign people who does not want us has a price. (Rabin 1994a)

In addition, Rabin distinguished between different groups of Palestinians and presented the extremist groups among the Palestinians as a common enemy of both Israel and the Palestinian Authority. This idea appeared in 22 percent of Rabin's speeches to local audiences and 33 percent of those to foreign audiences (Rosler 2012). In September 1995, he said "the enemies of yesterday share a common enemy today: the terrorism that sows death in our homes" (Rabin 1995e). Rabin even went so far as to say that Israeli extremists among the settlers were as bad as Arab terrorist and fundamentalist groups (Rosler 2012, 190). This distinction in Rabin's rhetoric was between the moderate forces, in his view a majority of both Israeli and Palestinian societies, and the extremist forces in both societies. Identical ideas appeared in Peres's rhetoric (Yadgar 2006). However, Israeli hawkish leaders from that period held the same pre-Oslo negative view about Palestinians, Arafat, and the PLO. Netanyahu often compared Arafat to Adolf Hitler, the Oslo agreement to the Munich agreement, and the West Bank to Sudetenland (Aronoff 2014, 53). Ironically, some anti-Oslo activists thought, like Rabin and Peres, that there was common ground between the Israeli government and the PLO leaders, but that both Arafat and Rabin acted to destroy Israel.[9]

Since 2000 and the collapse of the Oslo process, Israeli leaders' rhetoric—that of both doves and hawks—has returned to old perceptions of Israel and its rivals. To start, after 2000, the rhetoric shifted back to describing one Muslim coalition aiming to destroy Israel, a frequent historical tendency to reference a large homogeneous group such as the "axis of evil." This view was echoed by Ehud Olmert in his speech to the Knesset during the 2006 Lebanon War: he maintained that the war was against "the terror organizations operating from Lebanon and Gaza," which were "nothing but 'subcontractors' operating under the inspiration, permission, instigation, and financing of the terror-sponsoring and peace-rejecting regimes, the axis of evil, which stretches from Tehran to Damascus" (Olmert 2006c). Similarly, Netanyahu called both Hezbollah and Hamas "Iranian proxy" (Netanyahu 2013c, 2013q). Negative beliefs about the Arabs and the Palestinians were common in Netanyahu's speeches during the year 2013. In fact, 52 percent of his speeches in 2013 (46 percent for domestic audiences and 88 percent for foreign audiences) included negative portrayals of Arab and Muslim groups. Twenty of his speeches (34 percent of those given in 2013) attributed negative images to a general term for Arabs such as "the Arab world," "Israel's enemies," and "terror organizations," which illustrates the broader tendency after 2000 to look at the Arabs as one general hostile group (see also Aronoff 2014, 60–61, about this tendency in Netanyahu's rhetoric).[10]

Another common trend in the period after 2000 was to present all wars as self-defense, even when the balance of power was clearly in favor of Israel or when Israel escalated the conflict by reacting harshly and disproportionally to Arab actions. For example, Olmert said during the 2006 Lebanon War that Israel was "exercising self-defense in the most basic and essential sense" (Olmert 2006c). The Gaza Wars were also presented in leaders' rhetoric as self-defense.[11] Israeli leaders dismissed international criticism of Israel and its army for many Palestinian civilian casualties, using the strategy of adding arguments to bolster a positive self-image of Israel. One such argument was that this is what any nation would do, and Palestinian civilian casualties were presented as a natural consequence of any such warfare (Oren, Rothbart, and Korostelina 2009). As Yair Lapid said about the 2014 Gaza War, "Anyone who criticizes us must ask themselves one question: 'What would you do if someone came to your child's school with a gun in their hand and started shooting?'" (Lapid 2014). But the most common argument was that Palestinian civilian casualties were victims of their own leadership action, not the IDF. An example can be found in Olmert's speech following the 2009 Gaza War—which resulted in more than 1,000 Palestinian deaths, many of them civilians:

> Hamas has placed its military system in crowded residential neighborhoods, operated among a civilian population which has served as human shields and has acted under the aegis of mosques, schools and hospitals, while making the Palestinian population a hostage to its terrorist activities, with the understanding that Israel—as a country with supreme values—would not act. . . . We feel the pain of every Palestinian child and family member who fell victim to the cruel reality created by Hamas which transformed you into victims (Olmert 2009).

The idea that Israelis were "forced" to kill by their rivals (also expressed by Meir), then, continued in the period after 2000. In fact, this idea even appeared in writings of Israeli peace activists to justify attacks on Palestinian civilians. For example, singer and peace activist Achinoam Nini published a letter to the Palestinians in Gaza during the 2009 Gaza War. Like Olmert, she expressed her sorrow for the civilian casualties. Also like Olmert, she differentiated between the Hamas as an "ugly monster" who "rapes the minds of Palestinian children" and the rest of the Palestinians in

Gaza who, per Nini, were passive victims. However, she took these ideas even further in justifying the IDF actions, arguing that Hamas "forces" Palestinians to hate Israel (ignoring Israel's actions, such as the blockade of Gaza or the killing of civilians, as another potential cause for rage against Israel among the Palestinians): "I see you sometimes, out in the streets, demonstrating, yelling 'death to the Jews, death to Israel!!' But I don't believe you! . . . You want nothing of this but I guess you feel you have no choice! I see through your veil of fear my brothers, through your uncertainty and years of painful history" (Nini 2009). This is a good example of a "positive" attitude toward the Palestinians that still reinforced the mostly positive image of Israel and the superior Israeli as understanding what the Palestinians want better than they themselves do. This tendency continued later in Nini's letter:

> I know YOU know the truth!! And I know you cannot say it for fear of life so I will say it for you!! I fear nothing!! I am privileged to live in a democracy where women are not objects but presidents, where a singer can say and do as she pleases! I know you do not have this privilege (yet . . . but you will, inshallah, you will . . .). (Nini, 2009)

Nini then justified Israel's attacks in Gaza because the Palestinians "benefit" from these attacks that would free them from Hamas rule: "I can only wish for you that Israel will do the job we all know needs to be done, and finally RID YOU of this cancer, this virus, this monster called fantacism [*sic*], today, called Hamas" (Nini 2009).

There was, then, agreement among most Israeli leaders (as well as peace activists) that the IDF actions during these wars (including killing of civilians) were just, and a denial of claims criticizing the IDF actions. In this context, Israeli leaders from the period after Oslo, like leaders from earlier periods, maintained that all actions of the Israeli army were moral. For example, Olmert argued following the 2009 Gaza War, that while Hamas did not care even about their own people, "the State of Israel demonstrated great sensitivity in exercising its force in order to avoid, as much as possible, harming the civilian population not involved in terror," and that "there are not many countries which would act thusly" (Olmert 2009). Netanyahu echoed this assertion in 2010: "There is no army more moral than the IDF and we proved this time and again when faced with the most despicable enemies—those dedicated to death and barbarism, while we sanctify life and enlightenment" (Netanyahu 2010b).

Israeli leaders in the period after 2000 also expressed the belief that the Israeli society, not just its army, was morally superior than its neighboring states. Barak said in a 2002 interview that the Palestinians "don't suffer from the problem of telling lies that exists in Judeo-Christian culture. Truth is seen [to them] as an irrelevant category" (Morris 2002). In 67 percent of his 2013 speeches, Netanyahu presented a positive perception of the State of Israel as an advanced, moral, and peace-seeking country that stood as a sharp contrast to Arab or Muslim states, as seen in Table 2.1. The image of a villa in the jungle also appeared several times in his speeches. For example, in a 2011 speech in Jerusalem, he described Israel as "an island of progress in a region where there is no progress"[12] (Netanyahu 2011a).

However, the most common distinction between Israel and the Muslim Palestinians in Netanyahu's 2013 speeches was between Israel's desire for peace and a Muslim Palestinian lack thereof. Forty-five percent of Netanyahu's speeches during the year 2013 included this assertion (see Table 2.1). A typical example is this quotation: "Look at the story of the Israeli mountain climber—he did not think twice when he reached out his hand to his Turkish colleague and saved him from certain death just days ago. Unfortunately, the strong and I must say, natural desire of our people to extend our hand in peace is not always answered by governments in our region" (Netanyahu 2012c).[13] In 6 percent of his 2013 speeches, he delegitimized Israel's enemies—mainly Iran—by connecting them to Nazi Germany,[14] and spoke similarly of the Palestinians. Already in a 2012 speech, he said that "there is a legacy of hate and destruction among the Palestinians starting with the Mufti Haj Amin el-Husseini" who, according to Netanyahu, "was one of the leading architects of the Final Solution" (Netanyahu 2012a).[15] Recall that this contention also appeared in Ben-Gurion's rhetoric. In a controversial 2015 speech, Netanyahu went even further and said that it was the Palestinian mufti who gave Hitler the idea of exterminating the European Jews: "Hitler didn't want to exterminate the Jews at the time, he wanted to expel the Jew[s]. And Haj Amin el-Husseini went to Hitler and said, 'If you expel them, they'll all come here (to Palestine).' '[S]o what should I do with them?' [Hitler] asked, [el-Husseini] said: 'Burn them'" (Botelho 2015).

When the speech was criticized by politicians and scholars as baseless,[16] Netanyahu answered that "my intention was not to absolve Hitler of his responsibility. But rather to show that the forefathers of the Palestinian nation, without a country and without the so-called occupation, without land and without settlements, even then aspired to systematic incitement to exterminate the Jews" (Rudoren 2015). This idea that Palestinian actions against Israel had nothing to do with Israel's actions (e.g., Israel's settlements policy) was common in Netanyahu's rhetoric (Aronoff 2014, 50). Furthermore, this idea also appeared in the rhetoric of some of Netanyahu's main political competitors. For example, Lapid posted on his Facebook page in 2015 that when a Palestinian woman tries to stab an Israeli soldier she does not do it because of the Israeli occupation, "but because she wants to kill Jews because they are Jews" (Lapid 2015).

In sum, while the rhetoric of many Israeli leaders in the period after 2000 stands in contrast to the rhetoric of dovish leaders such as Rabin and Peres during the Oslo years, it echoes the beliefs and narratives that dominated Israeli leaders' rhetoric for years about the Arabs as motivated by mainly one aim—to destroy Israel. This perceived aim of the Arabs was explained as part of the Arabs' inherited aggression and had nothing to do with Israel's actions in the conflict. Israel, according to this view, was a purely peaceful nation protected by the most moral army in the world.

School Curricula

The 1950s Through the Late 1970s

Teaching negative beliefs about the Arabs was never an explicit articulated goal of the intended curriculum (unlike beliefs about Israel as a Jewish state). At times, the intended curriculum even called for acceptance of the "other" and coexistence between Arabs and Jews (see elaboration on this in Chapter 7). Yet most studies of the content of Israeli textbooks has shown that negative stereotypes and beliefs about the Arabs were common in Jewish school textbooks in the 1950s through the late 1970s. As with leaders' rhetoric, these beliefs were accompanied by positive self-images of the Jews as the opposite of the Arabs. Podeh (2002, 144) found that, in history textbooks from the 1950s until 1975, "a clear dichotomy was created between the western, civilized, peace-loving image of the Jews and the oriental, treacherous, belligerent, and backward image of the Arab" (see also Firer 1985). Historical events that contradicted this dichotomy were mostly ignored or marginalized. For example, several textbooks from this period completely ignored the killing of Palestinian civilians by Jewish fighters in the village of Dir Yassin in 1948. Other textbooks mentioned this event, but used the strategy of bolstering by stating that the Arabs used it as "an excuse for their frenzied and bloody agitation against Jews" (Podeh 2002, 105–106).

Similar conclusions were found in Bar-Gal's (1993, 1994) analysis of Arabs' representations in geography books from the 1950s until the 1980s. He found that the textbooks often negatively stereotyped Arabs as uncultured, unproductive, and aspiring to war. Arab citizens of Israel were described more positively—as a "minority" in Israel that became modern and developed. But as Bar-Gal notes, these relatively positive impressions "convey to students mostly a positive image of Israel than a positive image of Arabs" (Bar-Gal 1994, 230). More specifically, the description was that the State of Israel caused deep social changes in Arab society, rescuing the Arabs who lived in Israel from their "mediaeval world." Geography textbooks from the 1970s and 1980s also described the vast improvements that

Israeli authority had brought to inhabitants of the territories. Shnell (2013, 107) notes that geography textbooks from the 1950s depicted Jewish superiority in subduing nature as they built the Jewish homeland, in contrast to the Arabs' inability to transform the land and overcome its limitations. Similar messages were found in readers from this period (David 2012).

The 1980s and 1990s

By late 1970s, delegitimizing descriptions of Arabs had almost disappeared from school textbooks (Bar-Tal 1998; Firer 1985),[17] a trend that continued through the 1980s and strengthened in the late 1990s. These textbooks even included some more critical views of Israel's actions in the conflict, although the distinction between positive (Israelis) and negative (Arabs) remained. A comprehensive study of 360 Israeli textbooks across all grades and six majors used during the late stages of the Oslo process (1999–2000), conducted by the Institute for Monitoring Peace and Cultural Tolerance in School Education (IMPACT-SE), found many positive presentations of Islam and Arab culture, as well as references to Arabs' contribution to human civilization. Readers from this period incorporated several positive stories about Arabs (including some by Arab authors). Thus, "the student was exposed to seeing the Arabs as ordinary human beings, just like himself" (IMPACT-SE 2000). Most textbooks of this time presented Arab hostility toward the Jews as a result of the ongoing conflict—their claim for the land and desire to remain a majority—although a few books did consider it "an inherent hatred that is independent of political, military or economic circumstance." The study also found negative portrayals of Arabs in blaming them for the failure of contacts between Arabs and Jews, such as the Feisal-Weizmann Agreement of 1919, as well as for the outbreak of all Israeli-Arab wars. Similarly, only a few textbooks acknowledged the suffering of the Palestinians in the conflict such as the Palestinian refugees from the 1948 and 1967 Wars.

New history textbooks from the late 1990s merit special attention, and have been studied extensively by Podeh (2002); Firer, 'Adwān, and Pingel (2004); and Peled-Elhanan (2012). Podeh concluded that overall, history textbooks from the late 1990s presented a less biased image of the Arabs. In contrast to history textbooks from earlier years, Arabs were presented more humanely and "not only as mere spectators or as aggressors" (Podeh 2002, 149–150). Instead, the new textbooks acknowledged the suffering of the Palestinian refugees, including Bar-Navi and Naveh's (1999) history textbook that contains a photo of deprived Jewish immigrants opposite one of Palestinian refugees. This arrangement "may suggest a parallel between the fate of the Jewish and Palestinian refugees" (Bar-Navi and Naveh 1999, 110). Further, Podeh (2002) found that history textbooks from the late 1990s expressed a more critical view of the State of Israel and its history than in previous years. For example, the later textbooks noted a Jewish patronizing attitude toward the Arabs. They also pointed to the partial responsibility of Jewish forces for the creation of the Palestinian refugee problem during the 1948 War (while earlier textbooks considered the Palestinians alone to be responsible for their fate). One textbook mentioned some attacks on Palestinian civilians carried out by Jewish forces (e.g., the 1948 attacks in Dir Yassin, the 1953 IDF attack on the Jordanian village of Kibiya, and the 1956 attack at the village of Kafr Qassem) that were omitted from previous books (see a full review in Podeh 2002, 108–109).

However, Peled-Elhanan (2012) and Firer, 'Adwān, and Pingel (2004) analyzed the same textbooks and drew different conclusions. Peled-Elhanan's analysis of the two pictures of refugees (in Bar-Navi's and Naveh's 1999 book) noted that the Israeli photo was of a young family, whose eyes meet the viewer's eyes, while a smaller photograph showed a Palestinian refugee camp with an empty flooded street and distant unrecognizable figures. Thus, the students saw "one group of refugees as 'demanding' (and deserving) human beings . . . and the other as an impersonalized epidemic-like, human-less 'problem'" (Peled-Elhanan 2012, 101). So, while Podeh (2002) felt the photo arrangement presented a "parallel between the fate of the Jewish and Palestinian refugees," Peled-Elhanan (2012) interpreted it as a positive image of one group and a negative image of the other. Further, while the text acknowledged the difficult conditions for Palestinians in the refugee camps, this situation was described as a "self-directed phenomenon" that had nothing to do with Israel's actions in the war.

Both Peled-Elhanan (2012) and Firer, 'Adwān, and Pingel (2004) showed that despite the discussion of negative actions by the Jews, the new history textbooks from the late 1990s still diminished the importance of and even justified these events. Again, the strategy of bolstering was common in this context; one common justification was that these negative actions were explained by the situation of war. For instance, Bar-Navi (1998, 184), cited Nathan Yellin-Mor, commander of the Dir Yassin killers, who said: "I know that in the heat of battle things like that happen, and I know that people do not preplan it in advance. They kill because their friends have been killed and they want an instant revenge. I know that many nations and armies do such things." Firer, 'Adwān, and Pingel (2004, 41) added that while Arab violence was described using inherent permanent traits ("bloodshed riots"), Jewish violence against Palestinians (including the statement that thirty-three Palestinian settlements were intentionally evacuated by Jewish forces) was explained by external forces. Bar-Navi's book, for example, argues that "the reasons for the [Palestinian] flight can be summarized in one word: the war" (quoted in Firer, 'Adwān, and Pingel 2004, 50).[18]

Yet Peled-Elhanan (2009) and Firer, 'Adwān, and Pingel (2004) also found some of these textbooks to be critical of Israel's actions. For example, two pages in Bar-Navi's book (1998, 234–235) discussed relationships between Israel and Africa. The pages included three components: the main text, a photograph, and a green text box "window," each referencing a different period. The photograph displayed an Israeli woman showing a branch of an orange tree to two African men, with the caption that in the 1950s African students came to Israel to specialize in domains in which Israel had an exclusive knowledge. The main text referred to the 1970s, and noted that most African states broke off their relationships with Israel after the 1973 War due to Arab pressure. The green text box "window" criticized Israel's 1980 "Jerusalem Law" as "not only . . . unnecessary . . . but it was perceived as an open provocation against the Arabs and the whole world." Peled-Elhanan (2009) suggested that the combination of these three elements could influence not only how students referred to the Jerusalem Law but also how they interpreted the broader events of the 1970s: "While reading the editorial text, one may reason that perhaps it was not Nasser's conniving and the prices of oil that made the African countries break off their friendship with Israel but some (unmentioned) Israeli indiscretion that made Israel hateful in the eyes of the world" (p. 109). At the end of this double-page spread, the main text mentioned the Oslo Accords and asked: "Will the window of opportunities remain open, or will it be closed again? The answer is first and foremost in the hands of Israel itself" (Bar-Navi 1998, 289). Thus, contrary to speeches of many Israeli leaders, Bar-Navi's textbook maintained that Israel's actions influenced Arab and non-Arab countries' attitudes toward Israel.

Further, the new history textbooks blamed extremists in both nations for difficulties during the Oslo process, presenting a far more complex picture than the simple dichotomy of peace-loving Israelis and aggressive Palestinians used by previous textbooks. Naveh (1999) included a quotation by Joshua Sobol (1993) that "there were Palestinians who dreamt that the State of Israel would be liquidated. . . . Corresponding to them were Jews who dreamt that it would be possible to transfer the Palestinians, or at least to continue to rule them" (Firer, 'Adwān, and Pingel 2004, 85–86). They point out an assignment in Naveh's (1999) textbook asking students to write about the 1967 War from the point of view of an Egyptian soldier and a female refugee in Gaza. However, Firer, 'Adwān, and Pingel (2004) noted that there was no information in the textbook to help the students with this task, and stated that "such [an] assignment cannot be open to free discussion and inquiry in ordinary Israeli classrooms at present, not during the peace process and even more so, not after the recurrence of aggressive conflict since September 2000" (Firer, 'Adwān, and Pingel 2004, 90–91). It is not surprising, then, that some of these new history textbooks have since been banned or revised (see elaboration of this in Chapter 2). These decisions reflect a reversal of the 1990s trends toward more complex and empathetic portrayals of the Israeli-Arab relationship—a reversal that began following the outbreak of violence in the fall of 2000.

The Period After 2000

Peled-Elhanan (2012, 98) went so far as to argue that the generation of textbooks in the period after 2000 "manifests the same ideological stance and uses the same rhetorical devices that characterized the first generation of Israeli school books [from the 1950s and 1960s]." She asserted that textbooks from this period justified Israel's negative acts more than those from the late 1990s and used new ways to marginalize and excuse these acts. In discussing aggressive Israeli actions, some textbooks during the period after 2000 focused on the Palestinian portrayal of and response to these actions, but not on the actions themselves (which could be seen as a type of denial). One textbook said that Israeli violent acts against Palestinians "*became a myth in the Palestinian narrative* . . . and created a horrifying negative image of the Jewish conqueror *in the eyes of* Israel's Arabs" (Peled-Elhanan 2010, 393, emphasis in original). Other textbooks added new bolstering arguments ("The loud-speaker encouraging the inhabitants of Dir Yassin to leave the village did not work"). Peled-Elhanan (2010, 391) also noted a more dramatic revision in the way that events were portrayed in textbooks from 1999 to 2009. In Naveh (1999) the Palestinian village of Dir Yassin was described as "a friendly village whose inhabitants made a non-aggression agreement with the Hagana [the Jewish militia] and kept it meticulously," while Naveh, Vered, and Shahar (2009) described Dir Yassin as "one of the bases of the Arab forces that kept attacking the road to Jerusalem." This addition of negative actions by the victims served to justify and legitimize Israeli acts.

Given the relatively small number of textbooks that were analyzed in Peled-Elhanan's (2010) study, it is important to couple her study with a more comprehensive analysis of books from the period after 2000. One such comprehensive study of how Palestinians and Arabs were presented in Israeli textbooks was conducted by a joint Palestinian-Israeli research team. Their analysis of all books approved by the Israeli Ministry of Education for the year 2009 found that dehumanizing and demonizing characterizations of Arabs (as seen in textbooks from the 1950s and 1960s) were rare (Adwan, Bar-Tal, and Wexler 2016). However, the textbooks did often describe the Arabs negatively and blame them solely for the eruption and continuation of the conflict.[19] The more comprehensive study, then, failed to support Peled-Elhanan's (2012, 98) far-reaching conclusion that "the representation of Palestinians in Israeli history school books has made a full circle, from prejudiced biased and antagonistic representation in the 1950s to prejudiced biased and antagonistic representation in the 2000s." It showed that the negative stereotyping and delegitimization seen in textbooks from the 1950s and 1960s was rare in textbooks after 2000, and that those later books even included some positive references to Arabs' contributions to human civilization. Still, most of the textbooks presented Palestinians and Arabs as aiming to destroy Israel and blamed only the Arabs for the eruption of the conflict and lack of peace, just as Israeli leaders after 2000 have done.

The Public

Moral and Cultural Superiority of the Jews over the Arabs

As noted, negative stereotypes of Arabs were common in school textbooks in the 1950s and 1960s and appeared even in the rhetoric of leaders. The above review also indicated a significant reduction in negative stereotypes of Arabs in later years, although occasionally these stereotypes still appeared. Questions measuring the existence of such negative stereotypes of Arabs were asked mainly in polls conducted among children and youth (see a review in Bar-Tal and Teichman 2005), and were rare in polls of the Israeli adult population. Note that especially among adult respondents, the findings might not represent the actual prevalence of these beliefs, as adults tend to hide stereotypic thinking so as not to be considered racist. Despite these limitations, we can find some data about this issue.

In a 1968 Guttman poll, 60 percent of the respondents agreed with the statement that "the Arabs can progress a lot, but they will never attain the Jews' level of development." In June 1980, this percentage dropped to 37 percent and then rose somewhat to 44 percent in March 1987. Twenty years later in a 2007 Democracy Index poll, 55 percent of the respondents agreed with the statement: "Arabs cannot attain the Jews' level of cultural development." We can see, then, a clear decrease during the 1980s in the belief regarding the Arabs as backward and imminently inferior to the Jews, although a considerable part of the respondents still held this belief in 2007. Since the 1990s, several questions were asked about negative stereotypes of the Palestinians as violent, unintelligent, and untruthful. Peace Index polls during the Oslo process revealed that most of the respondents did not hold negative views of the Palestinians but by the end of 2000, with the eruption of violence between the two sides, a more negative image of the Palestinians as violent and dishonest was emerging (see Table 4.1).

Other surveys also indicated that following the second intifada, beliefs about the Palestinians and the Arabs as violent and dishonest became more common among the Israeli public. In November 2000, 78 percent of respondents in a Peace Index poll agreed with the statement that Palestinians had lit-

Table 4.1   The Image of Palestinians in Israeli Eyes, 1997–2000 (percentage)

	1997	1999	2000
Violent	39	37	68
Dishonest	42	35	51
Unintelligent	37	30	n/a

Source: Peace Index.

tle regard for human life and therefore persisted in using violence despite the high number of their own casualties. In a 2007 Democracy Index, 75 percent of the Jewish respondents agreed with the statement that "Arabs are inclined to violent behavior" (but only 43 percent agreed with the statement that "Arabs are not intelligent"). Finally, in a February 2016 Peace Index poll, 77 percent strongly or moderately agreed with the statement of Police Commissioner Roni Alsheikh that the Palestinian families' grief over their fatalities was not comparable to the grief of the Israeli families who lost their loved ones because "the Palestinians sanctify death while we sanctify life."[20] Following the violent events of the period after 2000, then, Israelis seemed to share the beliefs that appeared in the rhetoric of some leaders that depicted the Palestinians and Arabs as violent and with little regard for human life.

A further illustration of this trend can be found in 2002 interviews with 100 Israeli Jews (Bar-Tal, Raviv, and Abromovich forthcoming). These interviews were conducted during the violent period of the second intifada, which likely influenced the participants' attitudes toward Palestinians. Recall also that the participants were fifty-five years old or older at the time of the interviews, and hence attended school during a time when delegitimization of Arabs was common in school textbooks. The interviews found delegitimization of Arabs and Palestinians to be common among the participants. The main delegitimization labels associated with Palestinians were "animals," "barbarians," "inhuman," "murderers," and "criminals." For example, Participant 212 in the study by Bar-Tal, Raviv, and Abromovich (forthcoming) said "They are animals. That is all . . . I know where it comes from. . . . There are genes . . . they are savages." Participant 108 compared Palestinians to snakes and said that "they are not human beings." Participant 615 stated that the Arabs are "barbarous" and that "nothing can be done. That is the way they are." A few participants compared the Palestinians to Nazis, a comparison that, as I showed above, was common in their formative textbooks and in speeches. Participant 112 said that the Arabs were "worse than the Nazis." Participant 111, like Netanyahu, mentioned the mufti as an evidence to the Nazi nature of the Palestinians.[21] Another negative stereotype common in textbooks from the 1950s and 1960s, and which found expression in the 2002 interviews, was that Arabs were primitives and fools. Furthermore, many participants thought that this could not be changed—that the Palestinians would never be able to progress. For example, Participant 101 described the Palestinians as "primitive" and "illiterate." He then continued with the following observation: "With illiterate people, you cannot change them all at once, you need two generations, three generations, but they [the Palestinians] do not, they are not moving forward, they do not advance."

In contrast to descriptions of the Arabs, several participants in the study by Bar-Tal, Raviv, and Abromovich (forthcoming) emphasized how smart and enlightened the Jews were; for example, according to Participant 701, "like the Americans perhaps even more." Many participants described the smart and civilized Jews while comparing them to the backward fanatic Arabs. Participant 112 provided the following comparison: "Jews are successful . . . and there are poor Arabs, they make children and they do not care about them, like cats. But the Jews [are] more calculated, more careful and hard-working and smart." Several participants suggested, in line with some textbooks from the 1950s and 1960s, that the Jews enlightened the backward local Arabs. For example, Participant 101 said, "After the Six Day War, you know what we did for them. . . . After all, they learned everything from us . . . and we were smarter and more developed, of course, they were primitive people . . . they progressed only because of us, [only because of us they] opened their eyes."

But the most common negative stereotype of Arabs among the participants in the study by Bar-Tal, Raviv, and Abromovich (forthcoming) was that the Arabs were dishonest and liars that could not be trusted. Participant 215 argued, like Barak, that "their ideology is not telling the truth and to lie. It's part of their culture." Other participants attributed it not to Arab culture but to their very nature. For example, Participant 307 thought that "they are chronic liars, lying is natural to them as eating yogurt, they lie even when it is unnecessary, even when it does not help them, even when it is harmful to them." And Participant 108 said "they are known as crooks, they are liars, it's in their blood." Participant 101 provided the following example of "typical" Arab behavior: "They say that an Arab, if you come to his house, he would set a table for you and host you. As you leave his house, he'll put a knife in your back. This is exactly like that, just like that." This example appeared in several other interviews; for example, "with one hand they would say hello to you, with the other hand [they would] stab you" (Participant 111) and "You cannot believe them. . . . There is a saying, do not believe an Arab even after he is 40 years in the tomb" (Participant 402). Participant 213 said that "the Arab mentality is really different, not like ours. We are people with a sense of justice, with decency."

Another common difference between Jews and Arabs, according to the study participants, was that Arabs were vicious people who wanted to kill Jews while the Jews just wanted to defend themselves and live peacefully. Participant 504 said, "We do not kill for no reason. But the Arabs do not have any problem to kill or to burn or to do these things." Participant 112 argued, "[We] never kill. It happens during a war it happens, but [we] do not take a child and kill him intentionally. . . . We are not murderers. we are not such a people." In this regard, several participants argued that human life was worthless to Arabs while Jews cared deeply. Participant 502 summarized this argument: "We care more about life; we have something to lose. And there— human life [is] not considered. You can recruit a million [Arabs] easily and you can sacrifice these million [people]. Human lives do not count."

It must be noted that some participants in the study by Bar-Tal, Raviv, and Abromovich (forthcoming) did provide positive images of the Arabs that stood in sharp contrast to the opinions presented above. A few participants said that the Arabs were smart. Two said that they were honest. One of them, Participant 701, said that the Arabs "are very honest to do business with . . . they stand by their words. . . . If you treat them well they treat you well." Some participants even went so far as to say that Arabs were better than the Jews. For example, Participant 213 said "that they do not give up their land, I respect them for that, not what they do, but that the land is important for them, it makes me appreciate them about it. They know that the land is important, and unfortunately we do not always know that." However, these opinions were not common. More common, though, was criticism of Israeli Jews and society as racist. For example, Participant 703 thought that Israel "is a racist country. We are not tolerant people . . . [we are] aggressive people."

A critical view of the morality of the Israeli society also appeared in some public polls. Table 4.2 shows the percentage of respondents who thought that the Israeli society is a moral one. It shows that from 1975 to 1990, less than 40 percent of the respondents thought that Israel was a moral society, but that number increased significantly by 2016—another indication for strengthening of the villa in the jungle theme at that time. For the purposes of this book, it is important to note why respondents felt their society was less than moral. Would they point to the Israeli-Arab conflict and Israeli

Table 4.2 Perception of Israel as a Moral Society, 1975–2016 (percentage)

	1975	1983	1987	1988	1990	2016
Israeli society is a moral society	36	23	37	39	35	57

Sources: Guttman and Oren's 2016 Survey.

control over the territories as main cause for what they saw as a lack of morality in the Israeli society? In a 1979 Guttman survey, most respondents blamed the Israeli education system (74 percent), popular culture (76 percent), and political corruption (69 percent) for the perceived decline in the moral character of the State of Israel. Fifty-two percent faulted the security situation, and yet fewer respondents (38 percent) cited the situation in the territories. Similarly, in a 1987 survey, only 32 percent thought that "continued Israeli occupation of the West Bank will erode Israel's democratic humanitarian character" (Zemach 1987). In a January 2016 Peace Index, only 29 percent agreed with the statement that the ongoing control of the territories prevented Israel from being a real democracy. Israeli Jews thus were critical of the morality of Israeli society, but did not link it to the Israeli-Arab conflict and Israeli control of the territories (as did some dovish leaders, like Rabin). As for the effect of the occupation on IDF ethics, in 1986 most respondents in the NSPOP survey did *not* think that the IDF's actions in the territories were having a deleterious effect on morality of the IDF. However, that percentage sharply increased during the 1990s (from 25 percent in 1986 to 55 percent in 1992, and then a decline in 1995 to 45 percent[22]). It seems, then, that following the first intifada, more and more respondents believed actions in the territories were eroding the IDF's morality. However, this tendency changed in later years: 71 percent of respondents in a November 2017 Peace Index poll disagreed with the statement that "the IDF's continuing responsibility for many years to control the territories, amid ongoing friction with the Palestinian population, is damaging its moral values."

Overall, Israeli respondents (like their leaders) expressed high confidence in the ethics of IDF actions, especially in the period after 2000. For example, most respondents (64 percent) in a March 2009 Peace Index poll discounted the testimony of soldiers from the 2009 Gaza War in which IDF forces harmed, on orders, Palestinian civilians and structures. Likewise, and in line with leaders' rhetoric, 79 percent of respondents in a September 2009 Peace Index poll opposed the UN Goldstone Report's finding that, during that war, the IDF committed war crimes. An August 2014 Peace Index poll (following the 2014 Gaza War) indicated that only 6 percent of the respondents thought that the IDF used too much firepower during the operation, 48 percent regarded the use of firepower as appropriate, and 45 percent thought the IDF made too little use of it. In a February 2016 Peace Index poll, 90 percent of the respondents thought that the IDF was operating in a moral fashion in counteracting terror.[23]

Arabs' and Israel's Intentions—No Partner for Peace

As discussed earlier, a common argument in leaders' rhetoric and textbooks was that the Arabs wanted to destroy Israel while the Jews only wanted peace. According to Guttman polls, prior to Anwar Sadat's visit in 1977 around 80 percent of respondents believed the ultimate goal of the Arabs was to eradicate the State of Israel. This proportion dropped to 48 percent following the historic visit, but then rose again and remained around 70 percent until 1992 (see Figure 4.1). Since 1987, an NSPOP poll has asked respondents about several possible aims of the Arabs, including to recover some or all of the territories conquered by Israel in 1967, to conquer all of Israel, or to conquer all of Israel and destroy most of the Jews living there. As can be seen in Figure 4.1, over time most of the respondents thought that the Arabs' goal was not limited to control of the territories but to conquer all of Israel. In fact, the most common answer (sometimes over 50 percent) was that the Arabs wanted to conquer all of Israel and destroy the Jewish population. Varying through the years, this belief decreased in 1992 (before Oslo) and through 2000 before increasing again. By 2015, the percentage of respondents who thought the ultimate intention of the Arabs is to destroy Israel had returned to the pre-Oslo levels. A similar trend appeared regarding the Arabs' interest in peace (see Figure 4.2). During the 1970s, a significant majority of the respondents thought that the Arabs did not want peace, declining somewhat in 1977 and through the late 1980s. By that time, fewer questions in public polls referred to the "Arabs" and instead addressed specific Arab and Muslim groups—especially the Palestinians. This trend is discussed further in the next section.

Perceptions of the Arabs' intentions toward peace were linked to the idea that Arab aggression was unrelated to Israel's actions, and that the Palestinians were solely responsible for the continued conflict and lack of

Figure 4.1   Perceptions About Arabs' Ultimate Intentions, 1973–2015

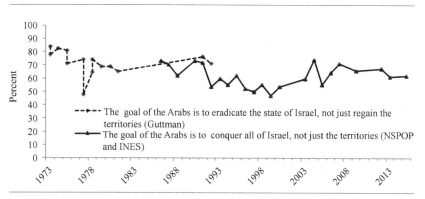

Sources: Guttman, NSPOP, and INES.

Figure 4.2   Perceptions About Arabs' Interest in Peace, 1967–1987 (percentage who say Arabs are not interested in peace with Israel)

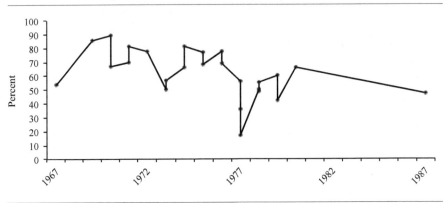

Source: Guttman.

peace. As shown in previous sections, for many years leaders and school textbooks indicated exactly that. Some questions in public polls specifically addressed this belief by asking respondents whether Arab (lack of) interest in peace was related to Israel's actions. As can be seen in Table 4.3, from 1975 to 2016 most respondents thought that an Israeli agreement to give up the territories would *not* affect Arab openness to peace.[24] Likewise, most surveys indicated that Israeli Jews indeed blamed the Palestinians for the absence of peace. A Peace Index survey in July 2000 showed that 67 percent of respondents believed the Palestinians were entirely or mainly responsible for the failure of the Camp David summit. In a 2002 poll, 84 percent of respondents thought the Palestinians were solely or mainly responsible for the deterioration in the relations between the two sides (Arian 2002). In a Peace Index poll in December 2012, 67 percent of the respondents agreed that "the peace process with the Palestinians is at a standstill for reasons that have nothing to do with Israel." Polls conducted in the Index of Arab-Jewish Relations in Israel from 2003 to 2012 indicated that an overwhelming majority of Jewish respondents held the Arabs responsible for the eruption and continuation of conflict (Smooha 2013). Finally, in a Peace Index poll in November 2013, 66 percent thought that the Israeli government wanted to reach a permanent peace settlement with the Palestinians while only 22 percent thought that the Palestinian Authority wanted such an agreement. It seems, then, that since 2000 the Israeli Jewish public has perceived, in line with leaders' speeches and textbooks, a distinction between Israel as the peace-loving country and Palestinians as opposing peace.

Table 4.3 Perceptions About Israel's Agreement to Give Up the Territories on Arabs' Willingness for Peace, 1975–2016 (percentage)

	1975	1977	1978	1979	1985	1988	2016
Israel's agreement to give up the territories would not increase Arabs' willingness for peace	91	69	77	79	87	78	85

Sources: Guttman and Oren's 2016 Survey.

Perceptions About Uniformity of the Arab World

Polls that I have discussed up to this point have referred to two national groups (the "Arabs" and the "Jews") without differentiating between subgroups of each society. However, questions in public polls did ask about the interest in peace among specific Arab countries and groups. A series of questions asked by the Guttman Institute from 1967 to 1993 addressed this issue. They indicated that even before Sadat's visit, around 50 percent of respondents felt that the Egyptians did not want peace, while between 80 to 90 percent felt similarly about the Palestinians and Syrians. In March 2007, a Peace Index poll asked respondents how hostile five different Arab countries were toward Israel. The findings indicate that only around 20 percent thought Egypt and Morocco were hostile toward Israel while an overwhelming majority saw Lebanon and Syria as hostile (74 percent and 80 percent, respectively).

Major events in the conflict had mainly short-term effects on perceptions of specific Arab states' interest in peace. The percentage of respondents who thought that Egypt did not want peace declined sharply (but briefly) after the 1973 War, especially after the 1974 Separation of Forces Agreements.[25] Sadat's 1977 visit to Jerusalem and the signing of the 1979 Israeli-Egyptian peace agreement seem to have triggered another extreme, yet brief, decline in the belief that the Egyptians had no interest in peace. Interestingly, these decreases were accompanied by mild declines in the same rate for the Syrians and the Palestinians, even though they were not involved in (and opposed) the Israeli-Egyptian peace process.

Since the 1990s, the focus has shifted mostly to the Palestinians. Overall, beliefs about Palestinians' attitudes toward Israel were negative, as summarized in Figure 4.3. From 1994 to 2010, a majority of respondents in the Peace Index survey felt that most Palestinians did not accept Israel's existence and would destroy it if they could.[26] At the same time, though, 64 percent in a 1999 NSPOP poll thought that Palestinians actually wanted peace. This percentage declined sharply after the second intifada (to around

40 percent). After 2006, with the separation between Hamas-controlled Gaza and the Fatah-controlled Palestinian Authority in the West Bank, public polls asked about the intentions of these two factions within the Palestinian leadership. The findings indicate that Israelis distinguished between Hamas and Fatah. Most respondents thought that Hamas's aim was to conquer all of Israel (most also thought that Hamas aimed to kill all Israeli Jews) while less than 50 percent felt that was Fatah's intention. Israeli Jews, then, felt less negatively about Fatah than Hamas. Ben Meir and Shaked (2007) stated that while many Israelis believed that the Palestinians—like the Israelis—wanted an end to the conflict, they also had little faith in the Palestinian leadership and perceived it as unwilling to compromise. Ben Meir and Shaked (2007) based this conclusion on NSPOP polls. However, data from other Israeli surveys did not support this claim. First, other surveys showed less positive beliefs toward the Palestinian public: far more Israelis believed the Palestinians intended to destroy Israel than those who perceived the Palestinians as seeking peace. Second, respondents perceived the intentions of most Palestinians as closer to those of Hamas than of Fatah (see Figure 4.3). According to these polls, then, Israelis saw Fatah's leadership as more moderate than Hamas, but they did not necessarily perceive Fatah's attitude as representative of most Palestinians. This view matches beliefs expressed in Netanyahu's speeches.

Figure 4.3   Perceptions About Palestinians' Ultimate Intentions and Desire, 1994–2016

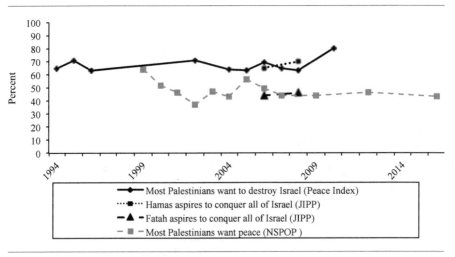

Sources: Peace Index, JIPP, and NSPOP.

Israel's Military Might

Like its leaders, the Israeli public expressed high confidence in the IDF's combat capability and Israel's military power, especially as compared to the Arabs. For example, in a 1973 Guttman survey (conducted at the beginning of the 1973 War) around 80 percent of respondents thought the Arabs were not good fighters. By the end of the war, this percentage had dropped to around 70 percent and stayed there until 1975, two years after the war (Stone 1982). Asked again twelve years later (during the first intifada in 1987–1988), little had changed in assessment of Arab fighting ability (67 percent in 1987 and 64 percent in 1988 thought that the Arabs were poor fighters). Israeli Jews, then, believed that the Arabs were poor combatants, although this belief weakened somewhat after Egyptian and Syrian achievements in battle at the beginning of the 1973 War.

By contrast, surveys showed positive impressions of Israel's power and the IDF. As seen in Table 4.4, a remarkable and consistent majority thought that the IDF was generally capable of coping with the security threats facing Israel, albeit with some decrease in 2007 and 2009. This finding is corroborated by a NSPOP question on Israel's ability to cope with specific challenges. These answers indicate a high degree of confidence in Israel's capability to cope with military challenges. Confidence was high regarding Israel's ability to cope successfully with war against Syria, terror attacks, and surface-to-surface missile attacks, but less so around the idea of war against all Arab states and successfully coping with a nuclear attack against Israel. Confidence regarding the latter two threats also decreased over time. For example, the percentage of Israeli Jews who believed that Israel had the ability to wage war successfully against all the Arab states dropped from 78 percent in 1985 to 58 percent in 1993 and to 48 percent in 2000. However, confidence in Israeli military superiority rose again in later years: 67 percent and 69 percent of the respondents thought that Israel had the ability to wage war successfully against all the Arab states in 2004 and 2013, respectively.[27]

Conclusion

A negative perception of the enemy (including delegitimization, attributing to the opponent extremely negative social categories that exclude it from the sphere of human groups) and a positive perception of one's own society as opposite images is a common situation in intractable conflict and by no means unique to the Israeli-Arab conflict. However, in this chapter I reviewed the specific details of these perceptions in the Israeli society. This review indicated that until the late 1970s leaders' rhetoric and textbooks

Table 4.4   Confidence in the IDF's Combat Capabilities, 1975–2013

	1975	1980	1984	1985	1988	1990	1991	2007	2009	2013
Percentage who expressed high confidence	92	93	92	92	88	92	87	83	80	89

Sources: Guttman (1975–1991), NSPOP (2007–2009), and Peace Index (2013).

presented Israelis as advanced, honest, brave, and peace seeking while Arabs were depicted as primitive, untrustworthy, cowardly, and cruel. At times, there even was delegitimization of Arabs and their leaders in these texts, especially through associations made between the Arabs and Nazis. Unfortunately, questions in public polls addressing negative stereotypes and delegitimization of Arabs were not common before the mid-1980s. Hence, there was not enough data about the occurrence of these beliefs among the public during the 1950s to 1980s period. However, since the late 1970s, stereotypical negative presentations decreased, and delegitimization of Arabs almost disappeared from textbooks (yet there are indications that latent and more sophisticated negative presentations of the Arabs existed in even the most progressive school textbooks from the 1990s). Public polls from the 1990s indicated that less than 60 percent held negative stereotypes of the Arabs and Palestinians as backward and imminently inferior to the Jews. Delegitimization of Palestinians through associations made between them and Nazis appeared in Netanyahu's rhetoric during the period after 2000. Interviews with 100 fifty-five- to seventy-five-year-old Israeli Jews (who attended school during a time when delegitimization of Arabs was common in school textbooks) conducted in 2002 revealed delegitimization of Arabs among this group, but there was not enough data about delegitimization of Arabs among the general Israeli public during this period.

While public polls data about delegitimization of Arabs among the Israeli public was partial, there is a clear indication that the Israeli ethos included a good (Israeli)–bad (Arab) theme that presented the Arabs as untrustworthy and aggressive in contrast to the honest and peace-seeking Israelis. The rhetoric of Israeli key leaders, such as Ben-Gurion, Meir, Begin, and Netanyahu, reduced each side's motivation and explanation to only one aim: for Arabs' behavior to destroy the State of Israel and for Israel's behavior to provide self-defense. Similarly, Arab hostility was explained in school textbooks by inherent traits while such Israeli action was justified by the situation. Public polls revealed that more than 60 percent agreed with these beliefs during the years 1973–1992. Some important changes appeared during the 1990s (when the reality of the conflict also changed). Public polls indicated that during this period the villa in the jungle theme weakened. They also revealed that the Israeli public tended to differentiate among different groups of Arabs, prior to any similar adjustment in their leaders' rhetoric or their school textbooks. But eventually during the 1993–1999 period (Oslo years), leaders' rhetoric and some textbooks suggested that not all Arab groups were enemies seeking to destroy Israel. They instead presented clear differences among different groups of Arabs and Palestinians, who formed distinct relationships with Israeli Jews, ranging from hostility and conflict to peace and cooperation. However, in the period after 2000, changes in the reality of the conflict saw a return to old portrayals in leaders' rhetoric in school textbooks and in public polls. Negative presentations became more common, as did the tendency to describe one hostile homogenous coalition of Arabs and to exclusively blame Arabs for the lack of peace. In addition, public polls, leaders' speeches, and school textbooks all continued to refer to the IDF as the most moral army in the world and used a variety of strategies (e.g., denial and bolstering) to cope with any potential clash between IDF actions and the image of Israel as a moral society.

It seems that this theme of the ethos was especially sensitive to major events in the conflict. While major events, such as Sadat's 1977 visit to Jerusalem and the 2000 second intifada, also influenced other themes of the ethos (see Chapter 2), their influence on the theme about Israel as a villa in the jungle was especially notable. A dramatic immediate change in public opinion appeared following Sadat's 1977 visit to Israel and the subsequent peace treaty with Egypt. A decline in delegitimization of Arabs in school textbooks also followed this event. Another weakening of the villa theme in public polls, leaders' rhetoric, and textbooks appeared during Oslo years but this theme strengthened again following the collapse of the Oslo process and the 2000 second intifada. In Chapter 9, I elaborate on the factors that explain the effects of these events on public opinion regarding the villa theme and other themes of the Israeli ethos.

Notes

1. I used the 2012 data because assessments of military intervention in politics, religious tensions, and ethnic tensions were not included in the 2014 and 2015 Israeli Democracy Indexes. Israel's ranking in civil liberties did not change from 2012 to 2013—again, like Lebanon (the 2015 index did not include an assessment of civil liberties).

2. For example, the 1964 Arab League summit ended with a decision to make "collective Arab military preparations" that "will constitute the ultimate practical means for the final liquidation of Israel" (Shlaim 2000, 230). That same year, the Palestinian National Council (PNC) issued the Palestinian National Charter, defining its aim to "eliminate Zionism in Palestine" and effectively calling for Israel's destruction. Shortly after the 1967 War, the Arab League summit in Khartoum

adopted a resolution committing themselves to not recognize Israel or negotiate with it.

3. By 1949, King Abdullah of Jordan was already involved in peace negotiations with Israel. Secret Egyptian-Israeli and Syrian-Israeli discussions regarding a possible bilateral peace treaty also occurred between 1948 and 1953.

4. From 1969 to 1973, King Hussein of Jordan secretly met eight times with Golda Meir. Hussein initially refused to participate in Egypt and Syria's 1973 War against Israel, and even warned Meir before the war began (Morris 2001).

5. Indeed, in October Jordan announced the "union" of its army with Egypt's and Syria's under the chairmanship of the Egyptian chief of staff. However, the talks between Israel, Britain, and France about a joint attack on Egypt started before this announcement (Morris 2001, 290), and Jordan and Syria did not help Egypt in the war.

6. While this quotation has been cited countless times, no primary source can be found for it (Rachlin 2015).

7. For example, Rabin said in the Knesset in 1985: "Most of the [Palestinian] population . . . wants to go on living with peace with us regardless of their political views" (Auerbach and Ben-Yehuda 1993, 151). Rosler (2012, 142–144) also found that, in his speeches during the years 1987–1990, Rabin differentiated between the PLO, which was perceived negatively, and the Palestinian population in the territories, which was perceived positively as a potential partner for peace.

8. For example, in a 1994 speech Rabin said that "our partners—the Egyptians, Jordanians, Palestinians, and the Chairman of the Palestine Liberation Organization, Mr. Yasser Arafat . . . have chosen the path of peace and are writing a new page in the annals of the Middle East" (Rabin 1994d). Rabin also said in September 1995, "King Hussein, President Mubarak, Chairman Arafat . . . we all love the same children, weep the same tears, hate the same enmity and pray for reconciliation. Peace has no borders" (Rosler 2012, 185)

9. For example, a poster of Mateh Ma'amatz (a settler action group) depicted Rabin's face in Arafat's kefiya headdress and labeled Rabin as "traitor." Another poster in anti-Oslo rallies showed Rabin as smiling at Arafat and washing his hands in blood. The caption associated Rabin with Palestinian terrorism (Peri 2000).

10. Eleven speeches (19 percent of the speeches that Netanyahu gave during 2013) attributed negative intentions and traits specifically to Iran, 8 speeches (14 percent) referred negatively to Palestinians, only 3 speeches (5 percent) referred to Hezbollah and the same number of speeches included negative references toward Syria.

11. During the 2009 Gaza War, Olmert said, "We make the unprecedented effort to fight for and realize our right of self-defense" (Olmert 2009).

12. An identical claim appeared also in Netanyahu's speeches during 2013: "In the Middle East, Israel has always been an island of stability and democracy in a sea of instability and despotism" (Netanyahu 2013j) and "the State of Israel is a beacon of democracy and progress in the entire region" (Netanyahu 2013k). The sharp distinction between Israel and its rivals also appeared in his speech in the UN General Assembly in 2012. This time, Netanyahu presented the conflict between Israel and its rivals as part of a global conflict between modern and medieval forces. He declared that "these forces clash around the globe, but nowhere more starkly than in the Middle East. Israel stands proudly with the forces of modernity." He then elaborated on Israel's merits as modern and advanced: "Israel protects human rights, its scientists won Nobel Prizes and it made the world a better place by preventing hunger in Africa and Asia." According to Netanyahu, all this stood in contrast to "the medieval forces of radical Islam" that "want to extinguish freedom. They want to end the modern world" (Netanyahu 2012b).

13. This theme of differentiation between the Israelis as peace seekers and the Palestinians who do not want peace was also common in Netanyahu's speeches abroad. For example, in his 2011 speech to the UN General Assembly, Netanyahu presented the many steps that Israel had taken in furtherance of peace—called for direct negotiations without preconditions, outlined a vision of peace of two states for two peoples, removed hundreds of roadblocks and checkpoints, frozen new buildings in the settlements for ten months—and after naming each step, he pointed to the lack of any response from the Palestinians ("there was no response") (Netanyahu 2011b).

14. Netanyahu used additional delegitimizing labels in describing Arab states and groups such as the image of wild animals. For example, he described Hezbollah's efforts to get advanced weapons from Syria as "hyenas feeding off a carcass—and the carcass is not even dead yet" (Netanyahu 2013d). In another speech, he called Palestinian terrorists "sub-human" (Netanyahu 2013f)

15. While a connection between el-Husseini and Nazi Germany indeed existed, according to Mattar (1988) the belief about strong ties between the Palestinians and the Nazis, as the one that Netanyahu expressed, exaggerates the scope and effectiveness of the relations between the Nazis and el-Husseini.

16. Historians such as Dina Porat have noted that hundreds of thousands of Jews were killed by the Nazis before the meeting between Hitler and el-Husseini took place, and that the order to carry out a Final Solution against the Jews was given in July 1941—months before their meeting. Netanyahu's political rival, Isaac Herzog, said the accusation was "a dangerous historical distortion," and he demanded that Netanyahu "correct it immediately" (Sterman and Ahren 2015).

17. Bar-Tal (1998), who analyzed the contents of all school textbooks used in all Grades 1–12 in 1994–1995, found only sporadic delegitimization of Arabs, although their negative stereotyping was prevalent and positive stereotypes were rare.

18. Podeh (2002, 138 note 225) noted the same trend.

19. Teff-Seker (2012) obtained somewhat different results about the presentation of Arabs and Palestinians in school textbooks during the period after 2000. She studied 149 textbooks for Grades 1–12 that were in use during the years 2009–2012. Her main conclusion was that the books "contain ample representation of the Palestinian point of view, their history, their positions and their rationale, without prejudice." Many of the examples that presented Arabs positively in her study, though, were from books published during the late 1990s. In addition, some of the examples that she cited for a balanced presentation of Palestinians without prejudice have been used in other studies as examples for negative presentations. This is because she referred to this negative description of Palestinians as "reality." For example, she claimed that "although books show the Palestinians (alongside other Arab nations) as the initiator of the 1948 War, as well as (most) pre-1948 Arab-Jewish violence, this can many times be attributed to historical facts" (Teff-Seker 2012, 8).

20. Also, according to a December 2013 Peace Index poll, on a scale of 0 (no trust at all) to 10 (full trust), 50 percent of the respondents chose 0, and the average score for trust in Palestinians was 3.09.

21. However, 62 percent of the Jewish respondents in an October 2015 Peace Index poll answered that they were not persuaded by Netanyahu's assertion that the Palestinian mufti was significantly responsible for the annihilation of the Jews in the Holocaust.

22. The answer was on a 7-point scale and the percentages are of those who chose the three most extreme negative ranks.

23. A Gallup poll that was conducted during the years 2008–2010 among 131 countries (including Israel) about the deliberate targeting of civilians by state and

nonstate actors, indicates that United States and Israel were ranked in first and second place regarding the percentage of respondents who saw military attacks on civilians as sometimes justified (49 percent and 43 percent, respectively). In most Arab countries, few respondents justified such attacks: Egypt (3 percent), Iraq (8 percent), Jordan (15 percent), and Lebanon (35 percent) ("Views of Violence" n.d.)

24. In addition, 71 percent of Jewish respondents in a November 2015 Peace Index poll thought that the signing of an Israeli-Palestinian peace settlement would not bring an end to Palestinian terror against Jews.

25. On this trend of a temporary decline in Israeli's perceptions of the lack of Arab interest in peace at the end of the Arab-Israeli wars, see also Stone (1982).

26. Additionally, most respondents in the Joint Israeli-Palestinian Poll during the years 2009–2012 thought that the Palestinians wanted to conquer all of Israel.

27. The confidence in Israeli superiority over the Palestinians and Israel's ability to cope with the second intifada was also very high. In an October 2007 Peace Index survey, 70 percent believed that if the current situation continued, Israeli society could hold out longer in terms of its internal fortitude than Palestinian society could. Similarly, 61 percent of Jewish respondents in a 2016 Democracy Index poll thought that if the current situation continued, Israeli society could hold out longer than Palestinian society could.

5

The Whole World
Is Against Us

A 2013 article by a well-known Israeli journalist—Ari Shavit—
in the liberal newspaper *Haaretz* revealed the story of an IDF fighter jet
flight over Auschwitz in 2003 (Shavit 2013). It focused on Amir Eshel, then
head of the Israeli Air Force, who, per Shavit, "became obsessed with a
question that drove him mad: Why didn't the American pilots who pho-
tographed Auschwitz bombard the camp from the air?" Following "a personal trauma during a routine training drill in Germany, when he found
himself feeling completely helpless when faced with a German nurse,"
Eshel "made up his mind to return to Auschwitz with strength, in a plane."
While the Polish authorities were not eager for an Israeli flyby over
Auschwitz, former Israeli Air Force commander Eliezer Shkedy ordered
Eshel to go ahead anyway, saying that "the last time the Poles told us what
to do was 60 years ago."

Eshel insisted that his partners in the Auschwitz flight have "a Holocaust background" and carried pages of testimony from twenty-one of the
victims who had arrived at Auschwitz from France precisely sixty years
before the flyby. During the flyby, 200 IDF soldiers and officers held a ceremony in Auschwitz. Prior to the ceremony, the delegation's commander
told the group: "The world knew about the existence of the site where
10,000 people were being murdered daily. The world could have shut down
the extermination camp, and the world did not do so." According to the article, "every squadron commander and every base commander in the air
force received a copy of the photograph of the flyby. Every general in the
general staff was sent a photograph of the flyby. The Shin Bet security service chief, the Mossad chief, the defense minister and the prime minister
received a photo of the flyby." On each copy of the photograph were the

words: "The Israel Air Force over Auschwitz—on behalf of the State of Israel and the Jewish people. To remember, not to forget, to rely only on ourselves" (Shavit 2013).

Shavit's (2013) article evoked many responses. Yehuda Bauer, a leading researcher in Holocaust studies, dismissed accusations that the Allies knew "everything there was to know" about Auschwitz during World War II. He maintained that Western intelligence had not trusted reports it received about killing by gas in Auschwitz and that, regardless, "it is surprising that the major general does not know that in 1944 there was not, in fact, a possibility for a precise bombardment that would hit the buildings in which the killing was taking place." He noted that the Nazis probably did not need gas to kill Jews, as they murdered between 250,000 and 400,000 Jews during the death marches. He also said the decision not to bomb Auschwitz was based on the doctrine of the Joint Chiefs of Staff in Washington that military means must not be used to bomb potentially nonmilitary targets. Bauer felt Shkedy's remark about the Poles was ignorant. "Despite all the anti-Semitism of large sectors of the Polish populace (and daring acts of rescue by a courageous minority), it was the Germans who issued orders, to the Jews and Poles alike, not the Poles." At the end of his response, Bauer concluded that "Auschwitz is the largest Jewish cemetery in our entire history. You do not fly over a cemetery as a gesture of mourning, and not even fury. Certainly not in a foreign, rather friendly, country, against its will. If foreign military planes were to fly over Israel for any reason whatsoever, in defiance of our demands, would Maj. Gen. Eshel not scramble the whole air force to intercept the alien planes?" (Bauer 2013).

This exchange illustrates another theme in the Israeli ethos: victimhood and siege beliefs (some of which are discussed in previous chapters). Chapters 3 and 4, respectively, showed that the Israeli ethos presents all Israeli actions during the conflict as self-defense in forced response to the Arabs. Per this view, then, Israel is the main victim in the Israeli-Arab conflict. In this chapter, I further explore the Israeli ethos's victimhood beliefs regarding relationships with the rest of the world, particularly on a common perception that Jews in general and the State of Israel in particular face a hostile world. As such, in this chapter, I refer to the phenomenon of *collective siege mentality*. While most societies have identified some rivals with negative intentions toward their own group, siege beliefs indicate that the rest of the world as a whole is hostile. Thus, they generalize the negative attribution to all out-groups—foes and allies alike—although sometimes they may identify one or two allies. This creates additional beliefs, such as that one's own group is "alone" in the world and cannot expect help from anyone in time of need (Bar-Tal and Antebi 1992a, 1992b; Bar-Tal n.d.). Though it is clear that the Israeli case influenced the conception of collective siege mentality (Bar-Tal and Antebi 1992a, 1992b; Bar-Tal n.d.), siege beliefs are found in other societies as well, including in Albania and Northern Ireland (Buckley and Kenney 1995; Volkan 1997).

In the Israeli case, siege beliefs are based on Jewish history, which includes constant persecutions and a systematic genocide (Holocaust). However, Jewish history also contains periods of a peaceful relationship between Jews and non-Jews such as the Jewish autonomy in Poland from the mid-sixteenth to eighteenth century, and the Golden Age of the Jews in Spain that lasted roughly from the tenth through twelfth centuries. As for the State of Israel, a full account of its foreign relations is beyond the scope of this book, but a brief review would reveal that the perception of mostly hostile interactions between Israel and the world is open to serious criticism. As noted, the State of Israel was established following a UN General Assembly resolution that called for the establishment of a Jewish state on November 29, 1947. Unusual for that period, both the Western bloc and the Soviet bloc supported the resolution. By 1967, Israel had "more diplomatic missions than any other state of her size and more than most of any size" (Brecher 1972, 37, 518).[1] This was despite efforts of the Arab states to isolate and malign it. Furthermore, during this period Israel had allies that, along with occasional disagreements, supported it with weapons and other aids. For example, during the 1948 War Israel received arms from Czechoslovakia (agreed to by the Soviet Union, which also gave Israel diplomatic support during the war). During the mid-1950s, a de facto alliance was forged between Israel and France; France sold Israel arms on a large scale in 1956 (to address the imbalance created by the 1955 Soviet arms deal with Egypt). Israel continued to receive conventional arms from France until early 1969 (Levey 2001). Also in 1957, France and Israel signed an agreement whereby France would provide the blueprints, technical assistance, and materials necessary for the building of a nuclear reactor. Israel promised to use the reactor for only peaceful purposes, but is believed to have used it to create a military nuclear option. Britain was also a source of arms for Israel during this time; Britain agreed to sell Israel its most modern tank in 1958 (Levey 2001). During the 1960s, the United States began to sell arms to Israel, including Hawk antiaircraft missiles and Phantoms, to counter the long-range bombers supplied to Egypt by the Soviet Union.[2] Security relations between the United States and Israel further deepened in the 1970s, as did economic and diplomatic relations. US aid increased from $269.6 million in 1968–1970 to $1.5 billion in 1971–1973, and the military portion increased from $140 million to $1.2 billion (Bar-Siman-Tov 1998; Freedman 2012). This support was vital to Israel during the 1973 War.[3]

Following the 1967 and the 1973 Wars, many countries broke diplomatic ties with Israel, leaving it relatively isolated internationally during the 1970s and 1980s. It was without diplomatic relations with the Soviet Union, India, China, any Eastern European country (except Romania), and any African country (except South Africa). It was also isolated in international organizations such as the United Nations. For example, in 1975, the General Assembly approved a resolution that listed Zionism as a form of racism (General Assembly Resolution 3379). At the same time, relationships strengthened between the United States and Israel, especially during the Ronald Reagan administration. From 1981 to 1988, the United States and Israel signed several public memorandums of understanding providing strategic, political, and economic cooperation, as well as designation of Israel as a major non-NATO ally.[4]

During the late 1980s and early 1990s, some thirty countries restored or established formal diplomatic ties with Israel, including Russia, all the countries of Eastern Europe, China, and India. Another thirty-five countries formalized ties following the signing of the Oslo Accords, including almost all countries on the African continent (S. Feldman and Shapir 2001, 70). Israel's position in international organizations also improved and, on December 16, 1991, UN Resolution 3379 was revoked, sponsored by eighty-six states and passed by a large margin (Manor 2010). In 2010, Israel became a member of the Organisation for Economic Co-operation and Development (OECD 2010). In 2016, the relationship with the United States became even stronger with a $38 billion ten-year deal for military assistance (Baker and Davis 2016). Even before this deal, Israel was already the largest cumulative recipient of US foreign assistance since World War II (Sharp 2015).

As shown below, some Israeli texts marginalized cooperation between Israel and other countries and emphasized conflict between Israel and the world. They indicated a *siege mentality*—a self-perception of Israel as a victim of unjust deeds, a high mistrust directed even against friendly states and allies, and the belief that Israel could only trust itself. Yet agreement with this theme in public polls and leaders' rhetoric was less constant than the agreement with other themes such as the Jewish state and security themes.

Leaders' Rhetoric

Liebman and Don Yihya (1983, 204–205) note that, in the early period of the state, Israeli leadership "avoided symbols that could be interpreted as placing Israel in a 'sacrificial' role in relation with other nations." The creation of Israel was perceived as breaking with the Jewish history of persecution, not its continuance and as "historical closure" to a Jewish tragic history. Israel's role, according to this perception, was to become "a beacon to other nations"—an example for them and a leader rather than a nation that separated itself from the rest of the world. The Israeli leader most closely associated with this idea was David Ben-Gurion (Brecher 1972; Liebman and Don-Yihya 1983). On other occasions, however, Ben-

Gurion expressed a negative view of the non-Jewish world and of international organizations such as the United Nations. Hence, he put forth a mixed message regarding siege beliefs. For example, he said in 1949 that "no state anywhere in the world is concerned about us. The world can live without us even if the entire Jewish race is eliminated from earth" (quoted in Barzilai 1996, 22). He also said that "our safety, shall not be done by anyone else" and that "in the field of security, more than any other field, we must remember the simple deep truth of our ancestors: 'if not me— then whom?'" (Saltzman 2016, 61). Ben-Gurion is also known as the creator of the phrase "um-shmum" that dismisses the United Nations.[5] Moshe Sharet strongly opposed this view and emphasized that "we owe our state to the United Nations" (Brecher 1972; Caplan 2001).

A review of sixty years of speeches by Israeli leaders revealed that siege beliefs appeared in the rhetoric of many of Ben-Gurion's successors. Rather than seeing the establishment of the State of Israel as a "historical closure," they often placed Israel's history and current state in an "historical circle" of eternal hate of Jews. In contradiction to presentation of the establishment of Israel as a normalization of Jewish history, this view asserted that Jews were doomed to isolation, even once they had their own state like any other nation. The only difference is that they now had an army with which to protect themselves from the world's hate.

Brecher (1972), who analyzed the perceptions and rhetoric of several Israeli leaders, found that many Israeli leaders during the 1950s and the 1960s (including Shimon Peres and Golda Meir) tended to share Ben-Gurion's negative view of the world and the United Nations. Bar-Tal and Antebi (1992a, 1992b) documented siege beliefs such as "no one will help us in time of needs" or "we cannot rely on other nations" in the writing and speeches of leaders, including Ben-Gurion, Meir, and Yitzhak Shamir. For example, Shamir explained, "We have plenty of 'friends' in the world who would like to see us dead, wounded, trampled, suppressed. And then it is possible to pity the wretched Jew, to commiserate with him" (Bar-Tal and Antebi 1992b, 264). Arian (1995) cites siege beliefs in the writing and rhetoric of Meir, Ben-Gurion, and especially Menachem Begin. Indeed, for Begin "the Holocaust meant that Israel has to be completely independent of the rest of the world and in total control over its international environment" (I. Peleg 1987, 64; see also Perlmutter 1987). Begin applied this attitude toward Israel's foes, but also its allies. For example, in a 1970 speech to the Knesset, Begin blamed the Americans for failing to save the Jews during World War II: "Six million Jews were exterminated during this generation, and the US did not save even one [of them]" (Naor 2003, 140). In 1980, he accused all European countries (with the exception of Denmark) of collaborating with the Nazis (I. Peleg 1987, 65). Gertz (2000) also found that siege beliefs were dominant in Begin's rhetoric. She notes that following the 1967 War, the narrative of "a people that dwells apart," while common mainly among leaders on the political right, also appeared in the subtext of those on the political left and center (see also Liebman and Don-Yihya 1983, 137–148, about this trend). Recall that at this time Israel was indeed isolated in the international community.

Yet during the 1990s, this narrative weakened, and other narratives coexisted with it. While siege narratives were still dominant in speeches of hawkish politicians like Shamir (see Aronoff 2014, 27), other leaders challenged the view of Israel as "a people dwelling alone." Rosler (2012) found that during the 1990s, Yitzhak Rabin often pointed to changes in international affairs and directly refuted siege beliefs. For example, in the Knesset in 1993, Rabin, while mentioning the improved relationship between Israel and the United States and Europe, claimed that "the train that travels towards peace has stopped this year at many stations that daily refute the time-worn canard 'the whole world is against us'" and that "we are no longer 'a people that dwelled alone'" (Caplan 2001, 167). Kimmerling's (1985) categorization of the two main political cultures in Israel summarized differences between dovish and hawkish leaders' rhetoric at that time. The "Eretz Yisrael approach" saw a relationship between Israel and a mostly hostile non-Jewish world while the "State of Israel approach" saw international relationships (including those between Israel and other nations) as a combination of conflicts and cooperation that, in part, were regulated by international organizations such as the United Nations.

However, this polarization among Israeli leaders seemed to fade somewhat after 2000. Following increasing violence in the Israeli-Palestinian conflict and a growing international criticism of Israel's actions in the conflict, siege beliefs strengthened again and have been found in the rhetoric of many Israeli leaders, including those on the political left and center. For example, in a 2007 speech Ehud Olmert said, "Let us not delude ourselves. All those honest people who have internalized consciousness of the Holocaust, its memory and its lessons, are *but a small portion* of the good, enlightened and moral of the human race" (Olmert 2007a, emphasis added). Siege beliefs were common also in the speeches and writings of Yair Lapid—both as a columnist and as a politician. His Facebook post from January 27, 2014, is typical: "Today is the International Holocaust Remembrance Day. The Holocaust has taught us . . . that we must survive on our own, because no one will come to save us." Likewise, in a 2014 speech in Berlin, which targeted a foreign audience but also was translated and distributed to Israeli audiences, Lapid (2014) expressed a mix of siege beliefs and liberal and universal values when discussing the lessons to be learned from the Holocaust. His first lesson was, "Train loads of Jews will never again depart from a platform anywhere in the world. The security of the State of Israel and its citizens must forever be in our hands alone." Lapid admitted that "we have friends, and I stand here among friends. The new Germany has proven its friendship to Israel time and again." However, he then added that "we must not, and we cannot, rely on anyone but ourselves." He did not explain why Israel still could not rely on Germany and other friendly countries, although his long opening description of the horrors of the Holocaust, including his family's personal story, may explain this high mistrust even in states currently friendly toward Israel. His second lesson, however, was that "no matter the circumstances we must always remain moral people . . . even when we have every reason to see only our own." He then maintained that the 2014 Gaza War "causes the two lessons we learned from the Holocaust to stand opposite one another." He dismissed international criticism of Israel's actions in the war—actions that resulted in many Palestinian civilian casualties—and contended that the IDF was the most moral army in the world and that Hamas was the "ultimate evil"—like the Nazis. In doing so, Lapid used the Holocaust to justify Israel's actions and dismiss international criticism. He explained that "some of the criticism [against Israel] stems from anti-Semitism" and from the critic's inability to accept the pure evil of the Nazi-like Hamas, exactly as the Jews and non-Jews during the Holocaust "didn't believe in the totality of evil." Lapid ended his speech by again emphasizing his belief in Israel as a victim of eternal evil: "We stand in the right place from which to say to the entire world: We will not board the train again. We will protect ourselves from evil" (Lapid 2014) and, in doing so, called on the world to stand with Israel as the main victim in the Israeli-Palestinian conflict.

Lapid's (2014) speech is a fine example of the strong connection between victimization beliefs and the villa in the jungle theme. In this aspect, Lapid's rhetoric was similar to the rhetoric of his main political rival—Netanyahu. Almost one-third of Netanyahu's speeches in 2013 incorporated references to siege beliefs (see Table 2.1).[6] He repeated the notion from the Passover Hagada that "in every generation, they [the other nations] rise up to destroy us." In a 2013 speech, he paraphrased another sentence from the Hagada: "In every generation, we must see ourselves as if we have survived the Holocaust and founded this country" (Netanyahu 2013e). His speech at the 2011 national ceremony opening the Holocaust Remembrance Day included ideas he brought up frequently and which represent overall use of siege beliefs in his rhetoric. In this speech, Netanyahu presented three lessons that must be taken from the Holocaust. The first lesson was similar to Lapid's first lesson—Israel should not ignore threats of annihilation from other countries. Netanyahu asked, "Has the world learned this lesson? I doubt it. Have we learned this lesson? I believe we have" (Netanyahu 2011a). He supported this conclusion with numerous historical examples from the expulsion of the Spanish Jews, the Holocaust, and Iran and Hezbollah to show that hate of Jews was eternal and that those who did not see it (mostly Jews themselves) were naively "bury[ing] their head in the sand." He relied again on this claim of eternal and widespread hate for Jews in his second lesson—that "we need to expose the true face of the hatred against our people."

In this speech, Netanyahu emphasized the *exceptionalism* of Jewish destiny. He did not present the Jews' situation as relevant to other dynamics between strong and weak groups in the world. Such a perception might imply that other small and defenseless ethnic groups have shared or could one day share the same fate as the Jews. It may also suggest that Israel should establish a coalition of other countries against its enemies. Neither did Netanyahu recognize any allies that stood by Israel during all these years as trustworthy in the future. Thus, in Netanyahu's perception, Israel stood alone in the world. It is not surprising, then, that his third lesson from the Holocaust was that "we must control our own fate" and that "if we do not have the ability to protect ourselves, *the world will not stand by our side*" (emphasis added). Netanyahu ended his 2011 speech with a warning that was reminiscent of Lapid's: "Let the world know, that when the People of Israel, and the IDF say 'never again'—we mean it" (Netanyahu 2011a). Note that he addressed every nation in "the world"—not just Israel's enemies. He saw Israel as standing alone against the whole world, not only against its enemies. In addition, while many of his 2013 speeches mentioned Iran's calls for the annihilation of the Jewish state, they ignored that Iran was one of the most internationally isolated countries at that time, and subject to heavy sanctions.

Indeed, the belief that Israel was a people dwelling alone, used by Lapid, Netanyahu, and other Israeli leaders, was especially emphasized in the context of the Holocaust. Rather than acknowledge the fact that the Allies defeated the Nazis and liberated the concentration camps, thus saving the lives of many Jews, Netanyahu argued that "the impotence of the world's nations" was one of the causes of the Holocaust (Netanyahu 2013c), and that "the rescue came late, too late"—the same idea expressed by Eshel, head of the Israeli Air Force, at the beginning of this chapter. In other speeches, Netanyahu shared Ben-Gurion's negative view of the UN and referred to Israel as the victim of biased international organizations. Netanyahu insisted that this situation was caused only by anti-Semitism and that there was nothing that Israel could do to change it.[7] In sum, Netanyahu and other Israeli leaders, including Begin, Shamir, and Lapid, presented two separate processes, one for world history and one for Jewish history; their *world history* process was one of repeated and inevitable anti-Semitism, no progress or change. The only change they acknowledged was in *Jewish history*—that Jews had learned to identify the "true" nature and intentions of the world and to defend themselves against it.[8]

School Curricula

The 1950s Through the Early 1990s

As with negative beliefs about the Arabs, siege beliefs were not explicitly included as declared goals in the intended curriculum. If anything, the curriculim's intent was often the opposite. For example, a stated aim of the first intended curriculum in history, drafted in 1954, was to imbue the student with "a sense of tolerance toward other nations and understanding of the importance of international organizations" (Kizel 2008, 27). The 1975 intended history curriculum also declared that one of its goals was to encourage tolerance toward different cultures and other nations (Kizel 2008, 40). However, various textbook analyses over time have shown this aim was rarely expressed in textbook content. David (2012) found siege beliefs about the Jews as the eternal victim of a hostile world in readers as early as 1900, but most notably in readers from the 1950s to the 1970s. These beliefs were invoked mainly in the context of the Holocaust but also appeared in the context of the Israeli-Arab conflict. One reader from the 1970s included a poem by Nathan Alterman that used the idea of the chosen people to criticize what it presented as the silence and passivity of other nations (and God) during the Holocaust: "As our children weep in the Shadow of the gallows / We have not heard the world's outrage."[9] The message was that Israel and the Jews could trust only themselves. As an eighth grade reader from the 1950s clearly stated, "We can rely only on ourselves, no nation in the world will help us in times of need" (David 2012, 224).

According to Firer (1985, 57), history textbooks used between 1948 and 1967 presented Jewish history according to siege mentality as an unbroken sequence of hate against Jews, with different antagonists over time. While she did find references to friendly interactions with other nations in history textbooks from 1967 to 1984, most were included in a "forgetfulness-illusion-punishment" narrative. In this narrative, the Jews forgot their harsh history with the world, deluded themselves that they could integrate with other nations, and eventually were subjected to anti-Semitism. History textbooks prior to 1967 presented anti-Semitism as an inborn trait of all non-Jewish people—part of their genetics that could not be changed. After 1967, these negative stereotypes of non-Jews disappeared. These textbooks focused less on anti-Semitic events prior to the Holocaust and relied primarily on the Holocaust as a major theme—a trend that increased the use of victimhood and siege beliefs in Israeli textbooks as discussed below.

Until 1994, history textbooks presented world history and Jewish history separately (both in content and in form). This situation contributed to the impression of Israel as a people dwelling alone and a history isolated from the world around it (Firer 1985). These textbooks included only a few topics from world history. Thus, Israeli children learned little about the history of the world beyond Europe, and even that study was partial and biased. Kizel (2008) notes in this regard that despite the inclusion of World War I, history textbooks did not mention the fate of the Armenians. Hence, Israeli children were not exposed to suffering of another ethnic group than the Jews.

The Mid-1990s Onward

The new 1994 history curriculum combined world history and Jewish history, lessening the presentation of Jewish history as isolated from world trends. It also added new topics, including ones from world history, such as the Cold War and decolonization. However, these issues were taught in isolation from Israel's history and "regarded as a series of far-away events, ignoring the regional case of Israelis liberating themselves from the British, and of Palestinians who regard the Israelis as occupiers" (Firer, 'Adwān, and Pingel 2004, 32). Furthermore, these changes occurred only in middle schools. Kizel (2008) states that no such change appeared in high school textbooks, which continued to emphasize only conflicts between Jews and other nations, although slightly less than before. Similarly, Bar-Tal (1998) found that victimization of the Jews was a leading theme in seven of the fourteen history textbooks for high school that were in use during the years 1994 and 1995.

The Special Case of Holocaust Studies in Israeli Schools

An increase in siege beliefs was linked to the strengthening of Holocaust studies in Israeli schools and the way the Holocaust was presented to students. Hence, in the rest of this section I focus on this specific issue. Porat (2004) notes that "until 1954, Israeli students did not study the Holocaust at all." He found that during the 1950s, "in the entire 12 years of schooling, only three lessons were devoted to the Holocaust." It was taught as part of world history, alongside the battles of World War II, and focused primarily on Jewish resistance to the Nazis. This presentation "gave readers the impression that Jews had joined the Allied Forces to face the Germans in the battlefield" (p. 621). The new 1970s history curriculum, however, situated the Holocaust within Jewish history (instead of world history). There was increased emphasis on Jews as victims of the Nazis, not just as fighters. Still, the Holocaust remained a minor topic. During the 1960s and 1970s, teaching of Holocaust was not required for high school students. Rather, it was one of several elective topics, such as "the French Revolution," chosen for study by only a few students (Porat 2004).

Everything changed in 1980 with the Holocaust Memory Law, which required that "all students graduating from Israeli schools be educated on consciousness of the memory of the Holocaust and Heroism" (Resnik 2003, 310; Porat 2004). Following this law, Israeli high school students were required to have at least thirty lessons on the Holocaust, and it became a mandatory unit on the matriculation exams (Segev 2000, 431). To ensure consistency of the lessons, only one Holocaust textbook for all high schools was approved. This book—*The Holocaust and Its Significance*—remained the main Holocaust textbook for at least fifteen years. In it, the Holocaust was presented as "an event that symbolized the Jews' uniqueness, their continuous victimization solely for the crime of being Jewish" (Porat 2004, 632). The book especially opposed any attempt to compare the Holocaust to genocide of other non-Jewish groups such as the Turkish killing of Armenians. Dror (2001), who analyzed educational items on the Holocaust as published by the Ministry of Education from the 1960s to the 1990s, also found that parallels between the Holocaust and other genocides were mostly ignored. Some history textbooks approved with the new 1995 national curriculum for middle schools again placed the Holocaust within discussion of World War II. However, one of these, *A World of Changes: A History Book for 9th Grade,* was later banned from use in Israel's educational system, and declared by the Knesset Committee of Education and Culture to have "overlooked the history of the Holocaust, Zionism and the State of Israel" (Porat 2004, 619).

Israeli students from different age groups were exposed to the Holocaust not just through formal learning in class, but also through extracurricular activities. Starting in 1963, schools were required to hold a ceremony on Holocaust Remembrance Day in the following format: "Six candles will be lit inside a large memorial candle stand (supplied by Yad Vashem) and appropriate prose and poetry passages will be read." In addition, schools were encouraged to invite camp survivors and resistance fighters "to relate their Holocaust experiences" (Ben-Amos and Bet-El 1999, 270). Ben-Amos and Bet-El (1999, 274), who studied Holocaust Remembrance Day assemblies at schools, found that these ceremonies included "many prose selections containing detailed information on the numerous perils and ordeals the narrator experienced." In 1969, schools were also instructed to visit the Holocaust commemorative centers such as Yad Vashem, Kibbutz Lohamei Hagettaot, and Kibbutz Yad Mordechai (Director-General's Circular 29/8 1969, as cited in Resnik 2003, 309–310).

Since the 1980s, the number of school extracurricular activities regarding the Holocaust increased significantly. More and more schools invited Holocaust survivors to tell their stories to the students, and the number of field trips to Holocaust museums and institutions increased (E. Cohen 2010, 15). In a 2010 survey of ninth and twelfth grade students, 95 percent reported having participated in school Holocaust Remembrance Day ceremonies, 78 percent had heard testimonies of Holocaust survivors who visited their school, and 85 percent had participated in school visits to museums and commemorative centers. Other commonly reported activities included watching Holocaust-related films (73 percent) and plays (82 percent) (E. Cohen 2010, 25–26).

Some researchers have suggested that high school tours of Holocaust sites in Poland, popular since the 1990s (as discussed in Chapter 3), also encouraged siege beliefs among students. For example, J. Feldman (2008, 60) contends that "the voyage is a civil religious pilgrimage, which transforms students into victims, victorious survivors, and finally, *olim* (immigrants; Ascenders) to the Land of Israel." According to J. Feldman (2002, 101), these trips included almost no contact with Poles, no attempt was made to meet local Jews, and students learned almost nothing about the modern life of the Polish Jewish community: "After all, he [current Polish Jew] or his parents experienced the Holocaust, yet he chose life in post-Holocaust Poland over immigration to Israel." This fact threatens beliefs about eternal hate for the Jews and Israel as the only safe place for Jews.

In 2014, the Education Ministry published a new curriculum for Holocaust studies in all grades beginning in kindergarten (Ministry of Education n.d.-b). The new curriculum presented no clear increase or decrease in exposure to the topic, however. On one hand, it made the subject mandatory for all age groups; previously required as part of the history curriculum for only higher grades.[10] On the other hand, it focused on making Holocaust studies age appropriate such that young children were not traumatized by how the subject was presented to them. Indeed, children as young as kindergarten were exposed to the Holocaust at school, even before the new curriculum, through extracurricular activities. Much of the instruction for kindergarten teachers in the 2014 program focused on limiting exposure to the subjects that might frighten young children such as avoiding content based on physical demonstrations in simulations and picture displays. In this sense, the 2014 program may actually have decreased the exposure of young Israeli children to the subject, at least in kindergarten classes.

Furthermore, siege beliefs were not dominant in the program's content for kindergartens and elementary schools. On the contrary, kindergarten teachers were advised to explain to the children that the Holocaust was "a difficult period that happened many years ago—a period even before the children and their parents were born" (Ministry of Education n.d.-a). The teachers were also asked to emphasize the fact that there were non-Jews who helped the Jews during this period. The tendency, then, was not to connect it to current attitudes of the "world" toward Jews. The program for kindergarten through third grade included seven lesson plans. Most of these were based on a story of a Holocaust survivor who was a child during the

Holocaust, and many of them included characters of "good" non-Jews who helped the Jewish child and her family.

The 2014 program's message for fifth through ninth grades was different. Teachers selected from twenty-five lesson plans, several of which promoted siege beliefs. For example, a lesson called "In Search for a Home" was intended for fifth to seventh grades ("In Search for a Home" n.d.). It was based on the stories of five survivors who left Europe for Israel after World War II. Student groups focused on one survivor and his decision to immigrate to Israel.[11] Two accounts included short references to American soldiers' kindness toward Jewish survivors. Two others mentioned liberation by the Soviet army, but focused mostly on Jewish Red Army soldiers. The option of immigrating to countries other than Israel was mentioned only briefly in a few stories. One, for example, mentioned that the narrator's brother was so impressed by the American soldiers that he wanted to and did eventually become an American citizen. Overall, though, the stories mainly presented Israel as the only place for Jews to be safe and to freely practice Jewish life. In fact, the lesson explicitly directed students' attention to this point by asking them to find the sentences explaining why each survivor chose to go to Israel and the meaning that Israel held for him or her. Some examples of such sentences in the stories follow.

> *Story 1*: I emptied the bag curbside. I thought to myself: Tomorrow the French will say "dirty Jews." What do I care, we're going to Palestine.
>
> *Story 2*: I started to understand that there is a place in the world that is whole mine. This is my country. I can go there on the street and I will not have to be worry. No one will call me "dirty Jew" anymore!
>
> *Story 3*: Naftali explained: Eretz Israel is the home of the Jews. From there we were expelled and this is where we need to go back. This is the only place in the world where Jews are not killed.

Siege beliefs could also be found where we would have least expected it—in a lesson about non-Jews saving Jews during the Holocaust ("In a Place Where There Are No Human Beings, Strive to Be One—Righteous" n.d.). Five cases were discussed during the lesson. The teachers were instructed to emphasize that these positive experiences were but exceptions to the hostility of the rest of the world (including the Allied forces) or indifference toward the extermination of the Jews. In the words of the teacher guidelines, these righteous actions were exceptions "especially because of the fact that Jews were persecuted in that time *everywhere, and there were almost no countries and societies that defended them*"(emphasis added). This idea was also repeated in specific stories. In the story of Raoul Wallenberg, the instructions for teachers noted: "Wallenberg's activities emphasize the fate of Hungarian Jews, that were sent to concentration camps relatively late, when the whole world knew about this intention [to kill the Jews] and its execution—knew and refrained from action. Wallenberg and diplomats from other countries have done to save the Jews of Budapest what the Allied forces did not do." The lesson also included the story of a small Dutch group that saved Jews in the Holocaust. The teacher was encouraged to use this story to discuss the fate of the Jewish community in Netherlands. In particular, teachers were instructed to correct "a common but incorrect assumption, created by the popularity of Anne Frank's Diary," that the Dutch people were friendly toward and protective of the Jews. Another story involved a small Polish group that saved Jews. The rescue of Danish Jews by the Danish people was briefly mentioned in the teacher guidelines, but it was not included among the five main case studies in the lesson plan.

Universal values and universal lessons from the Holocaust were presented in this lesson plan mostly at the individual level, as seen in the name of this lesson plan: "In a place where there are no human beings, strive to be one." Likewise, the moral earmarked for the lesson in teacher's instructions regarded the moral decisions of individuals who chose not to go with the flow and "do not erase their inner world." What is missing from this and other lessons in the 2014 program about the Holocaust was a message about the necessity of democracy and protection of human rights at the state level to guard the freedom of Jews and other minority groups. Instead, the main state-level message was the necessity of the existence of Israel as a state for the Jewish people with a strong army (e.g., a connection to two other themes in the ethos—the Jewish state and security).

The Public

Even though siege and victimhood beliefs were common in school textbooks and leaders' rhetoric, only a few questions in public polls have addressed this theme, and only since the early 1980s. In a 1982 survey, 40 percent of the respondents thought that the nations of the world were against Israel and 52 percent thought that it was impossible to generalize (only 5 percent thought the nations of the world supported Israel) (Liebman and Don-Yihya 1983). According to this survey, then, most respondents did not hold siege beliefs. A 1993 survey (prior to the Oslo Accords) included a question about the factors that contributed to the development of anti-Semitism. Most respondents (64–71 percent) thought that situational factors such as economic conditions in the external environment and the fact that the Jews were a minority among a non-Jewish majority contributed to a great extent to anti-Semitism. Fewer respondents, but still a majority (58 percent), thought that anti-Semitism was an expected trait of non-Jews—a view similar to that presented in pre-1967 school textbooks (S. Levy 1996).

NSPOP polls also addressed siege beliefs. In 1987, a clear majority (more than 60 percent) of respondents agreed that "Israel is and continues to be 'A people dwelling alone'" and that "world criticism of Israeli policy stems mainly from anti-Semitism," although only around 50 percent agreed with the harsher statement that "the whole world is against us." The agreement with these statements, however, declined significantly in the mid-1990s (before and during the Oslo process): the percentages of agreement with "Israel is and continues to be 'A people dwelling alone'" dropped from 72 percent in 1988 to 54 percent in 1994 (see Table 5.1). While this question was not included in NSPOP surveys after 1994, an identical question included in my 2016 survey showed a strengthening of siege beliefs among the public paralleling trends in leaders' rhetoric and school curricula (see Table 5.1).[12]

Another indication of siege beliefs after 2000 can be found in interviews conducted with 100 Israeli Jews in 2002, the second intifada when Israel faced international criticism (Bar-Tal, Raviv, and Abromovich forthcoming). Siege beliefs were common among the participants. Many echoed the rhetoric of Netanyahu's speeches in which history from different times and places was reduced to one phenomenon—the eternal hate of the world toward Jews. This phenomenon was also presented as something that only Jews—no other nation or ethnic group—experienced. The most common explanation for this situation that was offered during the interviews was that the "world" was jealous of the Jews—the chosen people. For example, Participant 501 in the study of Bar-Tal, Raviv, and Abromovich (forthcoming) stated, "They wanted to hurt us because we represent something supreme, something more advanced."[13] Participant 103 used an analogy from kindergarten to explain the situation of the Jews: "We were always special. [People] do not like the exception. Even in kindergarten [children] do not like the nerd kid on the one hand or those that are different." Many participants, such as Participant 212, argued that the hate of the "world" toward Israel was doomed to exist forever: "The world does not like Israel . . . for the world, we are a pain, if they could get rid of us they would have got rid of us."

Table 5.1   Agreement with Siege Beliefs, 1986–2016 (percentage)

	1986	1987	1988	1990	1991	1994	2016
The whole world is against us	40	51	52	46	43	34	51
Israel is and continues to be "a people dwelling alone"	n/a	70	72	69	68	54	71
World criticism of Israel stems from anti-Semitism	58	68	n/a	62	68	50	74

Sources: NSPOP and Oren's 2016 Survey.

As discussed earlier in this chapter, the perceived hostility of the world toward Israel included that of international organizations such as the United Nations. Indeed, public polls indicated that, like their leaders, Israelis had a relatively unfavorable attitude toward the UN. According to the 2016 European Social Survey (ESS), Israeli respondents were more likely to report no trust at all in the UN than any of the other countries surveyed. On a scale of trust ranging from 1 to 10, 33.2 percent of Israelis chose 1 (no trust at all)—see Table 5.2. The 2013 Pew Global Attitudes project survey also showed that Israelis had a negative view of the UN relative to most other countries. Ironically, Israel shared this attitude with the Palestinians and many of its Arab neighbors (see Table 5.3).

Conclusion

Several observers have pointed to the existence of siege beliefs, such as "the whole world is against us," "no one will help us in time of need," and "we cannot rely on other nations," in Israeli culture. Analyzing Israeli public and political discussion, they identified a strengthening of these beliefs in Israeli society since the late 1970s (Liebman and Don-Yihya 1983; Lustick 2017). The narrative connecting these beliefs was grounded in the traditional Jewish view of the gentile world as hostile, as well as the per-

Table 5.2   Lack of Trust in the UN, 2016

State	No Trust at All in UN (%)
Israel	33.2
Russian Federation	26.5
Italy	13.4
Spain	12.3
Slovenia	11.3
Austria	10.6
Portugal	8.5
France	8.3
Czech Republic	7.3
Estonia	7.1
United Kingdom	6.9
Germany	6.6
Belgium	6.2
Hungary	5.7
Poland	5.4
Switzerland	4.2
Lithuania	4.0
Norway	1.1

Source: European Social Survey Round 8 Data (2016).

Table 5.3   Unfavorable Attitudes Toward the UN, 2013

State	Percentage	State	Percentage
Israel	70	Mexico	27
Palestinian territories	69	Germany	27
Jordan	61	Argentina	26
Greece	58	Pakistan	25
Turkey	56	Canada	25
Egypt	52	Britain	24
China	45	Chile	23
Spain	44	Italy	20
Lebanon	40	Ghana	14
Japan	40	Philippines	13
France	36	South Korea	9
United States	31	Senegal	8
Russia	28		

Source: Pew Research Center (2013).

ception of the Holocaust as "uncovering the ferocious antisemitism lurking in the hearts and cultures of all non-Jews at all times" (Lustick 2017, 154). A related narrative described Israel as a state that fights for its existence against a Nazi-type enemy. International disagreement with this perception was perceived to be caused by eternal hate for the Jews, or at best as indifference to their suffering (Amir 2011, 12–13). Siege beliefs, then, were strongly linked to other themes in the ethos such as the goal of establishing a Jewish state as a safe place for the Jews, security beliefs, and the perception of Israel as a villa in the jungle.

In this chapter, I showed that siege beliefs were common in school curricula and in the rhetoric of leaders. Questions addressing this topic were not common; hence, our understanding of public agreement with this theme is partial and the polls could not prove researchers' findings about the strengthening of siege beliefs among the public during the 1970s, nor could they refute these findings. Nevertheless, public polls indicated that more than 60 percent of the public in the 1980s agreed with the statement that Israel was and continues to be a people dwelling alone. However, the prevalence of this theme in leaders' speeches varied over time, appearing infrequently in some periods—for example, during the 1990s, it appeared mainly in speeches of hawkish leaders, but was openly refuted by Rabin. Public polls also revealed declining agreement with this theme during the 1990s, but this trend reversed itself in later years. It seems then, that siege beliefs were less dominant in the Israeli ethos than other themes such as Israel as a Jewish state and security. Unlike the Jewish state theme, siege beliefs did not appear in texts like the Declaration of Independence (furthermore, the declaration refutes this theme), agreement with this theme in public polls was not as strong and consistent as agreement with the Jewish state theme (see Chapter 9 and Table 9.1), and public debate regarding this issue was wider as revealed in the debate about the 2003 IDF fighter jet flight over Auschwitz and Rabin's speeches during the late 1990s that challenged this theme of the ethos.

Public agreement with siege beliefs seemed to be influenced by major events and global trends—including those that contradict this view. In this vein, Liebman and Don-Yihya (1983, 142) argue that strengthening of siege beliefs during the 1970s was reinforced by the 1973 War and the international reaction to Israel. Israel's international isolation at that time was explained in the Israeli press as an expression of anti-Semitism while US support to Israel during the war was perceived mostly in terms of US self-interest. The decline in siege beliefs in the 1990s could be explained as a reaction to an opposite global trend when, following the end of the Cold War, some thirty countries restored or established formal diplomatic ties with Israel, including the Soviet Union (Rabin cited this fact when challenging siege beliefs) (see for example Caplan 2001, 167).

A 1988 well-known article by Israeli philosopher and historian Yehuda Elkana criticized the effect of siege beliefs on Israeli society. Elkana argued that the main factor that explains aggression of Israeli soldiers toward Palestinians during the first intifada was "a profound existential 'Angst' fed by a particular interpretation of the lessons of the Holocaust and the willingness to believe that the whole world is against us, and that we are an eternal victim." Regarding Holocaust studies in Israeli schools as I describe in this chapter, he stated:

> I see no greater threat to the future of the State of Israel than the fact that the Holocaust has systematically and forcefully penetrated the consciousness of the Israeli public, even the large segment that did not experience the Holocaust, as well as the generation that was born and grew up here [in Israel] . . . decade after decade, we sent every Israeli child on repeated visits to "Yad Vashem." What did we want those tender youths to do with this experience? We declaimed, insensitively and harshly, and without explanation: "Remember!" "Zechor!" To what purpose? What is the child supposed to do with these memories? Many of the pictures of those horrors are apt to be interpreted as a call to hate. "Zechor!" can easily be understood as a call for continuing and blind hatred. (Elkana 1988)

Several other scholars pointed to the negative effect of Israeli victimhood beliefs on the dynamic of the Israeli-Arab conflict. The mythical and apocalyptic perception of the Israeli-Arab conflict in the rhetoric of leaders like Begin, Shamir, and Netanyahu implied that the dispute is insoluble. Hence, it does not leave much room to negotiation (I. Peleg 1987). Siege beliefs become a psychological barrier in interaction between Israeli Jews and Palestinians, even among peace activists (Kahanoff 2016; Grob and Roth 2008). Furthermore, Amir (2011) showed that these beliefs were used in denial and suppression of injustices perpetrated by Israel not only with regard to Palestinians. These beliefs were also applied in the context of historical injustices perpetrated by Israeli governments or agencies associated with the state against others from *within* the Israeli Jewish society. A case in point is the whereabouts of the babies and young children of (mostly) Yemeni Jewish immigrants in the 1950s who disappeared postpartum or while being hospitalized or cared for by the state. Displays of pity and remorse toward these victims signified for the Israeli society at large as being weakness that Israel could not afford considering its situation as a people dwelling alone. As for the effect of siege beliefs regarding foreign policy in general, siege beliefs can sometimes alert a society to dangerous reality and untruthful allies, but it can also become a self-fulfilling prophecy when a combative foreign policy, driven by siege mentality, produces fierce backlash and further isolation of the state, which in turn further reinforces the siege mentality. The fact that siege mentality was not the most central theme in the Israeli ethos, however, may provide a path to break this circle in the Israeli case.

Notes

1. By this time, Israel had established a diplomatic and consular presence in nine Asian, twenty-nine African, seven Eastern European, twenty-one Western European, and fifteen Latin American countries, as well as in the United States, Canada, Australia, and New Zealand (Brecher 1972, 37, 518).

2. Nonetheless, there was friction between the United States and Israel during this period, primarily over Israel's nuclear program.

3. Yet the United States exploited Israel's dependence on its arms supply. For example, during the initial stages of war, the United States delayed arms delivery to restrict Israel's military activity.

4. During the Reagan administration, Israel received $22.9 billion from the United States, all grant aid. But there were also some difficulties between the two countries; for example, in the case of the US sale of an airborne warning and control system (AWACS) to Saudi Arabia, which Israel strongly opposed, and during Israel's invasion of Lebanon in 1982 (Freedman 2012).

5. It uses the Yiddish idiom of repeating a word and adding the prefix "shm" the second time, to indicate mockery of the original word. Since the Hebrew abbreviation of the United Nations is "um," the phrase "um-shmum" may be translated as "UN equals Zero."

6. It is important to note that in some of his speeches—mainly in speeches in front of foreign audiences—Netanyahu refuted the siege belief. For example, in his speech at the Knesset Special Session in Honor of the President of the French Republic, François Hollande, Netanyahu emphasized the friendship between Israel and France (Netanyahu 2013p). This tendency appeared also in a speech in front of an American audience (this time, he stated the friendship and support of the United States) (Netanyahu 2013j).

7. See, for example, "tikkun olam, fixing the world, does not protect us—it simply does not protect us because the beliefs against us persist . . . let no one delude themselves into thinking that if we reach an agreement with the Palestinians it would erase the wild slander against the Jewish state. Because the legacy of the Jews before this, for generations and generations, is the legacy of the Jewish state today" (Netanyahu 2013i).

8. See, for example, "The biggest change in our situation is not the threat to our existence. This threat is with us, our people, almost since the dawn of our existence, let alone in [our] exile. The most significant difference created here on this land during the past century, and especially since the creation of the state of Israel, is our ability to defend ourselves against these threats" (Netanyahu 2013r).

9. The translation to English is taken from Gorny (2011, 103).

10. A 2009 report by the state comptroller found that the subject of the Holocaust was introduced in most grades including kindergarten around the Holocaust Remembrance Day, but the Ministry of Education did not provide guidance and instructions for kindergarten teachers regarding the teaching of this topic. The issue of the Holocaust was also thought of as part of the subject of fatherland social studies and civics in second, third, and fourth grades and again without much instruction from the ministry (State Comptroller 2009).

11. Some of the content was taken from the same textbooks that were included in the program for first through fourth grades. But in the lesson for older students, the students read only a small section from the book and, hence, siege beliefs were much more dominant than in the lesson plans for younger children that presented them in the context of the entire book.

12. This trend also appeared in other surveys: Peace Index polls showed that 56 percent in August 2010 and 63 percent in August 2014 agreed with the statement that "the whole world is against us."

13. A similar idea appeared in a reader for religious schools from 2003, where a rabbi says, "God chose us among all nations because we are different. Just because we are different [other nations are] chasing and killing us" (David 2012, 344).

6

Patriotism
and National Unity

Like many other societies, Israeli popular culture includes numerous patriotic songs. One such song—"I Have No Other Country"—became popular in rallies on both the right and left of the political spectrum. Its composer, Ehud Manor, was awarded the Israel Prize for his contribution to Israeli songwriting, and the song was voted Manor's most popular in an online poll conducted by the newspaper *Yedioth Ahronoth* (Ynet 2005). Thus, it clearly resonates with the Israeli public. The song's message refers to a strong emotional attachment to the country and its language—it says that Hebrew is "impressed in my veins and soul." But most of all it expresses a sense of rootedness—the belief that a person should stay in his homeland, even when the country "seems to be changing," because "he has no other country." These ideas are also articulated in "Eretz" (which means country or land), another popular Israeli song. In "Eretz," Israel is the "land where we were born / Where we'll always stay / We will be here, come what may." Manor's song, "I Have No Other Country," however, clearly questions other aspects of patriotism such as pride in the country. It describes a situation when the country is wrong and in decline. Yet the narrator is proud of the history of the country and aims to help it to "renew its glorious days." As I show in this chapter, these ideas perfectly align with Israeli patriotism.

Patriotism—defined as identification with and loyalty to a "fatherland" to the extent of being ready to defend it and fight for it (Bar-Tal and Staub 1997; Sullivan, Fried, and Dietz 1992)—is a universal phenomenon. Its level, however, varies among different societies, and Bar-Tal (2013) maintains that ethos of societies in intractable conflict include a theme about patriotism. This general definition implies several distinctions. The first

139

distinction relates to the subject of patriotic attachment, which could be linked to a nation, a land, the heritage of the past, or a specific ideology. Another distinction is between dimensions or expressions of patriotism, some of them mentioned in the two songs above. Arad and Alon (2006) identified four dimensions of patriotism, of which three are relevant to our discussion: sacrifice, rootedness, and pride in the country.[1] A further relevant distinction is between blind and constructive patriotism. *Blind patriotism* is a rigid attachment to a country with unconditional loyalty and intolerance of criticism while *constructive patriotism* is characterized by a more critical attachment to the country that allows for criticism of the regime and its actions (Staub 1997).

In previous chapters, I touched on some aspects of patriotism that are included in the Israeli ethos: in Chapter 2, I explored the sense of connection between the Jewish people and the land of Israel, and in Chapter 3 the glorification of the army and the need to serve in it. In this chapter, I look at other aspects of patriotism, including a readiness to sacrifice one's own life for the country, the glorification of those who died in combat, pride in being an Israeli, a desire to live in Israel, and a condemnation of those who choose to emigrate. As I show, most of these aspects are indeed part of the Israeli ethos, but the agreement with some of these aspects is stronger than agreement with other aspects, and a decrease in the willingness to sacrifice for the state has appeared over the years. Finally, I discuss the related belief about preserving national unity in time of threat—another theme identified by Bar-Tal (2013) as common in the ethos of a society that is involved in intractable conflict. Unity, of course, is a universal value for all social groups and a precondition for social stability and the proper functioning of society. It is especially important in societies that are involved in intractable conflict, as it promotes the willingness of individuals to make sacrifices for the sake of the national struggle and is presented as essential condition for the society to endure the conflict. Unity beliefs, then, are highly linked to the security and patriotism themes of the ethos.

Leaders' Rhetoric

Prime ministers often praise their country. It is, however, important to note what aspects of their country they are especially proud of. As I noted in Chapter 5, David Ben-Gurion envisioned Israel as a state that would serve as an example to all other nations—as a light unto the world. He believed that Israel should and could play this role because the Jews have "uncommon intellectual and moral virtue." Benjamin Netanyahu also often expressed such pride in the Jewish people and Israel. He declared that "we are proud of the great light emanating from Zion, a light unto the people of

Israel, a light unto the nations; a light of progress, a light of prosperity, a light of a peace-seeking nation" (Netanyahu 2013e). In several speeches, Netanyahu, like Ben-Gurion, spoke about the "genius" of the Jewish people, referencing the large number of Jews who have won the Nobel Prize (Netanyahu 2013i). He expressed pride in Israel's exceptional moral values and, especially, Israel's democracy and technology. He proclaimed that "we in Israel are proud of our vibrant democracy and our strong democratic institutions" (Netanyahu 2013b). He also praised Israel's economy as an economic "miracle" (Netanyahu 2013o). Of Netanyahu's speeches in 2013, 28 percent expressed that Israel was a light unto the nations, 19 percent expressed pride in Israel's moral values and democracy, and 36 percent expressed pride in Israel's technology and economy.

Another dimension of patriotism common in Israeli political speeches over the years is sacrifice, which combines love for and loyalty to the country such that individuals are willing to risk their own safety for it and feel compelled to glorify those who died in its service. This theme appeared in the speeches of all the prime ministers. Here are several typical examples. Addressing the Knesset a week after the end of the 1967 War, Levi Eshkol glorified the IDF fallen soldiers: "They join the long chain of heroism and self-sacrifice with those who have offered themselves up entirely on the altar of Israel and its Land—a chain that will never be broken" (Eshkol 1967). Olmert said in 2006 of the fallen soldiers, "We are . . . brothers in self-sacrifice and love of the homeland" (Olmert 2006b). In his speech at the Knesset special session in memory of the Jewish prisoners in Mandatory Palestine who were sentenced to death by the British in 1947, Netanyahu repeated these themes: "From those who went to the gallows until today, from the 1930s through the reality of our current lives, the message of sacrifice and heroism didn't fall silent" (Netanyahu 2010a). He used the story of Moshe Barazani and Meir Feinstein, who were arrested and sentenced to death by the British but committed suicide together as they were being hanged. To Netanyahu, this was a story that expressed "sublime love for country and people. Yes, love of country, love of the homeland, love for their people."

While a sense of rootedness—the idea that Israelis should stay in Israel in any situation—was not a constant issue in leaders' rhetoric, it did appear several times over the years. The most notable expression of rootedness occurred when, during a television interview on Independence Day 1976, Rabin referred to emigrants from Israel as "the weakest of the weaklings" (E. Leshem and Shuval 1998, 507). In fact, the Hebrew word for such emigrants is *Yordim*—literally, people who are going downward. Later, he added that Yordim are "people who flight from the battle field, who in my eyes are deserters" (Man 1998). Begin also referred to emigration from Israel as a negative and unpatriotic act, saying to the Knesset in 1976 that "since the state was found we have lost [through emigration] four Divisions or 12 Brigades" (Y. Cohen 1988, 909). Emigration from Israel, then, was condemned as a lack of patriotism, especially in terms of the sacrifice and rootedness dimensions.

In 2013, following a series of reports on Israelis who left the country for financial reasons, Lapid criticized emigrants from Israel in his Facebook page, using both siege and patriotic beliefs:

> A word to all the people who are fed up and leaving for Europe, As it happens, you've caught me in Budapest. I came here to speak out in parliament against anti-Semitism and remind them how people here tried to murder my father only because the Jews had no state of their own, how they killed my grandfather in a concentration camp, how they starved my uncles, how my grandmother was saved from a death march at the last moment. So forgive me if I'm a bit impatient with people who are willing to throw the only state the Jews have into the garbage because it's easier to live in Berlin. (*Haaretz* 2013)

Finally, Israeli leaders stressed the theme of national unity, especially in the context of the Israeli-Arab conflict. In this context, they presented the Israeli society as one family and the IDF soldiers as "our sons" or "our children." In a 2006 speech (during the 2006 Lebanon War), Olmert addressed the families of IDF soldiers who were captured by Hamas and Hezbollah: "You, and mainly your children—*our children*—are always on my mind" (Olmert 2006c, emphasis added). Netanyahu spoke similarly in 2011, when a controversial prisoner exchange deal with Hamas released IDF soldier Gilad Shalit, who had spent more than five years in Hamas captivity:

> Citizens of Israel, today we are all united in joy and in pain. . . . In recent days, we have all seen national unity such as we have not seen in a long time. Unity is the source of Israel's strength, now and in the future. Today, we all rejoice in Gilad Shalit's return home to our free country, the State of Israel. Today, I can say, on behalf of all Israelis, in the spirit of the eternal values of the Jewish People: "*Your children shall return to their own border*" [Jeremiah 31:17]. (Netanyahu 2011c, emphasis added)

Israeli leaders also referenced national unity when they discussed common threats that all Israelis face, thus minimizing ethnic and other tensions among Israeli citizens. For example, Eshkol said, "Our people stood the test because it was united, because at the fateful hour it was able to concentrate its efforts and act as one man" (Eshkol 1967). During the Lebanon War, Ehud Olmert emphasized that "all of us—Jews, Muslims, Christians, Druze and Circassians—now stand as one person, as one nation, subjected together to the same hatred and malice, and fighting against it in consensus and partnership" (Olmert 2006c). As for Netanyahu, 22 percent of his

2013 speeches included references to national unity. In May 2013, he emphasized the importance of national unity when commemorating those lost in the 1948 sinking of the *Altalena,* which was shelled by the IDF after a dispute over division of its cargo, an event that symbolizes one of the most troubling frictions in Israeli Jewish society. Netanyahu said, "The lesson of Altalena for all of us [is] national unity." Likewise, he stressed the importance of national unity while referring to the security theme of the ethos: "All around us [there are] so many challenges, so many enemies, so many weapons stacked against us, we must at all costs and in any way to search for peace within our society. Peace within our society first and foremost." He also evoked the villa theme in the ethos while discussing the issue of Israeli national unity: "See what is happening around us today on our northern border. In Syria, Syrians are being slaughtered by Syrians, blood of tens of thousands of men, women, young, old, children—blood flowed like water by their brethren. We will never be like them, never we will raise our hands on each other" (Netanyahu 2013g).

This idea of the need for national unity can lead to blind patriotism and intolerance of criticism of the state or the army's actions, especially during a war. This idea was dominant in the 1950s and 1960s. During those years, the Israeli political system was extremely centralist with one dominant ruling party (Mapai, Ben-Gurion's party), and media that was subject to security censorship. But at that time, a lack of criticism during a war was also caused by a common belief that "the whole nation forms a front" meaning that everyone should support the government during the fighting—even if they oppose the war (Barzilai 1996). For example, during the 1956 War, Begin—who headed the main opposition party at that time, which criticized the timing of the war—declared: "For the purpose of this operation, no distinction need be drawn between government and opposition" (p. 40).[2] In the early stages of the 1982 Lebanon War, Shimon Peres and Yitzhak Rabin (who then headed the main opposition party) expressed similar idea. Peres spoke about the importance of a "united front" and Rabin said that "when shells and Katyushas fall and when there is loss of life and property, we must stand as one, on the elected government's making its decision" (Barzilai 1996, 138). But as the Lebanon War continued, the Labor party publicly criticized it. Menachem Begin referred to national unity beliefs when he addressed this situation in a 1983 speech in the Knesset: "Today I call on all factions that are loyal to the State to stand together in this trial, as we have stood in other times, so as to attain conditions which will indeed enable our soldiers to return to their homes and families and stand behind them. I ask that the same measure of unity which existed at the start of the fighting should continue until we reach the yearned for peace" (Begin 1983). As the war continued, Rabin opposed the belief that everyone should support the government during the fighting—even if the government is wrong. In a speech in June 1984 in the Knesset, Rabin said: "We oppose the Lebanon War. . . . There is no similarity, no resemblance between the war objectives presented to us and what actually happened on Lebanese soil" (Rabin 1984). However, a few months after this speech, Labor and Likud established a national unity government and Rabin become minister of defense.

Intolerance to criticism of Israel's actions during a war or of the IDF has been expressed today mainly regarding Israeli human rights organizations that criticize the IDF such as the Israeli nongovernmental organization (NGO) Breaking the Silence, which gathers testimony from IDF troops about alleged human rights abuses by soldiers. Netanyahu reputedly attacked this NGO. He said in the Knesset that Breaking the Silence "ties the hands of the State of Israel from defending itself" (Ravid 2015b). In May 2017, Netanyahu canceled a planned meeting with German foreign minister Sigmar Gabriel because Gabriel refused to call off a meeting with Breaking the Silence. Currently, Netanyahu has pushed for new legislation that would allow for closure or banning of groups critical of the IDF such as Breaking the Silence (Ahren 2017; Keinon 2017; Times of Israel Staff 2017). Yair Lapid, Netanyahu major political opponent, has also criticized Breaking the Silence. In a press conference, alongside a group of reserve IDF officers and combat soldiers, he explained that "criticism is constructive for our society, but there is a significant difference between criticism and defaming IDF officers and soldiers abroad. That is not criticism; that is undermining the foundations of the state" (Harkov 2015).[3]

School Curricula

Patriotism, and especially the sacrifice dimension, has been a dominant part of Israeli school curricula. This is not surprising given the ongoing conflict and mandatory military service in the country (three years for men, two for women, and many additional years of reserve service). Thus, schools have tended to focus not only on producing law-abiding citizens and prepping students for higher education but also on preparing students for military conscription after high school.

The 1950s Until the Early 1970s

Article 2 of the 1953 State Education Act called for all Jewish education in Israel to be based on "love of the homeland and loyalty to the State of Israel and the Jewish People." These declared aims appeared in the intended curriculum for numerous subjects during the 1950s and 1960s. For example, one of the stated aims of the 1954 history curriculum for elementary schools was "to instill [in students] a love of the State of

Israel and the desire to act for it and safeguard it" (Podeh 2002, 32). Instilling love for the fatherland was also among the goals of the 1950s' elementary school Bible curriculum (Hofman, Alpert, and Schnell 2007, 317), and the 1954 elementary school science and agriculture curriculum that included encouraging love for the country and cultivation of its land (Hofman, Alpert, and Schnell 2007, 320). In addition, the Ministry of Education introduced a specific subject called Fatherland (Moledet) to be taught in elementary schools with the aim "to instill in the heart [of the children] the love of the fatherland and a desire to cultivate and guard it, to develop loyalty to the state and willingness to defend it with all their heart and soul" (Dror 2004, 142).

Analysis of textbooks from the 1950s and the 1960s has found their content to be aligned with these goals, explicitly in encouraging patriotism. Bar-Gal (1993) showed that geography textbooks from the 1950s and 1960s glorified the sacrifice of the first Zionist settlers, describing them as dedicated and brave people who cultivated the land and defended themselves against Arab aggression. Likewise, Firer (1985) found that history textbooks from 1948 to 1967 glorified the first Zionist settlers and their sacrifice. They were presented as a role model to the students, holding a gun in one hand and a plow in the other. Most history textbooks from this period marginalized any trend contradicting this description—such as the high rate of emigration from Israel among the first Zionist pioneers. Furthermore, the need to sacrifice for the country was taught not just by glorifying the early pioneers (who arrived between 1881 and 1923) but also by condemning the fourth wave of Zionist immigration to Israel (1924–1926) as selfishly choosing the comfort of life in the cities (Firer 1985, 148–149).

The same trends were found in readers from this period. These readers included many stories about Jewish heroes, from biblical times to the Zionist pioneers, who sacrificed their individual interest (and sometimes their lives) for collective and national goals (David 2012, 123–134). Sacrifice was emphasized mainly in the context of the Israeli-Arab conflict. A seminal text popular in readers of this time was the poem "The Silver Platter" by Nathan Alterman, which recalls the Mount Sinai epiphany. At the end of a war, the nation gathers together, and a young girl and a boy dressed in battle gear slowly approach the gathering. When the nation asks who they are, the two reply: "We are the silver platter / upon which was served to you the Jewish state" (Raizen 1995, 22). The poem can be interpreted in several ways, and some scholars have suggested that it actually criticized the idea of sacrificing young life in a war (Miron 1992). As presented to and understood by the students, though, it seemed to glorify their young self-sacrifice and confirm it as necessary for the country. Another poem popular in readers from this period was "My Country," by Rachel (David 2012, 186), which highlighted general love of country and the importance of even a modest contribution such as planting a tree or writing a poem. Readers from this period praised bereaved parents for their willingness to sacrifice their children. For example, in a poem from a 1954 reader for seventh grade, a bereaved father says that he was designed not for lamentation but only to keep fighting (p. 240). There likewise were many references to national unity in readers from the 1950s, 1960s, and 1970s. They often described Israeli society as composed of Jewish immigrants from many places who shared the same Zionist dream, and as "brothers" and "sons" mostly portraying national unity as a positive experience that encouraged positive actions and commitment to the society. A poem in a 1965 third grade reader illustrated this trend well: "For my brother—I will open my home / and I will tell him: Come my brother! / This is my home, I built it— / for me and you" (p. 102).

Patriotic themes and the belief in national unity not only dominated textbook content but also informal education and extracurricular activities. In the early 1950s, the director of the Ministry of Education instructed schools to display commemorative plaques with the names of graduates who fell as soldiers. The goal of this act was "planting in [the pupils'] hearts healthy seedlings of love, devotion, and unswerving readiness to serve their nation and fatherland" (Ben-Amos, Bet-El, and Tlamim 1999, 268). A brochure with potential models of such monuments was sent to schools after the 1967 War. Many schools adopted the idea, and it is common to find such a memorial to fallen graduates in Israeli schools even today. The Ministry of Education also proscribed, in detail, a school assembly for the Memorial Day for the fallen soldiers. It included holiday attire, lowering the flag to half-mast, two minutes of silence during the wailing siren sounded throughout the country, listening to the radio broadcast of the education minister's, and concluding the ceremony by singing the national anthem. Studies of these school assemblies have found that the format has changed little over the years. The assemblies start with the siren, end with the anthem, and are comprised of seminal texts (e.g., the Bible and canonic poetry) emphasizing heroism and self-sacrifice (Lomsky-Feder 2004, 294).

Informal education in schools also included premilitary training, which began in the prestate era under the framework of the youth regiment (Gadna in Hebrew). During the early years of the state, Israeli educators agreed that schools should provide military education, and it was suggested that students should visit army camps and soldiers should visit schools (Ichilov 2004). After 1952, the Ministry of Education established the Gadna supervision that offered premilitary training in schools and intensive training in four Gadna centers. High school students and their teachers spent five days in these centers in simulated military boot camp training (Dror 2007).[4]

The Mid-1970s to the Late 1990s

By mid-1970s, the intended curriculum in most subjects emphasized academic and scientific goals over national and patriotic ones (Hofman, Alpert, and Schnell 2007). Textbook references to patriotism decreased significantly compared to the 1950s and 1960s. In readers (David 2012) and history textbooks (Firer 1985), for example, the early pioneer as a role model was replaced by the soldier figure. David (2012, 175) further found that readers from the 1980s and the 1990s included segments expressing ambivalence toward the country and patriotic sacrifice, as in the poem "Song of the Land" (Shir Eretz) by Natan Yonatan, which appeared in eighth grade readers from the 1980s and 1990s. The poem opens with a Bible quote ("A land that devours its inhabitants"), includes words of love for the country ("a land of milk, honey and blue sky") alongside the understanding that a heavy price is paid for this love ("its lovers gave her all they could offer"), and ends with a recognition of the country's negative deeds (a country "which itself even plunders the sheep of the poor"). David (2012, 246) also found a changed attitude toward bereaved parents. Instead of describing them as brave people who submissively accepted their tragic fate, readers from the 1980s and 1990s focused on their pain and daily coping with the loss of a child, rather than the patriotic message of such a death.

David (2012) also found fewer references to national unity in the readers from the 1980s and 1990s. Further, they sometimes acknowledged polarization in the society and the difficulties of new immigrants to Israel. Discussions of national unity relied on less positive rationales. While earlier readers described the common fate of Jews by using encouraging terms and positive actions ("all the people of Israel are responsible for one another"), in the 1980s and 1990s they focused instead on common suffering and victimization, especially in the context of the Holocaust. Resnik (2003, 306) identified a similar trend,[5] finding that since the 1980s, the memory of the Holocaust was used "as another means, among others (religious folklore, for instance), to promote the unity of the Jewish people."

Some changes were also documented in the content of school Memorial Day ceremonies. While their basic format has remained the same, Ben-Amos and Bet-El (2003) identified in the 1990s a decreased use of patriotic and heroic poems like "The Silver Platter" and an increased use of segments referencing parents' grief without the national patriotic lesson. Lomsky-Feder (2004), who studied these Memorial Day ceremonies in fifty schools from 1994 to 2003, found the same trend. Patriotic texts were fading out (Alterman's "The Silver Platter" featured in only 17 percent of the surveyed ceremonies), and the trend moved away from "the ritual of the ethos of sacrifice toward a focus on personal pain" (p. 298). This happened through a focus on the pain of the bereaved families to the point that "it sometimes seems that the mourners, rather than the fallen, are the protagonists of the ceremony" (p. 299). Some speeches of bereaved parents went so far as to challenge the patriotism in the death of a soldier in service to the state, no longer seeing military death as a meaningful act. In the words of a bereaved father addressing students at one Jerusalem high school: "Not one inch of land is worth human life" (p. 300). However, Lomsky-Feder (p. 301) notes that "critical texts mingle with the more canonical ones," and "despite the strong impression left by the painful protest texts, the conformist messages that follow tone them down, softening and neutralizing the criticism." Another trend Lomsky-Feder (2004) identified in the 1990s ceremonies was a new focus first and foremost on the school, and not the nation. Consequently, the ceremony creates a mythology based on "local heroes," who are actually represented as victims of war and not as heroes at all. However, Lomsky-Feder (p. 304) maintains that focusing on the mourning of the fallen soldiers still contributed to a sense of national unity because "the participants identify with the universal aspects of human experience—grief and mourning—escaping points of conflict by ignoring ideological disputes." It should also be noted that the above changes were limited mainly to secular high schools in wealthier towns and neighborhoods in the center of Israel. Ceremonies in elementary schools and in high schools in the periphery of Israel continued to follow the patriotic format as it was established in the 1950s.

Indeed, this decrease in patriotic messages in the curricula should not be overstated. Patriotism messages and beliefs about national unity certainly remained in textbooks. Readers from the 1980s and 1990s still included segments on love of country and glorification of fallen soldiers, including the same seminal texts from older textbooks such as "My Country" and "The Silver Platter." In addition, readers from the 1980s began to criticize emigration from Israel. For example, in a 1985 reader for fourth and fifth grades, a father tells his daughter that Israel is the state of the Jews and they should settle only there and never leave (David 2012, 201). Textbooks for young children changed less than those for older children. For example, Furman (1999, 155–156) cites the following text from a reader that was in use in first grade class during the 1980s:

Who is a Hero?
    Ronen said: "when I grow up I will be a pilot. I will fly in a plane way up high. Only a pilot is a hero." Avner said: "and when I grow up I will be a sailor. I will be the captain of a huge ship; the ship will guard our country's shores. Only a sailor is a hero." Uri said: "and I will be a simple soldier. A simple soldier is also a hero. He guards the State of Israel day and night. Who is right?"

The workbook included the following questions about this text:

Fill in the blanks: Ronen wants to be a ____ Avner wants to be a ____
Uri wants to be a ____ [...] I am ___ years old. In another ___ years I will
be a soldier.

With its emphasis on safeguarding the country, the above text could easily have appeared in textbooks from the 1950s. Patriotism messages were
especially strong in kindergarten classes (or even in prekindergarten). A
few studies from the 1980s and 1990s found that young Israeli children
were exposed to strong patriotic content and that their socialization into
the need to serve in the army began before first grade (Furman 1999;
Handelman 2004). Consider the celebration of Independence Day in a Tel
Aviv kindergarten class during the 1980s, as documented by Furman
(1999, 156–157). Toy soldiers and model tanks were displayed, along
with books such as *Father in Reserves*. The class attended a ceremony
with thirteen other local kindergartens, conducted primarily by an air
force unit that raised the national flag and marched. During a discussion
following the event, the teacher told the children, "We will all guard our
homeland and be brave soldiers."

Importantly, since the mid-1970s patriotic beliefs have been transferred to the pupils mostly through extracurricular activities. Following the
change in curricula and the decrease in patriotic lessons in textbooks discussed above, the education system often was blamed for a perceived lack
of patriotism among Israeli youths and a lack of commitment to Zionist
values. For example, a 1976 Knesset committee appointed to investigate
an increased rate of emigration from Israel concluded that "the education
system failed in instilling Jewish Zionist consciousness and in educating
for love of the homeland" (quoted in Podeh 2002, 42). Thus, the Ministry
of Education created various extracurricular activities—seminars, field
trips, and so on—to strengthen Jewish and Zionist consciousness. They
added requirements to the high school curriculum including eleventh grade
seminars on Judaism and Zionism and twelfth grade preparation for serving in the army (Dror 2007).

The Period After 2000

A few studies of early childhood programs after 2000 found that kindergarten teachers were emphasizing patriotic messages as they had done in
earlier years. Eldan (2006), who interviewed forty teachers from different
secular and religious kindergartens in the period after 2000, found that
teachers conveyed the importance of sacrifice for the country. The subject
Fatherland is still taught in elementary schools, but it has been merged
with social studies and civic studies. The goals of this subject are defined
differently than initially set out in the 1950s. It now contains academic and

scientific goals from the fields of sociology and geography (including local patriotism such as "knowing our neighborhood and town") and strengthening of the values of democracy, tolerance, and coexistence, as well as patriotic goals. However, the latter aim seems to take precedence. The first goal for the subject Fatherland, Social Studies and Civics, appearing in bold as published by the Ministry of Education, is that the students "would be aware to the fact that the state of Israel is a Jewish and democratic state. Will acknowledge the fact that the state of Israel is the only state of the Jewish people. And this is where [the Jewish people] exercises its right to establish an independent state according to the values of Judaism and Zionism and the lesson from the Holocaust" (Ministry of Education 2002, 13). Another goal for the subject is "love of the country and caring for what happens in it." This goal includes that the students "will foster a sense of belonging and attachment to the state of Israel and the land of Israel—to its landscape, its sites, and its inhabitants—their culture and beliefs—and its past" (p. 13).

The website of the Ministry of Education also provides suggestions for Fatherland lessons and other extracurricular activities to achieve these patriotic goals. School field trips, organized by the Shelah Department,[6] are considered a central means to transmit these patriotism beliefs to students.[7] A variety of trips to combat sites (Moreshet Krav) are offered so that the students "would see themselves as partners in this important mission when they are drafted" (Ministry of Education, Society and Youth Administration 2007, 78). One such school trip is to a 1948 battleground in the south of Israel. Per a ministry booklet with detailed instructions for the trip (Ministry of Education, the Society and Youth Administration n.d-b), the students learn how control of the territory (several uninhabited hills) is important and worth sacrificing for.[8] National unity is illustrated in the joint effort of fighters who immigrated to Israel from different places. Reading segments emphasizing patriotic beliefs about the need to sacrifice one's own life for the homeland are suggested for a short ceremony memorializing the battle's fallen soldiers. These include Alterman's poem that praises the sacrifice of Holocaust survivors who fell during the 1948 War, just after arriving in Israel.

The Shelah master plan also encourages high schools to participate in a six-day journey for eleventh graders: the Israeli Journey. Of the specific aims set out by the plan, the following emphasize patriotism and national goals: "To clarify and strengthen individual, Jewish and Zionist identity and pride"; "Restoring and fortifying the belief in the righteousness of our cause, within the hearts and minds of tomorrow's Israeli soldiers"; and "Arriving at a clear and motivational answer to the questions 'Why do I choose to live here?' and 'What am I fighting for?'" (Ministry of Education, Society and Youth Administration n.d.-c).

Furthermore, the program's rationale is clearly defined in patriotic terms and national needs, and echoes earlier years' statements about lack of patriotism among Israeli youth. The program identifies "worrisome trends" such as over 1 million Israelis who "have abandoned Israel for safer lands and the dreams of riches in the West," a low level of motivation among army recruits, and ignorance and indifference to Jewish tradition among Israeli youth—a trend that "is undermining national Jewish solidarity and love of the land of Israel." Without strong connection to the core Zionist values among Israeli youth, the program warns that "there is a serious danger of many of our youth questioning the purpose of living in the country and fighting for it." The program, then, emphasizes the importance of the sacrifice dimension of patriotism and presents the other dimensions (e.g., pride and love of the country), as well as beliefs about the justness of Israel's cause in the conflict, as the main factors that can contribute to the desire of young Israelis to sacrifice their life for the country. This idea guides the last three days of the journey.[9] The fourth day is dedicated to "the bond between the Jewish people and the land of Israel." The students tour "the Judean plain and the hills surrounding Jerusalem" (e.g., the territories) and visit biblical sites that are linked to the history of the Jewish people—hence, to the historical-biblical claims of the Jews to the land. The fifth day focuses on other justifications for Jewish right to the land such as the lesson of the Holocaust. On that day, the students visit Yad Vashem and Mount Herzl in Jerusalem. The sixth and final day is dedicated to "exploring and reinforcing Jewish identity." Participants visit the Western Wall and celebrate the Sabbath in Jerusalem. The Israeli Journey, then, follows the path of other school field trips in using direct experience with the sites to strengthen beliefs about the right of the Jews to the land by emphasizing the bond to the land, the bond to Jewish heritage, and the need to sacrifice for them (see Chapter 2).

Another recent trend relevant to patriotism, especially the sacrifice dimension, is the intensification of premilitary preparation in high schools. In 1999, the Ministry of Education made preparation for military service part of the formal curricula of eleventh and twelfth grades (Y. Levy, Lomsky-Feder, and Harel 2007). This was a reaction to what was considered to be a "motivation crisis." Although army service is mandatory for Israeli eighteen-year-olds, a slow decline in the readiness for combat units was already noted during the 1990s. Additionally, the number of graduates of elite secular schools who dropped out before or during their service for mental health reasons significantly increased. Against this background, the role of the Ministry of Education was redefined to encourage "meaningful service" in the army (Ministry of Education n.d.-c).

A 2007 circular issued by the director-general of the Education Ministry declared that it was the responsibility of the education system to prepare Israeli youth for army service (Ministry of Education 2007). It announced the establishment of "centers of preparation for meaningful service in the IDF" in local communities throughout Israel. These centers aimed to create "a supportive climate for meaningful army service" among parents, institutions and organizations in the community." The circular was followed by a document titled "Willingness and Readiness for IDF Service—A Collection of Programs, Issues and Activities" (Ministry of Education, Society and Youth Administration 2007), which provides one of the most comprehensive premilitary programs of the Ministry of Education. It targets not just the students but also significant figures in the students' environment, such as teachers, parents, and instructors in youth movements, and offers a variety of programs for during and after school hours. According to this document (p. 58), an IDF representative was to meet with each school principal to inform the principal about the rate of individuals that served in the army, and did not drop out for mental health or other reasons, among the school's graduates. The premilitary program for each school was to be adjusted according to this data. For example, "in schools with a low rate of draftees, the program would focus on increasing motivation to enlist. In schools with a high rate of draftees but with low rate of graduates who volunteer for command courses, the school pre-military program should address leadership."[10]

The document includes plans to strengthen teachers' willingness to deal with issues related to meaningful service in the army. It also includes a proposal for a parents' seminar to be run by the school.[11] Three kinds of activities are offered to the students. The first provides information about military service and the recruiting process through activities such as an IDF representative visiting the school. The second type, which includes activities like the five-day Gadna camp, lets students experience and prepare for army life. During this camp, for example, students and their teachers live as they would in a military boot camp, with a structured daily routine and military activities such as field subsistence, trekking, and shooting practice. The students are told that the IDF uniforms they wear "are real uniforms, uniforms that are worn by soldiers who fight or even die in them" (Paz 2008). It is important to note, however, that the Gadna camp is optional. The principal must approve the school's participation in this program and not all principals do so.[12]

The third activities are moral lessons meant to convince students that army service is "a right, not just obligation." These activities occur mainly during weekly homeroom lessons, and the 2007 document provides many moral lesson plans from which teachers may choose. The lesson "From Duty to Commitment" is representative of the spirit behind many of these lessons. In it, the students are presented with numerous statements about army service, are asked to choose the statement with which they most identify, and to sort the statements into three types of motivation to serve: personal, national-social, and mixed. According to the lesson plan, statements that involve "personal motives" include two positive statements in which combat unit service represents a test of one's abilities and builds character (by transforming the student from a spoiled and privileged child into a responsible adult). In another positive statement, a soldier notes that he chose his particular combat unit for its interesting activities, the high caliber of the other soldiers, and the unit's prestigious reputation. But there also are two negative statements about personal motives for army service: one statement rejects the idea that combat service should be valued as a test of one's abilities since there are other means to that goal; in the other, a soldier says he served only so as not to be considered "a parasite."

However, most of the statements in this lesson (10 statements) are categorized as "national." They include several positive patriotic statements ("I care about the state and want to contribute to it"), as well as negative ones ("What if there is a war?" and the guilt of not participating). Another statement refers to siege beliefs and anti-Semitism as the main motivation to serve in a combat unit:

> When I lived abroad, five youths dressed in black with a swastika appeared in the school and began to write Graffiti on the wall and threaten people. I was the only one who got out and started beating them. I was beaten but I survived. This episode left a deep impression on me. After that, I knew I am Jewish, and there was no doubt in my mind that I will come back to Israel to enlist in the IDF—to give something back to my country.

Another four statements are categorized as "mixed" motivations. One example is the following: "I think that we grow up with guilt feelings, because people who live before us paid with their life for [the existence of] the state. Now it is our turn. But the most meaningful motive is [one's] reputation in the society. The wish to act according to the accepted norms in the [Israeli] society. Serving in a combat unit is a natural thing for me. Everyone should have this experience." Note that several of the statements condemn those who do not choose combat service—these individuals are described as parasites, quitters, ungrateful, and unpatriotic. The lesson acknowledges that some students choose army service for mainly personal reasons and states, accordingly, that one of its goals is to help students "distinguish between personal motives and national-social motives and explore the possibility to combine both types of motives." However, the lesson's primary goal is a patriotic one: to "enhance the student's realization of their right and duty to protect the security of the state."

In sum, the education system in the period after 2000 clearly has remained committed to instilling patriotic beliefs in the hearts and minds of Israeli students, albeit in a different format than in earlier years. Instead of relying on textbook content, informal and extracurricular activities— field trips, the Israeli Journey program, and the school-based premilitary preparation plan—have aimed to address a perceived weakening of patriotic spirit by encouraging a willingness to sacrifice in Israeli youth.

The Public

The Level of Patriotism

Analysis of the level of patriotism among the public should be preceded by a discussion of the major issues associated with Israeli patriotism because, as I noted at the beginning of this chapter, patriotic attachment could be linked to different objects, such as a nation, a land, or a specific ideology. Attachment that focuses mostly on the land may allow patriotism to be shared by all groups that live in the country. Leaders' rhetoric and school curricula indicated attachment to the Jewish people and the Jewish heritage in the land of Israel. Thus, it excluded non-Jewish native residents of the land (e.g., Arabs) from Israeli patriotism. Questions about this topic were asked only during the 2000s. According to an Interdisciplinary Center (IDC) survey on patriotism during the years 2005–2009, the themes most associated with Israeli patriotism were "love of the land/country" (in 2007, 95 percent of the Jewish Israeli public said that this theme was a very important value related to patriotism), "the Hebrew language" (95 percent in 2007), and "Jerusalem" (95 percent in 2007). Surprisingly, "the ingathering of the exiles" and "Zionism" received moderate rankings (88 percent and 83 percent, respectively) (Ya'ar and Lipsky 2008). According to this survey, then, Israeli patriotism was related to both territory (the land of Israel, Jerusalem) and Jewish heritage (the Hebrew language).

As for the level of patriotism attachment, the IDC survey on patriotism from 2005 to 2009 asked respondents about the extent to which they saw themselves as Israeli patriots. In 2009, 71 percent of the respondents defined themselves as Israeli patriots (Ya'ar and Geva 2009). This was similar to levels in the United States: 74 percent of US citizens declared themselves "extremely patriotic" or "very patriotic" in a 2010 Gallup survey (Morales 2010). However, it should be noted that the term *patriot* has been ascribed a negative meaning, especially among dovish respondents. Among this group, patriotism has largely been associated with nationalistic and hawkish attitudes (Ya'ar and Lipsky 2008). These respondents therefore may have underreported their level of patriotism, and the level of patriotic attachment could well be much higher. Indeed, when asked directly how emotionally connected to Israel they felt, Israeli Jews ranked first among the thirty-seven countries that participated in the 2013 ISSP (see Table 6.1). Israeli Jews, then, were patriotic in terms of a strong emotional attachment to the country, but they did not necessarily recognize this feeling as patriotism.

Table 6.1   Emotional Attachment to the Country, 2013

State/Region	Very Emotionally Attached (%)	State/Region	Very Emotionally Attached (%)
Israel—Jews	75.8	United States	43.5
India	66.4	Mexico	40.9
Georgia	63.1	Sweden	40.8
Japan	61.6	Portugal	40.3
France	58.7	Israel—Arabs	40.1
Turkey	54.7	Philippines	38.7
Denmark	53.6	Taiwan	38.4
Norway	53.3	Croatia	37.7
Spain	48.8	South Africa	36.3
Iceland	48.7	Slovenia	36.1
Estonia	48.4	Ireland	35.4
Hungary	48.4	Germany—West	33.2
Finland	47.1	Latvia	32.8
Switzerland	46.0	Slovak Republic	31.7
South Korea	45.6	Germany—East	25.9
Belgium—Wallonia	44.8	Russia	24.3
Czech Republic	44.5	Great Britain	23.2
Belgium—Brussels	44.3	Lithuania	20.5
		Belgium—Flanders	11.7

Source: ISSP Research Group (2015).

Pride

The pride dimension of patriotism has been assessed in several international studies. In the 2001 WVS poll, 61 percent of Israeli Jewish[13] respondents noted that they were "very proud" to be Israelis (29 percent were "quite proud"). This placed Israel thirty-eighth (between Argentina and Spain) among the fifty-one nations surveyed. Therefore, surprisingly, and in contrast to the high level of pride in leaders' rhetoric and school curricula, public polls did not indicate a relatively high level of pride by Israeli Jews in their own nationality. Furthermore, in most Arab and Muslim countries, the proportion of respondents who were very proud of their nationality was higher; including in Egypt (82 percent were very proud to be Egyptians), Iran (90 percent), Iraq (77 percent), and Jordan (66 percent). The percentage of respondents who were very proud of their nationality was also higher in the United States (71 percent). A similar question was asked in the 2013 ISSP (see Table 6.2) and found that 59 percent of Israeli Jewish respondents were very proud to be Israeli—eighth among the thirty-seven countries surveyed. Unfortunately, this question was not asked frequently before 2001, so I could not assess change over time.[14] In the period after 2000, the question was asked annually as part of the Democracy Index and the IDC survey on patriotism (from 2003 to 2014). These surveys indicated that the rate of

Table 6.2   Pride in Nationality, 2013

State/Region	Very Proud (%)	State/Region	Very Proud (%)
Philippines	87.5	Great Britain	40.9
Georgia	78.0	Finland	38.8
India	78.0	South Korea	37.2
South Africa	70.3	Sweden	36.1
United States	70.1	Estonia	34.8
Turkey	69.1	Latvia	34.0
Ireland	59.4	Slovak Republic	32.9
Israel—Jews	58.8	France	32.8
Slovenia	50.2	Belgium—Brussels	31.2
Spain	49.8	Denmark	30.5
Mexico	49.4	Israel—Arabs	30.5
Iceland	47.4	Russia	30.0
Switzerland	47.3	Hungary	27.1
Croatia	46.3	Belgium—Flanders	25.4
Taiwan	45.4	Lithuania	25.2
Norway	45.0	Belgium—Wallonia	24.5
Japan	44.5	Czech Republic	19.8
Portugal	43.0	Germany—East	18.4
		Germany—West	17.0

Source: ISSP Research Group (2015).

respondents who were very proud to be Israeli was quite stable from 2003 until 2012—around 60 percent—with some mild increases in later years.[15]

The picture becomes more complex when addressing the specific sources of national pride. The 2013 ISSP survey asked the respondents how proud they were of their country's democracy, political influence in the world, economic achievement, social security system, technology, achievements in arts or literature, armed forces, and history (see Table 6.3). According to this survey, Israeli Jews expressed relatively low pride in Israel's democracy, international political influence, and social security system, in contrast with the rhetoric of leaders such as Netanyahu, who expressed great pride in Israel's democracy. However, Israeli Jews expressed higher pride in Israel's technology, army, and history. In these areas, Israel Jews ranked from third to fifth places among the other countries that participated in the survey (yet less than 60 percent expressed pride in each of these aspects of Israel).[16]

Rootedness

As discussed above, leaders' rhetoric and school textbooks over the years displayed the patriotic trait of rootedness and the belief that one should stay in their homeland because "he has no other country." A question about the

**Table 6.3 Pride in Specific Features of the Country Among
Israeli Jews, 2013**

	Very Proud (%)	Rank
Democracy of the country	15	15
Political influence in the world	11	12
Economic achievement	26	7
Social safety net	7	24
Arts or literature	27	19
Technology	55	3
Armed forces	53	4
History	54	5

Source: ISSP Research Group (2015).
Note: Rank is out of thirty-seven countries surveyed.

desire to stay in Israel was asked annually from 1967 to 2012 by several institutions, and most respondents (usually more than 60 percent) reported wanting to remain in Israel. This question was asked in a Guttman survey during the years 1967–1991 and it showed a downward trend at that period, while a similar question in the NSPOP survey during the years 1987–2004 and a question in Democracy Index surveys during the years 2003–2011 indicated milder downward trends in later years (see Figure 6.1). An IDC survey asked whether respondents would encourage their children to live in Israel: while the proportion of Jewish respondents from 2006 to 2009 who would encourage their children to stay in Israel was stable at around 80 percent, the rate of respondents who would strongly encourage their children to stay in Israel dropped from 69 percent in 2006 to 55 percent in 2009 (Ya'ar and Geva 2009).

How does the Israeli rate of respondents who want to emigrate from the country compare to other countries? The 2007 Gallup World Poll, conducted in 130 countries including Israel, looked at three categories: countries where there was a high desire to migrate (40–60 percent indicated a desire to leave), a moderate desire to migrate (20–39 percent), and low desire to migrate (1–19 percent) (Torres 2007). In 2007, 20 percent of Israelis expressed a desire to emigrate, placing them at the lowest end of the moderate category. Israel, then, did not stand out as a country with an exceptionally high or low rate of respondents interested in leaving the country.

As discussed earlier, Israelis who emigrated from Israel were at times condemned by politicians as traitors and unpatriotic. Unfortunately, only a few public polls addressed this issue. They indicated that few respondents agreed with that characterization. In a December 1986 poll, 57 percent of respondents agreed with the statement, "Emigrants are *not* traitors to their country" (Damian 1987; Friedberg and Kfir 2008, emphasis added). In

Figure 6.1   **Desire to Remain in Israel for the Long Term, 1973–2012 (percentage certain that they want to remain in Israel for the long term)**

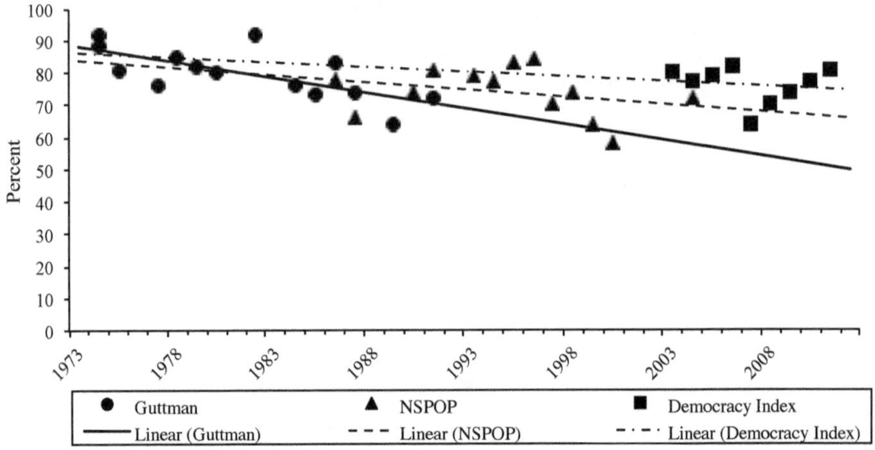

Sources: Guttman, NSPOP, and Democracy Index.

another survey, the percentage of respondents who felt that those who emi-grate from Israel were doing something wrong dropped from 70 percent in 1983 to 55 percent in 1986 (Zemach 1987, 25).[17] In late 2004, a Mina Zemach poll reported that 67 percent of Israeli respondents said that the choice to relocate abroad was acceptable (Ashley Sharon 2004).

Sacrifice for the Country

The dimension of sacrifice for the country was strong in leaders' rhetoric and school curricula and perceived as vital for a country involved in intractable conflict. As can be expected from a country with conscription, Israeli Jews had the highest percentage (in the 2004 ISSP survey) of respondents reporting that it was very important to serve in the army to be considered a good citizen (67 percent). Venezuela was in second place with 52 percent of respondents agreeing, and there were much lower rates in Russia and in the United States (47 percent and 44 percent, respectively). Some Israeli publications presented this finding as an indication of Israelis' exceptional willingness to sacrifice for their country (Arian, Atmor, and Hadar 2007). However, in international surveys asking directly about respondents' willingness to fight for their country in wartime, Israeli Jews' willingness was high, but not the highest.

In a 2001 WVS poll, Israel Jews ranked third in the percentage of respondents willing to fight for their country, with 89 percent willing to do so (Table 6.4). Unfortunately, no one survey included both Israel and most of its neighboring states and enemies, but the 2005–2009 WVS collected data from additional countries that did not participate in the 2001 survey. To an identical question in the 2007 Democracy Index, 79 percent of respondents said that they would fight for the country if war broke out. This ranked Israeli Jews sixteenth in the 2005–2009 WVS—between Malaysia and Mali. That was higher than the rate in the United States, Russia, many European countries (Poland, Hungary, France, and the United Kingdom), and Iran. But this rate was also lower than in Turkey, Vietnam, Taiwan, and China, Western European countries such as Finland and Sweden, and Arab countries such as Jordan and Egypt. In a 2014 Gallup year-end survey, Israel ranked in eighteenth place (like Lebanon) among sixty-three countries in the percentage of respondents who indicated that they would fight for their country (note that this figure comprised all Israeli citizens, including 25 percent of non-Jewish respondents). As in previous international surveys, other countries (e.g., India, Pakistan, China, Turkey, and Philippines) demonstrated a much higher percentage of respondents who would fight for the country, although not all (Israelis were more willing than in Ukraine, Russia, the United States, and South Korea). Importantly, even when the Israeli Arab population was included in the survey, the rate of respondents willing to fight for the country was higher in Israel than among the Palestinians in the territories.[18]

Table 6.4   Willingness to Fight for the Country, 2001–2004

State	%	State	%
Vietnam	94.0	Moldova	67.4
China	89.9	Puerto Rico	66.7
Israel—Jews	89.18	United States	64.8
Morocco	88.0	Bosnia and Herzegovina	61.1
Tanzania	86.9	Canada	60.1
Bangladesh	85.5	South Africa	58.3
Kyrgyzstan	85.2	Argentina	55.1
Philippines	83.5	Serbia	55.0
Singapore	77.5	Albania	54.6
Peru	76.5	Chile	54.4
Venezuela	76.3	Uganda	52.4
South Korea	74.4	Montenegro	47.6
India	73.7	Spain	37.3
Macedonia	71.8	Iraq	35.2
Mexico	67.4	Japan	15.6

Source: Inglehart et al. (2014).

As shown above, the percentage of Israeli Jewish respondents who were willing to fight for the country dropped from 89 percent in 2001 to 79 percent in 2007. An indication of changes over time in the willingness to sacrifice one's own life for the country was also found in a NSPOP survey that examined the agreement of respondents with the well-known Israeli phrase "it is good to die for our country."[19] Around 70 percent of respondents agreed with this phrase from 1987 to 1992, but that level declined to 62 percent in 1994 and again to 51 percent in my 2016 survey. The results, then, were consistent with the politicians' and educators' assessment that Israeli Jews' willingness to sacrifice their life for their country had declined over the years.

Another indication of the decline over time in beliefs about the need to sacrifice for the country can be seen in a question in Guttman surveys during 1967–1991. Respondents were asked if they agreed that "people in Israel should now be asked to be ready to make many concessions and lower their standard of living (buy less, pay more taxes, etc.) in sacrifice for the state" (see Figure 6.2). The percentage of respondents who agreed dropped from 79 percent in 1984 to around 50 percent during the period 1987–1991. When the identical question was asked from 2007 to 2010, the rate declined sharply to around only 30 percent. In sum, while the rate of Israeli Jews willing to fight for the country was above 60 percent and relatively high compared to other countries, there was some evidence of a decrease over time in respondents' willingness to sacrifice for their state.

Figure 6.2   Willingness to Make Personal Sacrifices for the Nation, 1967–2010

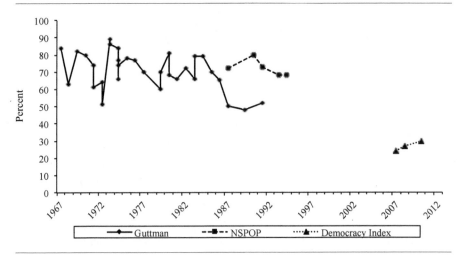

Sources: Guttman, NSPOP, and Democracy Index.

National Unity

From the 1950s to the 1980s, leaders' rhetoric and school curricula tended to minimize the magnitude and significance of tensions within the Israeli society, although a decline in this trend appeared in later years. Yet leaders and school textbooks emphasized the importance of national unity in times of war. In most years, Guttman polls that asked respondents to evaluate the relationship among various groups in the Israeli society indicated that most respondents thought the relationship between Mizrahim and Ashkenazim[20] and between new immigrants and "old timers" were good, but only a minority of the respondents thought that the relationship between religious and secular Jews was good—a tension mostly ignored in official texts (Oren 2005). More recently, a 2016 Democracy Index survey indicated that respondents perceived the tensions between religious and secular Jews, between rich and poor, and between the political right and left to be high (50 percent, 56 percent, 67 percent, respectively). However, when asked in a Democracy Index survey to evaluate the solidarity of Israel's Jewish society, most respondents (64 percent in 2011 and 68 percent in 2014) described solidarity in Jewish society as moderate or moderately high.

Of course, the perception of social solidarity within the Israeli society and its change over time has been influenced by many events and trends, not all related to the Israeli-Arab conflict. However, a sharp increase in positive assessment of relationships within society was observed during the 1967 War, the 1973 War, and the 1982 Lebanon War, possibly indicating a tendency to "rally around the flag" during wars. This has been documented in the United States during events such as World War II and the terror attacks of September 11 (Mueller 1973; Norris, Kern, and Just 2003; Zaller 1992). This aligned with findings from a NSPOP survey during the years 1986–1996 and my 2016 survey where the vast majority of respondents (more than 70 percent) thought that one must support the government in times of crisis, such as war, even if one differed with the government's policies (see Table 6.5). In addition, 37 percent of the respondents in the NSPOP 1986 survey said that criticism of the government should not be permitted under circumstances of war; 54 percent said that only subdued and restrained manner of criticism should be allowed; and 9 percent said that even vocal and strenuous opposition should be permitted. The public tended, then, to agree with a soft version of blind patriotism in time of war—that people should support the government even if they do not agree with it and that criticism of government should be limited. A harsher version of this belief (that forbids any kind of criticism) was supported by more than a third of the public in 1986; and in the November 2016 Peace Index, 55 percent of the Jewish respondents agreed that criticizing policy in times of security tension was illegitimate. Furthermore, in an international comparison, Israel had a relatively high percentage of respondents who thought that people should support their country even if it was wrong—similar to that found in Russia, but much higher than in the United States (see Table 6.6). Only Turkey and India had a higher percentage of respondents who agreed with this statement.

Table 6.5   Necessity of Supporting Government in Time of War, 1986–2016

	1986	1987	1988	1993	1996	2016
Percentage who think people should support the government in time of war	88	89	82	84	90	86

Sources: NSPOP and Oren's 2016 Survey.

Table 6.6   Blind Patriotism, 2013

State/Region	Strongly Agree that People Should Support Country Even if Wrong (%)	State/Region	Strongly Agree that People Should Support Country Even if Wrong (%)
India	35.3	Belgium—Wallonia	7.6
Turkey	32.5	United States	7.5
Israel—Jews	23.6	Belgium—Flanders	7.4
Russia	23.2	Iceland	7.4
South Korea	22.4	Slovenia	7.2
Georgia	19.0	Japan	6.9
South Africa	17.5	Switzerland	6.6
Estonia	15.2	Great Britain	5.4
Czech Republic	13.5	Portugal	5.3
Hungary	12.6	Germany—East	5.3
Belgium—Brussels	12.5	Latvia	5.3
Philippines	12.2	Germany—West	5.1
Denmark	11.2	Finland	4.3
Spain	11.2	Ireland	4.2
Croatia	11.1	Lithuania	3.6
France	10.3	Israel—Arabs	2.9
Slovak Republic	10.2	Norway	2.9
Mexico	9.1	Sweden	2.9
		Taiwan	2.7

Source: ISSP Research Group (2015).

Conclusion

Patriotism—a sense of belonging, love for, pride in, and concern for the well-being of one's society, as well as a willingness to sacrifice for it—is often a component of the ethos of societies in many different contexts. According to Bar-Tal (2013), a patriotism theme is especially common in the ethos of societies engaged in intractable conflicts and, as I demonstrated in this chapter, it features prominently in the Israeli ethos as well. Several key features of Israeli patriotism are worth mentioning. The first concerns the object of Israeli patriotism attachment. Eilam (2004) argues that Israeli patriotism prioritizes attachment to the Jewish nation over attachment to the land. My review of official texts and public polls, however, indicated that the attachment was to both territory (the land of Israel, Jerusalem) and Jewish heritage. Nonetheless, it still excluded non-Jewish native residents of the land (e.g., Arabs) from Israeli patriotism, as Eilam (2004) points' out.

Second, while more than 60 percent of the public agreed with some aspects of the three dimensions of patriotism (pride, rootedness, sacrifice), the public did not always reflect the same intensity of patriotism as found in leaders' rhetoric and school curricula. For example, while Israeli leaders expressed significant pride in Israel's heritage, democracy, economy, and technology, public polls revealed that Israeli Jews shared the pride for heritage and technology, but less so for Israeli democracy. Another gap between public sentiment and official texts relates to the rootedness dimension of patriotism—the belief that one should stay in his or her homeland "come what may." This belief appeared in leaders' rhetoric and school textbooks over the years (although less frequently than other dimensions of patriotism). However, public polls showed that while more than 60 percent of the respondents had no plans to ever emigrate from Israel (a rate that was not exceptionally high compared to other countries), unlike their leaders they did not tend to condemn those who did choose to emigrate.

Third, the willingness to sacrifice was the most common dimension of the patriotism expressed in leaders' rhetoric and school curricula. And when the prominence of the sacrifice dimension declined in school textbooks during the 1980s and 1990s, accompanied by a perceived weakening of patriotic spirit among young people, it was followed in the period after 2000 by a renewed focus on patriotism education, especially its sacrifice dimension, through school extracurricular activities. Public polls indeed supported this perception of a decline in the willingness to fight and make other personal sacrifices (e.g., higher taxes) for the country (albeit at 79 percent, Israeli Jews still ranked high compared to other countries in terms of willingness to fight for their country). This trend of decline was also evident in data about the proportion of draftees volunteering to serve in combat units: 69.8 percent of those drafted in November 2016 expressed interest in serving in combat units—a decline from 79 percent in November 2010. In addition, 26.3 percent of draft-age men and 43 percent of women in 2013 received exemptions from army service because of health or religious reasons (G. Cohen 2013; Harel 2017). This was a significant increase compared to the past: in 1980 only 12 percent of draft-age men received exemptions, and in 1990 16.6 percent (Barda 2007).[21] In June 2018, the IDF ombudsman wrote in his annual report that "the army is facing a serious crisis due to its inability to retain high-quality officers" (Kubovich 2018).

Declines in the sacrifice dimension over time can be attributed to several factors. Demographic shifts between different segments in Israeli society, as well as cultural shifts within some of these segments, provide some explanations. The ultra-Orthodox Jews, one of the groups exhibiting the lowest willingness to sacrifice among poll respondents,[22] refuse to serve in the IDF and are excused from service by law if they are full-time students at a recognized yeshiva. Thus, their constantly increasing share of the population will tend to depress the overall willingness to sacrifice numbers. Among secular Israeli Jews, a decline in willingness to sacrifice can be explained mostly by cultural shifts that have taken place since the late 1970s: idealism has given way to pragmatism, and worldwide trends elevating materialism, consumerism, individualism, and neoliberalism have influenced this segment of the population more so than others (Shafir and Peled 2002; First and Avraham 2007; Rebhun and Waxman 2000; Azaryahu 2000). In this context, army service is perceived in terms of self-fulfillment, and army draftees are treated as "clients" that need to be persuaded to serve in combat units. Among secular middle-class (mostly Ashkenazi) draftees, the willingness to serve in combat units decreased because such service became less relevant to acquiring the professional skills useful in the modern economy. On the other hand, ethnonational discourse offered the (mostly lower-class) Mizrahi Jews a meaningful sense of belonging as equal partners in Israeli society without making their membership conditional on contribution to the state through military sacrifice (Y. Levy 2012). Furthermore, given Israel's overwhelming military and technological superiority over its current main rivals (Hezbollah and the Palestinians), especially when it comes to air power, the expectation arose among the Israeli public that a war would be casualty free for the Israeli side (Finkel 2007), and that therefore sacrificing one's life in a military conflict was no longer necessary.

It is in this context that the change in the discourse surrounding bereavement should be viewed. As I noted above, in the 1980s and 1990s, leaders referred to fallen IDF soldiers as "our children" and school curricula described them mostly as victims, focusing on the mourning process rather than the patriotic meaning of such deaths. While this tendency contributed to national unity and the perception of Israel as one family, it also depicted soldiers not as responsible adults defending their homeland but rather as children in need of their parents' protection. The context of the child-centered culture in Israel may diminish Israelis' willingness to risk their lives or those of their children for the country and, thus, lead to a lower public tolerance for military casualties during war (on this trend in armies of Western countries, see H. Smith 2005). Indeed, in a 2017 speech, IDF chief of staff Gadi Eisenkot criticized this tendency to refer to an IDF soldier as a "confused little kid." Eisenkot argued that "an 18-year-old who enlists in the IDF isn't everyone's child, he isn't a baby who was taken prisoner. *He is a fighter, he is a soldier, he is called upon to put his life on the line*" (G. Cohen 2017, emphasis added).

The decline in the sacrifice dimension during the 1990s can also be explained by the weakening of other themes in the ethos at that time—security, villa in the jungle, and siege. Israel is a highly heterogeneous and sectarian society with myriad religious and ethnic tensions (much of the discord is within the Jewish society). Patriotism, and particularly its sacrifice dimension, is rooted in a shared attachment of all (Israeli Jewish) society segments to the Israeli ethos that I describe in this book. As I argue in the final chapter, taken as a whole, the message of the ethos to Israelis is that living by the sword is the only choice they have. Thus, the weakening of the ethos during the 1990s diminished the rationale and motivation to sacrifice one's own life for the country. In turn, concern by leaders as to the level of motivation for sacrifice among the population could have driven them to pursue peace agreements. Indeed, Rabin admitted that, when he sought to promote the Oslo agreements, he was influenced partly by reservists' attitudes toward army service and his concern that many would refuse to be called into active duty in a war over the territories (Peri 1999, 394).

In the period after 2000, with the resurgence of some themes in the ethos such as the villa in the jungle, security, and siege (a trend that may legitimize the use of force against the enemy), the preferred strategy to deal with lower public tolerance for military casualties shifted from pursuing peace to the use of overwhelming military force to reduce the risk to Israeli troops, often at the expense of increased civilian casualties on the enemy side. Y. Levy (2012) showed that the increase in the ratio of fatalities for Israeli soldiers and Palestinian civilians in Gaza (from one Israeli soldier to six Palestinian civilians in the first intifada to one to eighty-four in the 2009 Gaza War) was a result of a new military doctrine that prioritized protection of soldiers' lives over the obligation to avoid injuries to uninvolved civilians on the enemy side. At first, it included aerial bombardment and artillery attacks against any site from which rockets were fired on Israel, with the goal of eliminating the need for clearing out the launchers through a costly ground operation. Other means that were used to reduce soldiers' exposure to risk after a ground operation began included overwhelming aerial and artillery strikes prior to deployment of IDF forces to Gaza, use of Palestinian civilians as human shields to protect IDF soldiers, and returning fire toward the source of hostile fire even if civilians were known to be nearby (see also Oren 2012).[23] In a survey conducted in January 2009, more than 80 percent of respondents thought that the IDF had not used too much firepower during the 2009 Gaza War (Ben Meir 2009). The decline in the sacrifice dimension of patriotism, then, can both escalate and de-escalate the conflict, depending on the context of the other themes in the ethos.

Finally, despite the differences between the Israeli public and its leaders regarding the perception of the actual level of national unity in Israel, they have shared a strong belief in the need to preserve national unity in time of war and, relative to other states, the people have exhibited a high level of blind patriotism. Again, this tendency should be understood mainly in the context of other themes in the ethos. The demand to refrain from criticism has been justified in terms of the existential threat to Israel, as well as the concern that the enemy and the hostile international community will use such criticism against Israel.

Notes

1. The fourth dimension is the dimension of symbolism—for example, how important it is to fly the national flag on Independence Day.

2. Another party—Mapam—that had even stronger criticism of the 1956 War also decided to publicly support it, declaring that "once the decision was taken to launch the Suez Campaign, there emerged a situation calling for the people to unite in order to stand fast in battle" (Barzilai 1996, 43).

3. In response to Lapid, Knesset member Zehava Gal-On said that the soldiers who testified to Breaking the Silence were "patriots," and "true lovers of Israel," and that she was very proud of them (Harkov 2015).

4. Mandatory involvement of the army in schools is not unique to Israel. It existed, for example, in 1999 in Venezuela when President Hugo Chávez ordered that all school children receive military training, and in Taiwan in the 1980s when military officers provided two hours per week of military training in every senior school (Davies 2003; Harber 2004).

5. She studied Bible, history, literature, and civics curricula; teacher's guides for high school final examinations in Bible, history, civics, and literature; and circulars issued by the director-general of the Ministry of Education.

6. Shelah is the acronym of the Hebrew words for field/land, nation, and society.

7. This view is clearly formulated in the vision of this department as it appears on its website. Besides some account of democracy and personal self-fulfillment displayed in the section about the vision of the department, most of the vision of the Shelah Department stresses patriotism: the first goal is to instill love for the homeland and to strengthen Jewish Zionist identity in the education system from first grade to twelfth grade. The vision of the department also includes the goal of

strengthening the attachment of the students to the State of Israel and their sense of belonging to it (Ministry of Education Society and Youth Administration n.d.-a).

8. The teachers were instructed to tell the students that prior to the combat, the UN Security Council mediator in the Israeli-Arab 1948 War (Folke Bernadotte) submitted a proposal that suggested the inclusion of the Negev (a desert region in the south of Israel) in the Arab territory and that this proposal was influenced by the fact that the Egyptian army controlled some territories in this region. According to the booklet, the triumph of Israeli forces in this battle is the reason that the Negev is now part of the State of Israel.

9. The first and second days of the journey are in a remote wilderness region of Israel and include activities such as camping and team development. On the third day of the journey, the students are involved in volunteer work with charitable organizations in towns located at the periphery of Israel.

10. The percentage of a school's students who performed military or civilian national service was one of the criteria—together with other criteria such as matriculation results, dropout rates, and absorption of special education students—introduced by the Ministry of Education in a new differential incentive system to schools and teachers (Vered 2015). Also, in recent years, retired officers have been seen as the most appropriate choice for school leadership (Dahan-Kalev 2005).

11. These seminars aimed to enable parents to express their feelings regarding the drafting of their children so they could support their children in the best way during the enlisting process and army service.

12. On average, 19,000 high school students per year participated in the Gadna camp. This figure represented about a quarter of Israeli eleventh graders designated for mandatory military service (Paz 2008).

13. The survey was conducted among a sample of Israeli adult population, including Arabs. I calculated and displayed the finding for only the Jewish respondents.

14. In a 1986 survey, 82 percent of Israeli Jews definitely agreed with the statement "I am proud to be an Israeli" (Damian 1987).

15. The National Security Studies Center in Haifa University also studied the patriotic pride among Israeli Jews during the years 2000–2010. They used a different method. Respondents were asked to rate from 1 to 6 their acceptance of four phrases ("I love Israel and I am proud of Israel"; "When Israel is condemned abroad, I feel irritated about it"; "I am annoyed when the Israeli flag is being burned"; and "Israel has a just case in its disputes with other countries"). This survey also revealed relative stability in the level of patriotic pride during these years. The average score ranged from 4.8 to 5.1 (Lewin 2011).

16. This question was asked also in IDC surveys during the years 2006–2008. The findings of these surveys also showed that Israelis were mostly proud of Israel's technology and army, and the ranking had not changed much during those three years (Ya'ar and Lipsky 2008, 35).

17. The difference between the two findings may be attributed in part to the different wording of the questions. In 1983, the statement was, "Israelis who emigrate and settle in other countries are doing something wrong." In 1986, the statement was, "Israelis who leave Israel to live in other countries are doing something wrong." But the considerable gap between the two findings indicates that the different wording probably cannot fully explain this gap.

18. The IDC survey on patriotism contained a question about readiness to fight for the country, too. It was asked during the years 2006–2009 and yielded the same result each year: around 93 percent of the Jewish public was definitely willing or quite willing to fight for their country. Based on these results and the results of the 2001 WVS,

the IDC 2006 report concluded that Israel was leading among all other countries in the percentage of respondents who were ready to fight for the country. However, the wording of the IDC survey was different than the question in the WVS. In the WVS, the question was, "If it were to come to war, would you be willing to fight for your country?" and the respondents were offered two answers—yes or no. But in the IDC survey, the question was: "If another war erupts, would you agree to fight for the state *or participate in the war effort in another way if you cannot fight*?" (emphasis added). The IDC survey also offered four options as answers instead of two ("definitely agree," "almost certainly agree," "almost certainly not agree," "definitely not agree"). That could explain the higher rate of willingness to fight for the country in the IDC survey. But because of the different wording of the question, it is misleading to compare the IDC findings with results from WVS among other countries.

19. These are the reported last words of Yosef Terumpeldor—a well-known military Zionist hero—who was killed with seven of his comrades during a fight with the Arabs in the Jewish settlement Tel Hi in 1920.

20. *Mizrahim* (meaning oriental) is commonly used as a label for Jews of Asian or North African origin—primarily from Arab or Muslim countries. *Ashkenazim* is a name used toward Jews originally from Europe or from other Western countries

21. Although the fact that more people have been requesting exemptions is definitely a noteworthy societal trend, this number also is explained by the fact that the army has become more lenient in granting those exemptions due to the fact that they do not really need that many people.

22. Indeed, while 71 percent of religious respondents and 60 percent of traditional respondents in my 2016 survey agreed with the phrase "it is good to die for our country," only 45 percent of secular respondents and 40 percent of ultra-Orthodox respondents agreed with this sentiment.

23. Furthermore, Israeli policymakers prioritized protecting the lives of IDF soldiers over the protection of Israeli civilians. For example, they avoided large-scale ground operations in Gaza, as long as Israeli civilian casualties from Hamas rocket shelling were limited to Israeli communities near the Gaza border. IDF chief of staff Dan Halutz stated in a 2010 newspaper interview: "Today in the state of Israel it has become less legitimate that a soldier dies and more legitimate that a [Israeli] citizen dies. For us, a soldier at the age of 20 is 'our child' while a citizen heaven forbid killed in Sderot [a small town, less than a mile from Gaza] or Kiryat Shmona [a border town near the Lebanese border] is not 'our child'" (Y. Levy 2012, 141). Olmert himself expressed this strange moral differentiation between Israeli civilian casualties and those of Israeli combatants in his testimony before the Winograd Committee—an Israeli governmental commission convened to evaluate the conduct of political and military leaders concerning all aspects of the 2006 Lebanon War. He repeatedly cast Israeli soldiers as children. He described his emotional state when he authorized ground operations at the end of the war as the "worst moment of my life." Despite such sympathy expressed for the IDF soldiers, Olmert did not extend these sentiments to the Israeli civilians who he knew would be attacked by Hezbollah rockets, nor did he express remorse that, in the lead-up to the war, he predicted extensive suffering for Israeli civilians (Oren, Rothbart, and Korostelina 2009, 299).

7

Dreams of Peace

Numerous Israeli songs were written about peace, and many, ironically, were performed by military ensembles during their mandatory service as soldiers. Among them is the song "Flowers in Barrel" (Prahim ba-qaneh). Performed by the Artillery Ensemble in the early 1970s, it was inspired by the hippie revolution and the anti–Vietnam War movement (Regev 2004, 90) and its lyrics demonstrate popular Israeli beliefs about peace.[1] The song begins by describing the change of seasons from spring to summer and declaring that, at that time of the year, the last battle in the battlefield will end. The song's chorus evokes the biblical story of the battle of Gibeon—when the sun and the moon stood still in their courses, extending the day so that Joshua's army could defeat its enemies before nightfall. In the song, however, the sun and the moon stand still instead as peace arrives. During this time, according to the song, the barrels of tanks will hold flowers instead of shells and turrets will hold "girls" instead of soldiers, and "all the soldiers will return home to town."[2] The last verse describes again how the soldiers will return home and be welcomed by a festival of "young women, flowers, and songs." It ends with the prediction that "all those who suffered pain and bereavement / shall know no autumn and battle anymore." Like many other Israeli songs (see Chapter 3), this song presents the war as an inevitable and almost a natural phenomenon like the change of seasons. In contrast, peace is described as a utopic and unlikely scenario, a supernatural phenomenon associated with orbits ceasing and seasons vanishing. In other words, peace is a miracle, and not a realistic possibility. As such, there is nothing Israel can do to achieve peace, just as it cannot affect the seasons or the movement of the sun and the moon. All Israel can do is wish and dream for peace to appear.

According to Bar-Tal (2013, 200), the ethos of a society engaged in intractable conflict may include a peace theme that provides a positive expectation in times of suffering—and presents peace as a supreme goal. In this chapter, then, I examine whether the peace theme was indeed part of the Israeli ethos: whether it was presented as a major goal in leaders' rhetoric, school curricula, and public polls. Note that it is one thing to believe that Israel is a peace-loving society (a societal belief that is part of the villa in the jungle theme in the ethos) and another entirely different thing to set peace as a main value for the country. It also is one thing to merely *wish* for peace and another thing to *hope* for it—that is, to believe that peace is achievable and intend to work toward it (O. A. Leshem, Klar, and Flores 2016). Finally, I also look at any expressions of tension between the value of peace and other values, such as the need to keep national unity and security, and the way these tensions were addressed. In this vein, I show that peace was not always perceived in positive terms and sometimes was associated with negative feelings like anxiety.

Leaders' Rhetoric

Prior to the 1979 Israeli-Egyptian peace treaty, Israeli leaders' speeches referred to "peace with the Arabs" as a wish or a vision, often specifically using Hazon—the Hebrew word for vision, and not a realistic possibility. Peace was associated with the end of all wars and full cooperation between the countries, bringing economic prosperity to the region.[3] Furthermore, when talking about peace, Israeli leaders such as David Ben-Gurion often prioritized other values over peace. For example, in a 1952 speech Ben-Gurion maintained that peace with the Arabs "is one of our vital interests, but it is not the first and all-determining interest" (Shlaim 2000, 78). In 1958, Ben-Gurion said that "to achieve a permanent peace and cooperation with Israel's neighbors" was the second principle of Israeli foreign policy (the first was building good relations with any country friendly to Israel regardless of its domestic policies) (Israel 1958, vol. 24:1817). Then, in 1962, Ben-Gurion presented a different order of priorities that excluded peace with the Arabs altogether: the first was security needs of Israel; second, the ingathering of Jewish exiles; third, support for world Jews; and, fourth, helping new nations and strengthening peace seekers in the world (Ben-Gurion 1963, 448–449). However, in a different 1962 speech, he placed peace in the world and especially in the Middle East as the first goal and Israel's security needs came second (Israel 1962, vol. 34:3063). In Ben-Gurion's rhetoric, then, the centrality of peace with the Arabs varied widely.

Peace was a more consistently vital value in the rhetoric of Moshe Sharet, who criticized what he perceived as Ben-Gurion's preference for military over diplomatic means in dealing with the Israeli-Arab conflict. For example, in a 1957 speech, Sharet argued that "not even for one moment must the matter of peace vanish from our calculation" (Morris 2001, 280). Sharet also differed from Ben-Gurion in indicating that Israel needed to act for peace. He stressed that it was not enough to say that Israel wanted peace; Israel's government and army had to behave accordingly (Shlaim 2000, 107). In other words, he seemed to hope for peace, instead of just wishing for it.

Golda Meir's approach was closer to Ben-Gurion's, as her attitude toward peace was linked to the villa and security themes in the ethos. She contended that peace was unnecessary for Israel because Israel could live and even thrive in conflict while its enemies would pay a higher cost for the continued conflict. This can be seen in her 1969 speech in the Knesset, when she asserted that the security challenge "encouraged great activity" (Meir 1969). One reason that Meir's rhetoric did not assign peace a higher weight was her belief that peace depended only on change in the Arabs' minds. In 1969 she asked, "How many young men, Jews and Arabs, will have to pay with their lives for the *madness and irrationality of the Arab Leaders*" (Brecher 1972, 310, emphasis in the original).[4] Accordingly, Meir believed that peace would come only from Arab acceptance of all of Israel's terms, and that demands for compromise set by other countries, such as the US Rogers Plan, should be rejected because Israel could not compromise its existence. Furthermore, peace was sometimes associated with threat in Meir's rhetoric, such as her statement in a 1956 speech that she began to worry when she heard other countries talking about peace in the Middle East. How, she then asked, can the Jewish state with its tiny territory make any concessions? (Meir 1956). Thus, peace in Meir's rhetoric, especially if it involved Israeli concessions, had negative associations and feelings such as fear.

Yitzhak Rabin also expressed concern regarding peace (this time, in the context of the Israeli-Egyptian peace process). In his 1979 book, he dedicated an entire chapter to "the risks of peace" (Rabin and Peri 1996 [1979], 315). He stated that peace has many risks and, unlike Meir, he focused on risks beyond traditional military threats—the effect of peace on three important themes of the Israeli ethos: national unity, patriotism, and the goal of Israel as a Jewish state. Regarding the goal of Israel as a Jewish state, he noted that in the context of peace, "We will have to decide what will make our Jewish state a unique place in which to live and nurture future generations" (p. 336). He expressed further concern that the strong ties between Israel and diaspora Jews—that are based on the latter's firm stand behind Israel when it faces a "mortal threat"—will weaken because "Jews have always stood together in time of trials, while in tranquil days each [Jewish] community turned to tending its own garden [rather than helping Israel]"(p. 336) He also voiced concern about the way peace would affect unity among Israeli Jews: "What forces other than threat from beyond our borders will keep our people united in their vision and purpose?" he asked and added, "I have no doubt that the imminent threat from the outside was the most powerful force uniting the people of Israel. Now we live in a time of both peace and war, and we never experienced anything like it before. No one can predict how it will affect the motivation of our people, their readiness to bear heavy burdens" (p. 335). But while Rabin perceived these dangers as a "real threat to Israel existence," he ended his 1979 book with the notion that "the risks of peace are preferable by far to the grim certainties that await every nation in war" (p. 337). This view distinguished him from Meir and he repeated it, as shown below, during the 1990s. Begin expressed the same idea following the signing of the Israeli-Egyptian peace treaty: "I will not conceal from you—on the contrary—the fact that for this peace we made a great many sacrifices, some of them painful indeed. Why did we do this? Because we prefer sacrifices for peace to victims in war" (Begin 1979b).

After the peace treaty with Egypt, the focus shifted to the Israeli-Palestinian conflict and potential peace with the Palestinians. In this context, some Israeli leaders felt that peace with the Palestinians was not realistic and, like earlier leaders, prioritized other values such as security and Greater Israel. Yitzhak Shamir, for example, admitted in 1992 that peace with the Palestinians was not his main goal: "I would have carried on autonomy talks [with the Palestinians] for ten years, and meanwhile we would have reached half a million [Jewish] people in Judea and Samaria" (Shlaim 2000, 500). He also thought that security was more important than peace and stressed that "peace will be unattainable if Israel is weak" (p. 464). Shamir often qualified the term *peace* by adding other terms or conditions such as "peace in exchange to peace" and "peace with security."[5]

But other Israeli leaders, especially Rabin and Shimon Peres, expressed a different view regarding peace with the Palestinians. According to Rosler (2012), 27 percent of Rabin's speeches from 1992 to 1995 referred to peace. Rabin argued that peace between Israel and the Palestinians depended on a change in Israel's thinking and behavior, not just change on the Palestinian side, and he called for such a change. Rabin admitted that "much of what has been achieved in the State of Israel in all areas is a direct or indirect outcome of the necessity to defend our existence" (Rabin 1994c). Yet Rabin also emphasized the high cost of war.[6] He insisted that war was "not destined by fate or by God" and that Israel should actively try to achieve peace (Rabin 1995d).[7] In his rhetoric, peace with the Palestinians was a means to achieve other important values such as security and maintaining Israel as a Jewish and democratic state.[8] In a 1994 speech, he addressed the Israeli debate about peace with a military metaphor, "a battle without cannons in a war without fire," and argued that:

We will have to choose, on the one hand, between the road of zealousness, the tendency towards dreams of grandeur, the corruption of ethical and Jewish values as a result of ruling over another people . . . and, on the other hand, the road of maintaining a Jewish, democratic, liberal way of life, with consideration for the beliefs of others, even among ourselves, as well as side by side with us, with everyone living their lives according to their own faith. (Rabin 1994c)

Furthermore, during the 1990s Rabin preferred the value of peace over the value of national unity as Waxman concludes:

Aware of the peace process' domestic contentiousness, Rabin and Peres seemed ready to accept this as part of the price to be paid for eventual peace with the Palestinians. Israeli–Palestinian peace, for them, was Israel's most urgent national priority, and they were willing to pursue this even at the expense of domestic peace. Thus, if the demands of national unity stood in the way of peace, it was the former not the latter that was to be forsaken. (Waxman 2006b, 209)

However, a vision of a future peace agreement with the Palestinians was vague, not specific, in Rabin's speeches (Rosler 2012). He declared that it would include the establishment of a "Palestinian entity that is less than a state" and that Israel's borders would not be the pre-1967 borders (Rosler 2012, 184). During this period, Peres also referred often to peace. He presented a description of a new Middle East to include economic profits, an increased standard of living, regional openness, and vast business opportunities for all states (S. Peres and Naor 1993). As Yadgar (2006, 307) states, this description of peace "has become an icon of an utopian, abstract, and rather apolitical (that is, one that does not call for concrete political action) notion of peace in the Middle East." A similarly apolitical utopian peace appeared in speeches of former Israeli leaders, such as Meir, and even sporadically in the rhetoric of Benjamin Netanyahu.

But overall, peace was rarely even a wish in Netanyahu's speeches. Only 9 percent of his speeches in 2013 referred to peace, and most of these were in front of foreign audiences (see Table 2.1). Like Meir, Netanyahu argued that peace depended mostly on Palestinian willingness to recognize Israel's right to exist (hence, he linked it to the villa theme of the ethos). For example, he said that "the root of the problem is the [Palestinian] stubborn resistance to any settlement, a final peace settlement with the state of the Jewish people, because they always make demands, whether to enter negotiations or terminate negotiations that no responsible government can accept" (Netanyahu 2013a). Like earlier leaders, such as Shamir, Netanyahu co-opted peace by adding other terms and conditions such as "peace in exchange for peace," "peace with security," or "a true peace."[9] Several times he also prioritized national unity over peace with the Palestinians; for example, in 1996 he said that "the first and foremost peace that must be reached is peace at home, peace between us, peace among us" (Waxman 2006b, 210). While Netanyahu sometimes declared that Israel would agree to pay "painful prices" for peace (although he did not elaborate what this price was),[10] he also was pessimistic about the chance for peace with the Palestinians. In October 2015, during his appearance at the Foreign Affairs and Defense Committee of the Knesset, he said that Israel would "forever live by the sword" (Ravid 2015a). Thus, in his rhetoric, as in that of Israeli leaders from earlier years, peace remained more of a wish than a hope (e.g., realistic possibility).

Moreover, during the period after 2000, peace as a realistic option almost disappeared from the speeches of many Israeli leaders, and those from the political center and left, like Ehud Barak and Yair Lapid, shared Netanyahu's pessimism about the chances for peace. Lapid declared that "the perceived wisdom today is that peace between Israel and the Palestinians is not possible" (Times of Israel Staff 2016). More importantly, these politicians discussed separation from the Palestinians rather than peace. "Us over here, them over there" was Barak's declared new goal in 2001 after the failure of the Camp David summit (Waxman 2008, 86). "The answer is separation. As decisively as possible," Lapid said (Times of Israel Staff 2016). Thus, while they did call for action, it was not out of hope for peace or even a wish for it but rather from a desire for the rivals to disappear behind high walls.

School Curricula

The 1950s Through the Late 1970s

Of the eleven goals set forth by the 1953 State Education Act, one was to educate for "peace seeking and for tolerance in relations between people and between nations." But while other themes of the ethos that appeared in the act—like security, patriotism, and the goal of establishing a Jewish state in Israel—were integrated across as many school subjects as possible (history, geography, civics, etc.), peace was seldom included in textbooks. It was taught sporadically and with little connection to other school subjects. Until the 1970s, references to peace appeared mainly in readers, though infrequently (David 2012). Consistent with leaders' rhetoric from this period, peace appeared in the readers as a dream or a wish. One reader from the 1970s included the following poem: "Peace is a blessing / peace is a prayer / Peace is a word you would hear / anytime every day—every hour . . . but peace, a real peace / is a wish. This is a dream / we all ask for peace / always peace, no fight, no fire / Thus we all wish / Let there be peace on Israel" (p. 257).

The initial reaction of the Ministry of Education to the 1979 Israeli-Egyptian peace treaty was reticence. When interviewed about the educational aspects of this event, Education Minister Zvulun Hammer expressed concern that peace might threaten the Jewish identity of Israel and that peace "will eventually lead to our assimilation in the ocean of millions of Arabs" (Podeh 2002, 46). The Ministry of Education dedicated the 1978–1979 school year—during the Israeli-Egyptian peace process—to "celebrate the Jewish people's war for national independence and human justice in the Land of Israel" (Pinson, Levy, and Soker 2010, 262). It was war, then, that was "celebrated." Even after the treaty was signed in 1979, peace was not chosen as the annual theme. In 1981, following a demand from teachers, the ministry published "We and Our Neighbors"—the first textbook for elementary and middle school focused on coexistence and peace with the Arabs. While the text's introduction urged students to seek friendly relations with Arab neighbors, it also cautioned that this "should not diminish our right to feel commitment toward the homeland" (Podeh 2002, 50).

The 1980s and 1990s

Meaningful change did not appear until the mid-1980s. In 1984, the Ministry of Education introduced an ambitious new program—Education for Jewish-Arab Co-Existence. The program called for integrating subjects such as history of the Arab peoples, their culture, and Israeli-Arab relations into the educational process from kindergarten through twelfth grade. It initiated a review of all existing textbooks (for negative presentations of Arabs) and the development of new textbooks promoting the program's goals within three years. Indeed, David (2012) found increased references to peace in readers from the 1980s to the early 2000s. Many of these references still presented peace as a dream or a wish, but some (e.g., "The Song for Peace" by Yaacov Rotblit) noted that Israel should not just wish for peace, but also should act to bring it about: "Don't say the day [of peace] will come / Bring the day / because it is not a dream" (p. 258). In addition, a new optional topic was added to civics curriculum: "Education for Coexistence and Democracy." But this topic and another optional topic, "The Arab-Israeli Conflict," were seldom taught in classrooms (Firer, 'Adwān, and Pingel 2004).

The focus of the Education for Jewish-Arab Co-Existence program was on extracurricular activities. The Ministry of Education declared coexistence between Jews and Arabs as the theme of the 1985–1986 school year and established the Division for Democratic and Coexistence Education within the ministry. However, its focus was on democracy and conflicts between the Jewish majority and the Arab minority within Israel proper, not the relationship between Israeli Jews and the Palestinians in the territories, or the relationship between Israel and Arab countries (Podeh 2002; Vered

2016). Overall, extracurricular activities relating to coexistence between Jews and Arabs were provided by around sixty NGOs. These mainly encouraged interaction and common experiences of Arab and Jewish students through joint teaching and social activities such as sporadic meetings and weekly seminars. However, the Van Leer Foundation—a major provider of coexistence programs—noted that many teachers opposed these activities (Podeh 2002, 72) and that religious schools banned them altogether for fear of assimilation (Firer, 'Adwān, and Pingel 2004, 25; Podeh 2002, 52–53). It is not surprising, then, that only a few schools participated in these joint Jewish-Arab activities and that only 2–3 percent of the teachers participated in seminars to prepare for them (Podeh 2002, 52).

The ministry also encouraged schools to use the approximately 200 booklets on coexistence between Jews and Arabs published by NGOs. Firer, 'Adwān, and Pingel (2004) note that these booklets focused on topics such as Arab folklore and peace as a moral and a (Jewish) religious value. They referred only to the Arab Palestinian minority that were Israeli citizens and ignored the Palestinians in the territories (who were not Israeli citizens). Recall that during this time, the Israeli-Arab conflict was only an optional subject in civics studies and was taught by only a few teachers. Thus, the political aspect of the Israeli-Arab peace process was completely ignored.

In a 1991 Director-General Directive (DGD) from the Ministry of Education (again, under Hammer as minister of education), peace was presented mainly as a threat: "When the peace talks with Egypt were launched . . . reality came and struck us in the face, and the peace process began." As Pinson, Levy, and Soker (2010, 263) explain, the Hebrew phrase "reality struck us in the face" is a negative expression usually used to describe a situation where one's hopes are shattered by reality. In another 1991 DGD, peace was described as a "challenge" that Israel faces "in several frontiers" (p. 264). It identified peace as a threat to Israel's national unity because of its potential to trigger disputes and tensions within Israeli society—the 1991 DGDs, then, presented a contradiction between peace with the Palestinians and the value of national unity.

Some changes occurred during the Oslo process. "The Peace Process: Israel and the Middle East" was the 1994–1995 school year theme. According to a ministerial directive, the term *peace process* was to replace the term *Arab-Israeli conflict*. But Pinson, Levy, and Soker (2010, 264), who reviewed the DGD introducing the program, found that it presented peace as an unpleasant surprise, described in negative terms, and cautioned teachers "to be aware and alert to the fact that this is an emotionally loaded issue" that could cause "fear, anxiety and frustration" among the students. As before, this program's goal was first and foremost to deal with the potential threat to national unity, rather than to create dialogue between Israelis and the Palestinians. The 1994 program created a committee to propose curricular and textbook changes regarding the peace process. One curricular change, in 1994, was to move the optional civics topic, "The Israeli-Palestinian Conflict," to the history curriculum. Reflecting the optimism of this period, the change assumed that the conflict "belongs to the past and was no longer part of civic studies, which deals with the present" (Firer, 'Adwān, and Pingel 2004, 26). But change in textbooks was still to come. Bar-Tal's (1998) comprehensive study of Israeli school textbooks approved for 1994–1995 indicated that peace was rarely presented, and that only a few history books noted the 1979 peace agreement with Egypt.

In 1995, the Ministry of Education published a catalog of suggested extracurricular activities and teaching aids. Firer, 'Adwān, and Pingel's (2004, 22) reviews of this program identified several limitations. Most of the programs did not deal with the political aspects of the Israeli-Arab peace process or the price of this process for Israel.[11] Instead, the proposed activities referred to democracy and how the Jewish majority should treat the Arab minority in Israel, peace as a universal value, peace as reflected in literature and art, and so forth. Further, teachers regarded peace as a controversial topic and found it difficult to deal with in class. In any case, as Podeh (2002, 58) notes, "It was unreasonable to assume that students could absorb so much information on so many issues in one year, and consequently alter ingrained perceptions of the Other." Indeed, a change of government in 1996, when Hammer became again the minister of education, shifted the ministry's focus from peace education to Zionist and Jewish values.

The focus shifted again to peace education in 1999–2000 when Yosi Sarid, a politician from the dovish party Meretz and a well-known peace activist, became minister of education. He aimed to develop a program for "meaningful peace education" (Bar-Tal and Rosen 2009). New history textbooks were intended to present a more balanced description of the Israeli-Arab conflict (see Chapters 2 and 4), although almost none mentioned any Jewish and Arab contacts regarding peace other than the 1919 Feisal-Weizmann Agreement. Podeh (2002, 102) notes that "ignorance was not the cause, as contacts between the Jews and Abdallah had always been an open secret," and that an explanation for this omission may be the "mistaken perception of textbooks' writers that the history of the conflict was primarily of war and violence." Firer, 'Adwān, and Pingel (2004), who also analyzed these history textbooks, arrived at a similar conclusion as Podeh (2002). They cited the 1921–1929 period as an example:

> The eight years between 1921 and 1929 were a period of no clashes [between Jews and Arabs] and it hardly features in the textbooks. Infrequently, one or two sentences mention these years as an interlude between two "incidents." While admitting that some coexistence in everyday life was a reality for both nations for eight years, the authors are reserved in their conclusions. They regard coexistence as a superficial necessity for

people who live together, covering the conflict that burst out periodically. (Firer, 'Adwān, and Pingel 2004, 42)

However, the new history textbooks did reference the 1993 peace process with the Palestinians. Bar-Navi (1998) ended his discussion of the Oslo Accords by saying that in the Middle East "everything is possible, even the impossible," and then declared that the long-term war between Israel and the Arab world "is in its final stage" and "it is only a question of time" until it ends (quoted in Firer, 'Adwān, and Pingel 2004, 84). Naveh (1999) described in detail the terms of the Oslo Accords and the price that each side paid in this process. He incorporated in his book an article by Joshua Sobol (1993), which says that "climbing the route of peace starts with awaking from foolish dreams whose essence is the denial of the other's existence." The textbook asked the students about Sobol's text: "Do you agree with the writer's conclusion that peace is not a realization of a dream but rather an awakening from a foolish dream?" (Naveh 1999, 194–195). Naveh (1999, 195) concluded, like Bar-Navi (1998), with the declaration that "the process of mutual acknowledgment and acceptance of the other is irreversible." Both Naveh (1999) and Bar-Navi (1998), then, presented hope for peace through optimism that peace was possible and a perception of peace as a political arrangement that was based on mutual compromise. In the period after 2000, Firer, 'Adwān, and Pingel (2004, 85–86) wondered if these texts were still relevant given the changing reality of the conflict and the collapse of the Oslo peace process. Indeed, because of the change in reality and a more hawkish Israeli government, the 1999 plan for peace education was never executed and the new history textbooks were abandoned or revised (see Chapter 2). The focus shifted again to Zionism and Jewish studies.

The Period After 2000

Yuli Tamir, a well-known peace activist, served as minister of education from 2006 to 2009 and attempted to develop a new comprehensive program for coexistence between Jews and Arabs within Israel. A public committee appointed by Tamir submitted recommendations in 2009, suggesting a series of large-scale measures including teaching the history of the Israeli-Palestinian conflict along with the Palestinian national identity and its collective narrative (Vered 2015). However, with the appointment of a new minister of education, Gidon Saar (from the hawkish Likud party), these recommendations never matured into policy.

Indeed, the first decades of the 2000s brought an overall weakening of peace education (Vered 2015, 2016). The journal of the Israeli Association of Teachers, *Hed Haninuch,* dedicated an entire volume in 2011 to a comprehensive review of peace education in Israel. Most of the writers agreed that peace education in Israel was outweighed by national and security topics, and that teachers avoided peace education because it was considered a "political" and controversial issue. Orshak (2011) found that most history education in Israel focused on wars and conflict and that current Israeli history books included little about previous peace attempts, the history of coexistence between Jews and Arabs, or heroes who tried to bring peace. This tendency to focus on war heroes (rather than peace heroes) was also seen in school activities on Yitzhak Rabin Memorial Day. As a former IDF chief of staff, Rabin could be considered a war hero, but he also was a signer of the Oslo Accords, a co-winner of the Nobel Peace Prize along with Shimon Peres and Yasser Arafat, and he was assassinated following a peace rally by an Israeli Jewish man who opposed the Oslo process. However, lesson plans issued for this memorial day marginalized these facts and the events leading up to the assassination (James n.d.; Kashti and Skop 2014).[12] Levy (2014), who conducted in-depth interviews with forty teachers from 2009 to 2010, found that the interviewees felt they should avoid discussing the Israeli-Palestinian peace process in class because "those teachers who are interested in doing so find themselves in a conflict with the students. They are sometimes mocked, ignored or dismissed and singled out as being 'leftists,' in a derogative way" (p. 110). Peace education was considered to be "indoctrination" among Israeli students and teachers while Jewish and Zionist content was perceived as "values education" (p. 108).

In sum, hope for a feasible peace and a call for Israeli action were largely absent from school curricula throughout the history of the nation. The most serious attempts to introduce a systematic peace education program entailed two simultaneous conditions: a change in the reality of the conflict and a dovish minister of education. This happened in 1984–1986 following the Israeli-Egyptian peace treaty, and in 1994–1995 following the Oslo Accords. Both programs focused on extracurricular activities, and neither referred to peace as a concrete political process involving Israeli compromise. Both were also short-lived, as the reality of the conflict and the political situation in Israel changed rapidly. Furthermore, teachers were not eager to use materials on peace education, perceiving it as "political education." Tamir aptly summarizes this situation:

> Israel will continue to talk about peace and not educate for peace . . . a peace of white clouds and doves not peace of painful concessions and compromises; a peace as a poster torn off the wall a day after it was hanged there without leaving any mark; a peace that allows everyone to gather under its wings except the enemies whom we supposed to make peace with; a peace of disappointment, frustration, suspicion and fear, that shapes the national consciousness of future generations and keeps them away from peace; a peace that may quiet the conscience but not the land. (Tamir 2011, 46)

The Public

Peace as a Core Value: Tension Between
the Goal of Peace and Other Societal Beliefs

Some early polls about the centrality of peace indicated that peace was an important value and the main wish of Israelis. As early as 1962, in response to an open-ended survey question, 52 percent of Israeli participants mentioned "peace with the Arabs" as a national hope (none of the Egyptian participants expressed a hope for peace with Israel at that time) and another 16 percent mentioned "peace" (Antonovsky and Arian 1972). In a 1975 follow-up study, 14 percent of Israeli participants answered "peace with Arabs" and 58 percent "peace" (Katz 1980). Note, however, that because *hope* in Hebrew can mean also "wish," Jewish Israeli participants in this study probably reported their high wishes for peace, not a hope that included an expectation of peace.

Questions that ask respondents to rank values can provide an indication of the priority of peace as a value among Israeli Jews. Since 1988, a NSPOP time series survey has asked respondents to rank four values— democracy, peace, Greater Israel, and a Jewish majority in Israel. This question also has appeared in JIPP surveys during the years 2002–2012. The values "peace" and "Jewish majority" were the two highest ranked values in most years. From 1991 to 1994 and in 1998, peace was ranked as "the most important value," even greater than the value of "Jewish majority." Peace as a wish and a value, then, seemed to be more dominant among the Israeli public than in school curricula and leaders' rhetoric. However, since 2000, the prioritization of peace has decreased, with more respondents choosing "Jewish majority" over peace as the most important value. The erosion of peace as a value is even more notable when looking at the percentage of those who chose peace as the first or second choice, which dropped from 72 percent in 2000 to 57 percent in 2009 (for further discussion of the findings, see Ben Meir and Bagno-Moldavsky 2010; J. Shamir and Shamir 2000).

Other surveys asked respondents to rank peace against values such as economic growth, freedom, equality, national unity, and security. Recall that leaders' speeches often referred to the relationship between peace and security and national unity. In a 1971 survey conducted by Bar-Ilan University, a representative sample of Jewish Israelis were asked to name the main three important values from a list. Seventy-eight percent chose "peace" as one of the most important values, compared to 70 percent who chose "security," 33 percent who chose "freedom," 38 percent who chose "settlement of the country," and 8 percent who chose "equality." A different picture appeared in a JIPP survey in 2000 (before the second intifada) and 2001, as well as in my 2016 survey, in which respondents ranked the following goals: security, economic prosperity, democracy, peace, and a Jewish state. As shown in Table 3.3, the percentage of those who chose peace was lower than the percentage who chose security and the Jewish state, but higher than the percentage of those who chose democracy. According to a 2000 Gallup survey, 47 percent of Israelis felt that "preventing a rift in the nation" was more important than signing peace agreements with the Arabs, compared to 34 percent who believed the opposite (Waxman 2006b, 211). These findings, then, matched the findings of NSPOP surveys above (and leaders' rhetoric) that peace was secondary to other values in the Israeli ethos during the period after 2000.

Peace as a Hope

Leaders' rhetoric and school textbooks described peace as an abstract and vague wish rather than a concrete and policy-oriented option. Often, it was associated only with Arab concessions and agreement with Jewish goals and demands. Public polls presented a different picture. They showed a shift over time from the perception of peace in general terms to an increasingly concrete and policy-oriented one. This was seen even in the nature of the poll questions themselves. Until 1977, most questions regarding peace in Israeli polls presented peace in general vague terms and avoided policy implications (around 90 percent). After 1977, and especially after 1987, questions about peace more often included a set of policy options. By the years 1987–1991, only 18 percent of questions about peace and the territories were in general terms while 44 percent presented a set of policy options and 38 percent asked about different policy options and explicit trade-offs among those options. J. Shamir, Ziskind, and Blum-Kulka (1999), who conducted the study reported on in this paragraph, also found fewer references over time to abstract notions of "true peace" and "final peace," and more references to "peace agreements."

While some surveys in later years continued to ask questions about peace in general terms (for example, one NSPOP question from 1996 to 2012 asked if respondents agreed with the general principle of "land for peace"), most questions provided a detailed framework for potential peace. Two surveys—JIPP and NSPOP—asked respondents about their agreement with six elements of a peace agreement between Israel and the Palestinians (Ben Meir and Bagno-Moldavsky 2013, 88). Peace, then, was presented in more recent polls mainly in concrete terms and as involving concessions from all sides, including Israel—a tendency that was not common in school curricula. The findings indicated a substantial willingness for Israeli concessions as part of a peace deal, but they usually did not find agreement among a majority of respondents. Forty-four percent of respondents in a

1991 survey supported the general principle of "land for peace" (Israeli territorial concessions for peace with the Arabs). A time series NSPOP survey conducted from 1996 to 2012 also indicated that, in most of those years, less than 50 percent of respondents supported the principle of land for peace. That survey further showed that agreement with this principle declined from 48 percent in 2005 to only 30 percent in 2012. This decrease also appeared in questions about Israeli withdrawal from specific territories: a NSPOP time series survey indicated that only around 20–30 percent supported transferring areas such as Gush Etzion, the Jordan Valley, and western Samaria to the Palestinians, and that support for withdrawal from these areas declined from 2000 to 2012.[13] In addition, NSPOP data indicated that in 2012, 49 percent supported evacuation of only small and isolated settlements (down from 57 percent in 2004), and only 14 percent supported the evacuation of all settlements (a decrease from 20 percent in 2005) (Ben Meir and Bagno-Moldavsky 2013).

The decline in willingness for concessions as part of a peace agreement during the period after 2000 may have been caused by pessimism about the chances for peace. Before the mid-1980s, questions about the possibility of achieving actual peace between Israel and the Arabs were rare. This omission by itself may indicate that peace was perceived as a wish rather than a realistic option. Yet the few questions regarding this issue that were asked in a 1968–1969 Guttman survey revealed that between 45 and 50 percent of respondents thought peace between Israel and the Arabs was possible. These numbers may indicate relative optimism for peace following the 1967 War. However, in a later survey by the Dahaf Institute in 1981, after the Israeli-Egyptian peace treaty, only 32 percent thought that a peace agreement between Israel and all Arab states was possible.

NSPOP surveys showed that from 1986 to 2000, most respondents thought it would be possible to reach a peace agreement with an Arab country in three years, although this estimate dropped significantly after 2000: from 70 percent in 2000 to 21 percent in 2002 and 27 percent in 2007 (Ben Meir and Shaked 2007, 75). A Peace Index survey that asked respondents whether they believed there would be peace between Israel and the Arabs in the near future showed a similarly sharp decrease: from 40 percent in 2000 to 23 percent in 2001. Since 1994, NSPOP surveys have asked respondents about the likelihood of peace specifically with the Palestinians. The percentage of respondents who thought it was possible to reach a peace agreement with the Palestinians varied from a high of 44 percent in 2001 to a low of 29 percent in 2012 (Ben Meir and Bagno-Moldavsky 2013, 72). JIPP surveys that asked if lasting peace with the Palestinians was possible found a greater belief in this possibility: from 2000 to 2006, around 50 percent thought it was possible. But not only did that figure decline in 2012 (to only 31 percent), the question no longer even included the word "peace." It was replaced by "a final status settle-ment with the Palestinians."

Expectations from Peace

Leaders' rhetoric and school curricula often presented a maximalist ver-sion of peace (a new Middle East) rather than a minimalistic notion of peace (no war). A NSPOP time series question asked respondents to iden-tify the minimal conditions for peace (see Figure 7.1). In 1993, the most common answer (38 percent) was the exchange of ambassadors, in addi-tion to the absence of war and a peace treaty with security provisions. However, expectations for peace grew over time, and by 2000 only 18 per-cent of respondents would settle for that kind of peace. The most common answer (30 percent) was a more maximalist interpretation of peace: no war, a peace treaty with security provisions, the exchange of ambassadors, but also trade and tourism and a feeling of closeness between the citizens of the countries. My 2016 survey indicated that the expectations for peace were less ambitious at that time; by then, the most common response was quite minimal—a peace treaty with security provisions. However, almost 50 percent of respondents still chose the two maximalist answers, much like in 1996 (see Figure 7.1).

Figure 7.1   Minimal Conditions for Peace, 1994–2016

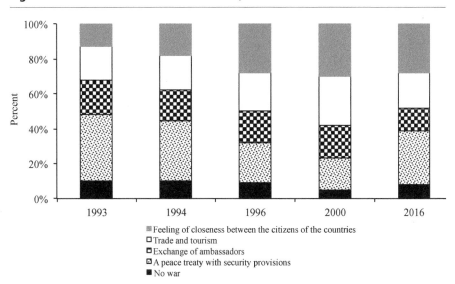

■ Feeling of closeness between the citizens of the countries
□ Trade and tourism
▣ Exchange of ambassadors
▨ A peace treaty with security provisions
■ No war

Sources: NSPOP (1993–2000) and Oren's 2016 Survey.

Conclusion

In this chapter, I showed that the belief in the value of peace did not meet the definition of a theme within the Israeli ethos, insofar as discussion of peace and its policy implications was not common in school curricula. Thus, an important criterion for a societal belief to be included in an ethos—namely, being imparted to the younger generation—was not met. Two attempts were made to introduce systematic peace education into school curricula: in 1984–1986 (several years after the Israeli-Egyptian peace treaty) and in 1994–1995 following the Oslo Accords. However, neither plan was fully implemented and few students participated in these programs. As for leaders' rhetoric, many leaders (e.g., Ben-Gurion, Meir, Shamir, Begin, and Netanyahu) tended to prioritize other values, such as security and national unity, over peace. In addition, references to peace in school curricula and speeches of Israeli leaders before 1977 were general, often in utopistic terms that avoided policy implications and the need for Israeli concessions (only Arab concessions were assumed). In contrast, public polls showed that the public gave greater priority to peace as a value or a wish, even prior to the Israeli-Egyptian peace treaty.

During the 1990s, leaders' rhetoric (especially for dovish leaders like Rabin) and public polls showed a new belief that Israel could and should act to promote peace more than it had done in the past. The polls also evidenced a perception on the part of respondents about an increased likelihood of peace coming about. The 1990s was the only period in which Israeli society hoped for peace rather than merely wishing for it. Public polls, as well as the speeches of some leaders (e.g., Peres), also showed high expectations for what peace might mean: regional economic cooperation and feelings of closeness among the citizens of the soon-to-be former rivals. But this optimism was short-lived: by the period after 2000, public polls and leaders' rhetoric revealed a lower perceived likelihood of peace. And while peace continued to be considered in practical terms, those terms related mostly to what Palestinians, rather than Israelis, would need to do for peace to be achieved. In other words, the belief had reemerged that peace could come about only if or when the Palestinians would be willing to meet Israel's conditions for peace, and that there was nothing Israel could do but wait for them to come around.

Why did the value of peace not feature more prominently in the ethos? In my view, the reason is that, much like the value of democracy, the value of peace clashed with core themes in the ethos. Peace was perceived by some leaders as a threat to Israel's security (see Chapter 3), and therefore those leaders (and some of the public) prioritized security over peace. Hope for peace also strongly challenged the villa theme in the ethos that depicted the Arabs as aiming to destroy Israel—meaning peace was unlikely and nothing but a dangerous illusion. In addition, many leaders warned that pursuing peace with the Palestinians could fray national unity, and even endanger the goal of a Jewish state—recall Rabin's worry and Hammer's concern about higher rates of intermarriage and assimilation (Podeh 2002, 46). In this context, peace was perceived as a threat regardless of whether a genuine desire for peace existed within Palestinian society.

More broadly, in this chapter I showed that the prospect of peace may sometimes engender negative feelings such as anxiety, and that a wish for peace does not necessarily lead to specific actions to promote it. Scholars such as Rumelili (2015), Mitzen (2006), and Steele (2008) have recognized that "states might actually come to prefer their ongoing, certain conflict to the unsettling condition of deep uncertainty as to the other's and one's own identity" (Mitzen 2006, 342)—a condition that often is created by a peace process. To further explore this trend, let us return to the concept of ontological security introduced in Chapter 1 and also discussed in Chapter 3. A peace process can generate ontological *in*security, which states seek to avoid. It challenges existing meaning systems such as ethos of conflict. The rhetoric of Israeli leaders, including Rabin, indeed expressed ontological anxiety about Israel's identity while discussing peace. Already in 1979, Rabin warned against the danger of "Israel losing her way because of the blessing of peace" and noted that "peace will demand that we change certain of our basic attitudes and philosophies" (Rabin and Peri 1996, 336).

I propose that for a peace process to succeed, either the ethos of conflict should remain mostly intact—as when a new enemy appears, or when a peace process resolves the conflict with one enemy but hostilities with other societies continue—or a new ethos should replace the ethos of conflict and provide a new meaning system and routines for the society. In the first process, the society can keep its ethos of conflict as a meaning system and the essence of its identity. The latter process (that involves new ethos) is risky because the prevailing ethos themes do not easily disappear and could be used by spoilers. In addition, a peace process may unleash clashes between various groups in the society regarding the construction of a new ethos. I discuss these ideas further in Chapter 9.

Notes

1. Dudu Barak was the lyricist and Efi Netzer the composer. The song was performed for Israeli soldiers; see https://www.youtube.com/watch?v=EwvAywMw93M. Guy Alon posted it July 5, 2011.
2. While all eighteen-year-old women must enlist in the Israeli army, during the 1970s women were not allowed any combat role. So, spotting a woman in the turret of an IDF tank was as unlikely as seeing flowers stuck in a barrel.

3. See, for example, "We will not stop to present to the people of the region and the world the vision of peace and cooperation that will bring social and economic progress to millions [of people] in this region who are living in poverty and degeneration" (Meir 1969).

4. See, also, "Nothing is lacking for the making of peace but the Arab persistence in denying Israel's very right to exist. Arab refusal to acquiesce in our existence in the Middle East, alongside the Arab States, abides. The only way to peace is through a change in that recalcitrance" (Meir 1970).

5. On this tendency among hawkish groups in Israel, see Wolfsfeld (1997, 117).

6. See, for example, "All our lives revolved around security. The struggle for survival hurts us: we lost trust, we suspected everyone, we have created an atmosphere of siege, we lived in a kind of political and economic ghetto. Withdrawn, we walked away, we doubted, we created patterns of tenacity and a gloomy world view" (Rabin 1995a).

7. See, for example, "The death and bereavement that we face often are not predetermined destiny. There is another way. We can at least try. This is the reason why we try in these days to achieve peace with the Palestinians, the Jordanians with Syria and Lebanon" (Rabin 1995c).

8. In a speech on July 13, 1992, Rabin explained that Israel needs peace with the Palestinians to be able to cope better with the Iranian nuclear threat (Rosler 2012, 186).

9. For example, "We need to sit down, raise the various demands and positions of both sides and try to reach genuine peace" (Netanyahu 2013h); "We all want genuine peace, stable and safe . . . stable and durable peace" (Netanyahu 2013l); "Genuine peace is the aspiration of every person in Israel" (Netanyahu 2013p).

10. For example, "I am ready to make difficult decisions to advance peace, but not those that will endanger the security of Israel's citizens" (Netanyahu 2013h).

11. Some items in the catalog were clearly against the peace process between Israel and the Palestinians. For example, a booklet titled "Outlook on Peace: Facts, Chances and Risks" began with nine examples of peace agreements, eight of which ultimately failed (the one successful peace agreement was the German unification— an emotionally problematic example for Israeli students because of the association with the Holocaust). After reading these examples, students were asked: "What happened to these treaties in the long run, in comparison to the hopes they had evoked? What can be learned from them concerning 'peace' in real life?" (Firer 2002, 11).

12. This tendency to glorify wars, but disregard peace processes, was found also in textbooks in the United States (Farnen 1994).

13. More specifically, support for withdrawal from Gush Etzion dropped from 33 percent in 2000 to 14.8 percent in 2009 and 20 percent in 2012; support for withdrawal from the Jordan Valley fell from 32 percent to 13.8 percent in 2009 and 22 percent in 2012; and withdrawal from western Samaria decreased from 51 percent to 26 percent in 2009 and 34 percent in 2012 (Ben Meir and Bagno-Moldavsky 2010, 2013).

PART 2

Explaining Policy Choices

8

The Prism of
Election Platforms

Thus far, I have discussed each theme of the ethos separately. In this chapter, I focus on the structure of the ethos as a whole. Specifically, I look at the relative importance of each theme within the ethos, the connections among ethos beliefs, and the strategies used to deal with contradictions among ethos beliefs and between ethos beliefs and other societal beliefs, if acknowledged. My analysis is based on election platforms and, in that sense, the chapter offers a new reading of the history of Israeli elections through the prism of the ethos of conflict. Such analysis provides a broad view that extends beyond the personal beliefs of a specific leader or the changes in the beliefs of one specific party.[1] Furthermore, it sheds light not only on the content and evolution of the ethos but also on the link between the ethos and preferred policy vis-à-vis the Israeli-Arab conflict and on the interplay between major conflict-related events and changes in the ethos.

As some observers have pointed out, political parties play a remarkably dominant role in Israel's political system (e.g., Inbar 1991). In addition, studies of Israeli election campaigns have shown that Israeli parties tend to reflect public preferences (M. Shamir and Shamir 2007). While the salience of party platforms is declining—the Likud party, which won the most votes in the 2013 and 2015 elections, did not publish platforms in those elections—for most of the period that is covered in this chapter (1969–2009), party platforms were an essential element in Israeli elections and the parties attributed great importance to them. Inbar (1991, 6), for example, argues that Israeli political parties draft their platforms "with a legalistic-Talmudic frame of mind; every possible shade of meaning is surveyed and evaluated. In the Israeli political culture . . . the wording of a platform is still deemed to be crucial."

Of course, the content of the party platform and its evolution is a result of debate among the different groups within the party. As a matter of process, a change in the platform may start out as a tactical rhetorical adjustment intended to solve a political problem or to achieve short-term goals. It is when such adjustments prove politically successful, and the new rhetoric becomes increasingly difficult to abandon, that the ideology of the party can truly be said to have shifted (Shelef 2010). This process can explain the different timing of changes in the platform of each party as a reaction to major events, such as the Israeli-Egyptian peace process, that my review in this chapter reveals. By focusing on the final product (the party platform), my analysis misses the struggle between those faithful to the party's original ideology and those who seek change as an attempt to deal with the political problem. However, this intraparty process does not occur in a vacuum. The political problems that trigger the adjustments in the first place, as well as the ultimate failure or success of the adjustments, are largely driven by shifts in public preferences and thus also by changes in societal beliefs and the ethos of the society that shapes these preferences. Indeed, the parties' election campaigns and platforms were often based on polls and focus groups that aimed to help the parties to identify public opinion (Mendilow 2003). Thus, a change observed in political platforms, especially if it persisted and was accompanied by changes in public polls, is another indicator of a change in the ethos.

Compared to other countries, Israel has known a relatively large number of small parties (Mendilow 2003). On average, twenty-five parties contested each election cycle in the period covered in this chapter, of which typically twelve garnered enough votes to be represented in parliament. Due to practical considerations such as space and breadth of topics covered, I chose to focus on the ethos as reflected in the political platforms of only the two main parties in each election.[2] One may reasonably wonder whether ignoring the platforms of the smaller parties impacted the validity of my analysis. Recall however that, as I indicated in Chapter 1, my focus was on mainstream politicians and the hegemonic discourse. Hence, parties that did not compete for the votes of the general electorate, but rather of specific subgroups within Israeli society (e.g., Yisrael B'Aliya that represented immigrants from the former Soviet Union, Gil that represented pensioners, Aguddat Israel that targeted only ultra-Orthodox voters of Ashkenazi ethnicity) were less relevant to my study. Second, over time the two main parties experienced mergers with other smaller parties. For example, in 1973 the main hawkish party Herut merged with the Liberal party, Free Center, National List, and the Labor Movement for Greater Israel to create the new main hawkish party Likud; the small parties Tzomet and Gesher merged with Likud in the 1996 elections; and in 1999, Gesher and the small party Meymad merged with the Labor party.[3] Furthermore, because Israel is a parliamentary democracy with a proportional representation system, coalition considerations have always influenced parties' actions. The prospect of a potential alliance with other parties to establish a ruling coalition following an election has influenced the rhetoric of the main parties during the election campaign, as have their efforts to appeal to voters of smaller mainstream parties (Mendilow 2003). In other words, the platforms of the two main parties have often reflected the political influence and relevance of other mainstream parties that either merged with the main party or were perceived as candidates for coalition building, which would at least in part incorporate the content of these parties' platforms. A final justification for my focus on only the two main parties was to ensure that this analysis remains accessible to non-specialists in Israeli affairs, by minimizing confusion with a multitude of Hebrew names and by exposing the big picture.

Turning to the election platforms of the two main parties, Table 8.1 presents the percentage of sentences in each platform that mentioned the ethos of conflict themes.[4] Reflecting their position as the core tenets of the Israeli ethos, the themes of Israel as a Jewish state and security featured most prominently in the platforms of both parties over the years. Themes such as villa in the jungle and peace were also common, but their presence varied over time. These variations and others are discussed further below.

The 1969 Elections

The platforms of the two main parties in the 1969 elections (Alignment, which won the elections, and Herut) began with a reference to Israel's victory in the 1967 War. Both texts followed the ethos themes closely in their depiction of the event: they emphasized the existential threat to Israel before the war, Arab aggression, and Israeli actions that were described as self-defense. Both platforms also hailed the bravery of the Israeli army and the solidarity among the Israeli people as the factors that contributed to Israel's victory. The two main differences between the platforms were Herut's assertion that, confronted with Arab aggression before the war, "the UN, as usual, did nothing. We were alone"—a reference to siege beliefs that did not exist in the Alignment platform; and Herut's declaration that, as a result of the war, "our fatherland was *liberated*" (Herut 1969, 1, emphasis added) also absent from the Alignment platform.

Overall, the 1969 platforms reflected a rather uniform view among the two parties when it came to the main elements of the Israeli-Arab conflict. In other words, the two platforms shared the same ethos of conflict. Both platforms contained a chapter about "Zionism and the Jewish People" (the first chapter in Herut platform; the fourth in Alignment platform). In those chapters, they highlighted the Israeli goal of establishing a Jewish state in

Table 8.1   References to Ethos Themes in Platforms (percentage of sentences that refer to each theme)

	1969	1973	1977	1981	1984	1988	1992	1996	1999	2003	2009
Labor											
Jewish state	18	25	29	31	27	24	16	18	36	23	33
Security	19	9	12	16	14	13	18	31	19	16	29
Villa	14	11	10	3	3	3	3	2	0	1	8
Victim	3	6	3	5	3	3	3	0	0	0	0
Patriotism	5	6	1	7	2	3	0	0	2	0	0
Unity	6	2	0	1	1	2	2	0	6	0	0
Peace	6	14	13	18	10	9	18	22	7	7	16
Likud											
Jewish state	9	21	36	30	31	38	18	29	36	36	34
Security	15	36	12	11	12	12	13	13	19	19	19
Villa	15	7	11	9	6	4	5	1	5	5	16
Victim	7	5	7	6	5	4	0	2	2	2	0
Patriotism	6	2	1	1	2	3	0	1	0	0	0
Unity	2	0	0	0	0	2	0	1	1	1	0
Peace	2	11	7	6	4	9	13	6	12	12	2

the ancient homeland of Eretz Israel. Herut's platform repeatedly evoked the idea that the national right of the Jewish people to the land of Israel is undeniable. This right was justified in both platforms through the use of historical and moral arguments. The main argument was that the land of Israel is the historic homeland of the Jewish people and that anti-Semitism in general and the Holocaust in particular demonstrate the need for the Jewish people to have a safe haven (Alignment 1969, 16; Herut 1969, 4). Yet the two parties differed about the territorial dimension of the Israeli sovereignty. While Herut's platform called for full Israeli sovereignty in the territories captured in the 1967 War (p. 3), no such demand appeared in the Alignment (1969) platform. This difference between the 1969 platforms clearly demonstrates that the goal of Greater Israel was not a part of the Israeli ethos, even when the pivotal 1967 War was fought just two years before.

However, the two platforms did take similar oppositional positions about the Palestinian claim to self-determination. Each denied the existence of a Palestinian entity or a Palestinian people (references in both texts to Palestinians included phrases such as "local population," "residents of the territories," and "the Arabs of the territories"). In addition, both platforms stated that Palestinian refugees should settle in Arab states (Alignment 1969, 14; Herut 1969, 5). Likewise, the two platforms agreed that the threat to the State of Israel was existential and they securitized mostly traditional threats like war and terror. Both expressed concern about future wars with Arab states and the danger posed to Israeli citizens from potential acts of terrorism. Having enumerated, in similar terms, the myriad threats faced by Israel, the two platforms placed considerable emphasis on the value of security. Both platforms dedicated an entire chapter to matters of security and expressed the need to subordinate many spheres of life to the security domain. Much similarity could also be found between the platforms when it came to the means to achieving security. Military means were seen as most effective in dealing with threats, and a need to strengthen the military was the logical corollary. The Herut platform, for example, highlighted the importance of building up the IDF in terms of "spirit, skill and modern equipment" (p. 6). The Alignment platform similarly listed strengthening the IDF as one of its top priorities (p. 8). The two platforms also shared a similar view of the importance to Israel's security of Jewish settlements in the territories (Alignment 1969, 9, 12; Herut 1969, 2).

Another theme featured in both 1969 platforms was that of Israel as a villa in the jungle, a notion also commonly found in school textbooks of that period. In each platform, the Arabs were portrayed as pursuing the extermination of Israel and its inhabitants and as having no interest in peace. Table 8.2 presents the specific terminology used in referring to Arab states or groups. As can be seen in the table, both platforms used general terms when discussing these Arab entities, primarily the terms *Arab states* and *the enemy*. These terms conveyed a perception that all Arabs are part of a single homogenous group (the Arab world) with no meaningful way to classify them into subgroups. Table 8.3 presents the actions ascribed to Arab states and groups. As can be expected, the platform of the dovish Alignment party tended to acknowledge more positive actions on behalf of the Arab entities than did the platform of the hawkish Herut party. However, the bulk of the references to Arab states and groups in the platforms of both parties described hostile actions. The Alignment platform, for example, stated that "Arab leaders, with their aggression toward Israel, keep rejecting any peace effort, and keep preparing to the next war" (Alignment 1969, 8).

Both 1969 platforms also stated that Palestinian terror groups operated at the behest of the Arab states and with their material support. For example,

Table 8.2   References to Arab States and Groups in Platforms (percentage)

	1969	1973	1977	1981	1984	1988	1992	1996	1999	2003	2009
Likud											
General	57	85	82	62	45	54	28	9	31	32	15
Specific	43	15	18	38	55	46	72	91	69	68	85
Labor											
General	84	77	47	21	22	22	38	23	29	25	33
Specific	16	23	53	79	78	78	62	77	71	75	67

Table 8.3   **Actions Related to Arab States and Groups in Platforms (percentage)**

	1969	1973	1977	1981	1984	1988	1992	1996	1999	2003	2009
Labor											
Friendly	24	35	65	52	43	53	71	59	71	50	28
Initiator	9	15	13	8	11	8	31	18	19	6	14
Receiver	15	20	52	44	32	45	40	41	52	44	14
Hostile	63	55	27	28	38	31	13	21	19	50	54
Initiator	34	45	17	12	19	14	4	11	5	6	9
Receiver	29	10	10	16	19	17	9	10	14	44	45
Neutral	9	5	3	5	3	1	–	–	5	–	9
No action	5	5	5	15	16	15	16	20	5	–	9
Likud											
Friendly	11	13	26	8	20	13	57	69	54	50	13
Initiator	5	–	–	–	–	–	23	39	21	21	–
Receiver	6	13	26	8	20	13	34	30	33	29	13
Hostile	68	37	35	46	40	40	20	23	21	23	67
Initiator	47	31	35	38	25	20	11	–	13	14	48
Receiver	21	6	–	8	15	20	9	23	8	9	19
Neutral	16	38	13	23	20	27	3	–	2	4	9
No action	5	12	26	23	20	20	20	8	23	23	11

the Alignment platform said that "Arab states, where the bases of Palestinian terror groups are located, are fully responsible for the terror actions of these groups" (Alignment 1969, 9). Similarly, the Herut platform declared that "the saboteur groups are nothing but means in the enduring aggression of Arab states and their army forces" (Herut 1969, 6). When it came to the Palestinian inhabitants of the territories, however, the Alignment platform presented a somewhat less negative image than the Herut platform. It said, for example, that "the inhabitants in the territories generally refrained from cooperation with terror organizations" (Alignment 1969, 10).

In contrast to the negative portrayal of the Arabs, both platforms presented a positive image of Israel and Israelis. Each praised Israel's embrace of Western values and ideals such as democracy. Both highlighted the humane attitude of Israel toward the Palestinian refugees in the territories and the Israeli efforts to provide for their welfare. Other sections in both platforms extolled the strength of the Israeli army and the courage of its soldiers, and emphasized the need for broad national consensus, especially in times of crisis or war. In discussing Israel's relations with the world at large, both platforms exemplified the dichotomy ever present in the Israeli attitudes toward the world: a strong desire to belong to the international community contrasted with a recitation of the many instances of hostility toward Israel and the Jews, in the past (the Holocaust) and the present (in the Soviet

Union and in Arab states). That said, siege was not a prevalent theme in the 1969 platforms. Likewise, the two platforms included few references to the value of and desire for peace (as can be expected, peace was more prominent in the Alignment platform; see Table 8.1). Both platforms expressed Israel's desire for peace, but neither of them presented it as an urgent need.

The two platforms differed in the ways they dealt with potential contradictions between the ethos beliefs and other societal beliefs. Herut's platform acknowledged a potential inconsistency between its belief in the need to maintain all territories under Israeli control (the value of Greater Israel) and the goal of Israel as a Jewish and democratic state. It tried to deal with the contradiction by using the strategy of bolstering—adding new cognitions to bolster one of the clashing beliefs. First, the platform stated that any resident of Eretz Israel who applied for Israeli citizenship, and demonstrated loyalty to the state, would be granted Israeli citizenship (Herut 1969, 3). However, should a majority of Palestinians obtain Israeli citizenship, the goal of maintaining a Jewish majority and a Jewish character for Israel would come under severe threat. Acknowledging this risk, the platform stated that large Jewish immigration from "trouble spots" where Jews were prosecuted, and even from the West, would enable Israel to preserve its Jewish majority (Herut 1969, 3). Herut's platform also acknowledged the potential inconsistency between its belief in the need to keep all territories under Israeli control and its argument that Israel was "constantly striving" for peace with the Arabs (which, in turn, might require territorial concessions). In another example of bolstering, the platform noted that Israel's willingness to give up some territory would never satisfy the Arabs since they did not have a genuine interest in peace (Herut 1969, 2).

As noted above, the 1969 Alignment platform did not call for Israeli sovereignty over the territories captured in the 1967 War. Yet it insisted on Israeli control over these territories (and their inhabitants)—a demand seemingly at odds with the platform's assertion of Israeli commitment to universal values such as "supporting any effort by small or large nations to achieve national freedom" (Alignment 1969, 14). Alignment's platform denied this inconsistency. First, it rejected the Palestinian claim to nationhood. Second, and in contrast to the Herut platform, Alignment left open the question of Palestinian judicial status under Israeli rule. It stated that, in these territories, there would be no Jordanian, Egyptian, or Syrian authority (Alignment 1969, 11). It also said that Israel would encourage the establishment of "democratic foundations" in the social and municipal life of these people (Alignment 1969, 11), and that the Israeli military administration in the territories would encourage a "social regime that is advanced and appropriate" (Alignment 1969, 12). In other words, the inherent contradiction between democracy and keeping a mass of people in the territories under military rule was mostly denied in the Alignment platform.

My review of the two 1969 platforms, then, provided a clear picture of the Israeli ethos at that time. This ethos was based on the goal of Israel as a Jewish state with a universal rejection of Palestinian self-determination. Israel was perceived as a villa in the jungle, living under an existential threat and as being the main victim in the conflict, while the Arabs were perceived as a single, undifferentiated, implacably hostile, and aggressive entity. Peace was viewed as a remote dream rather than a realistic near-term possibility. Both parties seemed to hold these beliefs and coped successfully with potential contradictions between the ethos beliefs and other societal beliefs by using strategies such as bolstering and denial. While both platforms noted traditional military threats to Israel, they did not mention a threat to identity. Hence, they did not indicate ontological anxiety. As such, the Israeli ethos had policy implications. So long as Israel had confidence in its ability to pursue all its goals, refused to accept Palestinian identity, and perceived peace in the near term to be unattainable, policy choices regarding the conflict tended to be centered on a military buildup and deterrence. For example, the Alignment platform declared that "we yearn for peace . . . but until peace comes we will have to hold our weapons and steadily develop our defense capacity and our ability to repel any enemy" (Alignment 1969, 6). Herut's platform expressed the same idea (Herut 1969, 6). Both platforms mentioned only Israeli demands from the Arabs,[5] and did not include any references to potential Israeli concessions or compromises. The possibility of a territorial compromise or the establishment of a Palestinian state did not exist in the 1969 platforms.

The 1973 Elections

The 1973 elections, which ended with another victory for Alignment (albeit smaller than in 1969), took place in December 1973, shortly after the 1973 War. Both parties discussed the war in their platforms. The Likud platform did not refer to the 1973 War as an Israeli victory (in contrast to the way that it described the 1967 War in its 1969 platform), but rather as having "negative military and political results" for Israel (Likud 1973, 1).[6] The Alignment platform did describe the war as an "IDF victory" (Alignment 1973, 3) and went on to suggest that the war proved once again to Arab leaders the futility of trying to defeat Israel militarily.

Both 1973 platforms reprised many of the ideas and sentences that appeared in previous versions, but some of the changes and additions exposed a growing contrast between the parties. Alignment's platform included new language that explicitly opposed Likud's demand of keeping all the territories under Israeli control (Alignment 1973, 3). Likud's platform, on the other hand, expressed even more emphatically its commitment to that goal. One of the first sentences in the platform now said: "The right of the Jewish people to the Land of Israel is an eternal right which cannot be denied. . . . Israel should enforce its sovereignty over all parts of the liberated territories of the Land of Israel" (Likud 1973, 2). The strong language here and elsewhere in the platform made it clear that this was now a core tenet of Likud and, with Alignment taking the opposite position, this issue emerged as one on which the two parties had significantly diverged since the previous election cycle. Furthermore, the 1973 Alignment platform for the first time mentioned the "Palestinians" and their national aspirations, albeit to declare that these aspirations could be realized only within Jordan (Alignment 1973, 4–5). So, while Alignment continued to oppose Palestinian demands, one could definitely see a difference from the Likud platform as well as from Alignment's own 1969 platform, both of which essentially ignored the existence of Palestinians and their national aspirations.

On the issue of security, the Alignment platform again broke new ground when it suggested the possibility of ensuring security through "borders that are established on territorial compromise in addition to demilitarized zones and political arrangements" (Alignment 1973, 4). In other words, it contemplated means other than military ones for ensuring Israel's security. Likud's platform, on the other hand, still advocated a reliance on military power and asserted that maintaining control of the territories was a security imperative, illuminating another area of divergence between the two parties.

Both 1973 platforms, to a large degree, continued to project a villa in the jungle image when contrasting Israel and its neighbors. The Alignment platform, for example, repeatedly blamed the Arabs for the absence of peace. And yet some cracks were beginning to appear on the villa's facade. The Likud platform warned about a "deep social, economic and moral crisis in Israel" (Likud 1973, 1). The Alignment platform spoke of "irregular actions" taking place in the territories in defiance of Israel's professed "humane policy" that respected the local population in the territories (Alignment 1973, 5). Both parties, then, presented a less glowing image of Israel when compared to previous platforms. This was probably influenced by the glooming public mood following the 1973 War, which ended with a death toll of 2,412 soldiers and a feeling of defeat. In contrast to the 1967 War, which was followed by economic growth and prosperity, the 1973 War triggered high inflation and negative economic impacts on Israeli civilians because of price increases, severe shortages of basic commodities, and income lost because of continuing mobilization (Stone 1982, 100–102).

Finally, the theme of peace featured more prominently in the 1973 platforms than it did in 1969 (see Table 8.1). Likud's 1973 platform, in contrast to its 1969 predecessor, mentioned peace in the introduction and declared the pursuit of peace to be one of the foundations of Likud policy. However, other than repeating a vague paragraph from its previous platform, Likud did not elaborate on what that peace might look like or what would be required of Israel to bring it about. As was the case with other issues, the 1973 Alignment platform took bolder steps in elevating and concretizing the notion of peace. Its first chapter was titled "Peace and Security" rather than only "Security" as was the case in 1969. More importantly, the 1973 platform sounded a more optimistic note about the prospects of reaching a peace agreement, associating those prospects with concrete conflict-related events. It stated that the upcoming peace conference (Geneva conference) presented an "opportunity for a transformation in Israel's relations with Arab states" (Alignment 1973, 4). In contrast to the Likud platform, the Alignment platform's discussion of the terms of a potential peace agreement was more detailed and concrete and included some new terms.[7] And contrary to its own previous platform, the 1973 Alignment platform raised the prospect of Israeli territorial concessions, albeit without elaboration on what territory might be in play beyond declaring that Israel would not return to its 1967 borders. Another innovation in the 1973 Alignment platform was a reference to a potential separate peace agreement between Israel and Jordan based on a two-states solution (Israel and a Jordanian-Palestinian state).

The Likud platform continued to argue that there was no contradiction between holding the territories and preserving Israel's Jewish and democratic nature. In a variation on its 1969 citizenship-related proposals, the 1973 platform declared that while every resident of the state would have the right to apply for Israeli citizenship, they would also be allowed to keep their previous citizenship and would not be obligated to take Israeli citizenship (Likud 1973, 2). Under this proposal, if the Palestinian residents of the territories were to retain their original Jordanian, Egyptian, or Syrian citizenship despite living under Israeli sovereignty, they would not be able to vote in Israeli elections and therefore would not threaten Israel's Jewish voting majority or its Jewish character. By effectively "outsourcing" the exercise of Palestinian individuals' democratic rights, the proposal sought to resolve the tensions between the value of Greater Israel and the values of democracy and a Jewish state. The Likud platform, then, added to its strategy of bolstering to solve the inconsistency between goals.

Seen as a whole, the 1973 Likud platform indicated that, at that point, the party was still holding on to the ethos beliefs and proposing what it considered plausible strategies to address the potential contradictions. It therefore did not feel the need to offer any new policy ideas regarding the Israeli-Arab conflict, and mostly recycled (literally in some cases) the same prescriptions from its 1969 platform: bolstering the military and enhancing deterrence. With regard to the upcoming Geneva conference, the Likud platform stated that "the international campaign that we are facing is vital to the future of the nation" (Likud 1973, 1). However, this campaign was presented mostly as a threat, rather than an opportunity, and the platform called for a mobilization of the Jewish people and of friends of Israel in the world, especially in the United States, to "prevent dictates and pressures" (Likud 1973, 1). The 1973 Alignment platform, on the other hand, did call for new policy—namely, territorial compromise—to advance the prospects of peace with the Arab states. Furthermore, territorial compromise was justified mainly in terms of two values in the ethos—peace and security. The platform stated that the Greater Israel idea thwarted the prospects of peace (Alignment 1973, 3), and that peace that was based on defensible borders would allow Israel to defend itself more effectively (Alignment 1973, 4).

In short, the 1973 War seemed to have stimulated changes chiefly in Alignment's perception of the ethos (although the centrality of peace also increased in Likud's 1973 platform). The outcome of the war raised hopes that Arab leaders had finally acknowledged that Israel could not be defeated militarily and would therefore be more amenable to a peaceful resolution of the conflict. In addition, the ideas expressed in the Alignment platform regarding demilitarized zones and political arrangements as a means to ensure security may have been inspired by the separation-of-forces negotiations that took place between Egyptian and Israeli officers starting on October 25, 1973. It is important to note, however, that the Alignment 1973 platform still echoed most of the ethos themes, including the villa in the jungle notion and the importance of security as a value. It did not recognize Palestinian self-determination as a nation, as was evident from its calls for a Jordanian-Palestinian state. And much like the Likud platform, it called for further strengthening of Israel's military and deterrence capabilities and reiterated its opposition to the establishment of an independent Palestinian state (Alignment 1973, 4).

The 1977 Elections

These elections proved to be a watershed moment in Israeli politics. It would be the first time since the establishment of Israel that a party of Alignment's political lineage and labor and socialist heritage would not garner enough seats to establish the ruling coalition. Instead, Likud won the most votes and forged a coalition that did not include Alignment. The cataclysmic 1973 War and its acrimonious aftermath, featuring many protests and the controversial Agranat Report, clearly had a substantial impact on the election results. It just as clearly influenced the two parties' views of the conflict, as was evident from their respective platforms for the 1977 election cycle. The Alignment platform made the assertion that the IDF had grown stronger as a result of the lessons it learned from the war (Alignment 1977, 1). It also posited that the Israeli-Egyptian and Israeli-Syrian separation-of-forces agreements could serve as a foundation for peace agreements with these neighbors (Alignment 1977, 2). It hailed the improvement in relationships with the United States and argued that Israel's earnest pursuit of peace was increasingly being recognized by the international community and had exposed the Arabs as the rejectionists and the ones responsible for the absence of peace (Alignment 1977, 2). While this portrayal was in line with some ethos themes (villa in the jungle), it also refuted others (siege).

Changes were evident in regard to the different components of the security theme. With respect to the nature of the threats to Israel, the Likud platform highlighted the dangers posed by the potential establishment of a Palestinian state, which, according to the platform, would serve as a base of hostility and aggression toward Israel and the "whole free world" (Likud 1977, 2). The 1977 Alignment platform, while continuing to express opposition to a Palestinian state, did not include it in a list of the threats. It did, however, for the first time, mention the threat posed by "lethal" weapons in the possession of Arab states (a reference to unconventional weapons) (Alignment 1977, 6). A difference could also be seen regarding the conditions for achieving security. The Alignment platform included, again for the first time, the principles of the Alon Plan (Alignment 1977, 4) that identified the areas of strategic importance to Israel. By incorporating the details of this plan, the Alignment platform provided more substance to its ideas about security as based on defensible borders and territorial compromise.[8] The almost exclusive reliance on military might that characterized past discussions of the means to achieving security seemed to have eroded somewhat in the 1977 platforms, with a recognition emerging of the importance and value of diplomacy. Thus, the Likud platform stated that there was a need for the "right combination of military and diplomatic means" to achieve security (Likud 1977, 4), although it provided no specificity as to what diplomatic means would be relevant or what it considered to be the right mix between the diplomatic and military components. The Alignment platform applauded the separation-of-forces agreements that it said brought "calm on all fronts and spared pointless bloodshed" (Alignment 1977, 2).

As if some light were finally able to penetrate the dense jungle surrounding the villa, willing observers were now able to discern the different entities comprising the Arab jungle. For the first time, most references to Arab states and groups in the 1977 Alignment platform were specific rather than general (see Table 8.2), indicating a shift in Alignment's perception of the Arab world from one homogenous hostile group to a more differentiating view of the Arabs. This image has remained mostly negative (the platform referred to "the Arab trait of aggression" on p. 2), but elsewhere the platform mentioned "expressions of willingness to make peace that are heard lately from the heads of Arab states" (Alignment 1977, 2). In addition, as can be seen in Table 8.3, both platforms showed an increase in references to Arabs in the context of friendly actions, although most of these were references to Arabs as receivers of friendly actions by Israelis. In other words, these positive references mainly reinforced a view of the Israeli self-image as a peace-loving country.

The 1977 Likud platform continued the party's attempts to resolve the potential inconsistency between the value of Greater Israel and the values of Jewish state, democracy, and peace by using the strategy of bolstering. Under the party's revised proposal, even if the Palestinians elected not to take Israeli citizenship, they would be allowed to have "cultural autonomy and full economic integration" (Likud 1977, 3), allowing them to partake of Israel's relative prosperity. This idea of autonomy, however, was vague. Menachem Begin, for example, insisted that it was only "personal" autonomy that would not give the Palestinians control over the territory as a national group (Sicherman 1991). On the matter of continued Israeli control of the territories being an impediment to peace, the platform promised that a Likud-led coalition government would undertake a publicity campaign among the Arab people "in order to make the Arabs realize that they do not need additional territories" (Likud 1977, 3). This campaign, according to the platform, would convince the Arabs that peace with Israel "will bring prosperity and progress to the Arab people" (Likud 1977, 3). In other words, the nature of the peace envisioned by the Likud platform was one in which the Arabs would be convinced to give up all of their goals in the conflict while no concessions would be asked of Israel.

In sum, my review of the 1977 platforms suggested that the differences between the two parties regarding the perception of the Israeli-Arab conflict remained much as they were in 1973. The two most significant changes in the 1977 platforms were the more differentiating view of the Arabs in the Alignment platform, and the new recognition in the Likud platform of the importance of diplomacy as a means for achieving security. In addition, some erosion was apparent in the theme of villa in the jungle. That change was consistent with the shift observed in both platforms from advocating the pursuit of a comprehensive resolution of the conflict with the entire Arab world toward contemplation of separate agreements with specific Arab nations. New language in the Likud platform expressed support for negotiating separate peace agreements with Egypt and Syria, although the terms of such agreements were largely left unspecified. Alignment similarly called for separate peace agreements with Jordan, Syria, and Egypt based on "territorial compromises *with each one of the neighboring Arab countries*" (Alignment 1977, 1, emphasis added). Again, this change could be linked to the Israeli-Egyptian and Israeli-Syrian separation-of-forces agreements (mentioned specifically as a foundation for peace in the Alignment platform) and also to public opinion that at that time showed a tendency to differentiate among different groups of Arabs (see Chapter 4). Note that these changes in platforms and public opinion preceded Anwar Sadat's visit to Jerusalem and the Israeli-Egyptian peace process.

The 1981 Elections

The 1981 elections resulted in what can be characterized as a tie between the major parties, with a slight edge toward Likud. The elections were held just two years after the successful consummation of the peace treaty with Egypt, and the impact of that momentous event was evident in both platforms. The Likud platform asserted that the agreement came about mostly because of Likud's successful policy. The Alignment platform put the Israeli-Egyptian peace process in a broader historical context and suggested that it was a result of Israeli military successes in the 1967 and 1973 Wars and, especially, the 1975 Israeli-Egyptian separation-of-forces agreement that "paved the road for Egyptian president Sadat's visit to Jerusalem" (Alignment 1981, 4). Both platforms, then, presented the peace agreement as resulting from Israel's policy, but Alignment's description of the event implicitly credited the Arab side with sincerity in its pursuit of peace.

While Likud's 1981 platform was in many ways similar to its previous platform (with some significant omissions, as shown below), more substantial changes were observable in the Alignment platform compared to its predecessor. References to the Israel-as-a-Jewish-state theme had always appeared in the Alignment platforms, but this time around they featured more prominently, in the first pages of the document. The first paragraph emphasized the "historical right of the Jewish people to establish its state in its homeland." The platform also declared that "Israel was always designated to be a Jewish state" (Alignment 1981, 3), and in its third sentence on page 1 referred to Israel's right to control Jerusalem, including East Jerusalem (in the 1977 platform, this issue appeared only on p. 28). Likud had always placed these Jewish state references at the beginning of its platforms, and so it was this time as well. Both 1981 platforms, then, started by emphasizing the value of Israel as a Jewish state, and this was the most prevalent theme of the ethos in each platform (see Table 8.1). This could be explained by the peace agreement with Egypt. In the 1979 Camp David Accords between Israel and Egypt, Israel recognized the "legitimate rights of the Palestinian people"—a statement that contradicted the theme in the ethos that indicated exclusive Jewish rights for the land. Both parties, then, may have felt the need to stress the Jewish theme that seemed to be "jeopardized" by the accords.[9]

This unanimity did not extend, however, to the platforms' attitudes toward the Palestinians. The Likud platform still did not recognize the

Palestinians as a national group and referred to them only as "Arab inhabitants of Judea, Samaria and Gaza" (Likud 1981, 2). A new entry in the platform said that the Camp David autonomy plan "would not constitute a state, sovereignty or self-determination in any form. Self-determination was given to the Arab people by the establishment of 21 Arab states," and that the autonomy arrangements for the Palestinians agreed on at Camp David were the best guarantee against the creation of a Palestinian state (Likud 1981, 3). In contrast, the Alignment platform included many references to "Palestinians" (see Table 8.2), but reiterated that self-determination for the Palestinians could be achieved only in a Jordanian-Palestinian state "which the majority of its [Jordan] citizens are Palestinians, as well as densely populated areas in Judea, Samaria and Gaza" (Alignment 1981, 5). Nevertheless, it expressed willingness to talk with Palestinian leaders and organizations that would recognize Israel and denounce terrorism (Alignment 1981, 6), demonstrating a growing recognition of Palestinians as a national group that had the right to participate in talks regarding its future. That was, however, provided that future did not lead to a Palestinian state: the 1981 Alignment platform included a new sentence that securitized the establishment of such a state and, in language similar to that found in Likud platforms, warned that such a state would "serve as a center of hostility and instigation that would endanger Israel and the whole region" (Alignment 1981, 5). Both 1981 platforms now securitized the possibility of a Palestinian state. This was probably a result of the Camp David Accords that referred to the future of the Palestinians in the territories (although it did not mention specifically the possibility of a Palestinian state). The Alignment platform also expanded on its 1977 discussion of the threat from unconventional weapons, speaking of "worrying signs of nuclear potential in the possession of belligerent Arab states" (Alignment 1981,10), and it reiterated its previous policy prescription—security based on defensible borders and territorial compromise. Despite the peace treaty with Egypt, then, threat perceptions remained high. Furthermore, as shown below, the Alignment platform, for the first time, mentioned a threat to Israel's national identity. Thus, it indicated ontological anxiety.

As the villa dwellers began to make inroads into the jungle, the centrality of the villa in the jungle theme started to recede, as reflected in both 1981 platforms (see Table 8.1). Both still decried the aggression of some elements in the Arab world and shared a negative image of the PLO (more so in the Likud platform). But some of the criticisms found in previous platforms were gone. The Alignment platform no longer complained about the Arabs' dismissal and rejection of Israeli peace initiatives and, instead, repeatedly mentioned the peace process with Egypt. Likud omitted its 1977 assertion that the PLO was established by the Arab states to advance their uniformly hostile intentions toward Israel. Indeed, with the advent of the peace agreement with Egypt, it would have been difficult to sustain the old image of the Arab world as being uniformly opposed to peace with Israel and refusing to tolerate its continued existence. Further evidence of the decline of the villa sentiment could be seen in the increased differentiation practiced in the Alignment platform between the different groups and entities within the Arab world (see Table 8.2).

The most significant transformation in both 1981 platforms, however, was undoubtedly with regard to the theme of peace. Not only did it feature more prominently in the platforms but the nature of the perceived peace had become more and more concrete and policy oriented. The Likud platform expressed its commitment to the Israeli-Egyptian peace agreement, promised to continue the negotiations regarding Palestinian autonomy and envisioned a potential Israeli-Syrian peace process. The Alignment platform stated that it would honor the Israeli-Egyptian peace agreement and, not to be outdone, suggested peace agreements with Jordan, Syria, and Lebanon might be in the offing.

Another significant development in Alignment's 1981 platform was its growing discussion of potential contradictions between values and goals. While previous platforms referred only to the trade-off between keeping the territories and peace, the 1981 platform pointed to tension between Israeli control of the territories and other goals. A new sentence in Alignment's platform contended that annexation of the territories, as advocated by Likud, "will transform Israel from a Jewish state to a bi-national state" (Alignment 1981, 4) and went on to say that "Alignment rejects the notion of permanent domination over the million and 200 thousand Palestinian-Arabs, the inhabitants of these territories" (Alignment 1981, 4) as offensive to the moral and societal essence of the State of Israel. Variations on this idea appeared three times in the platform (pp. 4, 6, 7). This contention indicated a threat to identity and, thus, a sense of ontological insecurity that was especially threatening (see Chapter 3). Israeli control of the territories was now presented in the Alignment platform as clashing with three values: peace, Israel as a Jewish state, and security (the latter in the sense that withdrawal from densely populated Palestinian areas, in the context of peace accords, would be a vital contribution to the security of Israel). In short, the 1981 platforms reflected a continuation of some of the trends witnessed in the 1977 elections: a weakening of the perception of Israel as a villa in the jungle surrounded by Arabs disinterested in peace, as well as an elevation of the value of peace and a concretization of its nature. Although Likud remained more loyal to the original ethos than Alignment, the peace process with Egypt transformed its platform as well. Likud's 1981 platform presented a less negative image of the Arabs and a perception of peace as a compromise (negotiation about Palestinian autonomy), not just an Israeli dictate.

The 1984 Elections

The 1984 elections—a close race with a small margin in favor of Alignment—ended with a national unity government and a power-sharing agreement between the parties. The elections took place while Israel was two years into the Lebanon War, and the platforms echoed the political effects of the war. The Likud platform described the war as an Israeli success, in which the terrorist bases in Lebanon were destroyed and the threat of terror in northern Israel was removed (Likud 1984, 2). The Alignment platform perceived the war as a "quagmire" (Alignment 1984, 14). It accuses the Likud-led government of going beyond the legitimate goal of defending northern Israel and trying to pursue unrealistic political goals. Despite these starkly different perspectives on the war, the effects on the ethos beliefs as reflected in both platforms appeared to have been mild. As before, the changes were to be found mainly in the Alignment platform.[10]

The war and its associated controversies likely inspired Alignment to expand its discussion of security themes and, specifically, to add a chapter dedicated to the IDF. In the chapter, the party paid tribute to military duty, military technological innovation, and the IDF moral code of conduct (Alignment 1984, 14–15), but at the same time took pains to assert the absolute authority of the elected civilian government over the military (Alignment 1984, 15). This was a not so subtle allusion to Alignment's belief that, in the Lebanon War, the Israeli government and parliament were misled by Defense Minister Ariel Sharon and IDF Chief of Staff Rafael Eytan about the war's goals and plans.

In what seemed like a late reaction to the Israeli-Egyptian peace agreement and to trends observed in Alignment platforms as early as 1977, the Likud platform finally started to "explore the jungle" and, thus, to reference specific Arab states and groups rather than use general terms like *Arabs* (see Table 8.2). While Likud continued to portray the same positive image of Israel as a villa in the jungle, the Alignment platform instead offered more mixed reviews. The introduction to the Alignment platform marveled at the miraculous nature of Israel's history and included many references to the belief that Israel must aim to be a light unto the nations "not only as an aspiration and as an obligation of the people to its destiny and its uniqueness among nations, but also as a vital condition for Israel's existence" (Alignment 1984, 8). At the same time, the platform did not shy away from discussing negative aspects of Israeli society and state. As shown above, it described the war as a "quagmire" (Alignment 1984, 14). It also mentioned the "Jewish terror group affair,"[11] which in its view offended Jewish and human moral values and was a result of chauvinism and a rejection of any territorial compromise (Alignment 1984, 12). The Alignment platform also refuted old beliefs about Israel as a cohesive society. Its introduction decried the social rift and the weakening of national consensus regarding questions of war and peace. Indeed, the Lebanon War provoked some of the most severe expressions of political violence in Israeli history.[12]

Finally, the Alignment platform returned to and expanded on its discussion of the inconsistency between Israel's control of the territories and some ethos beliefs, this time adding a paragraph on the tension about the value of Israel as a democratic state:

> The domination policies of the Likud government in Judea, Samaria, and Gaza have already caused alarming undermining of the democratic and moral values of the Israeli society regarding the rule of law, equality before the law, and the treatment of Israeli Arabs. The Alignment position is that maintaining a democratic regime in Israel, which is predicated upon equal rights for all of its citizens, is not consistent with permanent domination over the Arab Palestinian inhabitants of Judea, Samaria, and Gaza strip. (Alignment 1984, 12)

The platform twice repeated the idea that Israeli control of the territories endangered the goals of Israel as a Jewish and democratic state as well as Israel's security.[13] Alignment platform, then, intensified its securitization of Israel's control of the territories and the sense of ontological insecurity.

To conclude, the main change observed in the 1984 Alignment platform was the erosion in beliefs regarding a positive Israeli image and national unity. The main change in the 1984 Likud platform was a more nuanced view that distinguished among specific Arab groups. Some of these changes (e.g., erosion in beliefs about national unity) may be attributed to the Lebanon War. Other changes seemed to be influenced by other events such as the Jewish terror group affair and a delayed effect of the Israeli-Egyptian peace agreement.

The 1988 Elections

The 1988 elections, another close race that ended with a Likud victory, took place ten months into the first intifada, and the platforms showcased the initial processing and framing of this ongoing event. Both platforms referred to the intifada as localized riots, and to the IDF as the force attempting to restore law and order in the territories (Article 2.8 in Likud platform; Article 1.6.7 in Alignment platform). Alignment, for example, noted that "in the face of the disturbances in the territories, the task of the IDF and the security services is to bring about, rapidly and with determination, the enforcement of order and tranquility in Judea, Samaria and Gaza Strip" (Alignment 1988, 13). However, as shown below, the Alignment platform also assigned some responsibility for the eruption of the intifada to Israel's policies.

As in previous election cycles, the Alignment platform seemed to be more affected by the events in the conflict than the Likud platform. Nevertheless, some meaningful changes could be found in that platform as well. The 1988 Alignment platform opened with security beliefs—the first chapter, titled "Foreign Policy and Security Policy," included many paragraphs that praised the IDF (e.g., Articles 1.6.3–1.6.14; Article 1.6.17) and the way it was handling "the difficult situation in the territories" (Alignment 1988, 7). At the same time, the platform emphasized, more so than its predecessors, the importance of diplomacy and its superiority over military means in the quest for security. A sample of statements that expressed this belief includes, "Peace is an important element of security" (Alignment 1988, 7) "The solution to the Palestinian problem can only be political" (Alignment 1988, 8), and "This conflict can be resolved only by political means and not by force of arms" (Alignment 1988, 13).

The 1988 Alignment platform went further than before in its refutation of Israel as a villa in the jungle. In a sign that a mirror may have finally been installed in the villa (albeit one with partisan filters), the platform included explicit pronouncements that Israel (led by Likud) was responsible for the "political deadlock" in Israeli-Arab relations. Likud's peace policy was described as a "rejectionist policy" (Alignment 1988, 9), and the platform declared that "the outbreak in December 1987 of disturbances in the territories . . . was caused largely by the political paralysis imposed by the Likud" (Alignment 1988, 10). This was a totally different position from the one that characterized previous Alignment platforms, which placed all the blame for the absence of peace on the Arab side. This time around, the blame was apportioned to both sides. True, parties tend to criticize their political competitors and blame them for any problem a country is facing, but this was the first time that an argument placing the blame for the absence of peace on Israel had appeared in this context. Hence, it could serve as another indicator for the weakening of the villa theme at that time.

Other sections of the Alignment platform pushed back on the siege beliefs of the ethos. The emphasis on Israel's friendly relations with other states and on the goal of widening that circle was pronounced. Beyond the evergreen references to the friendship with the United States, there were references to the end of the Cold War and a positive view of the Soviet Union. Whereas the 1984 platform had included only four lines, mostly negative, about the Soviet Union, the 1988 platform devoted twenty-seven lines to, among other things, praising positive steps by the Soviets such as increasing the rate of immigration permits for Soviet Jews and exercising more tolerance for expressions of Jewish culture among Soviet Jews. The 1988 platform also dedicated forty-five lines to Israel's relationship with European countries (compared to only five in 1984) addressing the bad (the Holocaust, and the expulsion of Jews from Spain) and the good (the emancipation of

European Jews, and the current economic ties between Israel and Europe). Third world countries were also accorded increased attention, with fifty-seven lines versus only eight in 1984. The platform praised the friendly relations and economic cooperation with these countries and vowed to continue the "partnership in the fight for freedom and for a just society" (Alignment 1988, 17). The possibility of relations with China and Japan was also contemplated. Finally, two sentences from the 1984 platform, about anti-Israeli decisions at the UN and about the fact that the United States and other friendly countries were providing weapons to Arab states, did not appear in the 1988 platform.

As for the 1988 Likud platform, the main change was the omission of the proposal to allow the Palestinians to apply for Israeli citizenship. It is likely that the intensity of the first intifada drove home the realization that the Palestinians in the territories would not settle for a solution short of self-determination, making the Likud's vision untenable. Nevertheless, this change in the platform left the tensions between Likud's insistence on Israeli sovereignty over the territories and its commitment to a Jewish democratic state unresolved.

Although both 1988 platforms referred to the intifada mostly as an Israeli attempt to restore law and order in the territories (and not as an Israeli attempt to suppress a Palestinian popular demand for self-determination), the event seems to have weakened Alignment's confidence in some themes of the ethos such as villa in the jungle. It also seems to have strengthened Alignment's belief in diplomacy as the preferred means to achieve security. The weakening of siege beliefs evident in the 1988 Alignment platform is likely attributable to contemporaneous non-Israel-centric events such as the end of the Cold War. As in the past, the Likud platform tended to stick with the previous ethos of conflict while Alignment drew further away from it. However, the Likud platform for the first time exhibited a different approach for dealing with the potential inconsistency in its goals—it abandoned bolstering as the main strategy to solve the inconsistency and simply left it unresolved.

Numerous studies have pointed to the profound effects of the first intifada on Israeli politics. According to these studies, the intifada forced Israelis to see the implications of making no decision about the future of the territories and their inhabitants, and the tensions between this policy and other values such as Israel as a democratic state (J. Shamir and Shamir 2000). My historic review of the election platforms, however, revealed that this view had been expressed in Alignment platforms years before the intifada.[14] Instead, the Likud platform was most affected by this dose of reality: it shifted from coping with the inconsistency among its goals by using the strategy of bolstering to leaving this discrepancy unresolved probably because it was unable to articulate a tenable solution.

The 1992 Elections

The four years between the 1988 and the 1992 elections saw numerous major events in the Israeli-Arab conflict: the continuation of the first intifada, the Gulf War, and the Madrid conference. The elections ended with a clear victory for the Labor party (beginning with the 1992 elections, Alignment ran under the name "Labor"), and the platforms published in advance of the elections provide important insight into the impact these events had on the parties' view of the conflict. While neither platform mentioned the Gulf War directly, there were some indirect references that are discussed below. Both platforms, however, mentioned the first intifada (Likud 1992, 4; Labor 1992, 6). Both described Palestinian aggression and terrorist acts in the intifada and the role of the IDF in dealing with these challenges. Labor expressed the view that the most viable path to ending the intifada was by engaging in diplomacy and, ultimately, reaching a peace agreement with the Palestinians. Likud, on the other hand, continued to advocate for military measures. The discussion of the Madrid conference mixed in a bit of partisan posturing, with Likud calling it a triumph for its foreign policy (Likud 1992, 2), in line with the belief about Israel as a peace-loving state, and Labor deriding the conference as a "show" by a Likud government that had no real interest in peace (Labor 1992, 1).

For the first time in the period covered by this book, significant changes could be seen in both platforms, not only the Alignment (now Labor) platform as was the case in previous cycles. The frequency of the theme about Israel as a Jewish state decreased in both party platforms compared to past platforms (see Table 8.1). The declaration that opened the 1981, 1984, and 1988 Alignment platforms about "the historical right of the Jewish people to establish and maintain a state in its homeland" did not appear in the 1992 Labor platform. Additionally, the section about Jerusalem that appeared at the beginning of the 1981, 1984, and 1988 Alignment platforms was relegated to page 10 in 1992. A similar trend was apparent in the Likud platform which, unlike its earlier versions, did not open with declarations about the right of the Jewish people over Eretz Israel. Instead, it began with a statement about peace (a sentence about Jewish rights for the territories appeared in only the fifth paragraph). This trend matched election polls from this period, which indicated that peace was ranked in first place as the main value by more people (40 percent) than the values of a Jewish majority (28 percent) and of Greater Israel (only 14 percent) (J. Shamir and Shamir 2000, 216–217). Mendilow's (2003) analysis also indicates that the Likud 1992 campaign shifted its focus as the campaign progressed away from the value of Greater Israel, probably as a reaction to these trends in public opinion. As for Palestinian self-determination, Labor's platform included a new sentence that expressed explicit recognition of "Palestinian rights, including their national rights and their right to determine their future" (Labor 1992, 3–4). Likud's platform, in contrast, kept denying Palestinian self-determination rights—avoiding, in fact, the use of the term *Palestinians*—and insisted that such rights could be fulfilled in any of the existing twenty-one Arab states. As if to get them started on that path, the Likud platform stated that "Arab inhabitants of Judea and Samaria are Jordanian citizens" (Likud 1992, 2). It should be noted that this determination contradicted the abandonment by King Hussein of all Jordanian claims to the West Bank as of July 1988.[15] The gap between Labor and Likud on this issue, then, had widened.

Although both platforms objected to the idea of a separate Palestinian state, neither reprised past warnings about the threat that such a state might pose to Israel's security. In other words, both platforms presented desecuritization of the idea of a Palestinian state. The threat that now featured most prominently in both platforms was that of Arab states acquiring unconventional weapons (this threat was mentioned at least five times in the Labor platform—on pp. 2, 6, and 8). This shift in the perception of the nature of the threat, also observed in opinion polls, was likely influenced by the anxiety experienced by the Israeli public when Iraqi missiles, feared to be carrying chemical weapons, were fired on Israeli cities during the Gulf War. This event also contradicted the statement in previous platforms that Israeli control of the territories provided protection to the home front against missile attacks—since Iraqi missiles hit Israel despite its control of the territories. This experience may also have accounted for the increased centrality of the security theme in the 1992 Labor platform (see Table 8.1).

Dramatic changes were also observed regarding the theme of villa in the jungle. While references to hostile elements in the Muslim world remained in both 1992 platforms, on the whole the image of the Arabs was significantly more positive than in previous platforms. The negative references to the PLO were dropped from both platforms, and the Labor platform included a new commitment to change the law that forbade Israelis to have contact with PLO representatives (Labor 1992, 4). The Likud platform continued to expand its differentiation of the Arab and Muslim world, referring specifically not only to Egypt and Syria but also to Iran, Lebanon, Saudi Arabia, Kuwait, Morocco, and Tunisia. No longer were all of the Arabs perceived as enemies—rather, the Likud platform made a clear distinction among the different groups, based on the kind of relations they had established with Israel—from hostility to peace and cooperation. Indeed, a new sentence in the Likud platform can be seen to refute the old image of the Arabs as having no interest in peace with Israel. It mentioned the "Arab League members such as Kuwait, Saudi Arabia, Morocco and Tunisia" that "sat with Israel as part of the multinational peace negotiations" (Likud 1992, 2). It would seem that attending the peace conference in Madrid may have changed Likud's perception of some of the villa's neighbors. Another indication for the change can be seen in Table 8.3 that shows an increase (compared to previous platforms) in both parties' 1992 platforms in the percentage of references to friendly actions that were *initiated* by Arabs.

Labor's platform also reflected a further decline in the positive image of Israel. As noted above, it asserted that Israel, led by Likud, only "pretends" to have an interest in peace. It also mentioned the increasing corruption in Israeli society (Labor 1992, 1). Finally, for the first time, there was no reference in Labor's platform to "Israel's humane policy" in the territories. Most important, however, was the concern expressed in the platform that Israel might be losing its qualitative military edge in the region: "The need to preserve Israel's qualitative military superiority becomes even more acute when Arab states are increasingly acquiring high quality weapons and when IDF forces are being downsized due to budget cuts" (Labor 1992, 6). This may have been yet another reaction to the Gulf War and the Iraqi missile attacks on key targets in Israel. The two 1992 platforms celebrated the improvement in Israel's international status, and more than ever before expressed a desire to take part in international politics. Both platforms mentioned the fact that Israel was able to establish diplomatic relations with many countries that had refused to do so before. This theme was especially dominant in the Likud platform, which devoted its second chapter to this topic (before security—the subject of its third chapter). Both platforms, then, sharply contrasted with siege and isolationist notions that appeared in their older platforms.

Finally, in both 1992 platforms, there was an increase in the frequency of references to peace (see Table 8.1). Each platform stated at the outset its respective party's commitment to peace, and each presented a more optimistic view regarding the prospects of achieving peace. The Labor platform said that the chances for achieving peace had improved, and the Likud platform began with the declaration: "Yesterday it was Egypt, today it may be Jordan, Syria or Lebanon" (Likud 1992, 2). And more so than in the past, the Labor platform stressed the urgency of achieving peace with the Palestinians. It based this assessment on the emergence of new threats to Israel, and on the glaring inconsistency between Israeli control of the territories and core themes of the ethos:

> We want peace and *we need it*—in order to maintain a democratic regime, to secure a Jewish majority in the state of Israel, to create a humane society, and to assist with the absorption of immigrants, . . . and to increase economic growth. We know that *now more than ever, political deadlock and delaying the progress towards a peace agreement entails severe danger of wars and with them the danger of the introduction of new weapons of mass destruction to the region, and the transformation of local conflicts into a comprehensive regional conflict.* (Labor 1992, 2, emphasis added)

Expanding on its criticism of Israel's policy in the territories, the Labor platform argued (on page 1) that policy conflicted with the goal of a Jewish state not only because it endangered the preservation of a Jewish majority but also because it imperiled the goal of Israel as state for the Jews (a sanctuary for persecuted Jews from anywhere in the world). This was a reference to US demands for a settlement freeze in exchange for loan guarantees that Israel had asked for to help finance its absorption of new Jewish immigrants from the former Soviet Union. Finally, Labor also stated that Israeli control of the territories clashed with the goal of a welfare state (a goal promoted mainly by that party); its platform presented a list of altered priorities and advocated a shift of government spending away from settlement building in the territories and toward addressing social and economic needs in Israel proper.

Taken together, the two 1992 platforms reflected further erosion in the ethos of conflict that the parties had shared more than twenty years before; themes about peace, about villa in the jungle, and about the nature of the existential threat to Israel had significantly changed their content. Siege beliefs had lost most of their potency and peace (as a hope, not just as a wish) gained in stature as main value. This change was not sudden—rather, it was the product of a gradual process that began in the 1970s. The exact timing of this change was determined by many factors, some of them beyond the scope of this book (e.g., Shelef's 2010 explanation discussed at the beginning of this chapter). But they matched changes in the ethos as they appeared in public polls and, thus, changes in the ethos probably triggered this process and determined its direction. In addition, the process seems to have been accelerated by some major events such as the Gulf War and the Madrid conference.

These changes in the ethos of conflict that both parties shared had implications about the desirability of the status quo in the conflict. The heightened perception of the threat posed by unconventional weapons, the weakening of beliefs depicting Israel as a villa in the jungle that enjoyed technological and military superiority, and the fact that neither platform could cope successfully with the potential contradictions between the ethos beliefs and other societal beliefs (Greater Israel) or Israeli control of the territories all made the status quo less attractive than in the past. In addition, the desecuritization of the threat posed by the concept of a Palestinian state, the erosion in the perception of the Arab world as a uniformly hostile jungle, and the upsurge in optimism regarding the prospects of achieving peace created a context in which peaceful resolutions for the conflict seemed viable and desirable. It is not surprising, then, that both 1992 platforms introduced changes in the preferred policies vis-à-vis the Israeli-Arab conflict: Likud went beyond its 1988 platform, which referenced peace agreements with only Egypt, Syria, and Lebanon, and for the first time mentioned potential peace deals with Jordan as well as the "Arabs of Judea Samaria and Gaza" and "other Arab states" (Likud 1992, 2). Labor's platform included a detailed proposal for peace with Jordan, which was still based, as in the past, on the concept of a Jordanian-Palestinian state. Thus, Labor joined Likud in ignoring Jordan's proclaimed disassociation from the West Bank. The proposal, however, did include new provisions such as the freezing of settlement construction and Israeli willingness to negotiate mutual arms reductions (Labor 1992, 4). Labor's platform, hence, showed a greater willingness to compromise. At the same time, Labor's expectations as to the benefits of peace were higher than ever before: the platform envisioned a "new Middle East" with "a common market and joint projects in tourism, transportation and communication and with cooperation in the areas of energy, culture and science" (Labor 1992, 3). It is important to note that all of these changes in the ethos and preferred policies preceded the 1993 Oslo Accords—and they may, in fact, have been among its principal catalysts.

The 1996 Elections

The 1996 elections took place following the dramatic assassination of Yitzhak Rabin and as the Oslo process (after the Oslo Accords) was still unfolding. They resulted in a narrow and rather unexpected victory for Likud's leader Benjamin Netanyahu who, following a short-lived change in the electoral system, was the first ever to be elected prime minister in his personal capacity. However, Labor won the most seats in the Knesset—two seats more than Likud. The Likud platform included only a handful of references to the Oslo Accords. It promised to respect them but to "act to limit the *dangers these accords pose to Israel's security and future existence*" (Likud 1996, 3, emphasis added). In contrast, the Labor platform referred to the accords as a "breakthrough" (Labor 1996, 6) and exalted in the ensuing flurry of regional and international cooperation initiatives such as the Sharm-el-Sheikh Convention, the Casablanca Convention, the Amman Convention, and the Barcelona Convention (Labor 1996, 9). Notwithstanding these very different perspectives on Oslo, it is evident that both 1996 platforms largely continued the trends that began in 1992 of significant changes in the ethos themes.

Unlike previous Likud platforms, the 1996 platform did not include any explicit mention of the goal of Israeli sovereignty over all of the territories. In another first, it explicitly referred to "Palestinians" and "Palestinian authority" (Likud 1996, 3). The platform did reiterate, however, Likud's unwavering commitment to the value of a Jewish state and its steadfast conviction in the Jews' right to the entirety of the disputed lands.

Thus, it seems reasonable to conclude that the omission of the demand for Israeli control over the whole of the territories was not a result of a change of heart regarding the justness of Israel's claim to the territories but rather a bow to the realities of the Oslo Accords and the establishment of the Palestinian Authority in the West Bank and Gaza Strip. These events certainly challenged the idea of Greater Israel and forced Likud to make its choice between the value of Greater Israel and the value of peace. Put differently, the omission of the Greater Israel goal from Likud's 1996 platform did not indicate the party's complete abandonment of the goal but a decline in the salience of the goal for the party. This change resulted from a debate between ideological hard-liners and pragmatic members in the party that was influenced by public polls that showed prioritizing of other goals (e.g., peace) over the Greater Israel goal and support for a solution to the conflict with the Palestinians based on territorial compromise. These polls led pragmatic Likud members to conclude that, without a change in the party platform, the party would become "irrelevant" and be "condemn[ed] to many years in the wilderness of the opposition" (Mendilow 2003, 172–185; Shelef 2010, 166–171; Aronoff 2014, 45). Thus, this change was triggered by changes in shared beliefs in the society following the Oslo Accords.

Both 1996 platforms highlighted security (this was the central theme in the Labor platform—see Table 8.1). This increased focus on security was likely in response to the series of deadly suicide attacks carried out during 1994–1996 by Palestinians groups who opposed the peace process (and polls that indicated an increase in security concerns among the public). While acknowledging that these terrorist acts threatened the security of Israeli individuals, the Labor platform asserted that they did not threaten the existence of the State of Israel (Labor 1996, 5). The Likud platform securitized terrorism (Likud 1996, 3) and personal security along with other issues such as the threat of war with Syria, the need to preserve Israel's deterrence (Likud 1996, 9), and the threat of Iran's possession of unconventional weapons (Likud 1996, 9).

The changes in the villa in the jungle theme, which began in 1992 elections, continued to evolve in the 1996 elections. Both 1996 platforms presented a positive image of some Arab states. The Labor platform referred to states such as Egypt, Jordan, Morocco, Tunisia, Mauritania, Oman, and Qatar as "peace seeking Arab states" (Labor 1996, 8). But it also mentioned "fundamentalist Arab regimes" and the terrorist acts by Palestinian groups (Labor 1996, 6). In the Likud platform, Israel's relations with Arab states were discussed in the same chapter that covered Israel's relations with other countries in the world, including European countries. Arab states, hence, were no longer perceived as enemies. The platform mentioned Morocco and its contributions to the peace process. It stated that the Gulf states might establish relations with Israel based on mutual interests. Egypt was referred to as "the first Arab country to sign a peace agreement with Israel" and Jordan as the second (Likud 1996, 7). However, the platform also included negative references to the Palestinians and specifically to the Palestinian National Charter that, according to the Likud platform, still called for the destruction of Israel (Likud 1996, 3).[16] This ambivalent attitude toward the Arabs (more pronounced in the Likud platform) might be a result of the complex relations between Israel and the Palestinians at that time (the simultaneous existence of peace talks and terrorist acts).

As for peace, the 1996 Labor platform remained optimistic regarding the prospects for peace and suggested that it might be achieved by 2000 (Labor 1996, 3, 5). At the same time, the Labor platform expressed less willingness to compromise compared to 1992 (e.g., a new paragraph noted that any agreement would have to be approved in a referendum). The 1996 Likud platform was decidedly less optimistic and, accordingly, the frequency of the peace theme diminished relative to the previous platform (see Table 8.1). Furthermore, it emphasized the potential contradiction between peace and security. It mentioned the "dangers" that the Oslo Accords "pose to Israel's security and future existence" (Likud 1996, 3). Labor platforms, on the other hand, argued that peace was the main means for achieving security. For example, it stated that "a stable peace is itself an important security factor in the strength of the country"—this idea appeared three times in the platform (on pp. 3, 4, 5).

To sum up, the 1996 platforms reflected the continued weakening of the ethos themes in platforms. Changes in the Likud platform brought it even closer to Labor's perception of the Israeli-Arab conflict.[17] That is not to say that Likud wholly embraced Labor's dovish view of the conflict. Contrary to the Labor platform, it did not express explicit recognition of the Palestinians as a nation, it conveyed a more negative view of the Palestinian Authority, and it remained deeply skeptical about the prospects of resolving the conflict. These disparities matched the divergence in the parties' policy preferences regarding the idea of a Palestinian state. The Likud platform still opposed the idea of a sovereign independent Palestinian state and insisted that Israel should not agree to anything beyond an autonomy of some kind (Likud 1996, 3). The 1996 Labor platform, in contrast to its predecessors, did not express any objections to a Palestinian state, and in fact implicitly endorsed it when it declared that a government led by Labor would promote a separation between Israelis and Palestinians that would be based on security interests and "national identity aspirations on both sides" (Labor 1996, 7). Its commitment to the idea of a Jordanian-Palestinian state, then, was abandoned. It is also important to note that both parties did remain loyal to some themes in the original ethos: their platforms endorsed the goal of a Jewish state in Israel, identified at least some hostile groups within the Arab world, and reflected a broad consensus about the importance of the value of security. The

1996 platforms, then, represented a weakening of the ethos of conflict—but not its demise or its replacement by a broadly accepted ethos of peace.

The 1999 Elections

The 1999 elections, which ended with a landslide victory for Labor's leader Ehud Barak, took place during the later stages of the Oslo process. The Oslo process was discussed in the Likud platform mainly in the context of insisting on the need for reciprocity with the Palestinians and making sure they met in full their obligations under the agreement (Likud 1999, 4). The platform also boasted that Likud was able to reduce the size of territory that was turned over to the Palestinians as part of the Israeli-Palestinian agreements (Likud 1999, 6). The Labor platform described the Oslo Accords as the only viable mechanism for reaching a historic reconciliation between Israel and the Palestinians. However, like the Likud platform, the Labor platform stated that the accords were based on the principles of reciprocity (Labor 1999, 6). Thus, whereas in 1996 it was mainly Likud expressing doubts about the Oslo process, this time around the skepticism was shared by both parties. Accordingly, my review of the 1999 platforms revealed a resurgence of several of the dormant themes of the ethos of conflict.

The theme of Israel as a Jewish state was stronger in the 1999 platforms of both parties compared to the previous elections (see Table 8.1). In addition, the Likud platform contained a new paragraph stating that the Palestinians should abandon their claim to the Right of Return and that Palestinian refugees should be resettled in their current locations (in Arab states) (Likud 1999, 7). Thus, the explicit opposition to the Palestinian Right of Return, not seen in a Likud platform since 1984, reappeared in 1999. With potentially serious final status negotiations going on, Likud may have felt the need to restate its opposition to the Right of Return. While the Likud platform did not mention the goal of Israeli sovereignty over all the territories, it called for Israeli control of a large area of the territories and, especially, preservation of Israeli settlements there. It justified this goal based on the Jewish theme—the statement that the settlements represented Jewish rights for the land—and security arguments (Likud 1999, 7).

The security theme was more prevalent in the 1999 Labor platform than in 1996. Both 1999 platforms securitized terrorism (Likud 1999, 5; Labor 1999, 6), and the Labor platform omitted the previously present assertion that terrorism did not constitute a strategic threat. Moreover, there was no reference in the Labor platform to the threat of unconventional weapons in the possession of Iran or other Muslim states. The Labor platform, then, focused on terrorism and personal security as the main threat. The Likud platform repeatedly decried the "terror infrastructure" that was established within the areas under control of the Palestinian Authority, but it also mentioned other severe threats like the threat posed by the "presence of Palestinian security forces in proximity to Israeli civilian centers, Israeli government and strategic installations" (Likud 1999, 5), the threat of pollution of the water sources of Israel located in the territories (Likud 1999, 7), and the Israeli Air Force's need to control the airspace over the territories as protection in case of war (Likud 1999, 7). In a way, this can be seen as a reprisal of the warnings about the threatening nature of a Palestinian state that were featured in previous Likud platforms. Furthermore, the threat from a Palestinian state was more dominant in the 1999 Likud platform than any other type of threat. Thus, in both 1999 platforms, the focus of the threat discussion had shifted from unconventional weapons to the threat of Palestinian forces and terror groups. As dark clouds of doubt and distrust gathered in the skies, the jungle started to reacquire its ominous complexion. The Likud platform included new references to the Palestinian terror groups and to anti-Israeli sentiments in Palestinian media and education programs (Likud 1999, 5) while still acknowledging the existence of friendly Arab states such as Egypt and Jordan. The Labor platform, on the other hand, did not include any references to peaceful and friendly Arab states. Finally, the frequency of references to the peace value in the Labor platform had decreased compared to previous platforms (see Table 8.1). Also, the Labor platform was less optimistic about the prospects for peace and no longer promoted its vision of a new Middle East.

To conclude, both 1999 platforms exhibited a restrengthening of some themes in the ethos (villa in the jungle, Israel as a Jewish state, and security) with a change in content of the belief about the nature of the main threat to Israel—a shift from the threat of unconventional weapons in the possession of Muslim states to the threat of a Palestinian state. In a sense, this was back to basics for both platforms—a revitalization of the ethos of conflict as a whole. A corresponding shift was apparent in the policy prescriptions, especially in the Labor platform. The Labor party declared that Israel preferred the creation of a Jordanian-Palestinian confederation—a return of an idea that was dropped from the 1996 platform, and one that contradicted Labor's recognition of the Palestinians as a separate people.[18] The 1999 platform went on to say that a Palestinian state was not and would not be an Israeli goal. However, if a Palestinian state were ever to be established as part of an Israeli-Palestinian permanent agreement, it would be imperative that the political and security restrictions on that state ensure vital Israeli interests (Labor 1999, 8). Thus, although Labor expressed more willingness than Likud to accept the idea of a Palestinian state, much like Likud it insisted on placing political and security restrictions on the Palestinian sovereignty. The differences between the two parties regarding this issue can therefore be seen as less significant than might be apparent at first glance.

The ethos of conflict as presented in the 1999 Labor platform (with its emphasis on security threats and its highlighting of the contradictions between Israeli control of the territories and key societal beliefs such as the belief in Israel as a Jewish and democratic state) suggested that the status quo would not be an attractive option. Yet because of the resurgence of the villa in the jungle sentiment, peace was seen as a less feasible option than before. Labor thus found itself in a tough spot, with an ethos perceiving the current situation as undesirable and a need to find a solution other than a peace agreement. Indeed, a new paragraph in the 1999 Labor platform advocated unilateral "physical separation" between the two nations (Labor 1999, 8). This was a first reference to the idea of "disengagement" that would come to dominate election campaigns in later years. The platform grounded this approach in the perceived threat to Israel's identity (ontological insecurity) and personal security: "Predicated on the belief that a Jewish state should not dominate another nation, the Labor proposes to initiate physical disengagement between the two nations. . . . Only such disengagement will guarantee personal security to its citizens and will serve the political, security, and moral interests of Israel" (Labor 1999, 8). Again, these changes predated the collapse of the Oslo process that happened a year later.

The 2003 Elections

The 2003 elections marked the return to the pre-1996 proportional electoral system, and ended with a clear victory for Likud.[19] The intervening period between the 1999 and the 2003 elections was marked by two major events: the failed Camp David conference and the outbreak of violence in September 2000 (the second intifada), which was ongoing during the 2003 campaign. Surprisingly, the 2003 Likud platform was almost identical to its 1999 platform and did not mention any of these events. In contrast, the 2003 Labor platform was different from its predecessor.

As in previous elections, security was a major theme in the 2003 Labor platform (see Table 8.1) and was covered in its first chapter. It called for compulsory national service for all (Labor 2003, 2) including Orthodox Jews and Israeli Arabs. In addition, the emphasis on the threat of Palestinian terror groups continued in the 2003 elections.[20] More significant was Labor's new belief about the conditions for achieving security. The Labor platform still promoted diplomacy and a negotiated agreement with the Palestinians as the preferred method for achieving security; however, it also suggested that, should negotiations fail, security could be achieved by Israeli unilateral actions aimed at separating Israel from the Palestinians. In the words of the platform, "Two rivals need to engage with each other to reach a peace agreement, but security can be reached by the actions of only one side" (Labor 2003, 1). This approach was consistent with the fact that the 2003 platform, compared to previous Labor platforms, exhibited a significant strengthening of the villa in the jungle theme. As can be seen in Table 8.3, the Labor 2003 platform showed an increase in references to Arabs in the context of hostile actions (50 percent of references to Arabs were in the context of hostile actions, compared to only 19 percent of such references in 1999). Yet the platform referred to the Palestinians as a "nation" (Labor 2003, 4), an indication that the party did not dismiss the Palestinians' claim to self-determination.

Unlike previous platforms, there was no chapter with the title "peace," and the word "peace" seldom appeared in the 2003 Labor platform (being replaced, e.g., by "permanent settlement," "political negotiations," or "diplomatic horizon"). Ironically, in these elections peace was more frequently mentioned in the (reheated) platform of the hawkish Likud party than in that of the dovish Labor party. The Labor platform was also much more pessimistic about peace, remarking at one point that "the [Israeli] hopes for ending the Palestinian-Israeli conflict were dashed as a result of the waves of hatred, incitement, extreme violence, and terror unleashed on Israel under the patronage of the Palestinian Authority" (Labor 2003, 4).

The 2003 Labor platform, then, was characterized by an intensification of trends that were observed in the 1999 elections: a strengthening of the security theme, an emphasis on Palestinian terrorism, a strengthening of the villa in the jungle theme, and a weakening of peace beliefs amid pessimism about the prospects for peace. Thus, the tension between an urgent need to change the status quo of Israeli control of the territories, and pessimism regarding the prospects of a negotiated peace, carried over into the Labor platform and even seemed to intensify. The dual-track solution alluded to in the 1999 platform was further developed in 2003. On the one hand, the 2003 platform called for negotiation with the Palestinians and expressed more willingness than ever before to compromise for the sake of peace. It clearly accepted the idea of a Palestinian state, and this time around did not seek to impose any political or security restrictions on that state.[21] This acceptance was consistent with the Labor party's recognition of the Palestinians as a nation. Furthermore, for the first time, the Labor platform mentioned possible concessions on Jerusalem: the idea of a "special regime" in the old city and an insistence on Israeli sovereignty only in the Jewish quarter of the city (Labor 2003, 4). This was a significant change from the seemingly immutable position that featured in all previous Labor platforms—a unified Jerusalem under Israeli control—and was another indication of the weakening of united Jerusalem as a sacred goal. At the same time, Labor emphasized and further developed an idea that first appeared in its 1999 platform, that of a unilateral Israeli withdrawal from certain territories if negotiations failed. As in the 1999 platform, the rationale for this unilateral action was the perceived contradiction between democracy and Israeli control of the territories and the security theme of the ethos. According to the platform, Israeli withdrawal from some territories and the building of a separation barrier between Israel and the Palestinians "will bring more security for everyone" (Labor 2003, 1) and it also "will end Israeli control of another people" (Labor, 2003, 4).

The 2006 and 2009 Elections

In Israel's vibrant multiparty system, it was not unusual for new parties (often led by established politicians) to spring up, especially around election season. It was, however, unusual for such a newcomer to sweep into power. And yet that is exactly what took place in the 2006 elections. A new party—Kadima—was established by former prime minister and former Likud leader Ariel Sharon and other key figures from the two historically major parties—Likud and Labor.[22] Following the elections, Kadima became the largest party in the Knesset (with 29 of the 120 seats). As a result, and for the first time in Israel's history, the largest party in the Knesset was neither "Alignment/Labor" nor "Herut/Likud." Labor was the second largest with nineteen seats and Likud the third with only twelve seats. Following the 2006 elections, Kadima formed a government with Labor and other parties while Likud led the opposition. In the 2009 elections, Kadima again won the most seats in the Knesset (twenty-eight), followed closely by a resurgent Likud with twenty-seven seats. At the end of the day, it was Likud that formed a government with Labor (thirteen seats) and other parties while Kadima led the opposition. Given Kadima's prominent role in these elections, in this section I analyze its platform as well as the platforms of Labor and Likud. I combined my discussion of the 2006 and 2009 elections because both Likud and Labor issued only brief summaries instead of full platforms in the 2006 elections.

Of the major events in this time period, those most relevant to this discussion are Israel's 2005 unilateral withdrawal from Gaza (the "Disengagement," which entailed the removal of Jewish settlements), the 2006 Lebanon War, the takeover of Gaza by Hamas in 2007, and the 2009 Gaza War. Only the 2006 Kadima platform referred to the Disengagement, describing it as having created a "window of opportunity" for reaching a peace agreement with the Palestinians, by demonstrating Israel's willingness to compromise and yield territory (Kadima 2006, 2). All of the 2009 platforms mentioned the Lebanon and Gaza Wars. These events had a noticeable effect on security beliefs and on the villa in the jungle theme, as I demonstrate below.

As in previous elections, the goal of Israel as a Jewish state was the most prevalent in Labor and Likud 2009 platforms (see Table 8.1). However, this theme was especially central in the 2006 Kadima platform: Kadima's first sentence was dedicated to the goal of a Jewish state in Israel (compared to references in the second and third sections for Likud and the eighth section for Labor). All three parties in the 2006 and 2009 elections addressed the "State of the Jews" aspect of a "Jewish State"—they all had sections about the need to encourage Jewish immigration to Israel and Israel's responsibility for world Jews. They also all had sections about Jewish education and the goal of Israel as a state that would conform to Jewish traditions. However, the goal of preserving a Jewish majority in Israel was only emphasized in the Kadima documents (more on that below). None of the platforms avoided the term *Palestinians* or denied Palestinian nationality (e.g., by maintaining that Palestinians were Jordanians or "generic" Arabs—arguments seen in older platforms), but all expressed opposition to the Palestinian right of return.

There was consensus among the parties that a nuclear Iran was the main threat faced by Israel. The 2009 platforms also cited Palestinian terrorism and the threat of missile attacks by Hezbollah and Hamas—referring specifically to the Lebanon War and the Gaza War, respectively. For example, the 2009 Likud platform asserted that "Hezbollah has more weapons, and these weapons are more lethal, than ever before, and while there is a cease-fire in Gaza, Hamas continues to import huge amounts of ammunition, to prepare itself for another round of terrorism" (Likud, 2009 6). The 2009 Kadima platform identified yet another threat—that of non-Jewish immigrants[23]—and argued that "uncontrolled arrival of [non-Jewish] immigrants to Israel from other countries in our region and from elsewhere threatens public order and the Jewish and democratic character of the state" (Kadima 2009, 1).

But the parties differed in the way that they described the link between security and peace. Likud's 2006 summary and 2009 platform argued that overwhelming Israeli military superiority and deterrence were the best guarantors of the stability of any peace agreement. In contrast, Kadima argued that "the State of Israel has a clear interest in a peace agreement that would determine the permanent borders and would guarantee the national and security interests of the State of Israel" (Kadima 2006, 1). The 2009 Labor platform declared that "peace and security are linked" (Labor 2009, 1), but at the same time emphasized military means as the most effective in dealing with terror and Hamas.

The villa/jungle dichotomy was back with a vengeance in 2009, as evident in the Labor and Likud platforms. (See Table 8.1. For the dramatic increase in the Likud platform's references to Arabs in the context of hostile actions, see Table 8.3.) This resurgence was likely a reaction to the Lebanon and Gaza Wars. The Labor platform mentioned the "axis of evil"—Iran, Hezbollah, and Syria—and "terrorism incubators" in Gaza (Labor 2009, 2). It argued that Israel had a military advantage over its enemies and that the IDF had learned its lessons from the 2006 Lebanon War and degraded the military capabilities of Israel's rivals. Thus, in Labor's view, the villa towered over the hostile jungle. The axis of evil motif also featured in the Kadima platform, which argued that "the State of Israel is now fighting against an Islamic extremist coalition led by Iran, which also includes other countries and terrorist organizations such as Hamas and Hezbollah." But the platform differentiated between Arab groups and identified "pragmatic forces in our region" that Israel should cooperate with against "the extremist forces [that] are working to harm the citizens of Israel and are calling for Israel's destruction" (Kadima 2009, 1). The notion of villa in the jungle was especially prominent in the Likud summary and platform (see Table 8.1). The 2009 Likud platform referred to "the Iranian calls to wipe Israel off the map, Ahmadinejad's denial of the Holocaust and his promise to bring about a new one, the launching of missiles with 'Death to Israel' inscriptions" (Likud 2009, 6). The Palestinians also came under harsh criticism, with no differentiation among their various groups:

> We do not believe that the Palestinians are ready for an historic compromise that can end the conflict. There is no evidence that the Palestinians are ready to accept even the minimum requirements demanded by any Israeli leader. The Palestinians have rejected far-reaching concessions that we, the Israelis, proposed eight years ago, and their position has not changed or moderated since then, when it comes to the core issues. If anything, their position has become more extreme because of the weakness and laxity of the current government. (Likud 2009, 7)

Unlike their platforms from the 1990s, the Likud and Labor 2006 summaries and 2009 platforms seldom mentioned Israel's relations with the United States, the European Union, or any other non–Middle Eastern country. Neither did they invoke the kind of siege beliefs about a hostile world common in their platforms in the 1960s and 1970s. The 2009 Kadima platform did refer briefly to Israel's relations with the United States, Russia, the European Union, China, and India. More importantly, it explicitly refuted siege beliefs: "The perception that 'the whole world is against us' proved to be wrong in recent years, and while our positions are not always accepted [by other states], the world has a growing appreciation of Israel's right to defend itself. This appreciation will increase as Israel is perceived as willing to negotiate a peace agreement with its neighbors and not as a 'peace rejectionist,' as it was perceived in the past" (Kadima 2009, 3). As for the peace theme, all three parties declared in both 2006 and 2009 that peace was Israel's primary objective. They all referred to peace as a political solution that would require Israeli concessions.

Finally, the parties presented differing views about the potential clash between ethos beliefs and other societal beliefs or contexts. This tension was most vividly on display in the Kadima documents, both of which began with a statement about the clash between the idea of Greater Israel and the goal of Israel as a Jewish and democratic state: "The choice between letting every Jew settle anywhere within the Land of Israel, and maintaining the state of Israel as a national Jewish homeland, necessitates relinquishing parts of the Land of Israel" (Kadima 2006, 1). At the same time, Kadima continued to affirm the Jewish right to the whole land, in effect adopting a trade-off strategy—giving up the territorial goal to preserve a more important goal, namely, that of maintaining a Jewish and democratic state. Indeed, Kadima noted that "the ceding of parts of the Land of Israel does not constitute the abandonment of this ideology [the Greater Israel ideology], but the realization of an ideology which seeks to guaranty the existence of a Jewish democratic state in (parts of) the Land of Israel" (Kadima 2006, 1). The Labor summary and platform did not include an affirmation of Jewish rights to the disputed land and, as in the past, warned that Israeli occupation threatened Israel's future as a Jewish and democratic state and diminished its ability to fulfill its goal as a welfare country. In another echo of previous platforms, Labor called for changing the context of Israeli control of the territories to solve the contradictions between this context and Israeli goals. Likud, in contrast to Labor and Kadima, did not mention any clash between the Israeli ethos and other beliefs or contexts.

In sum, Kadima and Labor recognized the Palestinians as a separate people while Likud omitted its typical refutation of that notion. The three parties shared a perception of peace as a political solution that would require Israeli concessions. Accordingly, Kadima and Labor expressed explicit agreement with the idea of a Palestinian state while Likud neither opposed nor endorsed it. Labor and Kadima shared a sense of urgency and ontological anxiety, a conviction that peace with the Palestinians was the best means to achieve security, and a perception of a clash between the ethos and Israeli control of the territories. Thus, both supported peace negotiations with the Palestinians, though neither expressed the same confident optimism observed in platforms of the early 1990s regarding the outcome. In contrast to Labor and Kadima, Likud emphasized military means for achieving security and did not acknowledge any clash between the ethos and other societal beliefs or contexts. The perception of Israel as a villa in the jungle, with no differentiation among Arab groups, was more pronounced in the 2009 Likud platform, which declared emphatically that the Palestinians were not ready for peace. Thus, Likud advocated preservation of the status quo and an avoidance strategy—a policy of managing the conflict rather than trying to solve it.

Its 2009 platform declared that "Israel should focus its efforts on improving the daily lives of Palestinians. In particular, we need to help them develop their economic system" (Likud 2009, 7). The platform acknowledged that this policy would not resolve the conflict, but suggested that it would reduce the level of violence. It elaborated about Israel's demands, but did not envision that negotiations would resume in the short term.

Conclusion

In this chapter, I showed that the parties used the themes of ethos of conflict to explain and justify their policies and to criticize each other. However, some themes were more prevalent than others: Israel as a Jewish state and security were consistently the most dominant themes, villa in the jungle fluctuated in intensity, and themes such as siege and patriotism were less prevalent in the platforms of the surveyed period (1969–2009). My review also revealed some significant changes in the ethos over time. along with corresponding changes in the parties' preferred policies regarding the Israeli-Arab conflict.

In 1969, the two main parties shared one ethos that included five pillars—Israel as a Jewish state with exclusive rights to the land; the centrality of security, grounded in the perception of an existential threat; the view of Israel as a villa in the jungle; siege beliefs; and patriotism. At that time, the main points of contention between the parties concerned the territorial goal of the Jewish state as well as non-conflict-related matters such as social and economic issues. The parties also differed regarding the relative dominance of some themes (Jewish state and villa in the jungle were more dominant in Herut's platform). In addition, the platforms revealed a divergence in the parties' perceptions of potential contradictions between the ethos themes and other societal beliefs, and the strategies to cope with such contradictions. The Herut platform acknowledged a potential inconsistency between its goal of full Israeli sovereignty over the territories and the goal of Israel as a Jewish and democratic state, and it employed a strategy of bolstering to address this inconsistency. Alignment, for its part, denied any inconsistency between Israeli control of the territories and its declared commitment to "support any effort by small or large nations to achieve national freedom" (Alignment 1969, 14). The sharing of the ethos of conflict, specifically its core themes (Jewish state, security, and Israel as a villa in the jungle) and the fact that each party dealt successfully from their perspective with the potential contradictions, made preservation of the status quo through Israeli military superiority the preferred policy choice of both parties.

Starting in the early 1970s, however, the divergence between the two parties vis-à-vis the core ethos themes began to grow, reflecting a weakening of the ethos as a whole. Labor platforms openly refuted some of the main themes of the 1969 ethos (villa in the jungle and siege) and explicitly acknowledged the potential contradiction between Israeli control of the territories and major tenets of the ethos—Jewish state, security, and peace, as well as democracy and the goal of a welfare state. Labor adopted the strategy of changing the context of Israeli control of the territories to preserve these goals. Likud platforms did not initially stray as far from the 1969 ethos but, by the late 1980s and early 1990s, they had drawn much closer to the Labor positions. Thus, by the early 1990s, many of the beliefs that comprised the 1969 ethos were refuted by the platforms of both parties: the beliefs rejecting the Palestinian claims to self-determination, the image of Israel as a strong villa surrounded by Arabs who rejected peace and aspired to exterminate it, and the belief that "the whole world is against us." Peace beliefs became more dominant in the platforms of both parties. In addition, the content of beliefs about peace and about the nature of the existential threat to Israel changed significantly in the platforms of both parties: a shift in the perception of peace from an elusive aspiration to a realistic short-term prospect achievable by means of negotiations and compromise, and an elevation of the threat of unconventional weapons in the possession of Muslim states over that of a conventional war or Palestinian statehood, respectively. Finally, Likud abandoned its use of bolstering as a strategy for coping with the clash between ethos values and its embrace of a Greater Israel. These shifts had substantial policy implications: the perceived urgency and severity of the new threat, combined with a perception of corrosive contradictions between control of the territories and core ethos goals (which indicated a threat to identity and, hence, ontological anxiety) made the status quo of the Israeli-Palestinian conflict less desirable. And with the decline in the villa in the jungle sentiments and in siege beliefs, both parties expressed an unprecedented willingness to negotiate and compromise in the pursuit of peace.

The collapse of the Oslo process in 2000 heralded another major shift in the way that the Israeli ethos was reflected in election platforms. The platforms after 2000 reprised some themes from the 1960s and 1970s ethos but also differed from the early ethos in some meaningful ways. Like the 1969 platforms, the platforms after 2000 emphasized the goal of Israel as a Jewish state and security beliefs (that now highlighted both the danger of Palestinian terrorism and statehood and the threat of unconventional weapons). They also featured a resurgent perception of Israel as a villa in the jungle and a decline in peace beliefs and the optimism as to the prospects for peace. Contrary to the 1969 platforms, however, the platforms after 2000 recognized the existence of Palestinians as a national group, suggested means other than military for achieving security, and perceived peace as a political solution requiring compromises from both sides (including Israel). The platforms after 2000 differed in their villa in the jungle discourses: Kadima warned of an axis of evil—Iran, Hezbollah, and Syria—but also identified moderate Arab forces while Likud depicted a uniformly hostile Arab Muslim monolith, encompassing the Palestinians as well. Another important difference among platforms after 2000 was that Labor and especially Kadima still emphasized the contradiction between the idea of Greater Israel and the goal of Israel as a Jewish and democratic state, and called for changing the context of Israeli control of the territories to preserve the ethos goals. But Likud admitted no such contradiction. Yet Likud platforms stopped referring to the goal of establishing full Israeli sovereignty over the territories. Accordingly, the parties differed regarding their preferred policy. Kadima and Labor called for peace negotiations, based on the principle of two states—Israel and a Palestinian state—although they were not optimistic about the likelihood of a peace agreement (for a while they advocated unilateral separation from the Palestinians, but this idea disappeared from their platforms after Israel's Disengagement from Gaza and the subsequent takeover of the territory by Hamas). Likud, in contrast, did not see any prospects for progress in negotiations in the short term and advocated postponing those negotiations to an unspecified point in the future.

The changes in platforms that I described in this chapter were caused by many factors. Major events in the Israeli-Arab conflict triggered major changes, although other crucial factors that are beyond the scope of this book—such as the "evolutionary-dynamic" explanation described by Shelef (2010)—determined the timing of some of the changes, especially the delay effect on Likud platforms of some events. I further discuss the link between major events, ethos, and conflict resolution in the concluding chapter.

Notes

1. On changes in the beliefs of specific leaders see, for example, Ben-Yehuda and Auerbach(1991) and Aronof (2014). On changes in the beliefs of a specific party see, for example, Rynhold and Waxman (2008) and Inbar (1991).

2. I analyzed the platforms mainly through a thematic quality content analysis: first, by recoding election platforms according to the ethos themes; and, second, by comparative reading of the platforms that enabled me to identify year-over-year variations in each category. I also used quantitative content analysis to study the perceived relationships between Israel and the Arabs. I first searched for specific terminologies referring to Arab states and groups, then coded them according to the following categories: general references (such as "Arabs," "the enemy") and specific names such as Egypt, Syria, or Palestinians. I then used another linguistic approach to examine how the text referred to relationships between Israel and the Arabs. This analysis was based on a method developed by Franzosi (1994) for collecting narrative data, which organizes the textual data around a simple structure of

subject-action-object. I coded the actions related to these references according to their type (friendly, hostile, neutral) and the role of the Arabs (initiator/subject or recipient/object) with respect to the action.

3. The small right-wing party Yisrael Beiteinu merged into the Likud party before the 2012 elections. In the 2015 elections, the Ha'Tnuah party merged with the Labor party to run on a joint ticket called the Zionist Camp.

4. My coding was based on Bar-Tal's (1998) coding of ethos themes in school textbooks. The final coding book is available on request. The analysis refers only to sections in the platforms about Zionism, Jerusalem, security, peace, and foreign relations. Excluded from the analysis are platform sections that focused on other issues such as the economy, healthcare, housing, the environment and women's rights.

5. The Alignment platform, for example, mentioned nine Israeli conditions that had to be met in any potential peace deal between Israel and the Arab states. These included, among others, a united Jerusalem under Israeli control, borders that ensure Israel's vital interests, maintaining the Jewish character of Israel, and allowing unimpeded sailing for Israeli vessels through the Suez Canal. In addition, the platform emphasized that peace between Israel and Arab states should be a "true peace" and "comprehensive and lasting peace," not in the form of "partial and temporary agreements" (Alignment 1969, 13).

6. Beginning with the 1973 elections, Herut ran as part of a new party—Likud.

7. According to the Alignment platform, a peace agreement between Israel and the Arab states should include the following terms: cessation of any hostile acts; defensible borders with demilitarized zones; preservation of the Jewish character of Israel; Jerusalem united under Israeli control; and normal economic, social, and cultural relations between Israel and the Arab states.

8. The security zones that should stay under Israeli control, according to the Alignment platform, were "Greater Jerusalem, Golan Heights, Jordan Valley, Rafiah salient and Solomon region—Sharm-el-Sheikh region which is at the tip of the Sinai Peninsula" (Alignment 1977, 4).

9. J. Shamir and Shamir (2000, 220) used a similar explanation for the rise in respondents that chose "Jewish majority" as the main value in 1996 (and a decrease in those that chose "peace" as the main value that year). They argued that the public tended to rank higher "neglected" values over values that overemphasized in terms of policy and events.

10. One change in the Likud platform was the omission of the paragraph stating that Palestinian refugees should be resettled in the Arab states and not return to Israel. The absence of this paragraph, however, should not be interpreted as agreement with the Palestinian Right of Return demands. Rather, it is that at this point Likud took the opposition to the Right of Return for granted and did not feel the need to express it anymore.

11. Members of the Jewish Underground—a Jewish terrorist group formed by settlers in the West Bank—carried out a series of terror attacks including car bomb attacks against Palestinian mayors in 1980 and a terror attack at the Islamic College in Hebron in 1983 (three Palestinian students were killed). They also planted five bombs in five Palestinian buses, which were to convey civilians and tourists. Finally, they plotted to blow up the Dome of the Rock in Jerusalem. They were arrested in 1984 and three of the members in this group were sentenced to life in prison, but were released after seven years.

12. In February 1983, during a Peace Now rally in Jerusalem, a grenade was thrown into the crowd and one demonstrator was killed. This was a rare incident of political violence in Israeli politics.

13. For example, according to the Alignment platform, "Israeli security needs and the preservation of its unique national character, realization of Zionist goals and the aspiration to establish Israel as a westernized democratic society will guide the policies of the government towards permanent borders" (Alignment 1984, 9).

14. The 1988 Alignment platform repeated assertions from the 1984 platform that Israeli control of the territories would clash with the Israel as a Jewish and democratic state goal, security goal, and peace beliefs. It also added a new sentence: "A Jewish majority in most of the territory is preferable to the whole territory with the loss of the Jewish majority" (Alignment 1988, 7).

15. In a dramatic televised performance, on July 31, 1988, King Hussein proclaimed that "Jordan is not Palestine . . . the independent Palestine state will be established on the occupied Palestinian land, after it is liberated" (Peretz 1990).

16. Calls to destroy Israel were indeed included in the charter, but the charter was amended to remove them about a month before the elections (Israel Ministry of Foreign Affairs 1996).

17. Both parties presented similar views about the territories staying under Israel's control; they each insisted that Israel's eastern border should be the Jordan River and that Israel would keep the Golan Heights and "security zones" in the West Bank (Labor 1996, 6–7; Likud 1996, 3–4). Thus, the plan presented by Likud was similar in many ways to the Alon Plan that Labor adopted more than twenty years earlier, and included a willingness to withdraw from Gaza and some areas of the West Bank.

18. The 1999 Labor platform stated, "We acknowledge the Palestinian Authority and recognize its leaders as the representatives of the Palestinian people" (Labor 1999, 8).

19. In 2001 a special election for prime minister only took place; Ariel Sharon replaced Ehud Barak as prime minister, without any change in the Knesset composition.

20. Surprisingly, one of the few new sentences in the Likud platform pointed to a decrease in the perception of threat from Iran. It said that Israel followed with great interest the moderation trends in Iran and hoped that a permanent agreement with the Palestinians would stimulate a reconciliation process between Israel and other Arab and Muslim states (Likud 2003, 6).

21. However, the 2003 Labor platform, like the Likud platforms of 1999 and 2003, expressed explicit opposition to the Palestinian Right of Return (Labor 2003, 4).

22. However, Sharon was incapacitated by a stroke soon after forming Kadima and before the elections; he was succeeded by Olmert.

23. This is a reference to guest workers—from China, the Philippines, and Thailand—many of who are in Israel illegally, as well as refugees from Africa.

9

Conflict and Israel's Changing Political Culture

I was born in Israel and lived there into my adulthood. By 2018, when I finished writing this book, I had been living and raising my sons in the United States for seventeen years. I thus have, on the one hand, an intimate firsthand familiarity with the Israeli ethos and, on the other hand, enough distance and perspective to allow for a dispassionate analysis of the ethos and the socialization process that accompanies it. My study of the Israeli ethos focused on six main themes, inspired by Bar-Tal's (2013) framework about ethos of societies with prolonged exposure to intractable conflict: Israel as a Jewish state, Israel as a villa in the jungle, Israel as a small country under existential threat with national security as its main focus, Israel as a people dwelling alone (siege beliefs), strong patriotism, and peace beliefs. All of these themes, with the exception of the peace beliefs, were part of the Israeli ethos for most of the study period—they appeared in leaders' rhetoric, they were imparted to the younger generation in school curricula, and a majority of respondents in public polls agreed with them for long periods.

Together, the themes of the Israeli ethos provide one coherent prism for looking at the history and current reality of Israel and the Israeli-Arab conflict. To illustrate this, let us turn to a seminal text—Moshe Dayan's 1956 eulogy for Roi Rotberg, a member of Kibbutz Nahhal Oz on the southern border (near Gaza), who was killed by Palestinians. The eulogy portrayed Israel as a villa in the jungle by repeatedly contrasting Roi, for whom "the yearning for peace deafened his ears and he did not hear the voice of murder waiting in ambush," with "hundreds of thousands of [Arab] eyes and hands, praying for our weakness, to tear us to pieces" (quoted in Zertal 2005, 180). In a rare expression for its time, the eulogy noted the tragic fate of Palestinians in the refugee camps of Gaza, who saw "with their own eyes" how the Israelis made a homeland of the soil and the villages where they and their forebears once dwelt. Yet this apparent acknowledgment of Palestinian dispossession was not a source of guilt or regret for the speaker because of the justified right of the Jews to establish their state on this land. This right was justified by two arguments. First, the eulogy evoked the historical link of the Jews to the land; it compared Roi to the biblical hero Samson from the book of Judges—a brave Jewish warrior who fought against the Philistines in Gaza and who at one point lifted and carried the gates of Gaza (the same gates that Roi and his friends, according to the eulogy, now metaphorically carried on their shoulders). Thus, it suggested that the Jews were the original inhabitants of this territory, rather than the Palestinians who lived there prior to the arrival of Roi and his friends. The eulogy also justified the rebuilding of a Jewish state on this land as a safe haven for the "millions of Jews, who were exterminated because they had no country" and were "exhorting us to settle and build up a land for our people" (Zertal 2005, 180). In this worldview of a zero-sum nature, then, the suffering of the Palestinians was justified if the annihilation of the Jews was to be avoided. Siege beliefs were also reflected here: Dayan's speech did not mention any allies or friends of Israel. The only reference to the international community was a negative one—as the "ambassadors of scheming hypocrisy, who exhort us to lay down our arms" (Zertal 2005, 180). The conclusion was that Israelis must constantly be "armed and ready": "It is incumbent on us— morning and night—to be armed and ready. We are the generation of settlement, and without the steel helmet and the cannon's mouth we cannot plant a tree, nor build a house. There will be no life for our children if we do not dig shelters, and without barbed wire fence and machinegun we cannot pave roads nor drill for water" (Zertal 2005, 180).

Though Dayan spoke of living by the sword as being the fate of the current generation, there was nothing in his words to suggest that a different, more peaceful, future awaited the young children that now grew up surrounded by shelters, barbed wire fences, and machine guns. Sixty years later, the grandchildren of Dayan's listeners would still be fighting in Gaza and their great grandchildren would be hiding in shelters during missile attacks. The ethos as expressed in Dayan's speech helped Israeli Jews to accept this prolonged and harsh reality. It was presented to them as their "destiny," "fate," and "the only choice we have." Other societies also have seminal texts in the form of emotional speeches that were given during a fateful war.[1] The main aim of these addresses was to motivate people to fight and sacrifice their life for the nation. Dayan's speech, however, had another main purpose: "to persuade its audience to close its ears to other speeches—to the voice of peace" (Kochin 2012, 163). Peace was not a realistic option in Dayan's text. It was an illusion that might "blind" young Israelis and prevent them from seeing the "glint of the knife" or deafen their ears to the "sound of the lurking murderer" (Zertal 2005, 180). Like Delilah, who seduced Samson and cut his hair—the source of his extraordinary power—and thereby enabled the Philistines to overcome him, those who called on Israel to make peace with the Arabs were trying to seduce Israelis to lay down their arms so that the Arabs—the modern-day Philistines—could defeat and destroy them. Dayan argued, in other words, that Israelis must steel their hearts and avoid succumbing to false hopes and illusions of peace because "if the sword slips from our fists—our lives will be cut short" (Zertal 2005, 180).

Changes in the Israeli Ethos

The themes reflected in Dayan's speech have remained at the core of the Israeli ethos to this day. They have shown up in speeches of current Israeli leaders, such as Benjamin Netanyahu, and in school curricula. Public polls have indicated that many Israeli Jews agree with them. But my study also has revealed significant changes in the ethos over the years. The discussion of these changes that follows is organized by time periods, bookended by major events in the conflict: the 1967 War, Anwar Sadat's 1977 visit to Jerusalem, the first intifada, the Oslo process, and the second intifada. Table 9.1 lists these periods along with some of the findings in public polls on which this analysis was based.

The 1967 War Until Sadat's Visit in 1977

During this period, six core themes of the ethos (Israel as a Jewish state, Israel as a villa in the jungle, security, siege, patriotism, and national unity beliefs) were featured in leaders' speeches, were invoked in election platforms of parties from different political camps, and were imparted to the younger generation in school curricula. However, the Jewish state, security, and villa in the jungle themes were the most prevalent. Societal disagreements stayed mainly within the bounds of the ethos rather than disrupting it. Such was the case regarding one of the perennial disputes in Israeli society—the relationship between synagogue and state. Both sides agreed that Israel must have a Jewish character, and differed only about the application of this principle. Similarly, the controversies around the socioeconomic structure of the state took place within the framework of a general agreement about Zionist ideology, about the gravity of the external threats, and about the obligation of individuals to make sacrifices for the benefit of society; however, there was more consensus on sacrifices related to security than on the kind of economic sacrifices inherent in socialist societies (Horowitz and Lissak 1989).

Table 9.1   Endorsement of Four Themes in the Israeli Ethos, 1967–2016

Average Level of Agreement in Polls	Period 1 1967–1977	Period 2 1977–1987	Period 3 1987–1993	Period 4 1993–2000	Period 5 2000–2017
80% or more	Zionism (84%) Villa (81%) Patriotism (80%)	Zionism (91%)	Zionism (89%)		Zionism (80%)
60–79%		Patriotism (69%) Villa (68%)	Siege (70%) Villa (65%)	Zionism (72%)	Siege (71%) Villa (65%)
50–59%			Patriotism (50%)	Siege (54%) Villa (54%)	
Less than 50%					Patriotism (27%)

Notes: Zionism was measured by the question: "Are you a Zionist?" (Guttman and Dahaf). Villa was measured by two questions in two surveys: "There are those who claim that the Arabs' aim against Israel is not the return of occupied territories but the destruction of Israel. To what extent do you agree with this opinion?" (Guttman, polled during the years 1973–1981); and "What do you think is the ultimate goal of the Arabs: 1. Recapture some of the territory lost in the Six Day War, 2. Return of all territories lost in the Six Day War, 3. Conquer the State of Israel, or 4. Conquer the State of Israel and kill most of the Jews living there." (NSPOP, polled during the years 1986–2009). Patriotism was measured by the question: "There are those who claim that now we should ask people for many sacrifices. Do you agree with that?" (Guttman and Democracy Index). Siege was measured by the percentage of respondents who agreed with the statement: "Israel is and continues to be 'A people dwelling alone'" (NSPOP and Oren's 2016 Survey).

Despite the relative intertheme cognitive harmony that characterized the Israeli ethos in this period, it still held some potential internal contradictions. For example, maintaining that Israelis were militarily superior to their Arab enemies, both at the strategic level and in terms of the skill and commitment level of the individual soldiers (the essence of the villa in the jungle theme), did not necessarily fit with security beliefs implying an existential threat to the state. Levi Eshkol referred to this combination of power and vulnerability as "poor little Samson" (Shlaim 2000, 219). As exemplified in Dayan's speech, the way in which this contradiction was typically addressed was by asserting that Israel was indeed powerful enough to overcome the threats, provided that it did not let down its guard to allow the "sword to be knocked from our fists" (Zertal 2005, 180). Another tension in the Israeli ethos was between normalcy and uniqueness. On the one hand was a desire to be a nation like any other nation. (This was part of the justification for the establishment of the State of Israel—because it was the right of the Jewish nation like any other nation and because it put an end to the tragic fate of Jews in exile and returned them to the "normal course of history.") On the other hand, the ethos presented an ideal of Israel as a unique "light unto the nations," and siege beliefs asserted that the Jews were doomed to be the eternal Others (Brenner 2018). David Ben-Gurion argued that the two aspirations to normalcy and uniqueness "are apparently contradictory, but in fact they are complementary and interdependent." This was because Israel wanted to "be equal in rights in the family of nations" and to be a model state (quoted in Brenner 2018, 3). Hawkish leaders tended to downplay the wish to be a nation like any other nation and the justification that was linked to this desire, emphasizing instead siege beliefs and historical-religious justifications for the establishment of the State of Israel.

Potential contradictions also existed between the ethos and other societal beliefs, as between the values of democracy and Jewish state theme. This contradiction became especially apparent in the context of Israeli control of the territories captured in 1967, which were densely populated by Palestinians. Keeping masses of Palestinians under Israeli occupation without citizenship rights strained democratic norms. On the other hand, granting this sizable population full Israeli citizenship would threaten the goal of having a Jewish majority and a state with a Jewish character. This potential contradiction was mostly ignored in public polls and school curricula during this period while election platforms used the strategies of bolstering and denial to address it. The ethos, then, served as a meaning system for society and provided ontological security despite the perception of a high level of threat. In addition, numerous routines were based on this ethos such as the Israeli national calendar, a universal draft system, and school ceremonies.

The ethos in this early period reflected an Israeli view that the status quo vis-à-vis the conflict was sustainable—Israel was strong enough to withstand the Arab threats and, in any case, peace was not realizable in the foreseeable future. Accordingly, greater emphasis was placed on managing the conflict (e.g., a policy of military buildup and deterrence) than on solving it.

From Sadat's Visit to the First Intifada, 1977–1987

Sadat's visit and the ensuing peace agreement with Egypt brought substantial changes to the themes that composed the Israeli ethos in this second period of study. First, the beliefs that Jews had an exclusive right to the disputed land, and that Palestinians were not a people, weakened to such a degree that public polls on these issues no longer reflected a consensus. The dominance of the villa in the jungle theme declined (in public polls, election platforms, and school curricula), and some of its elements, specifically the tendency to view the whole Arab world as a single hostile entity, became significantly less pronounced. Societal beliefs about peace, while not part of the ethos, strengthened and their content shifted (mostly in polls and platforms, less so in school curricula): peace came to be regarded as a concrete political arrangement requiring concessions to and compromise with the other side. In addition, Labor party platforms stressed the inconsistency of the beliefs in Israel as a democratic and Jewish state and of peace on the one hand, and the context of "permanent forced Israeli control of the Palestinian inhabitants" on the other hand (Alignment 1981, 4). The main strategy used by Labor to solve this contradiction was to advocate for change in the context that was perceived as putting these values into conflict—namely, giving up Israeli control of densely populated areas in the territories. The Likud party, on the other hand, continued its use of bolstering to cope with this potential clash.

The main takeaway from the study of this period, hence, is that the ethos was no longer hegemonic as in the past. There were now manifestly distinct camps of hawks and doves, with diverging beliefs and policy prescriptions—the former supporting a Greater Israel and refusing to recognize Palestinians as a people, and the latter granting that recognition and advocating giving up sovereignty over some parts of the territories (both sides still opposed an independent Palestinian state). Thus, the peace process with Egypt weakened the ethos as a meaning system and increased ontological insecurity in society. (This was evidenced, for example, in a Labor platform that expressed anxiety based on threats to Israeli identity as a Jewish and democratic state). In Rumelili's (2015) terms, the changes in the ethos as described above indicated that, from the Israeli perspective, the conflict shifted from stable conflict to unstable conflict that involved both fear and ontological anxiety. But the ontological anxiety produced by the Israeli-Arab peace process was still limited. While the Israeli-Egyptian peace agreement indeed weakened beliefs that posited Egypt as an object of fear, Israeli perceptions of Palestinians and Syrians remained negative and they were considered as threats to Israel. Most of the previously discussed Israeli routines were not interrupted since the peace agreement with Egypt did not end the Israeli-Arab conflict or significantly alter Israel's basic self-perception as a villa in the jungle living under conditions of latent (and periodically active) war.

From the Eruption of the Intifada to the Onset of the Oslo Process, 1987–1993

During the 1980s, some of the core themes of the ethos lost their potency: the confidence in Israel's military superiority and its ability to prevail in a full-scale war (part of the villa in the jungle theme) seemed to be eroding in public polls, and similar concerns were expressed in election platforms. A decline was observed in patriotism as well (mostly in public polls, see Table 9.1). Toward the end of this period, a decline could also be seen in siege and in Arabs-would-exterminate-us-given-the-chance beliefs. At the same time, changes also appeared in the security theme, as it related to the perceived threats to Israel: the prospect of unconventional weapons in the hands of states such as Iraq and Iran became the main concern as well as the threat to Israeli identity from demographic trends. At the same time, fears about the dangers posed by a Palestinian state subsided somewhat (as can be seen in 1992 election platforms and public polls). More importantly, questions in Israeli public polls during this period asked the respondents to choose among competing values such as Greater Israel, democracy, peace, and Israel as a Jewish state. This reflected an increased public awareness of the potential contradictions among the values and the necessity of making mutually exclusive choices. Labor platforms manifested these concerns by repeatedly arguing that Israeli control of the territories endangered ethos themes like the belief in Israel as a Jewish state and the values of security and peace. By the end of the period, Likud had abandoned its use of bolstering as a strategy for coping with the clash between ethos values and its belief in the value of Greater Israel, and the party left this contradiction unresolved.

Below, I analyze the role of the intifada in these changes. For now, I focus on their implication regarding resolution of the Israeli-Arab conflict. These changes encouraged ripeness on the Israeli side and efforts to find a peaceful resolution of the conflict. First, as illustrated in the 1992 Labor platform, the continuation of the conflict was now perceived as riskier than before because of the emergence of a greater threat (unconventional weapons) and the diminished confidence in Israel's military superiority. The conflict was also perceived as costlier in terms of a threat to identity because of the awareness of contradictions between components of the ethos and Israeli control of the territories. This trend indicates ontological insecurity. Thus, the status quo became less desirable. Indeed, surveys from this period showed a decline in the rate of respondents who chose the alternative of status quo as the preferred solution to the conflict (J. Shamir and Shamir 2000). On the other hand, a decline in beliefs regarding the Arabs' genocidal intentions, and in Israel's international isolation, encouraged more optimism and hopes for peace. Indeed, Israelis' assessment of the chances of achieving peace increased from 57 percent in 1986 to 77 percent in 1991 (J. Shamir and Shamir 2000). In other words, the changes in the ethos were accompanied by increased motivation to end the conflict and optimism about the prospects of being able to achieve that—the two conditions for ripeness. If I had written my book in 1994, I could have ended with this optimistic observation, but the collapse of the Oslo process in 2000 and the eruption of the second intifada evidenced a more complex picture of the link between ethos, ontological insecurity, and peace.

The Oslo Process Years, 1993–2000

Many factors have influenced the collapse of the Oslo process, including those that concerned the Palestinian side. I suggest that the Israeli ethos of conflict, and its role in intensifying ontological insecurity in Israeli society during the peace process, was an additional and crucial factor in this failure. Rumelili (2015) argues that a peace process may challenge existing identity narratives, disrupt perceptions of self and Other, and interrupt established routines—all of these are crucial for ontological security. However, she offered few specifics regarding the way in which ontological insecurity triggered by a peace process may impact that process. For example, she and her coauthor argue that ontological insecurity during a peace process may cause the parties to "elevate minor aspects of the peace deal to existential threats" and that it may empower spoilers of the peace process "because the state of anxiety and uncertainty increases the attractiveness of the ideas, identities, and practices associated with conflict" (Rumelili and Çelik 2017, 3). In this situation, the *conflict in resolution* state (low level of fear and high level of ontological anxiety) may revert to *unstable conflict* (high level of both fear and anxiety) or *stable conflict* (high level of fear and low level of anxiety) rather than advance to *peace* (low level of both fear and anxiety).

These ideas about a peace process as a source of ontological insecurity and the implications for success or failure of the process were further developed by Lupovici (2015, 36). His analysis is especially relevant to this discussion because he applied these ideas to the failure of the Oslo process. He maintained that a peace process may threaten multiple identities of self and the measures required to address each of these threats might contradict each other or challenge other identities the society holds, causing what he called "ontological dissonance." Like other scholars who have been involved in this discussion about the role of ontological insecurity in peace processes, Lupovici did not provide a clear definition of collective identity and it was not always clear whether he referred to different elements within one collective identity of the society or to separate identities of subgroups within the society. This confusion was especially notable when he analyzed the Oslo process. He argues that negotiating Israeli control of the territories triggered ontological insecurity among Israelis because "for many Israeli Jews relinquishing parts of the 'homeland' and especially parts of Jerusalem, is a source of ontological insecurity as for them it questions the *meaning* of being a Jewish state" (p. 40, emphasis in original). However, as I demonstrated in Chapter 2, Israeli control of the territories was not a part of the Israeli ethos. It was a shared belief and a sacred goal only among a subgroup in Israeli society—the settlers. Similarly, Chapter 2 shows that the concept of united Jerusalem—keeping the Palestinian neighborhoods in East Jerusalem under Israeli control—was a pseudosacred goal for the Israeli public. Hence, the threat to Israel's identity in negotiating these issues may have been less severe than Lupovici suggests. Lupovici (2015, 41) also contended that negotiating the Palestinian Right of Return challenged Israel's identity as a "righteous actor" because it clashed with the Israeli narrative of the 1948 War. However, in Chapter 2 I established that during the Oslo period the Israeli public accepted, at least partially, the justness of the Palestinian demand for statehood, and at the same time grounded the justification for a Jewish state in the land on arguments that legitimized Israel's existence as a Jewish state irrespective of Palestinians' presence on that land prior to the Zionist immigration or Israel's actions during the 1948 War (e.g., the argument that the 1947 UN resolution on the establishment of an independent Jewish state recognized Jewish legal rights to rule the territory).

I propose that the ethos of conflict, as I presented in this book, provides a better framework to explain the potential of the Oslo process to produce ontological insecurity in Israeli society, which in turn served as a major obstacle for the peace process on the Israeli side. The prospect of a negotiated Right of Return challenged the goal of preserving a Jewish majority—a goal that, as shown in Chapter 2, was sacred to Israeli society—and reinforced the securitization of the demographic threat, including the threat concerning Israel's Palestinian citizens within the 1949 borders (which, as Lupovici (2015, 41) rightly argues, related to a threat to identity more so than a physical threat to the survival of the state).

But it was the broader context of the mere existence of peace with the Palestinians, rather than specific issues that were being negotiated between the parties, that threatened the essence of the Israeli ethos of conflict as the main meaning system in Israeli society. As discussed in Chapters 6 and 7, peace with the Palestinians was perceived as a divisive issue that threatened national unity. Indeed, this issue brought about the first (and only) assassination of an Israeli prime minister—Yitzhak Rabin—following a peace rally in 1995 by an Israeli Jewish man who opposed the Oslo process. In addition, as noted by Rabin as early as 1979 in his writing about the "risks of peace," a final peace settlement to end the Israeli-Arab conflict would have major consequences for Israeli identity and for Israel's role in regional and international politics (see also Lustick 2008; Oren 2010). Unlike the 1979 peace agreement with Egypt, a peace accord with the Palestinians would have the potential to end the Israeli-Arab conflict since this has been the main issue dissuading most other Arab and Muslim countries from establishing peaceful relations with Israel. As we saw in Chapter 4, for years the Israeli ethos presented Israel as an advanced and Westernized villa in the Mediterranean jungle. But following the Oslo Accords, the idea of Israel completely assimilating into the Middle East was within reach. Labor platforms, as discussed more thoroughly below, and even the 1999 Likud platform, hailed Israel's imminent assimilation into the Middle East. But what would that mean for Israel's geopolitical identity? Would it still be a Western villa, or would it take on a Middle Eastern identity, one perceived to be less committed to

Western values? Assimilation into the region also would have implications for the theme regarding Israel as a Jewish state; religious leaders expressed concern about interfaith marriages. Already in 1979 Rabin worried that the strong ties between Israel and diaspora Jews that were based on the latter's firm stand behind an Israel that faced a "mortal threat" would weaken in times of peace. He also wondered about Israel's national identity in this context—that Israel might merely become a state like any other in the region in which Jews lived (Waxman 2006a; Rabin and Peri 1996).

Furthermore, peace with the Palestinians would have forced Israeli society to reexamine its established routines, specifically those rooted in the ethos of conflict. As an international relations scholar, Rumelili focused on routines that relate to diplomatic patterns between states in conflict that have come to be taken for granted and thereby have become part of their national identities. In this vein, she said, "Just imagine an Israeli prime minister giving his/her annual speech at the United Nations following the resolution of the Israeli-Palestinian conflict: What would s/he say?" (Rumelili 2015, 18–19). But it is the disruption of domestic routines by a peace agreement that may cause ontological insecurity within the society. As noted, many Israeli ceremonies and practices have been based on the Israeli ethos of conflict. Just imagine an Israeli prime minister giving his or her annual speech at the main ceremony of Holocaust Remembrance Day or Independence Day: What would the prime minister say? What would happen to the narrative about Israel as the only safe place for the Jews in a reality of a peaceful Middle East where Israeli Jews are welcome to travel and live anywhere they want in the region? Thus, to provide the needed ontological security, new routines and narratives would have to be established, based on a new ethos. But what ethos would that be?

My review indicated that many themes of the Israeli ethos of conflict weakened during the Oslo years (Zionism, villa in the jungle, security, siege, and patriotism)—as evidenced by the fact that they received less support in public polls (see Table 9.1). Looking at the ethos as a whole, this was clearly the period when the ethos of conflict was at its weakest and peace beliefs among the public strengthened. Rabin attempted to establish a new ethos that regarded peace as a realistic prospect, as well as a core value that would necessitate a change in thinking and behavior not just on the part of the Palestinians but also on the Israeli side (see Chapter 7). In addition, as shown in Chapter 4, Rabin tried to replace the positive in-group negative out-group differentiation (the villa theme) with a new belief that differentiated between "extremists" and the supporters of the peace process—as a differentiation that existed in both the Israeli and the Palestinian societies. He challenged security themes that presented the Palestinians as an existential threat to Israel and, instead, promoted a belief in a powerful Israel that could afford to take calculated risks in pursuit of peace with a weaker rival (Rosler

2012, 2016). Shimon Peres presented a vision of Israeli assimilation into a new Middle East that is miraculously transformed from a jungle to an almost Western European model of democratic states with regional cooperation on security and economy matters. But these attempts to construct a new ethos had only partial success: while by the end of the period, most respondents (57 percent) accepted the idea of a Palestinian state (see Figure 9.1), a sizable proportion of respondents in public polls still agreed with the ethos of conflict themes; for example, in 1994, 55 percent of the respondents believed that the Arabs' goal was to exterminate Israel, 54 percent believed that Israel was "a people that shall dwell alone," and 67 percent saw a Palestinian state as a threat. Israelis also did not embrace Peres's goal of Israel's integration into the Middle East. In a February 1995 Peace Index poll, 50 percent of Jewish respondents preferred that Israel would politically integrate into Europe-America while only 29 percent preferred integration into the Middle East. The gap between those who preferred Israel to culturally integrate into Europe-America and those who favored the Middle East was even wider (64 percent compared to only 14 percent). There were also some attempts at that time to establish new domestic routines based on an alternative ethos of peace. Recall the new pattern of Memorial Day for fallen soldiers ceremonies in high schools during the Oslo period, discussed in Chapter 3, and the attempts to introduce peace education discussed in Chapter 7. But these attempts encountered resistance from teachers and students and, ultimately, floundered.

Figure 9.1   Opposition to the Creation of a Palestinian State, 1975–2015 (percentage)

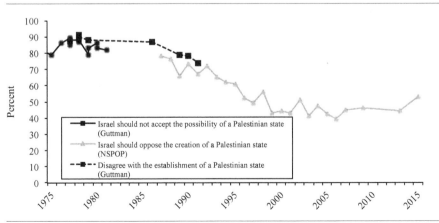

Sources: Guttman and NSPOP.

Finally, opposition forces used the ethos themes to attack the Oslo agreement. They used the ethos as a meaning system to highlight and criticize what they saw as the folly of conducting peace negotiations with the PLO while Palestinian groups were carrying out deadly suicide attacks against Israelis. In line with the villa and security themes, they emphasized that the Palestinians, including the PLO and its leader Yasser Arafat, could not be trusted and that the PLO supported and encouraged the terrorist acts. They pointed to the acts of terrorism committed against Israelis by Palestinians as evidence that peace would not bring security as Rabin maintained and, as shown in Chapter 3, securitized the threat from a Palestinian state as a state that would allow terrorists to enter Israel. Opponents of the Oslo Accords also argued that the peace process would strain Israel's national unity and "the peace within ourselves" (Lupovici 2015, 44). Netanyahu, for example, warned in 1995 that Israel was "approaching the abyss" and that "without agreed process of discussion among ourselves . . . we are liable to witness the dismembering of the nation" (Mendilow 2003, 175). As well, they deployed the Jewish sovereignty theme by emphasizing the fact that the accords would not have been ratified in the Knesset if not for the support of Israeli Palestinian members—in other words, they did not have the support of a "Jewish majority" in the Knesset (Rosler 2012; Waxman 2006a; Peri 2000).

Did the Oslo process shift Israel from a state of unstable conflict to one of conflict in resolution? Lupovici (2015, 38) asserted that this was the case during the Oslo years. My analysis, however, revealed that despite desecuritization of the threats of a Palestinian state, the perceived threats from terrorism and from unconventional weapons remained acute throughout this period. In other words, at that time Israel was still in an unstable conflict state. Thus, in theoretical terms, my study revealed that peace negotiations do not always lower the level of fear in the society as Rumelili (2015) assumed. When one of the parties perceives a complex of issues as potential existential threats and some of those existential threats still persist, the peace process will exist in an unstable state, further diminishing the chances for a successful outcome.

The Period After the Second Intifada, 2000–2017

Following the collapse of the Oslo Accords and the resurgence of violence (the second intifada), there was a commensurate strengthening of some of the themes of the ethos, specifically villa in the jungle (Arabs' intention to destroy Israel and Israel's military superiority), Zionism, and siege (these trends in public polls are shown in Table 9.1). Some of the more hard-line elements of the ethos, such as the belief in the Jews' exclusive right to the land and the rejection of Palestinian statehood—ideas that had faded over the preceding periods—also resurfaced. However, public polls have indicated that the agreement with the ethos themes in public polls has not been as strong as it was in the 1960s and 1970s, mainly because more people have been openly questioning the ethos than in the earlier period. In addition, the willingness to sacrifice for the nation has been much lower in this generation than it was in the 1960s and 1970s (see Table 9.1). So, while Israeli Jews have tended to accept the ethos perception about the nature of the conflict and its likely future, this ethos has been less successful, compared to the past, in motivating people to sacrifice and risk their lives for the state. Thus, Israeli society currently finds itself in the untenable position of having an ethos that suggests that Israel will forever live by the sword, combined with a declining willingness on the part of its members to pay the steep price of this situation. In addition, there is still high ontological anxiety in Israeli society because of securitization of identity issues such as the demographic threat (see Chapter 3). In other words, Israeli society has been unable to return to the stable conflict state of the 1960s and 1970s when the ethos provided ontological security despite the high level of fear, and it has remained stuck in the unstable conflict state with high levels of fear and ontological anxiety.

The changes in the ethos described above have fueled the search for ways, other than a negotiated peace agreement, to cope with the ontological insecurity and with the perceived contradictions between the ethos values and other societal beliefs in the context of Israeli control of the territories. The main strategy applied by Israeli society during this period has been avoidance. One element of avoidance is psychological (and physical if possible) distance from the cause of the dissonance. As Lupovici (2012, 830) notes, the separation wall between Israel proper and the territories that was built during this period has allowed "Israelis to avoid 'feeling' the conflict and the discomfort that accompanied the threat to its identities and the clash among them." One of Ariel Sharon's advisers stressed that Israeli society wanted the wall to serve as both "a physical and mental wall" separating them from the Palestinians (Bennet 2004). Thus, "Israeli Jews, literally and metaphorically, wanted to wall themselves off from their Palestinian neighbors" (Jacoby 2007; Waxman 2008, 87; see also Lustick 2008). This psychological distancing from the Palestinian problem has been discussed by several Israeli writers. For example, one columnist described how the separation wall "is nearby, yet as far away as the fence that India built in Kashmir." He then added, "Life without a fence was terrible, but at least it created a sense of urgency; that we have to do something to stop the killing; to solve the conflict; to make peace. The fence creates an illusion that we can 'manage' the conflict instead of resolving it" (Esteron 2004).

Another element of avoidance is to create ambiguity concerning the challenges to identity. Lupovici (2015, 44–45) contends that the solution Israelis have adopted to address ontological insecurity and ontological dissonance is avoidance in the form of creating ambiguities about the Palestinian Other by distinguishing between Hamas (that continues to serve as the Other) and Fatah (that is perceived as a partner to negotiations). However, my analysis has cast doubt on this assertion. The Likud 2009 platform did not differentiate between Hamas and Fatah, using the collective term *the Palestinians* instead (see Chapter 8). And public polls have indicated that while the public has perceived Fatah's leadership as more moderate than that of Hamas, it also has perceived Hamas as representative of Palestinians' intentions toward Israel more so than Fatah (see Chapter 4). I argue that the avoidance strategy is based on the differentiation between the *current* state of the Palestinians and their potential transformation in a distant *future*. This dual perception of the Palestinians is related to ambiguity concerning Israeli control of the territories, and it has encouraged actions toward the Palestinians that aim to make the conflict (and the dissonance) more tolerable rather than resolve it. It can be found in the 2009 Likud platform's assertion that the Palestinians (including Fatah) were not ready "to make the type of historic compromise that would end the conflict" (Likud 2009, 7). Therefore, the platform called for economic investment in the West Bank, acknowledging that "this will not resolve the conflict." Per this platform, peace negotiations with the Palestinians will occur only "when the time comes" (i.e., when the Palestinians will be ready). A proposal by author and peace activist A. B. Yehoshua provides another example of avoidance. While Yehoshua did not call for Israeli annexation of the territories, he proposed granting Israeli "residency" (not citizenship) to the Palestinians living in Area C of the West Bank, reasoning that it would "ease the burden of the occupation" because it would grant Palestinians partial but fundamental rights such as social security benefits, health care, unemployment benefits, and freedom of movement (Yehoshua 2016).[2] Plainly, this is an attempt to make the dissonance between the values of a Jewish state and democracy in the context of Israeli control of the territories more tolerable rather than resolving it, and to blur the nature of that control. The ambiguity concerning the nature of Israeli control of the territories is also manifested in the perception of the separation wall. Those whose ultimate goal is to annex the territories have argued that it is only a temporary solution for security reasons (Jacoby 2007). But a 2012 NSPOP survey indicated that 50 percent of respondents saw it as an element of an eventual permanent boundary (Ben Meir and Bagno-Moldavsky 2013, 87).

As the stubborn reality has made it more and more difficult to ignore the Palestinians, and as "chaos sprout up from under [the villa's] floor and into the living room" (Rosenblum 2007), there have been proposals aiming to address the perceived dissonance rather than avoid it. Israeli president Reuven Rivlin has recently expressed his support for the so-called one-state solution—full annexation of the territories and the granting of "full

Israeli citizenship" to the millions of Palestinians living there (Eisenbud 2017). Rivlin grounded his support for this approach in his commitment to the values of Greater Israel and democracy, seeming to prioritize these values over the goal of maintaining a Jewish majority. Other hawkish politicians have called for Israeli annexation of the territories without giving full citizenship rights to Palestinians,[3] preferring, in other words, the values of Greater Israel and a Jewish state over the value of democracy. As for public opinion, a small majority (53 percent) of respondents in a 2015 poll opposed the creation of a Palestinian state (see Figure 9.1). A June 2016 Peace Index poll regarding potential solutions to Israeli control of the territories did not mention this option at all. In that survey, 23 percent supported maintaining the status quo, 19 percent preferred Israeli annexation of the territories in which equal rights would be given to Israelis and Palestinians (as Rivlin suggested), and 32 percent expressed support for annexation without equal rights to Palestinians.

Major Events as a Cause of Change in the Ethos

As I noted throughout this book, the changes in the Israeli ethos were probably the result of a combination of factors such as demographic trends, global trends, and events that did not directly relate to the Israeli-Arab conflict. It is beyond the scope of the book to provide a comprehensive theoretical framework that could explain this complex interplay, although I hope that other researchers will undertake this challenge. In this section, I focus mainly on the effect of major events in the conflict on public opinion. Indeed, this book documents several immediate and dramatic changes in public opinion and election platforms following major events in the conflict. Two major events—the first intifada and the second intifada—were especially associated with changes in the Israeli ethos. Hence, I take a closer look at the factors that explain why these events had such a strong effect on Israeli public opinion.

Two types of factors are highly relevant to the analysis of the effect of these two major events: the first are factors that relate to the nature of the event itself, such as its duration and the level of threat that it generates. The second are factors that concern the way the event is framed by the media and by the leadership. In this vein, the term *major information* should be added to the term *major event*. Major information refers to information supplied by an epistemic authority (e.g., the prime minister, the media, and experts) about a matter of great relevance to the society, which may encourage people to reconsider their existing beliefs (Bar-Tal and Sharvit 2007).

As noted above, significant changes in the Israeli ethos of conflict occurred in the early 1990s following the first intifada. Specifically, during this time, there was a decline in the villa theme (the perceived intention of the Arabs to exterminate Israel and positive self-image of Israel), siege beliefs, and patriotism. More importantly, during this period the Israeli public became more conscious of the contradictions between their ethos and other societal beliefs. For example, there was a clash among the values of democracy, peace, and maintaining a Jewish majority, and an expressed preference for the strategy of changing the context that was perceived as putting these values into conflict with each other—by giving up the territories. All of these changes occurred even though the media referred to the intifada during most of its duration (at least until 1991) in a way that was consistent with prevailing beliefs. According to the law and order media frame of the event, the intifada was a massive outbreak of violence carried out by small local radical groups, as another plot against the existence of the State of Israel. Most Palestinians, according to this view, were quite content with the status quo and, hence, sought no more than local autonomy under continuing Israeli rule or as part of a Jordanian-Palestinian confederation. Israel's role and duty were defined as restoring law and order and protecting the lives and property of both Israelis and peaceful Palestinians (Nir and Roeh 1992; Akiba Cohen, Adoni, and Nossek 1993; Collins and Clark 1993; Loshitzky 1993; Wolfsfeld 1997). As such, this presentation of the intifada was consistent with the ethos of conflict themes such as the villa and security. This presentation of the event also was featured in the rhetoric of leaders such as Yitzhak Shamir and Rabin (Rosler 2012; Aronoff 2014). Rabin did express on occasion some differing perspectives, albeit mainly in speeches given to party members rather than when addressing the general public (Rosler 2012). For example, he spoke about Israel's "forced control" over the Palestinians and how it endangered the goal of a Jewish and democratic state. Labor election platforms from this period also included mixed messages about the intifada (see Chapter 8).

The relatively significant impact that the first intifada had on Israeli public opinion can be attributed in large measure to its prolonged duration (1987–1993). The intensity and magnitude of the Palestinian protest, sustained over such a long period, could hardly be interpreted as a set of local riots and gradually came to be recognized as a popular uprising. The event presented the Palestinians in the territories as a group with national awareness and motivation to fight for its rights. The contradiction between the values of democracy, peace, and maintaining a Jewish majority in the context of Israeli control of the territories could no longer be ignored or pushed aside using strategies like bolstering. The first intifada undermined both the "Palestinian autonomy under Israel rule" solution, preferred by Likud, and the "Jordanian option" solution, in which Jordan would maintain political authority in the West Bank under Israeli security supervision—a solution long advocated by Labor. Indeed, public polls from this period showed a decline in opposition to the idea of a Palestinian state, preceding a similar trend in leaders' rhetoric. In sum, in this case the duration of the event (the stubborn reality) may have eroded the influence of the associated major information regarding this event.

Other factors that related to the nature of the event may also explain this outcome. They include the fact that the intifada was perceived as a negative event that came as a surprise and generated some (but not extensive) fear among Israelis.[4] This explanation is based on literature in psychology, which indicates that negative events and information tend to garner more attention than positive ones and that they have a strong influence on evaluation, judgment, and action tendencies (Cacioppo and Berntson 1994; Ito et al. 1998; Pratto and John 1991). Moderate (but not extreme) fear focuses attention and sensitizes people to threatening cues and information (Hobfoll 1998; Doty, Peterson, and Winter 1991; Gordon and Arian 2001). Events in the international system during the intifada years also could have transformed Israelis' attitudes about the conflict and its ethos: the disintegration of the Soviet Union and the Eastern bloc (these events influenced siege beliefs); the resolution of other conflicts around the world such as in South Africa and Northern Ireland; the Gulf War, which increased fear of weapons of mass destruction and hence may have influenced security beliefs and self-image in the military might sense; and the 1991 Madrid conference, which refuted existing societal beliefs that the Arabs had no interest in attempting a peaceful resolution of the conflict. In other words, the fact that the first intifada was not exclusive on the world (and media) stage for its long duration may have also diluted the effect of the intifada-related major information.

While the first intifada weakened the ethos beliefs, the second intifada had the opposite effect of reinforcing them. The unsuccessful Camp David summit in 2000 and the eruption of the second intifada in its wake triggered a resurgence in ethos themes related to security, villa in the jungle, and self-victimization. These changes were caused by factors related to the major event along with major information. Like the first intifada, the second intifada was an intensive event that lasted several years and generated fear.[5] These features of the event increased its prospects of focusing people's attention on the threatening information that had the potential to reinforce the ethos of conflict themes. More specifically, the wave of Palestinian violence that killed many Israelis (by April 14, 2004, 943 Israelis—276 members of the security forces, 667 civilians—had lost their lives in this wave of violence, and 6,300 had been wounded) reinforced the image of the Palestinians as violent and opposed to the existence of Israel. The international condemnation of Israeli attempts to suppress the intifada had the potential to reinforce such beliefs as the whole world is against us and the Israeli sense of isolation.

But Israelis were probably also influenced by the way the events were framed by the media and leadership, and in this case there was one consistent message (Bar-Tal and Sharvit 2007; Halperin and Bar-Tal 2007). The failure of the Camp David summit was blamed solely on Palestinian leader Arafat. Prime minister Ehud Barak said that he had made Arafat an extremely generous offer at Camp David, which included 98 percent of the territories and even areas within Jerusalem, and Arafat had rejected the offer and unleashed a wave of terrorism with the aim of achieving by violence what he had been unable to obtain in the negotiations.[6] The media and Barak emphasized that these events exposed "the true face" of the Palestinians as having no interest in peace with Israel—in line with the villa theme of the ethos (Wolfsfeld 2003; Dor 2004). In line with security beliefs, leaders and the media presented the second intifada as a war for Israel's survival. They marginalized the high rate of Palestinian casualties in the intifada (by April 14, 2004, the violence had claimed over 2,720 lives and 25,000 wounded on the Palestinian side) and maintained that the IDF demonstrated self-restraint in the face of the Palestinian violence (Dor 2004; Shavit 2002). The argument that the Palestinian violence was due, in part, to the overwhelmingly forceful responses of the Israeli army was marginalized or denied. The public accepted the official framing of the event and adjusted its beliefs accordingly.[7] The fact that the second intifada was not exclusive on the world (and media) stage also contributed to its role in changing public opinion. Events such as the September 11 terrorist attacks in the United States reinforced the villa theme that presented the Palestinians as part of an axis of evil—a perception that appeared in leaders' and the media's framing of the two events (Bar-Tal and Sharvit 2007).

But while the ethos as a whole strengthened in the period after 2000, it did not go back to the levels seen in the 1960s and 1970s. Some of the reasons why have little to do with the second intifada. For example, the decline in patriotism was related to other factors, discussed in Chapter 6, such as the global trend of a shift from materialist to postmaterialist values that affected Israeli society as well. In addition, information from the second intifada, including the way that it was framed by leaders and the media, could not support previous attempts to cope with the clash between the value of a Jewish state and democracy in the context of Israeli control of the territories (e.g., the argument that the Palestinians were content with the status quo and sought no more than local autonomy under continuing Israeli rule). Israeli society, then, found itself on the one hand accepting the view that the conflict would last forever, and on the other hand lacking "the skills and sense of strength needed to withstand this conclusion" (Rosenblum 2011).

A final take from the analysis of changes in the Israeli ethos and major events in the conflict is that there was a reciprocal relationship between the Israeli ethos and the Israeli-Arab conflict context. My analysis showed only minor changes in public polls before the peace process with Egypt—it seems that this event shaped the Israeli ethos, rather than being a product of such a change. And yet there were meaningful changes in the content of election platforms before 1977, indicating shifts in beliefs, at least within Israel's political leadership. These shifts, in turn, may have made the leadership more receptive to the process and contributed to its success. As shown above, the changes in the ethos themes following the peace process with Egypt, and especially following the first intifada—a decline in the villa in the jungle and siege themes, and growing awareness of a contradiction between the ethos and the context of Israeli control of the territories—contributed to the mechanisms and conditions that made the Oslo Accords possible. The Oslo process brought about further changes in the ethos—an overall weakening. That trend was reversed, however, following the collapse of the process and the outbreak of the second intifada, with the ethos themes prominent anew in leaders' rhetoric, school curricula, and public opinion.

Top-Down and Bottom-Up Changes

This book is relevant to the scholarly discussion about leadership and social change. While scholars from diverse disciplines have dealt with the factors that make a leader transformational or effective, only a few have examined this issue within the context of conflict resolution and peace processes (Bargal and Sivan 2004; Rosler 2016; M. G. Hermann and Gerard 2009). To my knowledge, none have fully utilized the potential of recent scholarship about the social identity theory of leadership. Rather than seek the roots of effective leadership within fixed qualities of the leader (e.g., charisma or intellect) and the ability of the leader to satisfy the personal needs of followers, the social identity approach contends that "effective leadership is always about leaders and followers seeing themselves as bound together through their joint membership of the same group and working together to satisfy group needs and realize group ambitions" (S. A. Haslam and Reicher 2016, 23). Drawing on the social identity tradition in social psychology, this approach proposes that upon identifying with a group (like "Israelis"), individuals seek to elucidate the values and norms of the group and to conform to them. But in an uncertain and changing world, it is not always clear how one should react, and so people look for guidance as to what is appropriate. Thus, those who are seen to be uniquely representative of the shared values, norms, beliefs, and qualities that characterize the group and make it different from other groups—the prototypical group members—are more likely to emerge as leaders, and prototypical leaders will be perceived to be more effective leaders (S. A.

Haslam, Reicher, and Platow 2010; Hogg, Knippenberg, and Rast 2012; Reicher, Haslam, and Platow 2016). Since the ethos is a core component of collective identity that makes a society special and distinct from other societies, we can assume that those who are seen to exemplify the ethos of the society are in a privileged position to exert leadership.

Indeed, Israeli leaders have expressed the ethos themes in their rhetoric and presented themselves as representative of this ethos (sometimes referring to specific details in their individual biography to illustrate this), although different leaders have emphasized different themes of the ethos. For example, Menachem Begin emphasized the Jewish state and siege theme. Already in a famous 1952 speech to the Knesset, he referred to his own life experience and the tragic fate of his parents in the Holocaust using the grammatical term *we* instead of *I,* hence indicating that his individual experience mirrored collective memory and identity. He described himself and other Israelis as "we, the last generation for slavery and first for redemption . . . we who witnessed how the elderly father was thrown into the river with 500 other Jews from the city of Brisk in Lithuania and the river turned red from their blood; we who saw the old mother murdered in her hospital bed." Another typical example can be found in Begin's 1978 Nobel Peace Prize acceptance speech: "Here I stand in humility and with pride as a son of the Jewish people, as one of the generation of the Holocaust and Redemption" (Begin 1978b).

Rabin's image personified the security and patriotism themes of the Israeli ethos. His 1992 election campaign emphasized the fact that he commanded the Israeli army to its greatest victory, in 1967 (Mendilow 2003, 197). The opening lines of Rabin's 1994 Nobel Peace Prize acceptance speech emphasized these themes of the ethos while linking it to his biography:

> At an age when most youngsters are struggling to unravel the secrets of mathematics and the mysteries of the Bible; at an age when first love blooms; at the tender age of 16, I was handed a rifle so that I could defend myself—and also, unfortunately, so that I could kill in an hour of danger. That was not my dream. I wanted to be a water engineer. I studied in an agricultural school, and I thought that being a water engineer was an important profession in the parched Middle East. I still think so today. However, I was compelled to resort to the gun. (Rabin 1994d)

But effective leadership is more than being a prototypical group member; it involves actively shaping collective identity—when leaders become "entrepreneurs of social identity" and seek to define and even change the content of group identity (S. A. Haslam and Reicher 2016, 13). Social identity–based research into leadership has shown that prototypical leaders (especially new leaders—less so with established leaders) have some flexibility to diverge from group norms (Abrams et al. 2008), which may allow them to innovate and expand the horizons of the group (S. A. Haslam, Reicher, and Platow 2010). Applying these observations to leadership in the context of intractable conflict and the ethos of conflict, one can expect that leaders who are considered as representative of the ethos would have some leeway to change it. For example, Rabin tried to use his status as a prototypical group member to change the Israeli ethos and promote peace beliefs: "I, I.D. Number 30743, Retired Lieutenant-General Yitzhak Rabin, a soldier in the Israel Defense Forces, and a soldier in the army of peace; I, who sent regiments into the fire and soldiers to their deaths, I say to you. . . . Today we are embarking on a battle that has no dead and no wounded, no blood and no anguish. This is the only battle that is a pleasure to wage—the battle for peace" (Rabin 1994c).

A similar example can be found in Rabin's last speech that was delivered at a peace rally shortly before he was assassinated: "The path of peace is preferable to the path of war. I say this to you as someone who was a military man and minister of defense, and who saw the pain of the families of IDF soldiers." He continued, refuting the villa theme of the ethos: "I want to say bluntly, that we have found a partner for peace among the Palestinians as well: the PLO, which was an enemy, and has ceased to engage in terrorism" (Rabin 1995g). In his speeches, Rabin repeatedly tried to show how his individual biography mirrored that of the nation at large and then challenged themes of the ethos such as siege and security beliefs. He first confirmed siege beliefs, hinting at his own identity as a heroic native-born Israeli (Sabra), in a 1993 speech: "The establishment of the State of Israel gave birth to the new Jew, a Sabra: a strong man, a fighter, upright, with roots, one who beats those who rise against him. . . . Israeli superman . . . who can do anything, who is resourceful, sophisticated and a winner." He noted that "perhaps there was jealousy, perhaps the world could not get accustomed to the new Jew. . . . There was more than a grain of truth in the definition which followed our lives here for many years: 'The whole world is against us'" (Rabin 1993a). After that, Rabin revealed the negative aspects of this theme of the ethos: "We lost our trust in others. We suspected everyone and developed a siege mentality in a sort of political, economic and mental ghetto. We distanced ourselves, doubted, had reservations. We expressed stubbornness and perceived the world in gloomy colors" (Rabin 1993a). He went further, emphasizing that this theme of the ethos, which had been part of his identity and the Israeli collective identity for years, was not relevant anymore:

> In the last decade of the 20th century dramatic changes have taken place. Atlases of five years ago can no longer serve as school books. Empires have been wiped out, new states have emerged, new borders have been created, ideologies which were believed by hundreds of millions have broken down and collapsed like a house of cards. Everything has been altered. . . . In face of the new reality in a changing world, we must design

a new dimension for the Israeli image. This is a time of change: To open up, look around, talk, integrate. We must see the changing world with open eyes: The world is no longer against us. (Rabin 1993a)

In a 1995 speech, Rabin rephrased Joseph Trumpeldor's iconic patriotic words: "it is good to die for our country." As a war hero, Rabin said, "If there is no choice, if a sharp sword is placed on our neck . . . if our existence is at stake—there is no choice, we fight, we sacrifice life. But I also tell you: It is good to live for our country. The death and bereavement that we face often are not predetermined destiny" (Rabin 1995c). As I showed in this book, the ethos of conflict indeed weakened during Rabin's second term as prime minister (1992–1995), although he was not able during that time frame to replace the ethos of conflict with a new one.

Barak, like Rabin, used his image as prototypical Israeli to promote peace beliefs. The 1999 election campaign presented Barak as a leader whose personal identity embodied the Israeli national identity—especially the security and patriotism themes in the ethos—as a military hero and as a successor of Rabin (Mendilow 2003, 197–200). The Labor party platform included many photos in which Barak appeared in uniform, as well as photos of Barak with Rabin. The platform ended with Barak's biography noting that he was the most decorated IDF soldier. Like Rabin, Barak used this image to promote peace beliefs in his speeches:

> Almost my entire adult life has been spent in olive drab uniforms. I belong to the same generation of fighters which was educated according to the refrains of Nathan Alterman's poem, from which I quote: "In the mountains, in the mountains shines our light, we will climb up to the mountain. If the way is difficult and treacherous, even if more than one falls a casualty we will love you, land of our birth, forever, we are yours, in battle and in toil." Climbing the mountain of wars took determination, and persistence. Those same exact qualities are demanded of us today, in climbing the mountain of peace. (Barak 1999)

However, as shown above, after the failure of the Camp David summit and the eruption of the second intifada, then prime minister Barak changed his rhetoric and emphasized chiefly the villa theme of the ethos while de-emphasizing peace beliefs. Accordingly, public polls indicated a resurgence in ethos themes, including the villa theme. Barak nevertheless lost in the 2001 elections to Sharon—another army general who seemed to better represent the Israeli national identity at that time and the resurgent ethos of conflict.

Effective leaders influence a group's identity not only with their rhetoric but also with their actions. Such actions may include precipitating a major event (declaring war or signing a peace agreement), then influencing public opinion regarding the event with a symbolic gesture or rhetoric (major information). As an example, Waxman showed that Rabin purposefully chose to shake Arafat's hand during the 1993 Israel-PLO Declaration of Principles ceremony—an event witnessed on television by almost every Israeli—to change the Israeli identity as one of shaking hands rather than holding a gun. According to Waxman, "Rabin was signaling not only the beginning of a new era of peace and reconciliation between Israelis and Palestinians, but also the birth of a new Israeli national identity" (2006a, 101).

However, a major conclusion of my study is that these attempts may have unexpected results and that changes in public opinion do not always track with leaders' expectations and intentions. A case in point is Begin and the Camp David Accords that included Israel's recognition of the "legitimate rights of the Palestinian people." Begin's goal was to maintain Israeli control of the territories and to de facto annex them. From his perspective, the Camp David Accords and the Israeli-Egyptian peace treaty were designed mainly to separate the Israeli-Palestinian conflict from the conflict between Israel and Egypt and to reduce international pressure for Israeli concession on the issue of the territories (I. Peleg 1987). Begin intended to continue the government annexation activities in the territories during prolonged talks on "Autonomy for the Arab inhabitants of Judea, Samaria and the Gaza district" that he insisted was not recognition of Palestinian self-determination as a nation or a path to Palestinian statehood. He argued that Israel had exclusive rights to the land and that "this [the territories] is our land" (Begin 1978a, 1979a, 1979c). But as I demonstrated in this book, following the Camp David Accords and the Israeli-Egyptian peace treaty, public polls indicated erosion in the beliefs that denied Palestinian nationhood. Despite Begin's efforts, the value of Greater Israel was never part of the Israeli ethos.

In this book, I provided other examples where the public failed to embrace the content of the ethos themes as expressed in leaders' rhetoric. Polls have showed, for instance, that the Israeli public has tended less than politicians to perceive keeping Jerusalem united under Israeli control as a sacred goal. In another example, the main justification cited by respondents in 2016 for the creation of a Jewish state in the land of Israel was the acceptance by the nations of the world of the idea of a Jewish state—a justification that was not common in political speeches. Peace as a value was more dominant among the Israeli public during the 1970s and 1980s than in school curricula and leaders' rhetoric; siege beliefs were less prevalent among the public than they were in Netanyahu's rhetoric and the public expressed a lower level of patriotism compared to its leaders. The above examples are further evidence that Israeli society was sensitive to and influenced by global trends and ideas, even those that contradicted the official content.

It is more accurate, then, to describe the relationship between the leadership and followers as a two-way relationship. For example, public polls showed erosion in the ethos before Rabin became prime minister (this trend may have been one of the reasons for Rabin's 1992 election victory). Thus, Rabin intensified the trend of change in the Israeli ethos rather than creating it. This two-way process can be described as a "continuously evolving and dynamic process whereby reality feeds into identity, which feeds into leadership, which feeds back into reality. There is no natural starting point or finishing point to this process, and hence no element predominates over the others" (S. A. Haslam, Reicher, and Platow 2010, 142).

Furthermore, changes in group identity must be in line with core shared beliefs and values. A prototypical leader can influence the group's identity, but only up to a point: "Even the most prototypical leaders cannot go against clear, consensual, and long-standing group norms without throwing their prototypicality into question" (S. A. Haslam, Reicher, and Platow 2010, 106). As I argued above, Rabin and especially Peres (Rabin's successor who lost the 1996 election to Netanyahu) may have ventured too far ahead, especially with their ideas about the new Middle East. Opponents of the Oslo process repeatedly argued that rather than being prototypical Israelis, Rabin and Peres were more representative of the enemy—the Palestinians. Indeed, ads from Oslo years even depicted Rabin's face in Arafat's kefiya headdress. In 1997, after he overcame Peres in the 1996 elections and became prime minister, Netanyahu said that the supporters of Rabin, Peres, and the Oslo process "have forgotten what it means to be Jewish,"[8] indicating his belief that they drifted too far from Israel's national identity.

Effective leaders attempt to shape national identity not only with rhetoric, symbolic gestures, and major information but also by arranging ceremonies, holding commemorations, and shaping school curricula so as to reflect leadership's ideas about national identity. In this book, I demonstrated how the Israeli ethos themes were imparted to younger students (including very young children) through school textbooks, and in the period after 1980 mainly through extracurricular activities (although references to the ethos themes also continued to exist in textbooks from the period after 1980). It should be noted that the use of extracurricular school activities as a tool to encourage students to embrace the ethos themes is an important trend often ignored in studies that have analyzed only the content of school textbooks. Nevertheless, the effect of school activities on the beliefs of students is unclear. Firer (1985, 122) reported that, over the years, her students have challenged the justifications provided in their textbooks for the establishment of the State of Israel. They have wondered, for example, how the small number of Jews who emigrated to Israel before Zionism justifies their right to the land, especially given the fact that most of the Jews (then and now) prefer to live outside of Israel. Firer and other researchers also noted that students, especially in the period after 2000, have strongly resisted peace education and content that refutes the negative image of Palestinians, to the point that teachers have preferred to avoid this issue in class. Fuxman (2012) provides a complex picture of the influence of school textbooks on Israeli students. In

2008, he asked students if they agreed with the information regarding Israel's history presented in their textbooks. He found that some students said that their textbooks provided only facts. He concluded that students that referred to their textbooks as merely facts are likely to adhere to the narratives and beliefs in these textbooks rather than question them. However, another group of students in Fuxman's study thought that their textbooks were one-sided and wished that they could be exposed to the Palestinian narrative as well.

Literature in the field of political socialization has provided further evidence for the contention that students do not uniformly and automatically accept the ethos content as it appears in school textbooks. First, most models of youth political socialization have noted that children's and adolescents' political understandings are shaped by various sources (including family and community) as well as by the child's cognitive and social abilities at any given point in the developmental process (Raviv et al. 1999). Thus, each child may react differently to the content of ethos in their school curricula. Furthermore, there is evidence that children and youth may change their views about war and peace later in life. In the context of the Israeli-Arab conflict, Apfel and Simon (2000) noted critical changes in the political understanding of Israelis and Palestinians during the years from childhood to adolescence. As they grew older, their accounts of conflict-related events demonstrated an awareness of greater moral complexity. Raviv and colleagues (1999) found that when the Israeli children and adolescents in their studies were exposed to powerful personal experiences of war, their perceptions of war and peace changed to the extent of overriding previous influences of collective memory and myths that they had come across at school. Further research is needed, then, to gain a better understanding of Israeli students' internalization in the near and long term of the ethos content to which they are exposed at school.

In sum, the main conclusion of my study is that both Israelis and Palestinians will need to venture outside their respective villas to overcome their fear and mistrust of the jungle before the Israeli-Palestinian conflict can be reconciled. Major events in the conflict, global events and developments, demographic trends within each society, and courage and effectiveness of their leaderships will all exert influences on the ethos in ways that can either reinforce the barriers to peace or help knock them down. The ethos of conflict is not static; rather, it evolves over time. And its evolution is not necessarily a linear process. Neither is the road to peace.

Notes

1. Kochin (2012) compared Dayan's eulogy to the Gettysburg Address.
2. However, 62 percent of Jewish respondents in a June 2016 Peace Index poll, opposed Yehoshua's idea.

3. Miki Zohar, a Knesset member from the Likud party, suggested Israeli annexation of the West Bank with Palestinians having Israeli citizenship except the right to vote (*Haaretz* 2017).

4. In a 1992 survey, 83 percent of Israeli Jews reported being afraid that they or their relatives would be hurt by Arabs as they went about their everyday routines (Arian 1995).

5. In the spring of 2002, 92 percent reported being apprehensive that they or a member of their family might fall victim to a terrorist attack (by February 2004, this had fallen to 77 percent). Even in September 2004, when the terror attacks had declined significantly, 80.4 percent of bus riders were afraid of taking the bus and 59.8 percent of Israeli Jews were afraid to go to crowded places (Ben Simon 2004).

6. Numerous publications about the negotiations at Camp David presented a more complex picture of the failure of the talks and pointed to other causes for this failure, such as Barak's negotiation conduct and lack of US preparation (Ben-Ami 2006; Klein 2003). The assertion that Arafat planned the intifada was questioned by many experts, including Israeli security experts such as Ami Ayalon (former commander of the Israeli navy who served as head of the General Security Service until shortly before the eruption of the second intifada), Yuval Diskin (who at the time of the second intifada was deputy to the head of the General Security Service), Amos Malka (who headed the intelligence branch of the IDF during the early stages of the intifada), and Mati Steinberg (who served as adviser to the head of the General Security Service) (Rubinstein 2004; Halperin and Bar-Tal 2007).

7. In a May 2001 Peace Index poll, 70 percent of the Jewish public thought that Arafat personally lacked the will, or the capability, to sign an agreement to end the conflict with Israel, even if Israel agreed to all of his demands—and that he would make additional demands aimed at foiling the agreement.

8. Netanyahu made this comment when he visited the religious leader Rabbi Yitzchak Kadouri. Netanyahu did not know that an Israel Radio microphone was taping him. The comment triggered an angry uproar (Jewish Telegraphic Agency, 1997).

Appendix:
Main Surveys Used

Israeli Surveys

Guttman. The Louis Guttman Israel Institute of Applied Social Research (formerly the Institute for Public Opinion Research) conducted surveys from the early years of the State of Israel until 1997. Most of the data I cite in this book was taken from one of Guttman's main time series surveys, "The Continuing Survey of Social Problem Indicators," which was conducting surveys annually among representative samples of the urban Jewish population of Israel.

NSPOP. The National Security and Public Opinion Project (NSPOP) originates from the Institute for National Security Studies (INSS), incorporating the Jaffee Center for Strategic Studies. NSPOP has been conducted annually since 1984 among representative samples of the adult Jewish population of Israel. For more information, see the INSS website at http://www.inss.org.il/index.aspx?id=4414.

Peace Index. Peace Index polls are monthly polls that have been conducted by the Tami Steinmetz Center for Peace Research at Tel Aviv University since 1994. The Peace Index became a joint project of the Israel Democracy Institute's (IDI) Guttman Center for Public Opinion and Policy Research and Tel Aviv University's Evens Program in Mediation and Conflict Resolution in 2010. Surveys are conducted among a representative national sample of the entire adult population aged eighteen years and older (including the non-Jewish population), but the results for the Jewish only sample are also published. For more information, see the Peace Index website at http://www.peaceindex.org/DefaultEng.aspx.

Democracy Index. The Israeli Democracy Index surveys have been conducted annually since 2003 by IDI's Guttman Center for Public Opinion and Policy Research. Surveys are conducted among a representative sample of Israel's adult population (1,000 participants including non-Jewish representation), but the results for the Jewish only sample are also published.

JIPP. The Joint Israeli-Palestinian Poll (JIPP) was initiated in 2000 by the Truman Institute for the Advancement of Peace at the Hebrew University of Jerusalem and the Palestinian Center for Policy and Survey Research (PSR) in Ramallah. It is conducted among national representative Palestinian and Israeli samples. The results for the Israeli Jewish only sample are also published. For more information, see the Truman Institute website at http:// truman.huji.ac.il/?cmd=joint_polls.259.

INES. The Israel National Election Studies (INES) is a preelection survey that started in 1969. All surveys were conducted prior to Knesset elections and prime ministerial elections (held in 2001). At least one survey was carried out in each election year; in certain years more than one survey was conducted, and in a few cases a postelection survey was added. The sample has been changed over the years: during the years 1969–1977, it was conducted among the urban adult Jewish population (aged twenty years and older), eligible voters (in Greater Tel Aviv, Haifa, Jerusalem, and Beer Sheva). During the years 1981–1992, it was conducted among the adult Jewish population (aged eighteen years and older) eligible voters, not including Kibbutzim and localities beyond the 1967 Green Line. In 1996, the sample was of the adult population (aged eighteen years and older) eligible voters, not including Kibbutzim and localities beyond the 1967 Green Line (but for the first time also included non-Jewish respondents). Since 1999, the sample has been of eligible voters in Israel. The INES website allows researchers to analyze the data, and I calculated and displayed the Jewish only answers for the years 1996–2015. For more information, see the INES website at http://www.ines.tau.ac.il/.

Index of Arab-Jewish Relations. The Index of Arab-Jewish Relations in Israel was developed at the University of Haifa by Sammy Smooha of the Department of Sociology and Anthropology. Since its inception in 2003, the index has measured the attitudes of Arab and Jewish citizens toward each other and toward the state, drawing on representative national surveys. But the results for the Jewish only sample are also published. In 2012, the index became a joint enterprise of the University of Haifa and the Israel Democracy Institute.

National Resilience Survey. The National Resilience Survey has been conducted annually since 2000 by the National Security Studies Center at Haifa University. It encompasses a representative sample of the general

Israeli adult population. At each point in time, 2,000 respondents are sampled, of which approximately 1,600 are Jews. But the results for the Israeli Jewish only sample are also published. Every year, the survey focuses on five dimensions of the social component of national resilience, which are fear (from attacks by enemy states or terrorism), national optimism, militancy, patriotism, and confidence in national institutions. For more information, see the Herzliya Conference website at http://www.herzliyaconference .org/eng/?CategoryID=513&ArticleID=2542.

IDC. The Interdisciplinary Center (IDC) survey on patriotism in Israel, initiated by the Institute for Policy and Strategy at the Interdisciplinary Center Herzliya, has aimed to assess national strength and security with the intent of helping to formulate a national policy on contemporary issues. It was conducted annually during the years 2006–2009 among a random sample, who comprised a representative sample of the adult population in Israel, but the results for the Israeli Jewish only sample were also published.

Oren 2016 Survey. My 2016 survey was conducted on September 10, 2016, via an internet survey company among a representative sample of the Israeli Jewish population, not including Kibbutzim and localities beyond the 1967 Green Line (540 participants, 49 percent men, M age = 41.70 years, SD = 15.33; 59 percent were secular, 22 percent traditional, 11 percent religious, and 8 percent ultra-Orthodox Jews).

Rafi Smith Surveys, Dahaf Surveys, and Midgam Surveys. Smith Consulting, the Dahaf Institute, and Midgam Research and Consulting were the main Israeli commercial polling companies. Many of their political surveys are ordered by and published in Israeli main newspapers.

International Surveys

Pew. The Pew Global Attitude project conducts surveys in sixty-four countries. Data are available online from 2001. The Pew Global Attitude project bears no responsibility for the interpretations presented or conclusions reached based on analysis of the data. For more information, see the Pew Research Center website at http://www.pewglobal.org.

WVS. The World Values Survey started in 1981 and was conducted in almost 100 countries. Israel participated only in the 2001 round. For more information, see the World Values Survey website at http://www.world valuessurvey.org.

ISSP. The International Social Survey Programme started in 1984 and was conducted in fifty-seven nations. For more information, see the ISSP website at http://www.issp.org.

ESS. The European Social Survey started in 2002 and was conducted in thirty-six countries. For more information, see the European Social Survey website at http://www.europeansocialsurvey.org/.

Gallup World Poll. The Gallup World Poll started in 2005 and was conducted in more than 160 countries. For more information, see the Gallup website at http://www.gallup.com/services/170945/world-poll.aspx and http://www .gallup.com/178667/gallup-world-poll-work.aspx.

References

Abelson, Robert P. 1968. *Theories of Cognitive Consistency: A Sourcebook*. Chicago: Rand McNally.

Abrams, Dominic, Georgina Randsley de Moura, José M. Marques, and Paul Hutchison. 2008. "Innovation Credit: When Can Leaders Oppose Their Group's Norms?" *Journal of Personality and Social Psychology* 95 (3): 662–678. https://doi.org/10.1037/0022-3514.95.3.662.

Abulof, Uriel. 2014. "Deep Securitization and Israel's 'Demographic Demon.'" *International Political Sociology* 8 (4): 396–415. https://doi.org/10.1111/ips.12070.

———. 2015. *The Mortality and Morality of Nations*. New York: Cambridge University Press.

Adwan, Sami, Daniel Bar-Tal, and Bruce E. Wexler. 2016. "Portrayal of the Other in Palestinian and Israeli Schoolbooks: A Comparative Study." *Political Psychology* 37 (2): 201–217. https://doi.org/10.1111/pops.12227.

Ahren, Raphael. 2017. "Will German President Defy Netanyahu, Meet Breaking the Silence?" *Times of Israel,* May 1. https://www.timesofisrael.com/amid-nadir-in-ties-german-president-to-arrive-in-israel/.

Alignment. 1969. *Platform for the Seventh Knesset* [in Hebrew].

———. 1973. *Platform for the Eighth Knesset* [in Hebrew].

———. 1977. *Platform for the Ninth Knesset* [in Hebrew].

———. 1981. *Platform for the Tenth Knesset* [in Hebrew].

———. 1984. *Platform for the Eleventh Knesset* [in Hebrew].

———. 1988. *Platform for the Twelve Knesset* [in Hebrew]. http://web.nli.org.il/sites/NLI/Hebrew/collections/treasures/elections/all_elections/Pages/1988-data.aspx.

Amir, Ruth. 2011. *Who Is Afraid of Historical Redress? The Israeli Victim-Perpetrator Dichotomy*. Brighton, MA: Academic Studies Press.

Anshel, P. 2009. "Israel Challenges Palestinian Claim on Gaza War Dead." *Haaretz,* March 26.

Antonovsky, Aaron, and Alan Arian. 1972. *Hopes and Fears of Israelis: Consensus in a New Society*. Jerusalem: Jerusalem Academic Press.

Apfel, Roberta, and Bennett Simon. 2000. "Mitigating Discontents with Children in War: An Ongoing Psychoanalytic Inquiry." In *Cultures Under Siege: Collective*

Violence and Trauma, edited by Antonius C. G. M. Robben and Marcelo M. Suárez-Orozco, 102–130. New York: Cambridge University Press.

Arad, Uzi, and Gal Alon. 2006. "Patriotism and Israel's National Security." Working Paper. http://www.herzliyaconference.org/eng/_uploads/1388pat_e.pdf.

Arian, Asher. 1995. *Security Threatened: Surveying Israeli Opinion on Peace and War.* Cambridge: Cambridge University Press.

———. 2002. *Israeli Public Opinion on National Security* 2002. Tel Aviv: Tel Aviv University, Jaffe Center for Strategic Studies.

Arian, Asher, Nir Atmor, and Yael Hadar. 2007. *The 2007 Israeli Democracy Index.* Jerusalem: Israel Democracy Institute.

Armitage, David. 2007. *The Declaration of Independence: A Global History.* Cambridge, MA: Harvard University Press.

Aronoff, Yael. 2014. *The Political Psychology of Israeli Prime Ministers: When Hard-Liners Opt for Peace.* New York: Cambridge University Press.

Auerbach, Yehudit, and Hemda Ben-Yehuda. 1987. "Attitudes Towards an Existence Conflict: Begin and Dayan on the Palestinian Issue." *International Interactions* 13 (4): 323–351. https://doi.org/10.1080/03050628708434682.

———. 1993. "Attitudes to an Existence Conflict: Rabin and Sharon on the Palestinian Issue." In *Conflict and Social Psychology,* edited by Knud S. Larsen. 144–167. Newbury Park, CA: Sage.

Auerbach, Yehudit, and Charles W. Greenbaum. 2000. "Assessing Leader Credibility During a Peace Process: Rabin's Private Polls." *Journal of Peace Research* 37 (1): 31–50.

Azaryahu, Maoz. 2000. "The Golden Arches of McDonald's: On the 'Americanization' of Israel." *Israel Studies* 5 (1): 41–64. https://doi.org/10.1353/is.2000.0004.

Baker, Peter, and Julie Hirschfeld Davis. 2016. "U.S. Finalizes Deal to Give Israel $38 Billion in Military Aid." *New York Times,* September 13.

Barak, Ehud. 1996. "Address by Foreign Minister Ehud Barak to the Annual Plenary Session of the National Jewish Community Relations Advisory Council." February 11. http://mfa.gov.il/MFA/MFA-Archive/1996/Pages/FM%20Barak-%20Address%20to%20NJCRAC%20-%20Feb%2011-%201996.aspx.

———. 1999. "Address by Prime Minister Barak to the National Defense College." August 12. http://mfa.gov.il/MFA/ForeignPolicy/MFADocuments/Yearbook13/Pages/24%20Address%20by%20Prime%20Minister%20Barak%20to%20the%20National.aspx.

———. 2000. "Address by PM Barak on the Fifth Anniversary of the Assassination of Yitzhak Rabin November 8. http://mfa.gov.il/MFA/PressRoom/2000/Pages/Address%20by%20PM%20Barak%20on%20the%20Fifth%20Anniversary%20of%20th.aspx.

Barda, Moshe. 2007. "Data Regarding IDF Recruitment over the Years" [in Hebrew]. Jerusalem: Knesset Research and Information Center. https://www.knesset.gov.il/mmm/data/pdf/m01870.pdf.

Bargal, David, and Emmanurl Sivan. 2004. "Leadership and Reconciliation." In *From Conflict Resolution to Reconciliation,* edited by Yaacov Bar-Siman-Tov, 125–148. New York: Oxford University Press.

Bar-Gal, Yoram. 1993. "Boundaries as a Topic in Geographic Education." *Political Geography* 12: 421–435.

———. 1994. "The Image of the 'Palestinian' in Geography Textbooks in Israel." *Journal of Geography* 93: 224–232.

Bar-Navi, E. 1998. *The 20th Century: A History of the People of Israel in the Last Generations, for Grades 10–12* [in Hebrew]. Tel Aviv: Sifrei Tel Aviv.

Bar-Navi, E, and Eyal Naveh. 1999. *Modern Times, Part II: The History of the People of Israel, for Grades 10–12* [in Hebrew]. Tel Aviv: Sifrei Tel Aviv.

Bar-Siman-Tov, Yaacov. 1998. "The United States and Israel since 1948: A 'Special Relationship'?" *Diplomatic History* 22 (2): 231–262. https://doi.org/10.1111/1467-7709.00115.

Bar-Tal, Daniel. 1998. "The Rocky Road Toward Peace: Beliefs on Conflict in Israeli Textbooks." *Journal of Peace Research* 35: 723–742.

———. 2007. *Living with the Conflict, Socio-Psychological Analysis of the Jewish Society in Israel* [in Hebrew]. Jerusalem: Carmel.

———. 2013. *Intractable Conflicts: Socio-Psychological Foundations and Dynamics*. Cambridge: Cambridge University Press.

———. n.d. "Siege Mentality." Beyond Intractability. Accessed October 18, 2017. http://www.beyondintractability.org/essay/siege_mentality.

Bar-Tal, Daniel, and Dikla Antebi. 1992a. "Beliefs About Negative Intentions of the World: A Study of the Israeli Siege Mentality." *Political Psychology* 13: 633–645.

———. 1992b. "Siege Mentality in Israel." *International Journal of Intercultural Relations* 16: 251–275.

Bar-Tal, Daniel, and Phillip Hammack. 2012. "Conflict, Delegitimization, and Violence." In *The Oxford Handbook of Intergroup Conflict,* edited by Linda Tropp, 29–52. Oxford: Oxford University Press.

Bar-Tal, Daniel, Dan Jacobson, and Aaron S. Klieman. 1998. *Security Concerns: Insights from the Israeli Experience*. Stamford, CT: JAI Press.

Bar-Tal, Daniel, and Neta Oren. 2000. *Ethos as an Expression of Identity: Its Changes in Transition from Conflict to Peace in the Israeli Case*. Davis Occasional Papers, No. 83. Jerusalem: Leonard Davis Institute for International Relations, Hebrew University of Jerusalem.

Bar-Tal, Daniel, Neta Oren, and Rafi Nets-Zehngut. 2014. "Sociopsychological Analysis of Conflict-Supporting Narratives A General Framework." *Journal of Peace Research* 51 (5): 662–675. https://doi.org/10.1177/0022343314533984.

Bar-Tal, Daniel, Amiram Raviv, and Rinat Abromovich. Forthcoming. *Views of the Israeli-Palestinian Conflict by Jews: Interviews Following the Events of 2000* [in Hebrew]. Tel Aviv: Tami Steinmetz Center for Peace Research.

Bar-Tal, Daniel, Amiram Raviv, Alona Raviv, and Adi Dgani-Hirsh. 2009. "The Influence of the Ethos of Conflict on Israeli Jews' Interpretation of Jewish-Palestinian Encounters." *Journal of Conflict Resolution* 53: 94–118.

Bar-Tal, Daniel, and Yigal Rosen. 2009. "Peace Education in Societies Involved in Intractable Conflicts: Direct and Indirect Models." *Review of Educational Research* 79 (2): 557–575. https://doi.org/10.3102/0034654308330969.

Bar-Tal, Daniel, and Keren Sharvit. 2007. "Psychological Earthquake of the Israeli Jewish Society: Changing Opinions Following the Camp David Summit and Al Aqsa Intifada." In *The Israeli-Palestinian Conflict From Conflict Resolution to Conflict Management,* edited by Jacov Bar-Siman-Tov, 169–202. New York: Palgrave Macmillan.

Bar-Tal, Daniel, and Ervin Staub. 1997. *Patriotism in the Lives of Individuals and Nations*. Chicago: Nelson-Hall.

Bar-Tal, Daniel, and Yona Teichman. 2005. *Stereotypes and Prejudice in Conflict: Representation of Arabs in Israeli Jewish Society*. New York: Cambridge University Press.

Barzilai, Gad. 1996. *Wars, Internal Conflicts, and Political Order: A Jewish Democracy in the Middle East*. Albany: SUNY Press.

Bar-Zohar, Michael. 1979. *Ben-Gurion: A Biography*. New York: Delacorte Press.

Bauer, Yehuda. 2013. "The Israel Air Force Flyover at Auschwitz: A Crass, Super-ficial Display." *Haaretz,* October 8.

Beetham, David. 2006. "Parliament and Democracy in the Twenty-First Century: A Guide to Good Practice." Switzerland: Inter-Parliamentary Union. http://www .ipu.org/PDF/publications/democracy_en.pdf.

Begin, Menachem. 1977. "Prime Minister Begin Speech to Knesset Following His-toric Speech by Anwar Sadat." November 20. http://www.jewishvirtuallibrary .org/jsource/History/begintoknessetsadat.html.

———. 1978a. "Statement to the Knesset by Prime Minister Begin on the Camp David Agreements." September 25.

———. 1978b. "Menachem Begin—Nobel Lecture." December 10. https://www .nobelprize.org/nobel_prizes/peace/laureates/1978/begin-lecture.html.

———. 1979a. "Statement to the Knesset by Prime Minister Begin on the Israel-Egypt Peace Treaty." March 20. http://mfa.gov.il/MFA/ForeignPolicy/MFADocuments /Yearbook3/Pages/247%20Statement%20to%20the%20Knesset%20by%20Prime %20Minister%20Beg.aspx.

———. 1979b. "Telecast to the Nation by Prime Minister Begin on Independence Day, 1 May 1979." May 1. http://mfa.gov.il/MFA/ForeignPolicy/MFADocuments /Yearbook4/Pages/8%20Telecast%20to%20the%20Nation%20by%20Prime %20Minister%20Begin%20o.aspx.

———. 1979c. "Statement Issued by Prime Minister Begin on Israeli Settlements." June 11. http://mfa.gov.il/MFA/ForeignPolicy/MFADocuments/Yearbook4/Pages/23 %20Statement%20issued%20by%20Prime%20Minister%20Begin%20on%20Isr.aspx.

———. 1981. "Press Conference with Prime Minister Begin, I.D.F. Chief of Staff Eitan, I.A.F. Commander Ivri and Director of Military Intelligence Saguy." June 9. http:// mfa.gov.il/MFA/ForeignPolicy/MFADocuments/Yearbook5/Pages/28%20Press %20Conference%20with%20Prime%20Minister%20Begin-%20IDF.aspx.

———. 1982. "Address in the Knesset by Prime Minister Begin." Jerusalem, October 18. http://mfa.gov.il/MFA/ForeignPolicy/MFADocuments/Yearbook6/Pages/88%20Address %20in%20the%20Knesset%20by%20Prime%20Minister%20Begin-.aspx.

———. 1983. "Statement in the Knesset by Prime Minister Begin." Jerusalem, June 1. http://mfa.gov.il/MFA/ForeignPolicy/MFADocuments/Yearbook6/Pages/118 %20Statement%20in%20the%20Knesset%20by%20Prime%20Minister%20Beg.aspx.

Ben-Ami, Shlomo. 2006. *Scars of War, Wounds of Peace: The Israeli-Arab Tragedy.* Oxford: Oxford University Press.

Ben-Amos, Avner, and Ilana Bet-El. 1999. "Holocaust Day and Memorial Day in Israeli Schools: Ceremonies, Education and History." *Israel Studies* 4: 258–284.

———. 2003. "Education for Militarism—National Memorial Ceremony in Israeli Schools" [in Hebrew]. In *In the Name of Security,* edited by Uri Ben-Eliezer and Majid Al Haj, 369–400. Haifa: University of Haifa.

Ben-Amos, Avner, Ilana Bet-El, and Moshe Tlamim. 1999. "Holocaust Day and Memorial Day in Israeli Schools: Ceremonies, Education and History." *Israel Studies* 4 (1): 258–284.

Ben-Dor, Gabi, and Daphna Canetti. 2009. "The Social Aspect of National Security: Israeli Public Opinion After the Gaza War." Haifa: National Security Studies Center.

Ben-Dor, Gabi, Daphna Canetti, and Eran Halperin. 2007. "The Social Aspect of National Security: Israeli Public Opinion and the Second Lebanon War." Haifa: National Security Studies Center.

Ben-Dor, Gabi, Daphna Canetti, and Eyal Lewin. 2012. "The Social Component in National Resilience." Paper presented at the twelfth annual Herzliya Conference, Herzliya, January 30–February 2.

Ben-Eliezer, Uri, and Majid Al Haj, eds. 2003. *In the Name of Security* [in Hebrew]. Haifa: University of Haifa.

Ben-Gurion, David. 1956. "Ben-Gurion Speech to Knesset Reviewing the Sinai Campaign." November 7. http://www.jewishvirtuallibrary.org/jsource/History/bgsinai .html.

———. 1963. *The Eternity of Israel* [in Hebrew]. Tel Aviv: Hozaat sefarim Ayanot.

Ben Meir, Yehuda. 2009. "Operation Cast Lead: Political Dimensions and Public Opinion." *Strategic Assessment* 11 (4): 29–34.

———. 2014. "Operation Protective Edge: A Public Opinion Roller Coaster." In *The Lessons of Operation Protective Edge,* edited by Shlomo Brom and Anat Kurz, 129–134. http://www.inss.org.il/publication/the-lessons-of-operation-protective-edge/.

Ben Meir, Yehuda, and Olena Bagno-Moldavsky. 2010. "Vox Populi: Trends in Israeli Public Opinion on National Security, 2004–2009." Tel Aviv: Institute for National Security Studies.

———. 2013. "The Voice of the People: Israeli Public Opinion on National Security 2012." Tel Aviv: Institute for National Security Studies.

Ben Meir, Yehuda, and Dafna Shaked. 2007. "The People Speak: Israeli Public Opinion on National Security, 2005–2007." Tel Aviv: Institute for National Security Studies.

Bennet, James. 2004. "Sharon's Wars." *New York Times Magazine,* August 15.

Ben-Shaul, Nitzan S. 1997. *Mythical Expressions of Siege in Israeli Films.* Lewiston, NY: Edwin Mellen Press.

Ben Simon, D. 2004. "The Year When Optimism Was Lost" [in Hebrew]. *Haaretz.* September 15.

Ben-Yehuda, Hemda, and Yehudit Auerbach. 1991. "Attitudes to an Existence Conflict—Allon and Peres on the Palestinian Issue, 1967–1987." *Journal of Conflict Resolution* 35 (3): 519–546.

Blum, Gadi. 2006. "The Strengthening Plan: Interview with Benjamin Netanyahu" [in Hebrew]. *Yediot Aharnot,* October 13.

Botelho, Greg. 2015. "Netanyahu Criticized for Hitler, Mufti Holocaust Remarks." CNN, October 22. http://www.cnn.com/2015/10/21/middleeast/netanyahu-hitler -grand-mufti-holocaust/.

Brecher, Michael. 1972. *The Foreign Policy System of Israel: Setting, Images, Process.* New Haven, CT: Yale University Press.

Brenner, Michael. 2018. "A State Like Any Other State or a Light Unto the Nations?" *Israel Studies* 23 (3): 3–10.

Brom, Shlomo. 2007. "From Rejection to Acceptance: Israeli National Security Thinking and Palestinian Statehood." Washington, DC: United States Institute of Peace.

Brubaker, Rogers, and Frederick Cooper. 2000. "Beyond 'Identity.'" *Theory and Society* 29: 1–47.

Bruner, Jerome. 1991. "The Narrative Construction of Reality." *Critical Inquiry* 18: 1–21.

Buckley, Anthony D., and Mary Catherine Kenney. 1995. *Negotiating Identity: Rhetoric, Metaphor, and Social Drama in Northern Ireland.* Washington, DC: Smithsonian Institution Press.

Buzan, Barry, Ole Wæver, and Jaap de Wilde. 1998. *Security: A New Framework for Analysis.* Boulder, CO: Lynne Rienner.

Cacioppo, J. T., and G. G. Berntson. 1994. "Relationship Between Attitudes and Evaluative Space—A Critical-Review, with Emphasis on the Separability of Positive and Negative Substrates." *Psychological Bulletin* 115 (3): 401–423.

Caplan, Neil. 2001. "'Oum Shmoom' Revisited: Israeli Attitude Towards the UN and the Great Powers, 1948–1960." In *Global Politics: Essays in Honour of David Vital,* edited by David Vital, Abraham Ben-Zvi, and Aaron S. Klieman, 167–198. London: F. Cass.

Caspi, Mishael Maswari. 2001. *Take Now Thy Son: The Motif of the Aqedah.* North Richland Hills, TX: D & F Scott.

Central Intelligence Agency (CIA). n.d. "The World Factbook." Accessed November 11, 2018. https://www.cia.gov/library/publications/the-world-factbook/geos/is.html.

Cohen, Akiba A., Hanna Adoni, and Hillel Nossek. 1993. "Television News and the Intifada: A Comparative Study of Social Conflict." In *Framing the Intifada: People and Media,* edited by Akiba A. Cohen and Gadi Wolfsfeld, 116–141. Norwood, NJ: Ablex.

Cohen, Avner. 1998. *Israel and the Bomb.* New York: Columbia University Press.

Cohen, Eric. 2010. "Research on Teaching the Holocaust in Israeli High Schools: An Educational Research, 2007–2009" [in Hebrew]. Ramat-Gan: Bar-Ilan University.

Cohen, Gili. 2013. "Proportion of Teens Wanting to Serve in IDF Combat Units Drops Almost 10% in Three Years." *Haaretz,* November 8.

———. 2017. "IDF Chief on Hebron Shooter's Trial: Treating a Soldier Like a 'Confused Little Boy' Demeans the Army." *Haaretz,* January 3.

Cohen, Hillel. 2015. *Year Zero of the Arab-Israeli Conflict, 1929.* Waltham, MA: Brandeis University Press.

Cohen, Stanley. 2001. *States of Denial: Knowing About Atrocities and Suffering.* Cambridge, UK: Polity.

Cohen, Stuart A. 2008. *Israel and Its Army: From Cohesion to Confusion.* London: Routledge.

Cohen, Yinon. 1988. "War and Social Integration: The Effects of the Israeli-Arab Conflict on Jewish Emigration from Israel." *American Sociological Review* 53 (6): 908–918. https://doi.org/10.2307/2095899.

Collins, C., and Clark. 1993. "Structuring the Intifada in Al-Fajar and Jerusalem Post." In *Framing the Intifada: People and Media,* edited by Akiba A. Cohen and Gadi Wolfsfeld, 116–141. Norwood, NJ: Ablex.

Cuban, L. 1992. "Curriculum Stability and Change." In *Handbook of Research on Curriculum,* edited by P. W. Jackson, 216–247. New York: Macmillan.

Dahan-Kalev, Henriette. 2005. "'Generals' in Education: Military Men as School Principals." In *The Militarization of Education* [in Hebrew], edited by Hagit Gor, 109–130. Tel Aviv: Babel.

Damian, Natalia. 1987. "Israeli Public Opinion Regarding Emigration from Israel, Israelis Living Abroad, and the Policies Implemented to Encourage Their Return" [in Hebrew]. Jerusalem: Ministry of Aliah and Immigrant Absorption, Unit for Policy Planning and Research.

David, Ohad. 2012. "Sculpting the Face of a Nation Jewish-Israeli Identity in Twentieth-Century Hebrew Readers" [in Hebrew]. *Dor Ledor* 41: 30–427.

David, Ohad, and Daniel Bar-Tal. 2009. "A Sociopsychological Conception of Collective Identity: The Case of National Identity as an Example." *Personality and Social Psychology Review* 13: 354–379.

Davies, Lynn. 2003. *Education and Conflict: Complexity and Chaos.* London: Routledge.

Deutsch, K. W., and R. C. Merritt. 1965. "Effect of Events on National and International Images." In *International Behavior: A Social-Psychological Analysis,* edited by Herbert C. Kelman, 132–181. New York: Henry Holt.

Dor, Daniel. 2004. *Intifada Hits the Headlines: How the Israeli Press Misreported the Outbreak of the Second Palestinian Uprising.* Bloomington: Indiana University Press.

Doty, R. M., B. E. Peterson, and D. G. Winter. 1991. "Threat and Authoritarianism in the United States, 1978–1987." *Journal of Personality and Social Psychology* 61: 629–640.

Dror, Yuval. 2001. "Holocaust Curricula in Israeli Secondary Schools, 1960s–1990s: Historical Evaluation from the Moral Education Perspective." *Journal of Holocaust Education* 10 (2): 29–39. https://doi.org/10.1080/17504902.2001.11087129.

———. 2004. "The Israeli Education System as an Agent of Jewish Patriotism in Israel" [in Hebrew]. In *Patriotism in Israel,* edited by A. Ben-Amos and D. Bar-Tal, 137–174. Tel Aviv: Hakibuz Hamehuhad.

———. 2007. "The History of Israeli Non-Formal Education, 1920–2000: Dimensions Drawn from the Past." *Israel Studies Forum* 22 (1): 75–99.

Eagly, Alice, and Shelly Chaiken. 1993. *The Psychology of Attitudes.* Fort Worth, TX: Harcourt Brace Jovanovich.

Eilam, Y. 2004. "Patriotism and Zionism" [in Hebrew]. In *Patriotism: Homeland Love,* edited by Avner Ben-Amos and Daniel Bar-Tal, 29–60. Tel Aviv: Deyonon.

Eisenbud, Daniel. 2017. "Rivlin Supports Full Sovereignty in West Bank Blocs." *Jerusalem Post,* February 13.

Eldan, M. 2006. "Imparting Collective Memory by Secular and Religious Kindergarten Teachers" [in Hebrew]. Master's thesis, Tel Aviv University.

Elkana, Yehuda. 1988. "The Need to Forget" [in Hebrew]. *Haaretz,* March 2.

Eran Jona, Meytal. 2015. "Israelis' Perception of the IDF: A Split Between It as an Armed Force and as a Public Institution." Research Paper No. 15. College Park: Joseph and Alma Gildenhorn Institute for Israel Studies, University of Maryland, College Park.

Eriksen, T. H. 1995. "We and Us: Two Modes of Group Identification." *Journal of Peace Research* 32 (4): 427–436. https://doi.org/10.1177/0022343395032004004.

Eshkol, Levi. 1967. "Prime Minister Eshkol Reviews Six-Day War." Jerusalem, June 12. http://www.jewishvirtuallibrary.org/jsource/History/eshwar.html.

Esteron, Yoel. 2004. "Let's Dismantle the Fence." *Haaretz,* July 7.

European Commission. 2002. "Eurobarometer Number 56." Brussels: European Commission.

European Social Survey Round 8 Data. 2016. Data file edition 2.0. NSD—Norwegian Centre for Research Data, Norway. Data archive and distributor of ESS data for ESS ERIC.

Farnen, Russell Francis. 1994. "Nationality, Ethnicity, Political Socialization, and Public Policy: Some Cross-National Perspectives." In *Nationalism, Ethnicity, and Identity: Cross National and Comparative Perspectives,* edited by Russell Francis Farnen, 23–102. New Brunswick, NJ: Transaction.

Feldman, Jackie. 2002. "Marking the Boundaries of the Enclave: Defining the Israeli Collective Through the Poland 'Experience.'" *Israel Studies* 7 (2): 84–114.

———. 2008. *Above the Death Pits, Beneath the Flag: Youth Voyages to Poland and the Performance of the Israeli National Identity.* New York: Berghahn Books.

Feldman, Shai, and Yiftah Shapir, eds. 2001. *The Middle East Military Balance, 2000–2001.* Cambridge, MA: MIT Press.

Festinger, Leon. 1957. *A Theory of Cognitive Dissonance.* Evanston, IL: Row.

Finkel, Meir. 2007. "The Social Impact on the IDF's Doctrine and Culture" [in Hebrew]. *Ma'arachot* 412: 60–63.

Firer, Ruth. 1985. *The Agents of Zionist Education* [in Hebrew]. Tel Aviv: Sifriyat Poalim.

————. 2002. "Preventive Remedy: Tolerance Education—The Israeli Textbooks Case." Paper presented at the third global conference, Diversity Within Unity: Cultures of Violence, Prague, Czech Republic, August 12–16.

————. 2005. "Education Socialization." Paper presented at the Socialization for Conflict in the Israeli-Jewish Society Conference, Tel Aviv. May 31, https://www.youtube.com/watch?v=WX5GYGGr-eI.

Firer, Ruth, Sāmī 'Abd al-Razzāq 'Adwān, and Falk Pingel. 2004. *The Israeli-Palestinian Conflict in History and Civics Textbooks of Both Nations.* Hannover, Germany: Hahnsche.

First, Anat, and Eli Avraham. 2007. "Globalization/Americanization and Negotiating National Dreams: Representations of Culture and Economy in Israeli Advertising." *Israel Studies Forum* 22 (1): 54–74.

Franzosi, Roberto. 1994. "From Words to Numbers: A Set-Theory Framework for the Collection, Organization, and Analysis of Narrative Data." *Sociological Methodology* 24: 105–136.

Freedman, Robert Owen, ed. 2012. *Israel and the United States: Six Decades of US-Israeli Relations.* Boulder, CO: Westview Press.

Friedberg, A., and A. Kfir. 2008. "The Political Agenda and Policy-Making: The Case of Emigration from Israel." *International Journal of Public Administration* 31 (8): 819–844. https://doi.org/10.1080/01900690701696103.

Furman, Mirta. 1999. "Army and War: Collective Narratives of Early Childhood in Contemporary Israel." In *The Military and Militarism in Israeli Society,* edited by Edna Lomsky-Feder and Eyal Ben-Ari, 141–168. Albany: SUNY Press.

Fuxman, Shai. 2012. "Learning the Past, Understanding the Present, Shaping the Future: Israeli Adolescents' Narratives of the Israeli-Palestinian Conflict." Doctoral dissertation, Harvard University.

Gad, Ulrik, and Karen Petersen. 2011. "Concepts of Politics in Securitization Studies." *Security Dialogue* 42 (4–5): 315–328. https://doi.org/10.1177/0967010611418716.

Gadish, Michael. 2009. "Jewish-Israeli Identity in Naomi Shemer's Songs: Central Values of the Jewish-Israeli Imagined Community." *Miscelánea de Estudios Árabes y Hebraicos (MEAH)* 58: 41–85.

Gertz, Nurith. 2000. *Myths in Israeli Culture: Captives of a Dream.* Portland, OR: Vallentine Mitchell.

Ginges, J., S. Atran, D. Medin, and K. Shikaki. 2007. "Sacred Bounds on Rational Resolution of Violent Political Conflict." *Proceedings of the National Academy of Sciences* 104 (18): 7357–7360. https://doi.org/10.1073/pnas.0701768104.

Glickman, Hagit, Tal Raz, Tal Friman, Nurit Lipshtat, Netaniel Goldschmidt, and Mina Semach. 2011. "Evaluation of Youth Journeys to Poland in 2009: Cognitive, Value and Emotional Influences" [in Hebrew]. Tel Aviv: National Authority for Measurement and Evaluation in Education. http://cms.education.gov.il/EducationCMS/Units/Rama/HaarachatProjectim/Polin.htm.

Gordon, C., and A. Arian. 2001. "Threat and Decision Making." *Journal of Conflict Resolution* 45 (2): 196–215.

Gorny, Yosef. 2003. *Between Auschwitz and Jerusalem.* Portland, OR: Vallentine Mitchell.

————. 2011. *The Jewish Press and the Holocaust, 1939–1945: Palestine, Britain, the United States, and the Soviet Union.* New York: Cambridge University Press.

Grob, Leonard, and John K. Roth, eds. 2008. *Anguished Hope: Holocaust Scholars Confront the Palestinian-Israeli Conflict.* Grand Rapids, MI: William B. Eerdmans.

Haaretz. 1998. "Everybody Together: It Will Be Ok." April 29.

————. 2013. "Don't Scrap Home Because It's 'Easier to Live in Berlin,' Lapid Tells Israelis." October 1.

————. 2017. "Israeli Lawmaker: Only Palestinians Who Serve in Army Would Be Able to Vote in Binational State." March 6.

Hadashot. 1990. "Afraid of War" [in Hebrew]. September 19.

Haidt, Jonathan, Jesse Graham, and Craig Joseph. 2009. "Above and Below Left-Right: Ideological Narratives and Moral Foundations." *Psychological Inquiry* 20 (2–3): 110–119. https://doi.org/10.1080/10478400903028573.

Halperin, Eran, and Daniel Bar-Tal. 2007. "The Fall of the Peace Camp in Israel: The Influence of Prime Minister Ehud Barak on Israeli Public Opinion—July 2000–February 2001." *Conflict and Communication Online* 6 (2). http://www.cco.regener-online.de/2007_2/pdf/halperin.pdf.

Hamilton, David L., John M Levine, and Joel Thurston. 2014. "Perceiving Continuity and Change in Groups." In *Self Continuity: Individual and Collective Perspectives,* edited by Fabio Sani, 117–130. New York: Psychology Press.

Hammack, Phillip. 2009. "Exploring the Reproduction of Conflict Through Narrative: Israeli Youth Motivated to Participate in a Coexistence Program." *Peace and Conflict: Journal of Peace Psychology* 15 (1): 49–74.

Handelman, Don. 1990. *Models and Mirrors: Towards an Anthropology of Public Events.* Cambridge: Cambridge University Press.

————. 2004. *Nationalism and the Israeli State: Bureaucratic Logic in Public Events.* Oxford, UK: Berg.

Harber, Clive. 2004. *Schooling as Violence: How Schools Harm Pupils and Societies.* London: Routledge.

Harel, Amos. 2017. "Israeli Army Suffering Heavy Losses on the Front of Quality." *Haaretz,* January 14.

Harkov, Lehav. 2015. "Yair Lapid with Reservists: Breaking the Silence Crossed from Criticism to Subversion." *Jerusalem Post,* December 20.

Haslam, Nick. 2006. "Dehumanization: An Integrative Review." *Personality and Social Psychology Review* 10 (3): 252–264. https://doi.org/10.1207/s15327957pspr1003_4.

Haslam, S. Alexander, and Stephen D. Reicher. 2016. "Rethinking the Psychology of Leadership: From Personal Identity to Social Identity." *Daedalus* 145 (3): 21–34. https://doi.org/10.1162/DAED_a_00394.

Haslam, S. Alexander, Stephen D. Reicher, and Michael J. Platow. 2010. *The New Psychology of Leadership: Identity, Influence and Power.* Hove, UK: Psychology Press.

Hassner, Ron E. 2013. *War on Sacred Grounds.* Ithaca, NY: Cornell University Press.

Hattis Rolef, Shila. 2006. "Public Trust in Parliament—A Comparative Study" [in Hebrew]. Jerusalem: Knesset Information Division. https://www.knesset.gov.il/mmm/data/pdf/m01417.pdf.

Heider, Fritz. 1958. *The Psychology of Interpersonal Relations.* New York: Wiley.

Hermann, Margaret G., and Catherine Gerard. 2009. "The Contributions of Leadership to the Movement from Violence to Incorporation." In *Conflict Transformation and Peacebuilding: Moving from Violence to Sustainable Peace,* edited by Louis Kriesberg and B. W. Dayton, 30–44. London: Routledge.

Hermann, Tamar S., Chanan Cohen, Ella Heller, and Dana Bublil. 2015. *The Israeli Democracy Index 2015.* Jerusalem: Israel Democracy Institute.

Hermann, Tamar S., Ella Heller, Nir Atmor, and Yuval Lebel. 2013. *The Israeli Democracy Index 2013.* Jerusalem: Israel Democracy Institute.

Herut. 1969–2006. *Party Platforms* [in Hebrew]. http://www.infocenters.co.il/jabo/jabo_multimedia/%D7%94%20I/%D7%941%20_%2019_1.pdf.

Hobfoll, Stevan E. 1998. *Stress, Culture, and Community: The Psychology and Philosophy of Stress.* New York: Plenum Press.

Hofman, Amos, Bracha Alpert, and Izhak Schnell. 2007. "Education and Social Change: The Case of Israel's State Curriculum." *Curriculum Inquiry* 37: 303–328. https://doi.org/10.1111/j.1467-873X.2007.00389.x.

Hogg, Michael A., Daan van Knippenberg, and David E. Rast III. 2012. "The Social Identity Theory of Leadership: Theoretical Origins, Research Findings, and Conceptual Developments." *European Review of Social Psychology* 23 (1): 258–304. http://www.tandfonline.com/doi/abs/10.1080/10463283.2012.741134.

Horowitz, Dan. 1993. "The Israeli Concept of National Security." In *National Security and Democracy in Israel,* edited by A. Yaniv, 11–54. Boulder, CO: Lynne Rienner.

Horowitz, Dan, and Moshe Lissak. 1989. *Trouble in Utopia: The Overburdened Polity of Israel.* Albany: SUNY Press.

Huddy, Leonie, David O. Sears, and Jack S. Levy, eds. 2013. *The Oxford Handbook of Political Psychology,* 2nd ed. Oxford: Oxford University Press.

"Human Development Index (HDI) Human Development Reports." n.d. Accessed October 16, 2016. http://hdr.undp.org/en/content/human-development-index-hdi.

Ichilov, Orit. 2004. *Political Learning and Citizenship Education Under Conflict: The Political Socialization of Israeli and Palestinian Youngsters.* London: Routledge.

IMPACT-SE (Institute for Monitoring Peace and Cultural Tolerance in School Education). 2000. "Arabs, Islam and Palestinians in Israeli Textbooks." http://www.impact-se.org/wp-content/uploads/2016/04/Israel2000.pdf.

"In a Place Where There Are No Human Beings, Strive to Be One—Righteous" [in Hebrew]. n.d. Accessed October 21, 2016. http://education.yadvashem.org/zayin-tet/righteous.asp.

Inbar, Efraim. 1991. *War and Peace in Israeli Politics: Labor Party Positions on National Security.* Boulder, CO: Lynne Rienner.

Inglehart, R., C. Haerpfer, A. Moreno, C. Welzel, K. Kizilova, J. Diez-Medrano, M. Lagos, P. Norris, E. Ponarin, and B. Puranen et al., eds. 2014. World Values Survey: All Rounds— Country-Pooled Datafile Version. Madrid: JD Systems Institute. http://www.worldvaluessurvey.org/WVSDocumentationWVL.jsp.

Inglehart, Ronald. 1997. *Modernization and Postmodernization: Cultural, Economic, and Political Change in 43 Societies.* Princeton, NJ: Princeton University Press.

"In Search for a Home" [in Hebrew]. n.d. Accessed October 21, 2016. http://education.yadvashem.org/he-vav/home.asp.

Israel. 1958. *Divrei Haknesset.* Records of the Knesset, vol. 24.

———. 1962. *Divrei Haknesset.* Records of the Knesset, vol. 34.

Israel Ministry of Foreign Affairs. 1996. "The Amendment of the Palestinian Covenant—Arafat Letter-04-May-96." Accessed November 19, 2018. http://www.mfa.gov.il/mfa/foreignpolicy/peace/mfadocuments/pages/the%20amendment%20of%20the%20palestinian%20covenant-%20arafat.aspx.

———. n.d. "Declaration of Establishment of State of Israel." Accessed November 28, 2016. http://www.mfa.gov.il/mfa/foreignpolicy/peace/guide/pages/declaration%20of%20establishment%20of%20state%20of%20israel.aspx.

Israeli, Zipi, and Udi Dekel. 2018. "The Future of Jerusalem: Between Public Opinion and Policy." INSS Insight No. 1057. Tel Aviv: The Institute for National Security Studies, Tel-Aviv University.

ISSP Research Group. 2012. International Social Survey Programme: Environment III—ISSP 2010. GESIS Data Archive, Cologne. ZA5500 Data file Version 2.0.0, doi:10.4232/1.11418.

ISSP Research Group. 2015. International Social Survey Programme: National Identity III—ISSP 2013. GESIS Data Archive, Cologne. ZA5950 Data file Version 2.0.0, doi:10.4232/1.12312.

Ito, T. A., J. T. Larsen, N. K. Smith, and J. T. Cacioppo. 1998. "Negative Information Weighs More Heavily on the Brain: The Negativity Bias in Evaluative Categorizations." *Journal of Personality and Social Psychology* 75 (4): 887–900.

Jacoby, Tami Amanda. 2007. *Bridging the Barrier: Israeli Unilateral Disengagement.* Burlington, VT: Ashgate.

Jamal, Amal. 2007. "Nationalizing States and the Constitution of 'Hollow Citizenship': Israel and Its Palestinian Citizens." *Ethnopolitics* 6 (4): 471–493. https://doi.org/10.1080/17449050701448647.

James, Marisa. n.d. "'And Nobody Says Anything': 20 Years of Commemorating the Rabin Assassination." Accessed October 25, 2016. https://www.academia.edu/10331012/_And_Nobody_Says_Anything_20_Years_of_Commemorating_the_Rabin_Assassination.

Jewish Telegraphic Agency. 1997. "Netanyahu Remarks on Leftists Spur New Internal Controversy." https://www.jta.org/1997/10/23/archive/netanyahu-remarks-on-leftists-spur-new-internal-controversy-3.

Jost, John T., Christopher M. Federico, and Jaime L. Napier. 2009. "Political Ideology: Its Structure, Functions, and Elective Affinities." *Annual Review of Psychology* 60 (1): 307–337. https://doi.org/10.1146/annurev.psych.60.110707.163600.

Kadima. 2006. *Action Plan* [in Hebrew]. https://www.idi.org.il/media/6739/kadima-17.pdf.

———. 2009. *Action Plan* [in Hebrew].

Kahanoff, Maya. 2016. *Jews and Arabs in Israel Encountering Their Identities: Transformations in Dialogue.* Lanham, MD: Lexington Books.

Kashti, Or. 2010. "Education Ministry Revising Textbook for Being Too Critical of Israel." *Haaretz*, August 29.

Kashti, Or, and Yarden Skop. 2014. "As Schools Remember Rabin, Teachers Describe Rising Hatred." *Haaretz,* November 14.

Katz, R. 1980. *Patterns of Concerns of the Israeli—Trends 1962–1975.* Jerusalem: Institute of Applied Social Research.

Keinon, Herb. 2017. "Benjamin Netanyahu Sets Policy: We Won't Meet Diplomats Who Meet with Breaking the Silence." *Jerusalem Post,* April 25.

Kimmerling, Baruch. 1984. "Making Conflict a Routine: A Cumulative Effect of the Arab-Jewish Conflict upon the Israeli Society." In *Israeli Society and Its Defense Establishment: The Social and Political Impact of a Protracted Violent Conflict,* edited by Moshe Lissak, 13–45. London: F. Cass.

———. 1985. "Between the Primordial and the Civil Definitions of the Collective Identity: 'Eretz Israel' or the State of Israel?" In *Comparative Social Dynamics: Essays in Honor of S. N. Eisenstadt,* edited by S. N. Eisenstadt, Erik Cohen, Moshe Lissak, and Uri Almagor, 262–283. Boulder, CO: Westview Press.

———. 2001. *The Invention and Decline of Israeliness: State, Society, and the Military.* Berkeley: University of California Press.

———. 2008. *Clash of Identities: Explorations in Israeli and Palestinian Societies.* New York: Columbia University Press.

Kishon, Ephraim. 1961. "Happy Birthday to the State of Israel." *Atlantic Monthly,* November.

———. 2004. "Israel: My Only Country!" World Security Network, March 8. http://www.worldsecuritynetwork.com/Broader-Middle-East-Israel-Palestine/Kishon-Ephraim/Israel-My-only-Country.

Kizel, Arie. 2008. *Subservient History: A Critical Analysis of History Curricula and Textbooks in Israel, 1948–2006* [in Hebrew]. Tel Aviv: Mofet.

Klar, Yechiel, Noa Schori-Eyal, and Yonat Klar. 2013. "The 'Never Again' State of Israel: The Emergence of the Holocaust as a Core Feature of Israeli Identity and Its Four Incongruent Voices." *Journal of Social Issues* 69 (1): 125–143. https://doi.org/10.1111/josi.12007.

Klein, Menachem. 2003. *The Jerusalem Problem: The Struggle for Permanent Status*. Gainesville: University Press of Florida.

Kochin, Michael S. 2012. *Five Chapters on Rhetoric: Character, Action, Things, Nothing, and Art*. University Park: Penn State University Press.

Kress, Gunther, and Frances Christie. 1989. *Linguistic Processes in Sociocultural Practice,* 2nd ed. Oxford: Oxford University Press.

Krippendorff, Klaus. 2012. *Content Analysis: An Introduction to Its Methodology*. Thousand Oaks, CA: Sage.

Kruglanski, Arie W. 1989. *Lay Epistemics and Human Knowledge: Cognitive and Motivational Bases*. Perspectives in Social Psychology Series. New York: Plenum Press.

Kubovich, Yaniv. 2018. "Israeli Military Watchdog Warns: IDF in Crisis, Best Career Officers Leaving." *Haaretz,* June 27.

Labor. 1992. *Platform for the Thirteenth Knesset* [in Hebrew].

———. 1996. *Platform for the Fourteenth Knesset* [in Hebrew]. http://web.nli.org.il/sites/NLI/Hebrew/collections/treasures/elections/all_elections/Documents/matzayim-miflagot/14—avoda.pdf.

———. 1999. *The Essence of Barak's Plan for Better Israel* [in Hebrew].

———. 2003. *Platform for the Sixteenth Knesset* [in Hebrew]. https://www.idi.org.il/policy/parties-and-elections/elections/2003/.

———. 2009. *Platform for the Eighteenth Knesset* [in Hebrew].

Landau, Noa. 2017. "Yair Lapid Says Jerusalem Is Non-Negotiable Even If It Means No Peace." *Haaretz,* December 25.

Landau, Simha. 1998. "Security-Related Stress and the Quality of Life." In *Security Concerns: Insights from the Israeli Experience,* edited by Daniel Bar-Tal, Dan Jacobson, and Aaron S. Klieman, 289–310. Stamford, CT: JAI Press.

Landman, Shiri. 2010. "Barriers to Peace: Protected Values in the Israeli-Palestinian Conflict." In *Barriers to Peace in the Israeli-Palestinian Conflict,* edited by Jacov Bar-Siman-Tov, 135–177. Jerusalem: Jerusalem Institute for Israel Studies.

Lapid, Yair. 2001. "To Be an Israeli" [in Hebrew]. *Ma'ariv,* December 7.

———. 2014. "On the Holocaust." *Huffington Post,* August 20. https://www.huffingtonpost.com/yair-lapid/on-the-holocaust-from-a-s_b_5735850.html.

———. 2015. "Yair Lapid—Timeline Facebook." October 18. https://www.facebook.com/YairLapid/posts/1022009854524032.

Laqueur, Walter, and Barry Rubin, eds. 2008. *The Israel-Arab Reader: A Documentary History of the Middle East Conflict,* 7th ed. New York: Penguin Books.

Leshem, Elazar, and Judith T. Shuval, eds. 1998. *Immigration to Israel: Sociological Perspectives*. New Brunswick, NJ: Transaction.

Leshem, Oded Adomi, Yechiel Klar, and Thomas Edward Flores. 2016. "Instilling Hope for Peace During Intractable Conflicts." *Social Psychological and Personality Science* 7 (4): 303–311. https://doi.org/10.1177/1948550615626776.

Levey, Zach. 2001. "Israeli Foreign Policy and the Arms Race in the Middle East, 1950–1960." *Journal of Strategic Studies* 24 (1): 29–48. https://doi.org/10.1080/01402390108437821.

Levy, Gal. 2014. "Is There a Place for Peace Education? Political Education and Citizenship Activism in Israeli Schools." *Journal of Peace Education* 11 (1): 101–119. https://doi.org/10.1080/17400201.2013.865598.

Levy, Shlomit. 1996. *Israeli Perceptions of Antisemitism*. Jerusalem: Vidal Sassoon International Center for the Study of Antisemitism, Hebrew University of Jerusalem.

Levy, Yagil. 2012. *Israel's Death Hierarchy: Casualty Aversion in a Militarized Democracy*. New York: NYU Press.

Levy, Yagil, Edna Lomsky-Feder, and Noa Harel. 2007. "From 'Obligatory Militarism' to 'Contractual Militarism'—Competing Models of Citizenship." *Israel Studies* 12 (1): 127–148.

Lewin, Eyal. 2011. *Patriotism: Insights from Israel*. Amherst, NY: Cambria Press.

Liebman, Charles S., and Eliezer Don-Yihya. 1983. *Civil Religion in Israel: Traditional Judaism and Political Culture in the Jewish State*. Berkeley: University of California Press.

Likud. 1973–2006. *Platform for the Knesset* [in Hebrew]. http://www.infocenters .co.il/jabo/jabo_multimedia/%D7%94%201/%D7%941%20_%2019_1.pdf.

———. 2009. *Platform for the Eighteenth Knesset* [in Hebrew]. https://www.idi .org.il/media/6698/likud-18.pdf.

Loizides, Neophytos. 2015. "Ontological Security and Ethnic Adaptation in Cyprus." In *Conflict Resolution and Ontological Security: Peace Anxieties,* edited by Bahar Rumelili, 71–94. London: Routledge.

Lomsky-Feder, Edna. 2004. "The Memorial Ceremony in Israeli Schools: Between the State and Civil Society." *British Journal of Sociology of Education* 25 (3): 291–305. https://doi.org/10.1080/0142569042000216954.

Loshitzky, Y. 1993. "Images of Intifada Television News: The Case of Nahalin." In *Framing the Intifada : People and Media*, edited by Akiba A. Cohen and Gadi Wolfsfeld, 116–141. Norwood, NJ: Ablex.

Lupovici, Amir. 2012. "Ontological Dissonance, Clashing Identities, and Israel's Unilateral Steps Towards the Palestinians." *Review of International Studies* 38 (4): 809–833. https://doi.org/10.1017/S0260210511000222.

———. 2014a. "The Limits of Securitization Theory: Observational Criticism and the Curious Absence of Israel." *International Studies Review* 16 (3): 390–410. https://doi.org/10.1111/misr.12150.

———. 2014b. "Securitization Climax: Putting the Iranian Nuclear Project at the Top of the Israeli Public Agenda (2009–2012)." *Foreign Policy Analysis* 12 (3): 413–432. https://doi.org/10.1111/fpa.12081.

———. 2015. "Ontological Security and the Israeli-Palestinian Peace Process." In *Conflict Resolution and Ontological Security: Peace Anxieties,* edited by Bahar Rumelili, 33–51. London: Routledge.

Lustick, Ian S. 1993. *Unsettled States, Disputed Lands: Britain and Ireland, France and Algeria, Israel and the West Bank-Gaza*. Ithaca, NY: Cornell University Press.

———. 1996a. "The Fetish of Jerusalem: A Hegemonic Analysis." In *Israel in Comparative Perspective: Challenging the Conventional Wisdom,* edited by Michael N. Barnett, 143–171. Albany: SUNY Press.

———. 1996b. "Hegemonic Beliefs and Territorial Rights." *International Journal of Intercultural Relations, Prejudice, Discrimination and Conflict* 20 (3): 479–492. https://doi.org/10.1016/0147-1767(96)00030-2.

———. 2008. "Abandoning the Iron Wall: Israel and 'The Middle Eastern Muck.'" *Middle East Policy* 15 (3): 30–56. https://doi.org/10.1111/j.1475-4967.2008.00357.x.

————. 2015. "Making Sense of the Nakba: Ari Shavit, Baruch Marzel, and Zionist Claims to Territory." *Journal of Palestine Studies* 44 (2): 7–27. https://doi.org/10.1525/jps.2015.44.2.7.

————. 2017. "The Holocaust in Israeli Political Culture: Four Constructions and Their Consequences." *Contemporary Jewry* 37 (1): 125–170. https://doi.org/10.1007/s12397-017-9208-7.

Magal, Tamir, Neta Oren, Daniel Bar-Tal, and Eran Halperin. 2013. "Psychological Legitimization—Views of the Israeli Occupation by Jews in Israel: Data and Implications." In *The Impacts of Lasting Occupation: Lessons from Israeli Society,* edited by Daniel Bar-Tal and Itzhak Shnell. 122–186. Oxford: Oxford University Press.

Man, Rafi. 1998. *It Is Inconceivable* [in Hebrew]. Tel Aviv: Maariv.

————. 2012. "The Arabs Are the Same Arabs and the Sea Is the Same Sea" [in Hebrew]. *Footnotes to History* (blog), July 1. https://rafimann.wordpress.com/2012/07/01/.

Manor, Yohanan. 2010. "The 1975 'Zionism Is Racism' Resolution: The Rise, Fall, and Resurgence of a Libel." Jerusalem Center for Public Affairs, May 2. http://jcpa.org/article/the-1975-zionism-is-racism-resolution-the-rise-fall-and-resurgence-of-a-libel/.

Mattar, Philip. 1988. *The Mufti of Jerusalem: Al-Hajj Amin Al-Husayni and the Palestinian National Movement,* rev. ed. New York: Columbia University Press.

Maynard, Jonathan Leader, and Matto Mildenberger. 2018. "Convergence and Divergence in the Study of Ideology: A Critical Review." *British Journal of Political Science* 48 (2): 563–589. https://doi.org/10.1017/S0007123415000654.

McAdams, Dan P. 2006. *The Redemptive Self: Stories Americans Live By.* Oxford: Oxford University Press.

McClosky, Herbert, and John Zaller. 1984. *The American Ethos: Public Attitudes Toward Capitalism and Democracy.* Cambridge, MA: Harvard University Press.

Meir, Golda. 1956. "Golda Meir's Speech at the Zionist Congress." Jerusalem, May. http://www.golda.gov.il/archive/home/he/100/2/1241335691.html.

————.1969. "Peace Among Equals." Jerusalem, December 15. http://goldameir.org.il/archive/home/he/1/1199356423/shalom-beyn-shavim.PDF.pdf.

————. 1970. "For the Attainment of Peace: Address to the Israeli Knesset." Tel Aviv, May 26. http://gos.sbc.edu/m/meir.html.

Mendilow, Jonathan. 2003. *Ideology, Party Change, and Electoral Campaigns in Israel, 1965–2001.* Albany: SUNY Press.

Merom, Gil. 1998. "Outside History? Israel's Security Dilemma in a Comparative Perspective." In *Security Concerns: Insights from the Israeli Experience,* edited by Daniel Bar-Tal, Dan Jacobson, and Aaron S. Klieman, 37–54. Stamford, CT: JAI Press.

Midgam Research and Consulting. 2014. "Public Poll Findings." Commissioned by the S. Daniel Abraham Center for Middle East Peace. http://www.centerpeace.org/wp-content/uploads/2014/06/Israeli-Public-Opinion-Poll-June-2014-Midgam.pdf.

Miller, Elhanan. 2015. "Palestinians Fume over Netanyahu's 'United Jerusalem' Statement." *Times of Israel,* May 19. http://www.timesofisrael.com/palestinians-fume-over-netanyahus-united-jerusalem-statement/.

Ministry of Education. 2002. "The Curriculum: Fatherland Society and Civic Studies for Elementary School (Second to Fourth Grades)" [in Hebrew]. http://cms.education.gov.il/educationcms/units/tochniyot_limudim/moledet/tochniyhalimudim/tochnitlimudim.htm.

————. 2007. "Circular Issued by the Director-General of the Education Ministry Number 68" [in Hebrew]. November. http://cms.education.gov.il/EducationCMS/Applications/Mankal/EtsMedorim/7/7-1/HodaotVmeyda/H-2013-6-7-1-1.htm.

————. 2008. "A Master Plan Program for Knowledge of the Country and Patriotism" [in Hebrew]. http://cms.education.gov.il/NR/rdonlyres/5C0B8D67-323D -4F35-A892-F9008182229C/97337/tochliba.pdf.

————. n.d.-a. "Educational Guidelines for Dealing with the Holocaust in Kindergarten" [in Hebrew]. Accessed October 21, 2016. http://cms.education.gov.il /EducationCMS/Units/Moe/Shoa/ganeyeldim/ganim.htm.

————. n.d.-b. "Memory Lane: An Educational Program About the Holocaust" [in Hebrew]. Accessed October 21, 2016. http://cms.education.gov.il/EducationCMS /UNITS/Moe/Shoa/hpnew.htm.

————. n.d.-c. "Preparation for 'Meaningful Service' in the Army" [in Hebrew]. Accessed November 15, 2016. http://cms.education.gov.il/EducationCMS/Units /Noar/TechumeiHaminhal/ChinuchChevrathi/zahalsherut.htm.

Ministry of Education, Society and Youth Administration. 2007. "Willingness and Readiness for IDF Service: A Collection of Programs, Themes and Activities" [in Hebrew]. http://cms.education.gov.il/EducationCMS/Units/Noar/KatalogPirsumim /HachanaLezahal/ogdan.htm.

————. n.d.-a. "About Shelah" [in Hebrew]. Accessed November 16, 2018. http:// edu.gov.il/noar/minhal/departments/shelah/Pages/purpose.aspx.

————. n.d.-b. "The Bokim" [in Hebrew]. Accessed November 2, 2016. http:// cms.education.gov.il/EducationCMS/Units/Noar/KatalogPirsumim/hacharath HaartsVeahavathHaMoledeth/Habokhim.htm.

————. n.d.-c. "The Israeli Journey" [in Hebrew]. Accessed November 3, 2016. http://cms.education.gov.il/EducationCMS/Units/Noar/TechumeiHaminhal/Shelach /masaisraeli.htm.

Miron, Dan. 1992. *Facing the Silent Brother* [in Hebrew]. Jerusalem: Keter.

Mitzen, Jennifer. 2006. "Ontological Security in World Politics: State Identity and the Security Dilemma." *European Journal of International Relations* 12 (3): 341–370. https://doi.org/10.1177/1354066106067346.

Morales, Lymari. 2010. "One in Three Americans 'Extremely Patriotic.'" Gallup, July 2. http://www.gallup.com/poll/141110/One-Three-Americans-Extremely-Patriotic.aspx.

Morris, Benny. 2001. *Righteous Victims: A History of the Zionist-Arab Conflict, 1881–2001*. New York: Vintage Books.

————. 2002. "Camp David and After: An Exchange (An Interview with Ehud Barak)." *New York Review of Books,* June 13.

Mueller, John E. 1973. *War, Presidents, and Public Opinion.* New York: Wiley.

Muslih, M. 1997. "A Study of PLO Peace Initiatives, 1974–1988." In *The PLO and Israel: From Armed Conflict to Political Solution, 1964–1994,* edited by Avraham Sela and Moshe Ma'oz, 37–53. New York: St. Martin's Press.

Naor, Arye. 1999. "The Security Argument in the Territorial Debate in Israel: Rhetoric and Policy." *Israel Studies* 4 (2): 150–177.

————. 2003. "Lessons of the Holocaust Versus Territories for Peace, 1967–2001." *Israel Studies* 8 (1): 130–152.

Nasie, Meytal, Aurel Harrison Diamond, and Daniel Bar-Tal. 2016. "Young Children in Intractable Conflicts: The Israeli Case." *Personality and Social Psychology Review* 20 (4): 365–392. https://doi.org/10.1177/1088868315607800.

Naveh, Eyal. 1999. *The Twentieth Century: On the Verge of Tomorrow* [in Hebrew]. Tel Aviv: Tel-Aviv Books.

Naveh, Eyal, Neomi Vered, and David Shahar. 2009. *Nationality in Israel and the Nations: Building a State in the Middle East* [in Hebrew]. Tel Aviv: Rehes.

Naveh, Eyal, and Esther Yogev. 2002. *Histories, Towards Dialogue with Yesterday* [in Hebrew]. Tel Aviv: Baval.

Navon, Daniel. 2015. "'We Are a People, One People': How 1967 Transformed Holocaust Memory and Jewish Identity in Israel and the US." *Journal of Historical Sociology* 28 (3): 342–373. https://doi.org/10.1111/johs.12075.

Netanyahu, Benjamin. 2009a. "Address by Prime Minister Benjamin Netanyahu Begin-Sadat Center at Bar-Ilan University June 14, 2009." June 14. http://www.pmo.gov.il/MediaCenter/Speeches/Pages/speechbarilan140609.aspx.

———. 2009b. "PM Netanyahu's Speech at the UN General Assembly." New York, September 24. http://www.pmo.gov.il/MediaCenter/Speeches/Pages/speechUM240909.aspx.

———. 2010a. "Prime Minister Benjamin Netanyahu's Speech at the Knesset Special Session in Memory of the Jewish Prisoners Hung from the Gallows." March 9. http://www.pmo.gov.il/MediaCenter/Speeches/Pages/speechgardom090310.aspx.

———. 2010b. "PM Netanyahu's Speech at the National Security College Commencement Ceremony at Mount Scopus." Jerusalem, July 27. http://www.pmo.gov.il/English/MediaCenter/Speeches/Pages/speechmabal270710.aspx.

———. 2011a. "Prime Minister Benjamin Netanyahu's Address at the National Ceremony Opening the Holocaust and Heroism Remembrance Day at Yad Vashem." Jerusalem, May 1. http://www.pmo.gov.il/MediaCenter/Speeches/Pages/speechshoa010511.aspx.

———. 2011b. "Remarks by PM Benjamin Netanyahu to the U.N. General Assembly." New York, September 23. http://mfa.gov.il/MFA/PressRoom/2011/Pages/Remarks_PM_Netanyahu_UN_General%20_Assembly_23-Sep-2011.aspx.

———. 2011c. "PM Netanyahu's Remarks Following the Release of Gilad Shalit." October 18. http://www.pmo.gov.il/MediaCenter/Speeches/Pages/speechshalit181011.aspx.

———. 2012a. "PM Netanyahu's Speech at the Special Knesset Session Marking International Holocaust Remembrance Day." Jerusalem, January 24. http://www.pmo.gov.il/MediaCenter/Speeches/Pages/speechsoah240112.aspx.

———. 2012b. "Prime Minister Netanyahu's Speech at Holocaust Remembrance Day." Jerusalem, April 19. http://www.pmo.gov.il/MediaCenter/Speeches/Pages/speechholo180412.aspx.

———. 2012c. "Prime Minister Benjamin Netanyahu's Speech at the Institute for the National Security Studies' Conference on Security Challenges." May 29. http://www.pmo.gov.il/MediaCenter/Speeches/Pages/speechbitachon290512.aspx.

———. 2013a. "Address by PM Netanyahu at the Foreign Ministry Ambassadors' Conference." January 3. http://www.pmo.gov.il/MediaCenter/Speeches/Pages/speechamba030113.aspx.

———. 2013b. "PM Netanyahu's Remarks to the Taglit-Birthright Israel 'Mega Event.'" January 7. http://www.pmo.gov.il/MediaCenter/Speeches/Pages/speechtaglit070113.aspx.

———. 2013c. "Address by PM Netanyahu to the Jewish Agency Board of Governors." February 18. http://www.pmo.gov.il/MediaCenter/Speeches/Pages/speechsochnut180213.aspx.

———. 2013d. "Prime Minister Netanyahu's Address Before AIPAC 2013." March 4. http://www.pmo.gov.il/MediaCenter/Speeches/Pages/speechaipac040313.aspx.

———. 2013e. "Address by Prime Minister Benjamin Netanyahu at the Holocaust Remembrance Day Ceremony." April 7. http://www.pmo.gov.il/MediaCenter/Speeches/Pages/speechholo070413.aspx.

———. 2013f. "Address by Prime Minister Benjamin Netanyahu at the Memorial Day Ceremony." April 15. http://www.pmo.gov.il/MediaCenter/Speeches/Pages/speecheiva150413.aspx.

————. 2013g. "Prime Minister Benjamin Netanyahu's Speech at the Memorial Ceremony for Altalena Victims." May 26. http://www.pmo.gov.il/MediaCenter /Speeches/Pages/speechaltalena260513.aspx.

————. 2013h. "Prime Minister Benjamin Netanyahu's Remarks at the 40 Signatures Knesset Session." June 6. http://www.pmo.gov.il/MediaCenter/Speeches /Pages/speech40sugn050613.aspx.

————. 2013i. "Prime Minister Benjamin Netanyahu's Speech at the State Memorial Ceremony for Benjamin Zeev Herzl." Jerusalem, June 27. http://www .pmo.gov.il/MediaCenter/Speeches/Pages/speachhertzel270613.aspx.

————. 2013j. "PM Netanyahu's Remarks at the Fourth of July Reception." July 4. http://www.pmo.gov.il/English/MediaCenter/Speeches/Pages/speechUSind040713 .aspx.

————. 2013k. "Prime Minister Benjamin Netanyahu's Address at the Naval Course Graduation Ceremony." September 11. http://www.pmo.gov.il/MediaCenter /Speeches/Pages/eventhovlim110913.aspx.

————. 2013l. "Prime Minister Netanyahu's Statement at the Opening of the Winter Knesset Session." October 14. http://www.pmo.gov.il/MediaCenter/Speeches /Pages/speechknesster141013.aspx.

————. 2013m. "Prime Minister Benjamin Netanyahu's Remarks at the State Memorial Ceremony for the Late Prime Minister Yitzhak Rabin at Mount Herzl." October 16. http://www.pmo.gov.il/MediaCenter/Speeches/Pages /speechherzl161013.aspx.

————. 2013n. "Prime Minister Benjamin Netanyahu's Speech at the Knesset Special Session in Honor of Yitzhak Rabin." Jerusalem, October 16. http://www .pmo.gov.il/MediaCenter/Speeches/Pages/speechrabin161013.aspx.

————. 2013o. "Address by Prime Minister Benjamin Netanyahu at the Ceremony for the Appointment of Dr. Karnit Flug as Governor of the Bank of Israel." November 13. http://www.pmo.gov.il/MediaCenter/Speeches/Pages/speechflug131113.aspx.

————. 2013p. "Prime Minister Benjamin Netanyahu's Speech at the Knesset Special Session in Honor of the President of the French Republic, Francois Hollande." November 18. http://www.pmo.gov.il/MediaCenter/Speeches/Pages /speechfrance181113.aspx.

————. 2013q. "PM Netanyahu's Address to the Saban Forum." December 8. http://www.pmo.gov.il/MediaCenter/Speeches/Pages/speechsaban081213.aspx.

————. 2013r. "Prime Minister Benjamin Netanyahu's Address at the Flight School Graduation Ceremony." December 26. http://www.pmo.gov.il/MediaCenter /Speeches/Pages/speechwings261213.aspx.

Nets-Zehngut, Rafi. 2012. "The Passing of Time and the Collective Memory of Conflicts: The Case of Israel and the 1948 Palestinian Exodus." *Peace and Change* 37 (2): 253–285. https://doi.org/10.1111/j.1468-0130.2011.00745.x.

Neuberger, Benyamin. 2000. "Israel: A Liberal Democracy with Four Flaws" [in Hebrew]. In *The State of Israel: Between Judaism and Democracy,* edited by Joseph E. David, 289–310. Jerusalem: Israel Democracy Institute.

Nini, Achinoam. 2009. "A Letter to My Palestinian Brothers in Gaza and Everywhere." *Blog de Uriol108* (blog), March 6. http://uriol108.blogspot.com/2009 /01/noah-letter-to-my-palestinian-brothers.html.

Nir, R., and I. Roeh. 1992. "Intifada Coverage in the Israeli Press: Popular and Quality Papers Assume a Rhetoric of Conformity." *Discourse and Society* 3: 47–60.

Norris, Pippa, Montague Kern, and Marion R. Just. 2003. *Framing Terrorism: The News Media, the Government, and the Public.* New York: Routledge.

Novick, Peter. 2000. *The Holocaust in American Life.* Boston: Mariner Books.

OECD (Organisation for Economic Co-operation and Development). 2010. "Accession: Estonia, Israel and Slovenia Invited to Join OECD." May 10. http://www .oecd.org/about/membersandpartners/accessionestoniaisraelandsloveniainvited tojoinoecd.htm.

Olmert, Ehud. 2006a. "Address by Acting PM Ehud Olmert to the 6th Herzliya Conference." January 24. http://www.mfa.gov.il/mfa/pressroom/2006/pages /address%20by%20acting%20pm%20ehud%20olmert%20to%20the%206th Conflict%20herzliya%20conference%2024-jan-2006.aspx.

———. 2006b. "Interim Prime Minister Ehud Olmert's Speech at the State Memorial Service for Israel's Fallen Soldiers at Mount Herzl." Jerusalem, May 2. http://www.pmo.gov.il/MediaCenter/Speeches/Pages/speechher020506.aspx.

———. 2006c. "Address by Prime Minister Ehud Olmert." Jerusalem, July 17. http://www.pmo.gov.il/MediaCenter/Speeches/Pages/speechkneset170706.aspx.

———. 2007a. "Prime Minister Ehud Olmert's Speech at the Opening Ceremony of the Holocaust Martyrs' and Heroes' Remembrance Day." Jerusalem, April 15. http://www.pmo.gov.il/MediaCenter/Speeches/Pages/speechyadva150407.aspx.

———. 2007b. "Prime Minister Ehud Olmert's Speech at the Knesset Session Marking the 60th Anniversary of the U.N. Resolution on Partition." Jerusalem, December 3. http://www.pmo.gov.il/MediaCenter/Speeches/Pages/speechkness031207.aspx.

———. 2008. "Prime Minister Ehud Olmert's Speech at the Institute for National Security Studies Annual Conference." December 18. http://www.pmo.gov.il /MediaCenter/Speeches/Pages/speechdef181208.aspx.

———. 2009. "PM Olmert's Statement After the Cabinet Meeting." Jerusalem, January 17. http://www.pmo.gov.il/MediaCenter/Speeches/Pages/speechcabinet 170109.aspx.

Oren, Neta. 2004. "Changes in the Israeli Social Beliefs of Conflict, 1967–2000." *Palestine Israel Journal of Politics, Economics, and Culture* 11 (3, 4). http:// www.pij.org/details.php?id=312.

———. 2005. "The Impact of Major Events in the Arab-Israeli Conflict on the Ethos of Conflict of the Israeli Jewish Society (1967–2000)" [in Hebrew]. Doctoral dissertation, Tel Aviv University.

———. 2010. "Israeli Identity Formation and the Arab-Israeli Conflict in Election Platforms, 1969–2006." *Journal of Peace Research* 47: 193–204.

———. 2012. "Israeli Soldiers' Perceptions of Palestinian Civilians During the 2009 Gaza War." In *Civilians and Modern War: Armed Conflict and the Ideology of Violence,* edited by Daniel Rothbart, Karina V. Korostelina, and Mohammed Cherkaoui, 130–145. New York: Routledge.

———. 2016. "The Jewish-Israeli Ethos of Conflict." In *A Social Psychology Perspective on the Israeli-Palestinian Conflict,* edited by Keren Sharvit and Eran Halperin, 115–132. Cham, Switzerland: Springer International Publishing.

Oren, Neta, and Daniel Bar-Tal. 2006. "Ethos and Identity: Expressions and Changes in the Israeli Jewish Society." *Estudios de Psicología* 27: 293–316.

———. 2007. "The Detrimental Dynamics of Delegitimization in Intractable Conflicts: The Israeli-Palestinian Case." *International Journal of Intercultural Relations* 31 (1): 111–126.

———. 2014. "Collective Identity and Intractable Conflict." In *Identity Process Theory: Identity, Social Action and Social Change,* by Rusi Jaspal and Glynis M. Breakwell, 222–253. Cambridge: Cambridge University Press.

Oren, Neta, Daniel Bar-Tal, and Ohad David. 2004. "Conflict, Identity and Ethos: The Israeli-Palestinian Case." In *The Psychology of Ethnic and Cultural Conflict,* edited by Yueh-Ting Lee, 133–154. Westport, CT: Praeger.

Oren, Neta, Rafi Nets-Zehngut, and Daniel Bar-Tal. 2015. "Construction of the Israeli-Jewish Conflict-Supportive Narrative and the Struggle over Its Dominance." *Political Psychology* 36 (2): 215–230. https://doi.org/10.1111/pops.12266.

Oren, Neta, Daniel Rothbart, and Karina V. Korostelina. 2009. "Striking Civilian Targets During the Lebanon War—A Social Psychological Analysis of Israeli Decision Makers." *Peace and Conflict: Journal of Peace Psychology* 15: 281–303.

Orshak, Oki. 2011. "Look Back in Peace" [in Hebrew]. *Hed Haninuch* 85: 82–84.

Paez, D., and J. H. Liu. 2011. "Collective Memory of Conflicts." In *Intergroup Conflicts and Their Resolution: A Social Psychological Perspective,* edited by Daniel Bar-Tal, 105–124. New York: Psychology Press.

Paz, Shelly. 2008. "Gadna Pre-Army Program Tries to Restore IDF's Appeal." *Jerusalem Post,* April 13.

Pedahzur, Ami. 2004. *The Israeli Defending Democracy* [in Hebrew]. Jerusalem: Carmel.

Pedatzur, Reuven. 1998. "Ben-Gurion's Enduring Legacy." In *Security Concerns: Insights from the Israeli Experience,* edited by Daniel Bar-Tal, Dan Jacobson, and Aaron S. Klieman, 139–167. Stamford, CT: JAI Press.

Peled, Yoav. 2008. "The Evolution of Israeli Citizenship: An Overview." *Citizenship Studies* 12 (3): 335–345. https://doi.org/10.1080/13621020802015487.

Peled-Elhanan, Nurit. 2009. "Layout as Punctuation of Semiosis: Some Examples from Israeli Schoolbooks." *Visual Communication* 8 (1): 91–116. https://doi.org/10.1177/1470357208099149.

———. 2010. "Legitimation of Massacres in Israeli School History Books." *Discourse and Society* 21 (4): 377–404. DOI: 10.1177/0957926510366195.

———. 2012. *Palestine in Israeli School Books: Ideology and Propaganda in Education.* London: I. B. Tauris.

Peleg, Avraham. 1971. "Public Poll" [in Hebrew]. *Maariv,* April 28.

Peleg, Ilan. 1987. *Begin's Foreign Policy, 1977–1983.* Westport, CT: Greenwood Press.

———. 2007. *Democratizing the Hegemonic State: Political Transformation in the Age of Identity.* New York: Cambridge University Press.

Peleg, Ilan, and Dov Waxman. 2011. *Israel's Palestinians: The Conflict Within.* New York: Cambridge University Press.

Peres, Shimon, and Arye Naor. 1993. *The New Middle East.* New York: Henry Holt.

Peres, Yohanan, and Ephraim Yuchtman-Yaar. 1992. *Trends in Israeli Democracy: The Public's View.* Boulder, CO: Lynne Rienner.

Peretz, Don. 1990. *Intifada.* Boulder, CO: Westview Press.

Peri, Yoram. 1999. "Civil-Military Relations in Israel in Crisis" [in Hebrew]. *Megamot* 39 (4): 375–399.

———. 2000. *The Assassination of Yitzhak Rabin.* Stanford, CA: Stanford University Press.

Perlmutter, Amos. 1987. *The Life and Times of Menachem Begin.* Garden City, NY: Doubleday.

Pew Research Center. 2007. "Spring 2007 Survey Data." http://www.pewglobal.org/2007/05/28/spring-2007-survey-data/.

———. 2013. "Spring 2013 Survey Data." http://www.pewglobal.org/dataset/spring-2013-survey-data/.

———. 2016. "Israel's Religiously Divided Society." http://assets.pewresearch.org/wp-content/uploads/sites/11/2016/03/Israel-Survey-Full-Report.pdf.

Pinson, Halleli. 2007. "Inclusive Curriculum? Challenges to the Role of Civic Education in a Jewish and Democratic State." *Curriculum Inquiry* 37: 351–382. https://doi.org/10.1111/j.1467-873X.2007.00391.x.

———. 2013. "From a Jewish and Democratic State to a Jewish State, Period." Association for Civil Rights in Israel. http://www.acri.org.il/he/wp-content /uploads/2013/12/Pinson-Report-summary-en.pdf.

Pinson, Halleli, Gal Levy, and Zeev Soker. 2010. "Peace as a Surprise, Peace as a Disturbance: The Israeli-Arab Conflict in Official Documents." *Educational Review* 62 (3): 255–269.

Podeh, Elie. 2002. *The Arab-Israeli Conflict in Israeli History Textbooks, 1948–2000.* Westport, CT: Bergin and Garvey.

———. 2005. "Demonization of the Other." *The New East* 45: 151–208.

Porat, Dan A. 2004. "From the Scandal to the Holocaust in Israeli Education." *Journal of Contemporary History* 39 (4): 619–636.

Pratto, F., and O. P. John. 1991. "Automatic Vigilance—The Attention-Grabbing Power of Negative Social Information." *Journal of Personality and Social Psychology* 61 (3): 380–391.

Pruitt, Dean G., and Sung Hee Kim. 2004. *Social Conflict: Escalation, Stalemate, and Settlement.* Boston: McGraw-Hill.

Rabin, Yitzhak. 1984. "Statement in the Knesset by MK Rabin." Jerusalem, June 12. https://www.knesset.gov.il/rabin/heb/Rab_RabinSpeech2.htm.

———. 1993a. "Address by Prime Minister Rabin at the National Defense College, 12 August 1993." August 12. http://www.israel.org/MFA/ForeignPolicy/MFADocuments /Yearbook9/Pages/101%20Address%20by%20Prime%20Minister%20Rabin%20at %20the%20Nationa.aspx.

———. 1993b. "Statement in the Knesset by Prime Minister Rabin on the Israel-PLO Declaration of Principles." Jerusalem, September 21. http://mfa.gov.il /MFA/ForeignPolicy/MFADocuments/Yearbook9/Pages/110%20Statement%20in %20the%20Knesset%20by%20Prime%20Minister%20Rab.aspx.

———. 1994a. "Statement by the Prime Minister Rabin at the Opening of the Knesset's Summer Session—18 April 1994." April 18. http://www.mfa.gov.il/MFA /ForeignPolicy/MFADocuments/Yearbook9/Pages/179%20Statement%20by %20the%20Prime%20Minister%20Rabin%20at%20the%20O.aspx.

———. 1994b. "PM Yitzhak Rabin's Speech at the Officers Graduation Ceremony." July 13. http://www.rabincenter.org.il/Items/01783/12d.pdf.

———. 1994c. "Address by Prime Minister Yitzhak Rabin at the Levi Eshkol Creativity Awards Ceremony." October 6. http://www.rabincenter.org.il/Items /01101/RabinAddressatLeviEshkolCreativityAwards.pdf.

———. 1994d. "Address by Prime Minister Yitzhak Rabin upon Receiving the Nobel Peace Prize." Oslo, December 10. http://www.rabincenter.org.il/Items /01102/RabinAddressatNobelPeacePrize.pdf.

———. 1995a. *Rodef Shalom: The Peace Speeches of Yitsḥaḳ Rabin* [in Hebrew]. Tel Aviv: Zemorah-Bitan.

———. 1995b. "Rabin's Remarks on Beit Lid Bombing." January 23. http://www .jewishagency.org/rabin/content/23541.

———. 1995c. "It Is Good to Live for Our Country." Tel Hai, March 13. http:// www.rabincenter.org.il/Items/01765/7h.pdf.

———. 1995d. "Remarks by Prime Minister Rabin on Israel Radio and Television on Ramat Gan Attack." July 24. http://www.mfa.gov.il/MFA/ForeignPolicy /MFADocuments/Yearbook10/Pages/Remarks%20by%20Prime%20Minister %20Rabin%20on%20Israel%20Radio%20an.aspx.

———. 1995e. "Rabin's Addresses at the Signing Ceremony of the Israel-Palestinian Interim Agreement." Washington, DC, September 28. https://unispal.un.org/DPA /DPR/unispal.nsf/0/B770FD94C1F167FD85256E3700565C2E.

―――. 1995f. "PM Rabin Speech to Knesset on Ratification of Oslo Peace Accords." October 5. http://www.jewishvirtuallibrary.org/jsource/History/rabinoslospeech.html.

―――. 1995g. "Address by Prime Minister Yitzhak Rabin at a Peace Rally." Tel Aviv, November 4. http://www.rabincenter.org.il/Items/01103/RabinAddressat apeacerally.pdf.

Rabin, Yitzhak, and Yoram Peri. 1996 [1979]. *The Rabin Memoirs.* Berkeley: University of California Press. (Originally published as Rabin, Yitzhak. *The Rabin Memoirs.* Boston: Little, Brown, 1979.)

Rachlin, Harvey. 2015. "Misquoting Golda Meir: What She Might Not Have Said." *Haaretz,* June 16.

Raizen, Esther, 1995. *No Rattling of Sabers: An Anthology of Israeli War Poetry.* Austin: Center for Middle Eastern Studies, University of Texas at Austin.

Ravid, Barak. 2011. "Netanyahu: Israel Needs to Separate from the Palestinians." *Haaretz,* June 21.

―――. 2015a. "Netanyahu: I Don't Want a Binational State, but We Need to Control All of the Territory for the Foreseeable Future." *Haaretz,* October 26.

―――. 2015b. "Herzog Calls on Netanyahu to Defend Rivlin During Fiery Knesset Session." *Haaretz,* December 16.

―――. 2016. "Netanyahu: We'll Surround Israel with Fences 'To Defend Ourselves Against Wild Beasts.'" *Haaretz,* February 9.

Raviv, Amiram, Daniel Bar-Tal, Leah Koren-Silvershatz, and Alona Raviv. 1999. "Beliefs About War, Conflict, and Peace in Israel as a Function of Developmental, Cultural, and Situational Factors." In *How Children Understand War and Peace: A Call for International Peace Education,* edited by Amiram Raviv, Louis Oppenheimer, and Daniel Bar-Tal, 161–189. San Francisco: Jossey-Bass.

Rebhun, Uzi, and Chaim Isaac Waxman. 2000. "The 'Americanization' of Israel: A Demographic, Cultural and Political Evaluation." *Israel Studies* 5 (1): 65–91. https://doi.org/10.1353/is.2000.0018.

Regev, Motti. 2004. *Popular Music and National Culture in Israel.* Berkeley: University of California Press.

Reicher, Stephen D., S. Alexander Haslam, and Michael J. Platow. 2016. "Social Psychology." In *The Oxford Handbook of Political Leadership,* edited by R. A. W. Rhodes and Paul 't Hart, 149–160. Oxford: Oxford University Press.

Resnik, Julia. 2003. "'Sites of Memory' of the Holocaust: Shaping National Memory in the Education System in Israel." *Nations and Nationalism* 9 (2): 297–317. https://doi.org/10.1111/1469-8219.00087.

Rhodes, R. A. W., and Paul 't Hart. 2016. "Puzzles of Political Leadership." In *The Oxford Handbook of Political Leadership,* reprint ed., edited by R. A. W. Rhodes and Paul 't Hart, 1–24. Oxford: Oxford University Press.

Roccas, Sonia, Lilach Sagiv, Shalom Schwartz, Nir Halevy, and Roy Eidelson. 2008. "Toward a Unifying Model of Identification with Groups: Integrating Theoretical Perspectives." *Personality and Social Psychology Review* 12 (3): 280–306.

Rosenblum, Doron. 2007. "It's a Jungle Out There." *Haaretz,* June 15.

―――. 2011. "It's the Occupation, Stupid." *Haaretz,* July 15.

Rosler, Nimrod. 2012. "Political Context, Social Challenges, and Leadership: Rhetorical Expressions of Psycho-Social Roles of Leaders in Intractable Conflict and Its Resolution Process—The Israeli-Palestinian Case." Doctoral dissertation, Hebrew University of Jerusalem.

―――. 2016. "Leadership and Peacemaking: Yitzhak Rabin and the Oslo Accords." *International Journal of Intercultural Relations* 54: 55–67.

Rubinstein, Danny. 2004. "The Stronger Side Creates Reality." *Haaretz,* June 16.

Rudoren, Jodi. 2015. "Netanyahu Denounced for Saying Palestinian Inspired Holocaust." *New York Times,* October 21.

Rumelili, Bahar, ed. 2015. *Conflict Resolution and Ontological Security: Peace Anxieties.* New York: Routledge.

Rumelili, Bahar, and Ayşe Betül Çelik. 2017. "Ontological Insecurity in Asymmetric Conflicts: Reflections on Agonistic Peace in Turkey's Kurdish Issue." *Security Dialogue* 48 (4): 1–18. https://doi.org/10.1177/0967010617695715.

Rynhold, Jonathan, and Dov Waxman. 2008. "Ideological Change and Israel's Disengagement from Gaza." *Political Science Quarterly* 123 (1): 11–37.

Saltzman, Ilai Z. 2016. "Making War, Thinking History: David Ben-Gurion, Analogical Reasoning and the Suez Crisis." *Israel Affairs* 22 (1): 45–68. https://doi.org/10.1080/13537121.2015.1111638.

Schnell, Izhak. 2013. "Geographical Ramifications of the Occupation for Israeli Society." In *The Impacts of Lasting Occupation: Lessons from Israeli Society,* edited by Daniel Bar-Tal and Itzhak Shnell, 93–121. Oxford: Oxford University Press.

Sears, D. O. 2002. "Long-Term Psychological Consequences of Political Events." In *Political Psychology,* edited by K. R. Monroe, 249–269. Mahwah, NJ: Erlbaum.

Segal, Jerome M. 2001. "Clearing Up the Right-of-Return Confusion." *Middle East Policy* 8 (2): 23–31. https://doi.org/10.1111/1475-4967.00015.

Segal, Jerome M., Shlomit Levy, Nadar Izzat Sa'id, and Elihu Katz. 2000. *Negotiating Jerusalem.* New York: SUNY Press.

Segev, Tom. 2000. *The Seventh Million: The Israelis and the Holocaust.* New York: Henry Holt.

Sobol, Joshua. 1993. "Sobering Up from a Dream" [in Hebrew]. *Haaretz,* September 9.

Shachar, Yoram. 2002. "The Early Drafts of the Declaration of Independence" [in Hebrew]. *Tel-Aviv University Law Review* 26: 523–600.

———. 2009. "Jefferson Goes East: The American Origins of the Israeli Declaration of Independence." *Theoretical Inquiries in Law* 10 (2): 589–618.

Shafir, Gershon, and Yoav Peled. 2002. *Being Israeli: The Dynamics of Multiple Citizenship.* New York: Cambridge University Press.

Shamir, Jacob, and Michal Shamir. 2000. *The Anatomy of Public Opinion.* Ann Arbor: University of Michigan Press.

Shamir, Jacob, Neta Ziskind, and Shoshana Blum-Kulka. 1999. "What's in a Question? A Content Analysis of Survey Questions." *Communication Review* 3: 1–25.

Shamir, Michal, and Asher Arian. 1994. "Competing Values and Policy Choices—Israeli Public-Opinion on Foreign and Security Affairs." *British Journal of Political Science* 24 (2): 249–271.

Shamir, Michal, and Jacob Shamir. 2007. "The Israeli-Palestinian Conflict in Israeli Elections." *International Political Science Review* 28 (4): 469–491.

Shapira, Anita. 2000. "Hirbet Hizah: Between Remembrance and Forgetting." *Jewish Social Studies* 7 (1): 1–62. https://doi.org/10.1353/jss.2000.0022.

Sharon, Ariel. 2001. "Inauguration Speech of Prime Minister Ariel Sharon in the Knesset." March 7. http://www.mfa.gov.il/mfa/pressroom/2001/pages/inauguration%20speech%20of%20prime%20minister%20ariel%20sharon.aspx.

———. 2002. "Excerpts from Speech by PM Sharon to the Likud Congress—23-Oct-2002." Jerusalem, October 23. http://mfa.gov.il/MFA/PressRoom/2002/Pages/Excerpts%20from%20Speech%20by%20PM%20Sharon%20to%20the%20Likud%20Con.aspx.

———. 2004. "Prime Minister Ariel Sharon's Address to the Knesset—The Vote on the Disengagement Plan." Jerusalem, October 25. http://www.mfa.gov.il/MFA/PressRoom/2004/Pages/PM%20Sharon%20Knesset%20speech%20-%20Vote%20on%20Disengagement%20Plan%2025-Oct-2004.aspx.

Sharon, Ashley. 2004. "Shades of Grey." *Jerusalem Report,* December 13.

Sharp, Jeremy. 2015. "U.S. Foreign Aid to Israel." Congressional Research Service. https://Conflict fas.org/sgp/crs/mideast/RL33222.pdf.

Shavit, Ari. 2002. "The Enemy Within." *Haaretz,* August 29.

———. 2005. "Listen to Me: Interview with Ehud Barak." *Haaretz,* May 20.

———. 2006. "The End of the Third Way." *Haaretz,* July 13.

———. 2013. "IAF Commander Talks About a Mission that Shaped Israel's Future Decisions." *Haaretz,* September 10.

Sheikh, Hammad, Jeremy Ginges, and S. Atran. 2013. "Sacred Values in Intergroup Conflict: Resistance to Social Influence, Temporal Discounting, and Exit Strategies." *Annals of the New York Academy of Sciences* 1299: 11–24.

Shelef, Nadav G. 2010. *Evolving Nationalism: Homeland, Identity, and Religion in Israel, 1925–2005.* Ithaca, NY: Cornell University Press.

Shlaim, Avi. 2000. *The Iron Wall: Israel and the Arab World.* New York: Norton.

Shnell, Itzhak. 2013. "Geographical Ramifications of the Occupation for Israeli Society." In *The Impacts of Lasting Occupation: Lessons from Israeli Society,* edited by Daniel Bar-Tal and Itzhak Shnell, 93–121. New York: Oxford University Press.

Shohat, Ella. 1989. *Israeli Cinema: East/West and the Politics of Representation.* Austin: University of Texas Press.

Shor, Yitzhak. 1993. "New Poll: Education Second National Priorities after Security" [in Hebrew]. *Al Hamishmar,* April 22.

Sicherman, Harvey. 1991. *Palestinian Self-Government: Its Past and Its Future.* Washington, DC: Washington Institute for Near East Policy.

Smith, Anthony D. 1999. *Myths and Memories of the Nation.* New York: Oxford University Press.

Smith, Hugh. 2005. "What Costs Will Democracies Bear? A Review of Popular Theories of Casualty Aversion." *Armed Forces and Society* 31 (4): 487–512. https://doi.org/10.1177/0095327X0503100403.

Smith, Rafi, and Olga Paniel. 2014. "Public Poll Findings: Political Issues." Commissioned by the S. Daniel Abraham Center for Middle East Peace. http://www.centerpeace.org/explore/polls/.

Smooha, Sammy. 1990. "Minority Status in an Ethnic Democracy: The Status of the Arab Minority in Israel." *Ethnic and Racial Studies* 13 (3): 389–413. https://doi.org/10.1080/01419870.1990.9993679.

———. 2013. *Still Playing by the Rules: Index of Arab-Jewish Relations in Israel 2012. Findings and Conclusions.* Jerusalem: The Israel Democracy Institute.

Soen, Dan, and Nitza Davidovich. 2011. "Israeli Youth Pilgrimages to Poland: Rationale and Polemics." *Images* 9 (17–18): 5–27. https://doi.org/10.14746/i.2011.17.18.01.

State Comptroller. 2009. "State Comptroller Report 2009" [in Hebrew]. http://www.mevaker.gov.il/(X(1)S(j2bia2yrlnepwneb3cqf4fd4))/he/Reports/Pages/292.aspx?AspxAutoDetectCookieSupport=1.

Staub, Ervin. 1997. "Blind Versus Constructive Patriotism: Moving from Embeddedness in the Group to Critical Loyalty and Action." In *Patriotism in the Lives of Individuals and Nations,* edited by Daniel Bar-Tal and Ervin Staub, 213–228. Chicago: Nelson-Hall.

Stauber, Roni. 2007. *The Holocaust in Israeli Public Debate in the 1950s: Ideology and Memory.* Portland, OR: Vallentine Mitchell.

Steele, Brent J. 2008. *Ontological Security in International Relations: Self-Identity and the IR State.* New York: Routledge.

Stein, K. W. 1991. "The Intifada and the Uprising of 1936–1939: A Comparison of the Palestinian Arab Communities." In *The Intifada: Its Impact on Israel, the Arab World, and the Superpowers,* edited by R. O. Freedman, 3–36. Miami: International University Press.

Sterman, Adiv, and Raphael Ahren. 2015. "Netanyahu Blames Jerusalem Mufti for Holocaust, Is Accused of 'Absolving Hitler.'" *Times of Israel,* October 21. http://www.timesofisrael.com/netanyahu-accused-of-absolving-hitler-for-holocaust/.

Stone, Russell A. 1982. *Social Change in Israel: Attitudes and Events, 1967–1979.* New York: Praeger.

Sucharov, Mira M. 2005. *The International Self: Psychoanalysis and the Search for Israeli-Palestinian Peace.* Albany: SUNY Press.

Sullivan, J. L., A. Fried, and M. G. Dietz. 1992. "Patriotism, Politics, and the Presidential Election of 1988." *American Journal of Political Science* 36 (1): 200–234.

Szobel, Ilana. n.d. "Ilana Szobel: Modern Hebrew Literature—Writing the Holocaust." Schusterman Center for Israel Studies. Accessed November 29, 2016. http://blogs.brandeis.edu/siis/lecture-22-ilana-szobel/.

Tabibyan, K. 1999. *Journey into the Past: Chapters in History for Grades 8–10* [in Hebrew]. Tel Aviv: Matah/Education Ministry.

Tal, David. 2004. "Between Intuition and Professionalism: Israeli Military Leadership During the 1948 Palestine War." *Journal of Military History* 68 (3): 885–909. https://doi.org/10.1353/jmh.2004.0147.

Tamir, Yuli. 2011. "Peace and No Peace" [in Hebrew]. *Hed Haninuch* 85: 44–46.

Teff-Seker, Yael. 2012. "Peace, Tolerance and the Palestinian 'Other' in Israeli Textbooks" [in Hebrew]. Institute for Monitoring Peace and Cultural Tolerance in School Education. http://www.impact-se.org/reports/israel/.

Tetlock, Philip E. 2003. "Thinking the Unthinkable: Sacred Values and Taboo Cognitions." *Trends in Cognitive Sciences* 7 (7): 320–324. https://doi.org/10.1016/S1364-6613(03)00135-9.

Times of Israel Staff. 2016. "To Save Israel, Lapid Pitches 'Separation' from Palestinians." *Times of Israel,* January 25. http://www.timesofisrael.com/to-save-israel-lapid-pitches-separation-from-palestinians/.

———. 2017. "Government Advancing Bill to Ban Breaking the Silence." *Times of Israel,* October 16. https://www.timesofisrael.com/government-advancing-bill-to-ban-breaking-the-silence-report/.

Torres, Gerver. 2007. "Gallup World Poll and Migration." Gallup. http://www.un.org/esa/population/meetings/sixthcoord2007/Gallup_World_Poll.pdf.

Tzahor, Ze'ev. 1995. "Ben-Gurion's Mythopoetics." In *The Shaping of Israeli Identity: Myth, Memory, and Trauma,* edited by David Ohana and Robert S. Wistrich, 61–84. Portland, OR: F. Cass.

Urian, Dan. 2013. *The Arab in Israeli Drama and Theatre.* New York: Routledge.

Van Leeuwen, Theo. 2005. *Introducing Social Semiotics.* New York: Routledge.

Vered, Soli. 2015. "Peace Education in Israel: An Educational Goal in the Test of Reality." *Journal of Peace Education* 12 (2): 138–53. https://doi.org/10.1080/17400201.2014.991913.

———. 2016. "Peace Education Between Theory and Practice: The Israeli Case." In A *Social Psychology Perspective on the Israeli-Palestinian Conflict,* edited by Keren Sharvit and Eran Halperin, 199–216. Cham, Switzerland: Springer.

Vergun, Yuval. 2008. "Student Delegations to Poland" [in Hebrew]. Jerusalem: Knesset Research and Information Center. https://www.knesset.gov.il/mmm/data/pdf/m02040.pdf.

"Views of Violence." n.d. Gallup. Accessed October 17, 2016. http://www.gallup
.com/poll/157067/views-violence.aspx.

Volkan, Vamik D. 1997. *Bloodlines: From Ethnic Pride to Ethnic Terrorism.* New
York: Farrar, Straus and Giroux.

Waxman, Dov. 2006a. *The Pursuit of Peace and the Crisis of Israeli Identity:
Defending/Defining the Nation.* New York: Palgrave Macmillan.

———. 2006b. "Israel's Dilemma: Unity or Peace?" *Israel Affairs* 12 (2): 200–220.
https://doi.org/10.1080/13537120500535100.

———. 2008. "From Controversy to Consensus: Cultural Conflict and the Israeli
Debate over Territorial Withdrawal." *Israel Studies* 13 (2): 73–96.

———. 2014. "Identity Matters." In *Democracy and Conflict Resolution: The
Dilemmas of Israel's Peacemaking,* edited by Miriam Fendius Elman, Oded Hak-
lai, and Hendrik Spruyt, 133–156. Syracuse, NY: Syracuse University Press.

Weitz, Yechiam. 2013. "Even Ben-Gurion Exploited the Holocaust When It Suited
Him." *Haaretz,* October 31.

Wertsch, James V. 2002. *Voices of Collective Remembering.* Cambridge: Cambridge
University Press.

White, Ralph K. 1968. *Nobody Wanted War: Misperception in Vietnam and Other
Wars.* Garden City, NY: Doubleday.

Wimmer, Andreas. 2002. *Nationalist Exclusion and Ethnic Conflict: Shadows of
Modernity.* New York: Cambridge University Press.

Wolfsfeld, Gadi. 1997. *Media and Political Conflict: News from the Middle East.*
New York: Cambridge University Press.

———. 2003. *Media and the Path to Peace.* New York: Cambridge University
Press.

Ya'akobi, D. 1999. *A World of Changes: A History Book for 9th Grade* [in Hebrew].
Jerusalem: Education Ministry, Curriculum Division and Ma'a'lot.

Ya'ar, Ephraim, and Meno Geva. 2009. "Findings of Survey on Patriotism in
Israel—2009." Paper presented at the Ninth Herzliya Conference on National
Resilience and Security. Herzliya, Israel. February 2–4.

Ya'ar, Ephraim, and Jonatan Lipsky. 2008. "IDB Survey on Patriotism—2008."
Paper presented at the Eighth Herzliya Conference. Herzliya, Israel. January
20–23. http://herzliyaconference.org/eng/_Uploads/2115patriotism08(5).pdf.

Yadgar, Y. 2006. "A Myth of Peace: 'The Vision of the New Middle East' and Its
Transformations in the Israeli Political and Public Spheres." *Journal of Peace
Research* 43 (3): 297–312.

Yedioth Ahronoth. 1986. "A Majority Against Investigation of the Shin Bet Chief
and Support Giving Priority to Security" [in Hebrew]. May 30.

Yehoshua, A. B. 2016. "Reducing the Malignancy of the Israeli Occupation." *Haaretz,*
December 31.

Ynet. 2005. "Manor's Most Popular Song: 'I Have No Other Country'" [in Hebrew].
April 13. http://www.ynet.co.il/articles/0,7340,L-3072043,00.html.

Yogev, Esther. 2010. "A Crossroads: History Textbooks and Curricula in Israel." *Journal of Peace Education* 7 (1): 1–14. https://doi.org/10.1080/17400200903370852.

Young, James E. 1990. "When a Day Remembers: A Performative History of 'Yom
Ha-Shoah.'" *History and Memory* 2 (2): 54–75.

Yuchtman-Ya'Ar, Ephraim. 2002. "Value Priorities in Israeli Society: An Examination of Inglehart's Theory of Modernization and Cultural Variation." *Comparative Sociology* 1 (3): 347–367. https://doi.org/10.1163/156913302100418637.

Yuchtman-Yaar, Ephraim, and Yohanan Peres. 2000. *Between Consent and Dissent:
Democracy and Peace in the Israeli Mind.* Lanham, MD: Rowman and Littlefield.

Zaller, John. 1992. *The Nature and Origins of Mass Opinion*. New York: Cambridge University Press.

Zalmenson-Levy, Galia. 2005. "The Teaching of the Book of Joshua and the Occupation" [in Hebrew]. In *Militarism and Education,* edited by Hagit Gur-Zeev, 131–145. Tel Aviv: Baval.

Zarakol, Ayşe. 2010. "Ontological (In)Security and State Denial of Historical Crimes: Turkey and Japan." *International Relations* 24 (1): 3–23. https://doi .org/10.1177/0047117809359040.

Zartman, I. William. 2000. "Ripeness: The Hurting Stalemate and Beyond." In *International Conflict Resolution After the Cold War,* edited by Paul C. Stern and Daniel Druckman, 225–250. Washington, DC: National Academy Press.

Zemach, Mina. 1987. *Through Israeli Eyes: Attitudes Towards Judaism, American Jewry, Zionism and the Arab-Israeli Conflict*. New York: American Jewish Committee, Institute of Human Relations.

Zertal, Idith. 2005. *Israel's Holocaust and the Politics of Nationhood*. New York: Cambridge University Press.

Zerubavel, Eviatar. 2003. *Time Maps: Collective Memory and the Social Shape of the Past*. Chicago: University of Chicago Press.

Zerubavel, Yael. 1995. *Recovered Roots: Collective Memory and the Making of Israeli National Tradition*. Chicago: University of Chicago Press.

Index

About the Book

In a country whose citizens have experienced prolonged exposure to intractable conflict, are there unique features to be found in Israeli society's core beliefs? And how—and to what effect—have those beliefs changed across the decades? To answer these questions, Neta Oren deeply explores Israel's political culture.

Oren focuses especially on two circular processes: the two-way relationship between the course of the Arab-Israeli conflict and Israel's national identity; and efforts by leaders to shape that national identity while, in turn, shifts in public opinion exert influence on leadership positions. Drawing on extensive data including speeches, party platforms, school texts and curriculums, and public opinion polls, she offers both a unique analysis and a rich reference resource.

Neta Oren is visiting scholar at the School for Conflict Analysis and Resolution, George Mason University.